The Use of Data in School Counseling

D1451460

To my grandchildren.

The Use of Data in School Counseling

Hatching Results for Students, Programs, and the Profession

Trish Hatch

*Forewords by Denise Greene-Wilkinson
and Cheryl Holcomb-McCoy*

CORWIN
A SAGE Company

CORWIN
A SAGE Company

FOR INFORMATION:

Corwin
A SAGE Company
2455 Teller Road
Thousand Oaks, California 91320
(800) 233-9936
www.corwin.com

SAGE Publications Ltd.
1 Oliver's Yard
55 City Road
London EC1Y 1SP
United Kingdom

SAGE Publications India Pvt. Ltd.
B 1/I 1 Mohan Cooperative Industrial Area
Mathura Road, New Delhi 110 044
India

SAGE Publications Asia-Pacific Pte. Ltd.
3 Church Street
#10-04 Samsung Hub
Singapore 049483

Copyright © 2014 by Corwin

All rights reserved. When forms and sample documents are included, their use is authorized only by educators, local school sites, and/or noncommercial or nonprofit entities that have purchased the book. Except for that usage, no part of this book may be reproduced or utilized in any form or by any means, electronic or mechanical, including photocopying, recording, or by any information storage and retrieval system, without permission in writing from the publisher.

Printed in the United States of America

A catalog record of this book is available from the Library of Congress.

ISBN 978-1-4522-9025-6

This book is printed on acid-free paper.

Acquisitions Editor: Jessica Allan
Associate Editor: Kimberly Greenberg
Editorial Assistant: Cesar Reyes
Copy Editor: Cate Huisman
Typesetter: C&M Digitals (P) Ltd.
Proofreader: Dennis W. Webb
Indexer: Sheila Bodell
Cover Designer: Rose Storey

SUSTAINABLE FORESTRY INITIATIVE
Certified Chain of Custody
Promoting Sustainable Forestry
www.sfiprogram.org
SFI-01268
SFI label applies to text stock

15 16 17 10 9 8 7 6 5 4 3

Contents

Additional materials and resources related to
The Use of Data in School Counseling can be found at
http://www.corwin.com/useofdata

Foreword

Denise Greene-Wilkinson

*T*he *Use of Data in School Counseling* is a refreshing, timely look at the importance of our school counselors with guidance and practical advice on how to make counselors an integral part of today's education team.

Spend any time talking with Trish Hatch, and three things will become immediately evident: Her passion for the profession is boundless, her understanding of the complex growing role of the counselor is both deep and intricate, and her vision and understanding of the expanding web of school leadership is refreshing.

As principals work with their leadership teams to move their schools forward, understanding the integral role of the counselor as a school leader, as well as a member of the team, is critical during this time of school reform. In this book you'll find not only the research necessary to make the decisions we make but solid hands-on advice on how to deliver the best for each student by incorporating the knowledge and skills of your school's counselor.

School counselors, teachers, and administrators will welcome this book.

Hatch speaks directly to their daily tasks with students. She develops a rich and comprehensive case for action plans and intentional guidance. This book begins and ends with the student. No matter what our role in a school is, the fact of the matter is our students get up every day and come to school; there would be no "us" without "them."

This book also offers an expansive view of the role counselors play in developing a positive school climate, not only in the venue of socioemotional learning, but in curriculum implementation. Again, the school counselor is a part of the education team, not an add-on.

Hatch provides practical courses of action, solid advice, and typical stories taken from the field. She also goes beyond the practical when she invites readers to view themselves as agents of change. Nothing speaks louder than Chapter 8, with its focus on social justice and using your data to tell your story, the story regarding fairness for all students in all aspects of their education. Hatch states, "Students will be advantaged or disadvantaged by the voices and actions of school counselors and other educators."

One of my reasons for running for the presidency of the National Association of Secondary School Principals was to take back the national conversation on education, the conversation that says that schools are pulling themselves out of the muck and mire of poor quality education. I believe that our schools are not moving from bad to good, but from good to great—and that great schools are the result of great leadership teams. Hatch emphasizes that this team approach results in better educational opportunities for our students.

Hatch ends where she begins, with the concept that being a counselor is a good and worthy work. Education is at a turning point. Important changes are being made every day by educators throughout the country. We must continue to build on the many miracles that Trish Hatch extols throughout this book.

—Denise Greene-Wilkinson

President, National Association
of Secondary School Principals

Foreword

Cheryl Holcomb-McCoy

Education has always been at the heart of opportunity in this country. But it is especially so today. And that is why it is so critical to understand the impact that school counselors and their programs can have on students' choices and decisions about their futures—particularly college and career options. We have arrived at an important turning point in American education and more specifically in the school counseling profession, and Trish Hatch understands this important moment in our history. We live in a world where a college degree is becoming the new high school diploma. And, many jobs that didn't require a college degree in the past are increasingly requiring one now. This "up-credentialing" helps explain why the work of school counselors is so significant. In many of today's schools, school counselors are often the college and career experts, and students and parents (particularly in low-resourced communities) rely on counselors for not only advice and guidance but also the knowledge of how to navigate the career and college-going process.

Trish Hatch's career has focused primarily on assisting school counselors in recognizing their capacity to make sure that every student receives an opportunity to acquire a "great education." She recognizes that our profession's hallmark is our ability to ensure that all students, regardless of their background and circumstance, recognize their potential and promise for a productive career and life. In this role, Trish is a venerable leader in school counseling. Her vision and confidence are backed by her specific ideas of how to improve school counseling practice and by her strengths as a talented former counselor and school administrator. She recognizes the importance of clear and concise strategic plans that counselors need in order to ensure that every child receives the assistance and attention needed—(she calls it "intentional guidance"!). And, she has revolutionized school counseling by empowering counselors to place data-based decision making and social justice advocacy at the core of their work.

When discussing the use of data in school counseling, there is no one more prolific than Trish Hatch. From afar, I have respected and admired Trish's work because of its utility and practical application to the daily ups and downs of being a school counselor. She has enabled novice as well as experienced counselors to embrace new concepts and frameworks for doing their work. And, I've tried to determine why school counselors listen so attentively to her. Well, it's because she genuinely cares about the profession, she's energetic, compassionate, and she has "walked in their shoes."

This book, *The Use of Data in School Counseling: Hatching Results for Students, Programs, and the Profession,"* is a treasure for practicing, novice, and aspiring school counselors. It integrates Trish's insights about data-driven school counseling, the Common Core standards, elements of systemic change versus individual change, and rich case studies that link these concepts to actual practice. Trish truly has the gift of making these often complex concepts less difficult to understand and applicable to real-life situations.

School counselors will find this book helpful because of its emphasis on everyday counseling practices and interventions. Counselors who are particularly interested in the eradication of inequities in schools will also be delighted by the contents of the book. Intentional guidance, social justice advocacy, access and opportunity gaps, and using data to cause systemic change are all explored. The book is replete with wonderful examples and stories from counselors as well as the voices of transformative leaders (e.g., Reese House) in the field.

Trish Hatch writes in this book and demonstrates in her life that all students deserve an opportunity. ("Every Student Gets Every *Thing!*") We should all be profoundly grateful for Trish's passion for education, school counseling, and all students' success. As school counselors, we must rededicate ourselves to strong counseling programs that help every student fulfill his or her promise. Thanks to Trish for writing a book that will help us take constructive action to realize that dream!

—*Cheryl Holcomb-McCoy*

Vice Dean of Academic Affairs, Professor,
School of Education
Johns Hopkins University
Author, *School Counseling to
Close the Achievement Gap:
A Social Justice Framework for Success*

Acknowledgments

It has taken many years to finish this work and there are many people to thank. First, thank you to everyone at the American School Counselor Association, for the incredible opportunity to co-author the original ASCA National Model. Thank you to the pioneers in the profession e.g. Norm Gysbers and Pat Henderson, Robert Myrick, and C.D. "Curly" and Sharon Johnson who generously contributed their life's work to the ASCA Model. Special appreciation to Curly and Sherri Johnson for your mentorship early in my career and for teaching me the real meaning of "results."

Thank you to the many administrators and school counselors in Moreno Valley Unified School District for supporting this work long before it was popular; particularly to Lori Holland, for your dedicated and humble assistance with the ASCA Model.

When your profession is your "life," mentors, colleagues, coauthors, and friends become hard to separate. I am incredibly grateful to so many "teachers" in my life, especially Douglas Mitchell, Lloyd Campbell, Patricia Chandler, Louise Bigbie, Reese House, Carol Dahir, Patricia Martin, Carolyn Stone, Carey Dimmitt, Jay Carey, Sheila Deam, Katie Gray, Dawn Stevenson, Peggy Hines, Judy Bowers, Stuart Chen-Hayes, Tim Poynton, Robert Bardwell, Erin Mason, Laura Owen, Carol Robinson-Zañartu, Gerald Monk, Joey Nuñez Estrada, Kathy Cohn, Ric Hovda, and Joe Johnson for your advice, encouragement, and support.

Thank you to my colleagues in the Department of Counseling and School Psychology at San Diego State University for supporting the school counseling program. Thanks also to the fieldwork supervisors and adjunct instructors for your commitment to our students and their contributions shared in this text and online.

Thank you to the counselor educators, school counselors, counselor supervisors and administrators throughout the country who provided valuable feedback and suggestions during and following trainings and throughout the process of writing this book. Space would not allow me to list you all, please refer to the online acknowledgements.

Specific thanks to the reviewers of this text (mentioned on the following page) for your thoughtful comments and terrific suggestions.

Many thanks to those who provided testimonials, examples, and samples (some in the on-line appendix), especially: Gail Smith, Julie Hartline, Debbie Stark, Gary Hensley Candy Reed, Heather Fried, Freida Trujillo, Steven Bossett, Felipe Zañartu, Richard Eberheart, Danielle Duarte, Robert Stelmar, Sarah Pelham, Gayle Cicero, Lisa DeGregorio, Krish Mohip, Mike Smilonich, Monica Loyce, Nicole Pablo, Kathie Huisenfeldt, Lauren Aponte, Tracy Calimquim and Camille Sta Elena, Melisa Monteon, Nickie Miyazono Corley, Bryant Strause, Andrew Springsteen, Jovianne Pereyra, and Andrea Lin.

Many special thanks to Barbara Smith, for your amazing contribution to Chapter 12.

I am very grateful to those who provided specific feedback and/or editing at various stages: Vanessa Crawford, Mariko Cavey, Laura Romo, Cathia Sanchez, Kathy Ng, Kristen Caldwell, Tara Galvin, the SDSU graduate students, particularly the classes of 2013 and 2014 (who read it cover to cover).

Thank you to Denise Greene-Wilkinson and Cheryl Holcomb-McCoy for your forewords; I am humbled by your endorsements.

Thank you to everyone at Corwin, particularly, Jessica Allen, Heidi Arndt, Cate Huisman, Kim Greenberg, and Amy Schroller for your patience and persistence.

To my brother, Paul Meyers, thank you for being my best friend, colleague, mentor, advisor, and ally. Thank you Melody, for managing me; I'm not sure what I'd do without you.

To my three amazing sons, Brian, Michael, and Greg; you bring incredible joy, inspire me and continue to teach me every day.

Finally, and so very importantly, thank you to my beautiful parents, John and Kathleen Meyers, for your never-ending model of unconditional love and support.

Publisher's Acknowledgments

Corwin would like to thank the following individuals for taking the time to provide their editorial insight and guidance:

Jennifer Betters-Bubon
Assistant Professor
University of Wisconsin–Whitewater
Whitewater, WI

Ricardo Cooke
Assistant Principal
Steele Canyon High School
Spring Valley, CA

Jacob D. Hornberger
School Counselor
Sharp Middle School
Butler, KY

Franciene Sabens
School Counselor
Chester High School
Chester, IL

Chris Wood
Admissions Counselor
Wartburg College
Cedar Falls, IA

Brett Zyromski
Assistant Professor
Department of Counseling, Social Work, and Leadership
Northern Kentucky University
Highland Heights, KY

About the Author

 **Trish Hatch**, PhD is the author of *The Use of Data in School Counseling: Hatching Results for Students, Programs, and the Profession* (2014), co-author of *The ASCA National Model: A Framework for School Counseling Programs* (ASCA, 2003; 2005), and co-author of *Evidence-Based Practice in School Counseling: Making a Difference With Data-Driven Practices* (Dimmit, Carey, and Hatch, 2007).

Dr. Hatch is Director of the School Counseling Program and Associate Professor at San Diego State University and Executive Director of the Center for Excellence in School Counseling and Leadership (CESCaL) in the College of Education at SDSU. She has served on multiple state and national school counseling research summit steering committees and is one of five original panel members for the National Panel for Evidenced-Based School Counseling Practices (2004–2006). Dr. Hatch currently serves on the advisory council for the Evidence-Based School Counseling Conference (2013–2014).

Dr. Hatch has successfully co-authored 13 elementary and secondary school counseling (ESSC) grants awarding more than $16,000,000 in federal funds to school districts. In addition to providing external evaluation, she provides professional development for school counselors, social workers, school psychologists, and administrators on successful implementation of ESSC grants. Since 2007, Dr. Hatch has provided more than 250 full days of training to more than 100 school districts in 20 states on the use of data in school counseling to create efficient and effective evidenced-based school counseling programs that align with the ASCA National Model.

A former school counselor and administrator, Dr. Hatch served in multiple leadership roles including Supervisor/Post Secondary Level Vice President of the American School Counselor Association (ASCA) and President of the California School Counselor Association. She has received various state and national awards including the ASCA Mary Gehrke Lifetime Achievement Award and the ASCA Administrator of the Year Award.

As President and CEO of Hatching Results™ LLC, Dr. Hatch has gathered a team of expert school counselors and counselor educators who provide training and consulting on evidenced-based practice and the use of data to improve outcomes for students, programs, and the profession. Please visit us at www.hatchingresults.com.

Learning Targets

This text will prepare readers to

CHAPTER 1

Attitudes

- *Believe* in the importance of developing schoolwide counseling core curriculum action plans
- *Believe all* students deserve to receive school counseling curriculum
- *Believe* in the importance of school counselors taking an active role in core implementation

Knowledge

- *Explain* the purpose behind standards-based education
- *Understand* why guidance curriculum is now called school counseling curriculum
- *Identify* the Common Core action steps for school counselors as recommended by Achieve.

Skills

- *Develop* a schoolwide core curriculum action plan
- *Locate* Common Core information on the achieve.org website
- *Analyze* a Schoolwide Core Curriculum Action Plan and make suggestions for improvement

CHAPTER 2

Attitudes

- *Care* about helping every single student
- *Believe* "some students need more"
- *Believe* in the importance of using data to drive interventions

Knowledge

- *Define* intentional guidance
- *Identify* the professional competencies aligning with the intentional guidance activity
- *Explain* how intentional guidance aligns with dropout prevention

Skills

- *Draw* a four-tiered RTI pyramid
- *Draw and label* the evidence-based model in school counseling practice
- *Conduct* a discussion on intentional guidance versus intentional school counseling

CHAPTER 3

Attitudes

- *Believe* in the value of collecting data
- *Believe* using data can effect change in students
- *Believe* it is important to chart goals, objectives, and outcomes

Knowledge

- *Identify* accessible sources of school data
- *Identify* achievement-related data
- *Describe* the purpose of data collection

Skills

- *Locate* data via online data resources
- *Draw* a visual that explains data linkages
- *Create* reasonable, measureable outcome goals

CHAPTER 4

Attitudes

- *Believe* it is important to disaggregate data
- *Believe* it is important for school counselors to be experts in certain data sets
- *Believe* it is important to use data to design interventions

Knowledge

- *Compare and contrast* process, perception, and results data
- *Explain* the ASK acronym
- *Define* immediate, intermediate, and long-range data

Skills

- *Draw* the Hatching Results conceptual diagram
- *Explain* the conceptual diagram for intentional guidance
- *Create* the conceptual diagram for systems change

CHAPTER 5

Attitudes

- *Believe* in the importance of including both perception and results data in action plans
- *Believe* efforts should be made to align lesson delivery with subject areas
- *Believe* in the importance of administrator collaboration and approval of action plans

Knowledge

- *Describe* the prongs of the two-pronged approach
- *Explain* the guidelines for using curriculum and intentional guidance action plans
- *Discuss* priorities and considerations when developing action plans

Skills

- *Create* a curriculum action plan for their school
- *Create* an intentional guidance action plan for their school
- *Evaluate* an action plan and provide feedback

CHAPTER 6

Attitudes

- *Believe* in the importance of using referral forms
- *Believe* surveying at-risk students will provide for better-targeted interventions
- *Believe* using the fishnet approach will help students receive more appropriate interventions

Knowledge

- *Describe ways* to garner faculty input on school counseling core curriculum
- *Define* when and how to use the fishnet approach
- *Identify* which group curriculum is evidence based

Skills

- *Construct* curriculum surveys for parents and teachers
- *Create* surveys for at-risk students
- *Create* pre/post conference surveys for students and parents
- *Create* school counselor referral forms
- *Create* a menu of services
- *Locate* free online curriculum resources

CHAPTER 7

Attitudes

- *Believe* school counselors are teachers too
- *Believe* school counselors must assess the impact of their lessons
- *Believe* creating pre/post tests is a well-developed skill that requires practice

Knowledge

- *Differentiate* between the three types of questions used on pre/post tests and when to use each one
- *Explain* the difference between construct validity and content validity
- *Identify* the difference between surveys and pre/post tests

Skills

- *Create* a pre/post test assessing students' attitudes, knowledge, and skills
- *Create* a post-only test
- *Critique* a colleague's pre/post test

Chapter 8

Attitudes

- *Care* deeply about access and equity for *all* students
- *Believe* students are advantaged or disadvantaged by the voices and actions of school counselors
- *Believe* risk taking is no longer optional behavior

Knowledge

- *Define* the school counselor's role as a social justice agent for change
- *Describe* the role of data in systems and policy reform
- *Identify* an example of an opportunity gap

Skills

- *Facilitate* a discussion about data
- *Recognize* achievement gaps for specific student populations
- *Identify* a system issue as opposed to student issue
- *Prepare* and present a PowerPoint of schoolwide data to faculty

Chapter 9

Attitudes

- *Believe* in the importance of planning and calendaring
- *Believe* in the importance of prioritizing activities "worth a master's degree"
- *Believe* in importance of creating an annual agreement

Knowledge

- *Explain* the professional responsibilities of school counselors
- *Explain* the difference between a starter and a utility player
- *Discuss* methods of assigning students to counselors
- *Explain* strategic planning of office hours
- *Describe* how student-to-counselor ratios affect schedule planning
- *Define* the school counselor's role in discipline
- *Define* the school counselor's role in SST, 504 plan, and IEP teams
- *Define* the school counselor's role in master schedule building

Skills

- *Create* a detailed monthly calendar of events and activities
- *Draft* a list of responsibilities for secretaries and assistants
- *Create* an annual agreement

- *Initiate* a "Counselor of the Day" system for urgent needs at their school
- *Plan* and organize meetings with colleagues
- *Complete* a "Plates Are Full" activity

CHAPTER 10

Attitudes

- *Believe in the value of* creating and completing results reports
- *Believe* sharing program results can lead to systemic change

Knowledge

- *Describe* the difference between program evaluation and research
- *Identify and explain* five reasons why measuring results is important
- *Discuss* the concept of "impact over time"
- *Differentiate* between "improvement" and "increase" when calculating percentages

Skills

- *Create* a results report for their district
- *Calculate* percentage improvement in school data
- *Create* graphs and charts reporting school data

CHAPTER 11

Attitudes

- *Believe* data collection does not have to be a daunting process
- *Believe* in the importance of starting with measuring one thing well.

Knowledge

- *Identify* the steps to creating a core curriculum Flashlight PowerPoint
- *Identify* the steps to creating an intentional guidance Flashlight PowerPoint
- *Demonstrate* where to locate instructions for what to say during a staff presentation

Skills

- *Create* a Flashlight PowerPoint
- *Present* a Flashlight PowerPoint to teachers and school administrators
- *Complete* a Flashlight rating scale rubric

CHAPTER 12

Attitudes

- *Believe* in the importance of assembling Flashlight Packages
- *Believe* in adapting Flashlight Packages to fit the needs of their district
- *Believe* they can create Flashlight Packages (just like Barbara!)

Knowledge

- *List* the components of a Flashlight Package
- *Describe* the benefits of a Flashlight PowerPoint
- *Identify* CESCaL's website as a Flashlight resource

Skills

- *Complete* a Flashlight Package
- *Provide* an evaluation critiquing their Flashlight or a colleague's
- *Write* a reflection on your Flashlight experience

CHAPTER 13

Attitudes

- *Believe* they are owners, not renters
- *Believe* in the importance of professional association membership
- *Believe* obstacles present valuable opportunities for learning and growth

Knowledge

- *Define* the Bermuda Triangle
- *Describe* what it really means to be a "professional"
- *Describe* the role of "context" and "mechanism" in meaningful outcomes
- *Explain* the "pilots, passengers, prisoners, and hijackers (P³H)" analogy

Skills

- *Complete* the obstacles and opportunities worksheet
- *Identify* themselves as a pilot, passenger, prisoner, or hijacker
- *Identify* the content or mechanism concerns you face
  And finally,
- *Write* and *share* their stories about ways in which they have used data to hatch results for students, programs, or the profession (Send to: trish@hatchingresults .com)

Introduction

PART ONE

The Miracle

In solution-focused counseling, it's called the "miracle question." School counselors pose an exercise of imagination to students: "Suppose you woke up one morning and by some miracle everything you ever wanted, everything good you could ever imagine for yourself, had actually happened—your life had turned out exactly the way you wanted it" (Mason, 2008). Sklare's version reads, "If a miracle happened tonight and you woke up tomorrow and your problem was solved, what would be the first sign that this had occurred? What would you be doing differently? What else would be different after the miracle?" (2004, p. 69).

Suppose *you*, the school counselor, woke up one morning, and by some miracle everything you ever wanted for your profession, everything good you could ever imagine for yourself as a school counselor, had actually happened—and your professional career had turned out exactly the way you wanted it. Imagine further that you woke up tomorrow and your day-to-day professional school counseling problems were solved.

What would be the first sign that this occurred?

What might you do differently as a school counselor?

What else would be different after the miracle?

Sklare (2004) describes a ripple effect that might occur in relationships and poses the following questions:

Who would notice the change in you?

What might they notice?

How would they respond?

How would you then respond to them?

Until quite recently, school counselors have been largely left out of educational reform. Not mentioned in Goals 2000 or No Child Left Behind, school counselors have largely felt marginalized and ancillary in schools despite strong efforts by professional associations for inclusion (Bridgeland & Bruce, 2011). As a former school counselor and administrator and now a counselor educator, one of my miracles was to imagine the school counseling profession legitimized by its consistent and accurate (program and ratio) representation and inclusion in all state and national education reform documents. If school counseling were legitimized, the first sign would be more school counselors implementing programs and activities to benefit students, rather than performing nonschool counseling activities. The school counseling program would be different, because it would be seen as an integral part of the total educational program for students' success (ASCA, 2003, 2005). Teachers, students, parents, superintendents, policymakers, and legislators would notice the change in the performance of school counselors and in the outcomes of the students they serve. They would respond by holding school counselors, the school counseling program, and the profession of school counseling in such high regard that classroom-by-classroom, school-by-school, district-by-district, and ultimately in each state, one-by-one, stakeholders would demand legislation mandating school counseling programs.

The First Miracle

I woke up on March 24, 2010, to a call from my colleague Gary Hensley, who invited me on behalf of the Pearson Foundation to participate in "an intimate gathering of business, civic, education and philanthropic leaders to discuss the high school dropout and college/workforce readiness crisis and to devise an effective roadmap for change" (G. Hensley, personal communication). Gary *knew I was an undying advocate for school counseling.* He called at the last minute, informing me of an important meeting that would be held at the *Newseum* in Washington, DC, about dropout prevention. He was concerned no one would be in attendance to represent school counselors! Initially I suggested he call the American School Counseling Association (ASCA), but he explained it was too late, because everyone had to be approved in advance. However, because I was already consulting with Pearson, he could invite me in. Would I drop everything on my agenda to attend? Yes! *Someone*, I thought, has to represent school counselors, or yet another national document leaving the profession of school counseling behind will be written. I was given clear instructions the next day:

> Before the Roundtable event, we will circulate summaries of what each attending organization is doing to combat the high school dropout crisis. These summaries will lay the foundation for a candid and productive conversation focused on action and on the legislative agenda, and tools that have increased the number of students who graduate high school prepared for success, and together determine immediate next steps that can be taken to effect change. We look forward to seeing you there (G. Hensley, personal communication, March 25, 2010).

Fully prepared, I wore my "really important person" outfit and I took a picture in the room and again in the elevator. I even took a picture of the meeting room (see Figures 0.1, 0.2, and 0.3).

Figure 0.1 My "Really Important Person" Outfit in the Room

Figure 0.2 My "Really Important Person" Outfit in the Elevator

Figure 0.3 The Meeting Room

The event was "designed to be an intimate gathering of thought leaders who are prepared to have an action-forcing conversation" (G. Hensley, personal communication, March 25, 2010). As it began, we were each asked what we "thought" should take place to effect change in the dropout epidemic. I looked to my left and realized I was sitting next to Robert Balfanz, senior research scientist at Johns Hopkins University and national expert focusing on America's dropout crisis, chronic absenteeism, and the warning signs of impending dropout (Johns Hopkins University School of Education, 2012). I had about 20 things I was prepared to say, so I was relieved when the facilitator started with Balfanz and went the other direction, inviting each person, one by one, to share her or his thoughts. Each mentioned issues I was planning to address: early warning systems, the use of data to effect change, providing evidence-based intervention, and so forth. The ideas continued to be spoken around the room from Margaret Spellings, former U.S. Secretary of Education; Michael Brown from City Year; John Bridgeland, Civic Enterprises; Dan Domenech, American Association of School Administrators; Dane Linn, National Governors Association; Alma Powell, America's Promise Alliance; and many others (Balfanz, Bridgeland, Moore, & Fox, 2010, pp. 72–73). Each had suggestions for what to do about the dropout problem. Recommendations were made for systems, policies, practices, and people who should be included in the document, but none of the 50 people, not *one* person, mentioned the role of the school counselor. When it was my turn to speak, I knew why I was *really* there. I realized a miracle had occurred, and I was present at that moment to state, not once, but probably 50 times that day, once for every person who failed to mention it, that professional school counselors are perfectly positioned to provide all of the prevention and intervention activities previously suggested: to use data to drive decision making, to develop mechanisms that trigger appropriate interventions as early as elementary school in attendance, behavior, and achievement—I said it all. I promoted the role of the professional school counselor relentlessly. When the words *teachers* and *administrators* were being recorded on chart paper, I raised my hand and said "and school counselors." At the end of the day, as one might imagine, all I had to do was raise my hand and the recorder would affirm, "yes, and school counselors." As pleased as I was with the momentary inclusion, I left uncertain the words would make it to print.

In June 2010 I received a summary of the insights and collective wisdom from the conference titled the *Roundtable Summary Findings*. I anxiously skimmed it, and there it was:

- Regular, individualized student data needs to be shared with teachers, **counselors**, administrators, and parents married with prompt interventions (G. Hensley, personal communication, June 16, 2010).

Included in the draft of the Civic Marshall Plan was the following:

- **Early Warning Systems with Appropriate Interventions in Dropout Factory Schools.** Widespread adoption of individualized student data—tracking early warning indicators of potential dropout as early as 3rd grade, such as attendance, behavior (personal/social as well as work skills and study habits), grades in reading and math, and test scores, with regular reporting to teachers, **counselors**, administrators, and parents to identify individual students who are off-track and need regular or more intensive interventions (G. Hensley, personal communication, June 16, 2010).

I was delighted to see counselors mentioned, but I desperately wanted *school counselors*. So I revised the document in multiple places, adding *school counselors* or *educators* (at least *educators* includes school counselors) with tracked changes, and sent it back.

replicable? What is scalable?

- What is the current role of school counselors in student achievement? How do we implement best practices to ensure they are consistently integrated into dropout prevention, held accountable for early identification, data driven and evidence based interventions, and measuring student outcomes

> Deleted: guidance

> Deleted: ?

- Better understanding of the role of supports in a student's life: what is the potential impact of parents and other supports in a child's life to impact their decision to stay in school?
- Research on teacher/school counselor (or educators) preparation/quality. We know that good teachers/counselors matter, but we do not know how to train teachers/counselors to be effective.

> Deleted: to

A few months later, on November 13, 2010, I just *happened* to be at another Pearson meeting in Philadelphia with Laura Moore, who was writing the original Grad Nation report. I asked her if the Grad Nation report was out yet. She shared that she was actually reviewing the final copy edits *that night!* I froze. Dare I ask? I took a deep breath and said, "Could you do a quick search for the word *counselor?*" Sure enough, it was there on pages 17 and 62! Rejoice! But, again, only *counselor*, not *school counselor!* Arg! I turned to her and said: "You **must** add the word *school!*" (At this point I didn't care that I was "should, ought, and musting" her; there was no more time for politeness.) She hesitated a bit, as if unsure she had that authority. Finally, she said, "I'll try." I **watched her** as she typed *school* in front of *counselor*, and I hoped for a miracle.

Building a Grad Nation was released in November 2010, and the words *school counselor* were included in the text—twice (Balfanz et al., 2010):

Build Early Warning and Intervention Systems. States, school districts, and schools should collect individualized student data to track early warning indicators of potential dropouts as early as elementary and middle school with regular reports to administrators, teachers, **school counselors**, and parents to identify students who are off-track and need regular or more intensive supports. (p. 17)

Build Early Warning Systems with Appropriate Interventions. School districts should collect individualized student data to track early warning indicators of potential dropout as early as elementary and middle school, including attendance, behavior, grades in reading and math, and benchmark test scores, and regularly report this information to teachers, **school counselors**, administrators, and parents to identify individual students who are off-track and need both moderate and more intensive interventions. (p. 62)

Some might imagine this entire event was simply coincidence, or as my colleague John Krumboltz would say, "planned happenstance" (Krumboltz, 2009). I think it was a *miracle* that I met Gary, that he was invited to that meeting, and that he thought of me and I was able to go. It is a *miracle* I spoke last at the meeting and that later Laura Moore was at a different meeting for something *else* that I just *happened* to be at a few *days* before publication and that she just *happened* to be the final editor. Yes, *miracles*. I wondered about this ripple effect: Who might notice? How would they respond? Would it change anything?

More Miracles

In 2011, Secretary of Education Arne Duncan called on school counselors to "own the turf" of college and career readiness and implored school counselors to take on a leadership role within their schools to become a central part of educational reform in preparing all students to be college- and career-ready (College Board, 2011). When I was first saw the YouTube video clip link of Duncan, I was so excited I forwarded it to all of my e-mail contacts, because it was a great sign! I wondered how school counselors would act. As of March 2013, there are only 950 hits (30+ of them are mine) on this video. But the miracle *did* occur—the Secretary of Education said it was time to listen to school counselors and to place them in real leadership roles within schools, and yet, in a room full of more than 150 school counselors and administrators I met with two years later, only a handful had seen it and or understood the potential power and professional responsibility of that endorsement. So far they have not noticed.

In 2012, *Building a Grad Nation* (Balfanz, Bridgeland, Bruce, & Fox, 2012) mentioned school counselors 33 times, positioning school counselors as "ready to lead." The document outlines the challenge in school counseling due to unclear missions and the need to better define the role of the school counselor. It reports,

The College Board joined the Civic Marshall Plan Leadership Council and is working to fill important gaps, like tapping the talents of counselors to be part of the high school and college completion missions. The College Board National Office for School Counselor Advocacy (NOSCA) is working to better define the role of the school counselor and support them in their success. (2012, p. 61)

Wow! That is great news! Finally, this miracle document states, "Educators, including Teachers, *School Counselors* and Administrators: Quality schools with engaged teachers, counselors, and other administrators are critical to children's education attainment" (p. 89). It calls for the development and support of highly effective counselors and includes counselor preparation and evaluation as an action item (Balfanz et al., 2012).

On December 16, 2012, I woke up to watch David Gregory (*I love him*), and I saw Randi Weingarten, president, American Federation of Teachers (AFT) on *Meet the Press*. She was addressing the horror of the Sandy Hook tragedy. At 49:03 minutes into the program she said,

We can actually *do* things in schools. We can have more guidance counselors, we can have more social workers, psychologists, all of whom have been cut . . . we can do wrap-around services . . . more of these things to de-stigmatize mental illness and have more access. (Verdugo, 2012)

Stop! Rewind! Did she really just *say* that on national TV?! Might this lead to another miracle? One that would ensure more school counselors for prevention and intervention?

On December 18, 2012, Achieve released *Implementing the Common Core Standards: The Role of the School Counselor*, noting,

> As part of a school team consisting of administrators, teachers, parents, and students, school counselors have a critical role to play in the successful implementation of the new standards. School counselors are uniquely positioned to influence and implement many of the schoolwide goals and initiatives to ensure that all students are college- and career-ready. (p. 7)

Seriously? This is an *amazing* document that aligns with the ASCA National Model and supports the professional role of the school counselor—a miracle!

On January 16, 2013, President Barack Obama announced his policy proposal to protect children titled *Now is the time* (2013). Among other actions, the plan calls for funding to support the hiring of school counselors, social workers, and psychologists to implement evidenced-based policies and to help create safer schools. Miracle!

If the "miracle" *has* occurred, and these are all signs that the profession of school counseling *has* begun to be legitimized, one might ask, What are school counselors doing differently? Has anyone noticed a change in the school counselor? What, if anything, is different after these miracles?

Or, is it possible that these events are not miracles,
but rather simply the way these types of things play out in the political world of
problems, policies, and politics?

PART TWO

Problems, Policies, and Politics

John Kingdon's classic political science text, *Agendas, Alternatives, and Public Policies* (1984) describes an approach to policy formation as resulting from three "streams," the *problem* stream, the *policy* stream, and the *politics* stream. When the streams "couple," a policy window is opened, and policy change can occur. Problem streams are often brought to attention when public matters, such as the Sandy Hook tragedy, require the attention of politicians. The policy stream consists of proposals for change (such as gun control legislation) that are waiting for the right time to be implemented. Political streams refer to the issues of those who garner the political clout or authority to make change at the opportune time (after inauguration, a war is won, or an act of terrorism, for example). Typically, these streams run parallel to each other and are unrelated, until a problem is serious enough to draw attention at the same time that a well-vetted solution or policy is available and the political climate is ripe for change. When the Sandy Hook tragedy occurred, a "policy window" or opportunity emerged. The policy window, according to Kingdon, is a very dynamic time, with multiple policy solutions (*Now is the time,* for example) waiting their turn for review, floating in what Kingdon calls the "primeval soup."

Policy windows of opportunity are often open for only a short time while various "actors," whom Kingdon calls "policy entrepreneurs," strive to ensure their idea is heard and placed on the decision agenda. Decision makers like the president are busy and powerful people who spend their days shifting attention from one problem or policy to another. Policy entrepreneurs (who may be politicians, researchers, private citizens, or lobbyists for ASCA and the School Resource Officers Association) work inside or outside an organization in both the policy and problem streams on a specific set of issues, and are prepared, when the problem occurs, to propose a solution swiftly and promptly to the decision maker. If a policy is presented to the decision maker before the strongest members of the community have agreed to its central tenets, it may fail. For instance, it is unknown at press time if the president's proposal to require universal background checks for gun sales will pass into law.

Further inspection of the *Now is the time* (2013) proposal reveals school safety funds can be used to hire school counselors *or* other professionals:

> Each school is different and should have the flexibility to address its most pressing needs. Some schools will want trained and armed police; others may prefer increased counseling services. Either way, each district should be able to *choose* [emphasis added] what is best to protect its own students. (p. 10)

The program will give $150 million to school districts and law enforcement agencies to hire school resource officers, school psychologists, social workers, and counselors:

> Not every school will want police officers or additional school counselors, but we should do what we can to help schools get the staff they determine they need to stay safe. (p. 11)

"Choose." Yes. "Choose what is best" and "get the staff *they* determine they need." How will they determine? Will school counselors be considered?

According to Kingdon (1984), if the problem, the policy, and the political climate do not come together at the precise time, the window may be lost (e.g., funding for safer schools or gun control measures) as the streams begin to decouple. Therefore, he proposes that rather than lose the opportunity altogether, experienced policy entrepreneurs must become specialists in educating and preparing those with an interest in or voice on these issues prior to decision-making time. Kingdon holds that successful entrepreneurs possess persistence, technical expertise, political know-how, and a willingness to invest the necessary resources to promote their solution. Likewise, in schools and with school boards, school counselors must possess the technical expertise to begin to educate and prepare those with decision-making power when the time comes for local funding allocations.

Let's imagine the next miracle occurs, and $150 million or more is allocated for safer schools. What are the chances school districts nationwide will actually choose to spend their school safety funds on school counselors? *Are school counselors already doing things differently?* What do decision makers *notice and value* in the role and function of the school counselor over other choices? Enough for the profession to garner the soft money funding? Have school counselors earned this public endorsement, approval, and encouragement?

In some school districts and states, miracles are already occurring. In Georgia, HB 283, which called for at least one school counselor for every 450 students, was signed into law by the governor on May 7, 2013 (http://www.legis.ga.gov/Legislation/20132014/137066.pdf). Over the next five years (2013–2018) in Washington state, policymakers will decide how to spend billions in more funding to improve K–12 education to comply with the state supreme court's decision in *McCleary v. State* (Stang, 2013). Decisions on how these funds will be spent could result in a huge reduction in student-to-counselor ratios (Reykdal, n.d.). Although Florida's passage of SB 154 resulted in victory for only one of four goals (changing the title of a school counselor to Certified School Counselor), SB 154 received great attention when arguments for reduced ratios and more defined roles and functions were debated on the floor of both the House and Senate (http://fsca-legislation.blogspot.com/).

From: GailCounselor Smith <Gailcounselor.Smith@cobbk12.org>
Subject: Counselor Ratios in Georgia
Date: March 7, 2013 12:39:28 PM PST
To: "thatch@mail.sdsu.edu" <thatch@mail.sdsu.edu>

Hi Trish,

I just mailed my permission to reprint the Cobb success story in your book. Hopefully, you will receive it within a day or two. I have some other great Georgia news you might be interested in.

Two years ago, our state began restructuring how positions are allocated and funded. Last spring, Julie and I presented to the sub-committee that was in charge of making recommendations concerning student support groups. We asked them to level the school counseling ratios in Georgia to 1 to 400 (right now they are ES—1:462, MS—1:624, HS—1:400) and to provide funding for all sub-group segments (the state presently does not provide funding for special education, remedial education, ESOL, or advanced content segments).

The sub-committee came back with a proposal to fund school counselors at 1:450 and to add funding for special

(Continued)

(Continued)

education and ESOL in 2015 and funding for remedial education and advanced content in 2016. The full commission agreed with the proposal (it was ranked second to an overhaul of our state's technology infrastructure) and now this recommendation is in a bill that has cleared our House and is presently waiting on Senate approval. The decrease in counselor ratios over the next three years represents approximately $31 million.

During the hearing, one of the representatives asked us for data to show our effectiveness. Julie reached out to the RAMP schools in Georgia for their data reports (and of course we used data from Cobb), and at the next committee meeting, we used this data to support our request for a change in the ratios. Apparently, the data helped to persuade the committee to lower our ratios.

We are extremely excited that our request to lower the ratios and to provide full funding for school counselors is finally coming to fruition, especially during a time when budgets are being cut. At the same time we are cautious because the bill needs approval from the Senate and the governor's signature, but we are being told that he is in support of the change.

Anyway—this would not have happened had our state not been prepared to talk about the role of the counselor impacting student achievement.

I will keep you posted as this bill makes its way to the governor. Hope all is well on your side of the continent!

Gail M. Smith
School Counseling Supervisor
Cobb County School District
770.514.3832

"School counselors are uniquely qualified to assist students with overcoming barriers to learning."

However, this type of good news is most certainly not the case nationwide. While training in Chicago Public Schools recently, I learned that despite the best efforts of passionate school counselors and central office leaders who are working very hard to support the shift to appropriate professional school counselor responsibilities, far too many elementary school counselors are still primarily performing the role of "special education caseworker."

In California, school counselors are struggling with unbearably high counselor-to-student caseloads (1:700 at the high school level in some districts), as the state bears the highest student-to-school counselor ratio in the nation (EdSource, 2013).

If the goal was for each district or state, one by one, to mandate school counseling, what technical assistance would be necessary for school counselors to begin the process of becoming policy entrepreneurs for funding or to align their responsibilities with the recommendations of *Implementing the Common Core Standards: The Role of the School Counselor* (Achieve, 2012a)? What initial steps would school counselors need to take to begin the process of accountability in order to prove the role worthy of reduced ratios or more appropriately legislated responsibilities? How might school counselors overcome their *historical struggle with professional illegitimacy* and become vital imperative leaders, advocates, and systems-change agents in schools across the nation and the globe?

If *this* miracle were to occur,

> *What would be the first sign that this occurred?*
>
> *What might they do differently as school counselors?*
>
> *What would be different after the miracle?*
>
> *Who would notice the change in school counselors?*
>
> *What might they notice? And how would they respond?*
>
> *How would policymakers then respond to them?*

◆ ◆ ◆

PART THREE

The Bermuda Triangle of School Counseling
(Adapted from Hatch, 2002, 2008)

Throughout the history of the profession, school counselors have struggled to secure a legitimate position as being integral to the educational mission of schools, where their roles and functions are perceived as indispensable to the school system when budget cuts arise. School counselors are often excluded from meaningful conversations impacting students, systems in schools, use of resources, or their own role (Hatch, 2002). In many schools, counselors are assigned noncounseling duties that detract from their professional work. This marginalization is in large part due to uncertainty about the value of school counseling, which is related to a lack of clear, compelling documentation of the impact of the school counseling program on student outcomes. It is widely accepted that teachers are central to achieving quality educational outcomes. Opinion is less certain in the case of school counselors. Understanding the complexity of the counselor's role through the lenses of organizational, institutional, and political theory in school systems was the focus of my dissertation (Hatch, 2002). Each of these three theoretical perspectives might compose one point of the triangle in what could be called the *"Bermuda Triangle of School Counseling."* What purportedly happens in the middle of the Bermuda Triangle (Figure 0.4)? *Things **disappear**.*

Figure 0.4   The Bermuda Triangle of School Counseling

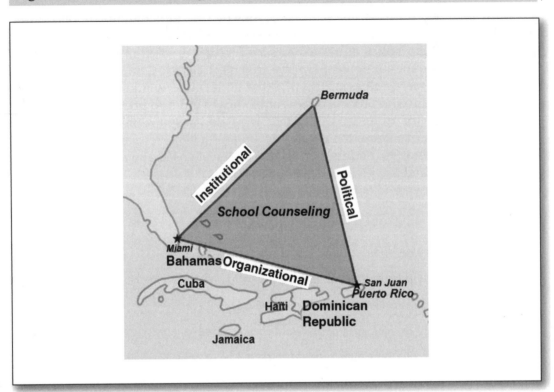

Organizational Theory—Efficiency and Effectiveness

Organizational theory concerns itself with how *effective* an organization is in accomplishing its goals and achieving the results or outcomes it intends to produce. Organizational theory is also grounded in *internal efficiency.* Rowan and Miskel (1999) theorize that organizational performance is often the main determinant of organizational survival. If a program is perceived as inefficient, it is often eliminated, or responsibilities of program personnel are shifted. Programs that are perceived as efficient, however, survive and frequently grow. Efficiency is the ratio of the amount of work performed to the amount of work or energy used (Efficiency, 2013).

Unfortunately school counselors still consider the use of data, collecting results, and reporting accountability as less important than other responsibilities, and they perform "random acts of guidance" rather than intentional acts of guidance (Hatch & Chen-Hayes, 2008). They maintain the status quo of doing things the way they have always been done. Many do not measure the impact of their activities and do not know whether or not they are achieving the desired outcomes of the school.

This is not necessarily all the school counselors' fault. Despite historical trends to promote standards (Campbell & Dahir, 1997) and accountability (Gysbers, 2010; Johnson & Johnson, 2001), despite a decade of the ASCA National Model (2002, 2005, 2012a), and despite the existence of a National Office for School Counselor Advocacy (NOSCA), far too many school counseling training programs still vary in philosophy, program standards, use of data, and adherence to models, competencies, and outcomes (Hines & Lemon, 2011). Far too many train mental health workers who may have a class or two in schools rather than a program in school counseling. As a result, many school counselors are ill prepared to implement comprehensive programs, and this has resulted in little consistency or predictability in services for students site-to-site or district-to-district (Hatch & Chen-Hayes, 2008).

When evidence of constancy or contribution to the efficiency and effectiveness within the "organizational machine" of school is lacking, administrators or others may decide it is appropriate to eliminate positions or shift responsibilities to support what is perceived to be more efficiency within the system (Hatch, 2002).

Many of the organizational challenges in school counseling can be addressed by focusing on program evaluation and program improvement, including asking questions such as these: What is the most efficient and effective use of a school counselor's time when teaching high school graduation requirements? Seeing each student one on one? In small groups? In a classroom session? In a multipurpose room? How are these decisions made? Measuring the impact of curriculum delivery on students in a variety of settings provides important feedback concerning what works, what does not, and what can be done differently in the future. In this way, school counselors continually refine their activities and programs and become more time-efficient in meeting their program goals and objectives. From an organizational theory perspective, when administrators

> Imagine that the organization called "school" needs to test its students and therefore requires testing materials to be counted and collected. These are absolute priorities in the organization; they must be accomplished. The organizational leader needs to find someone he or she can count on to complete this important and necessary task. It is reasonable to assume the leader will scan the available faculty resources to determine which employee, if the current duties were reassigned, would be most able to take on this task with the least amount of disruptions to the overall function of the organization. Might the leaders select the school counselor? If it is perceived by the leader that the testing needs outweigh the contributions that would otherwise be afforded the organization by the school counselor, it is reasonable that the leader selects the counselor for these tasks. If, on the other hand, the school counselor is performing duties that the leader determines are actively contributing to accomplishing the central goals of the organization (student achievement) such that lack of completion of these vital duties would negatively impact the goals of the organization, the leader will most likely utilize other faculty resources.

have evidence of how the work of school counselors helps support the capacity of the school to attain important educational goals for students, they become stronger advocates for protecting the role and function of school counselors during budget cutbacks, and they are less likely to assign school counselors duties that detract from their appropriate professional work.

Institutional theory focuses on an organization's effort to gain legitimacy both operationally and socially (Ogawa, 1992, 1994). *Legitimacy* exists operationally when structural elements such as standards, policies, and procedures are in place to specifically delineate norms and routines. *Social legitimacy* exists when organizational members are contributing to the cultural pressures that lead to the creation of structural elements such as job descriptions or evaluation tools. When members are involved in decision making and are part of the influential policy-making team, they are considered socially legitimate.

Many school districts lack job descriptions, appropriate evaluation tools, policies, and procedures manuals for school counselors, and/or they lack language specifying student-to-school-counselor ratios in budget documents. This lack of structural inclusion in district policies is an example of the profession's need for additional social legitimacy from an institutional theory perspective. Social legitimacy is present when school counselors are an indispensable part of the policy-making team responsible for the decision-making process of creating these structures. If school counselors are seen as indispensable to the organization, it will be evident by their inclusion in the important conversations and in the structural elements mentioned above. Thus, social legitimacy will lead to *operational legitimacy.*

Once school counselors earn social legitimacy as policy actors, they are more likely to be included in the process of decision making. Subsequently, school counselors can contribute to the *operational institutionalization* of the structural elements and processes of establishing new policies and procedures that support the appropriate role of the school counselor. When visiting a school site where school counselors have institutional legitimacy, one would find artifacts such as brochures, pamphlets, school handbooks, accreditation reports, and other similar materials on display for parents and other interested community members, illustrating the important responsibilities of the professional school counselors and their vital role in the educational system. Statewide laws, education codes, and policies would also reflect the essential role and appropriate ratios for school counselors.

Politics, as defined by Wirt and Kirst (2001), is a "form of social conflict rooted in group differences over values about the use of public resources to meet private needs" (p. 4). Political decisions often hinge on two important weighted components: *value* and *resources.* When a program is highly valued, it is said to have earned *social capital,* and resources are more likely to be allocated to fund it year to year. However, when a program is not valued, it can easily be cut from the budget during a tough fiscal year. Each year, school districts must determine which programs to fund and which ones to eliminate.

Many stakeholders in education are vying for a limited allocation of resources. Thus, it is critical for school counselors to operate within the system much as a politician operates (ala Kingdon)—by anticipating and nullifying the "competing demands from school constituencies that have been organized to seek their share of valued allocations from the school system" (Wirt & Kirst, 1997, p. 59). If school counselors share their program results strategically, they can begin to leverage the steady flow of support necessary to substantiate that their value is worth the school's and district's resources. This approach requires developing a marketing strategy—one that ensures school counselors are not only collecting and reporting student outcomes and results but also communicating them in a manner that improves their social capital.

The quest for political legitimacy within the school is an attempt to leverage the social capital necessary to obtain the resources, authority, rights, and responsibilities of a legitimate profession. Schools are also political systems, where some individuals have more power and influence than others in determining how finite resources are distributed and in establishing the institution's policies, procedures, structures, and routines. The school counseling program will earn political legitimacy and social capital as the program's value is believed to be worth the cost resource.

Many of the current professional challenges in the school-counseling profession today are the consequences of organizational inefficiency, institutional illegitimacy, and subsequent political devaluing (Hatch, 2008). What steps are necessary within the profession to resolve these concerns and avoid the Bermuda Triangle of school counseling?

First, the school counseling programs must increase their internal efficiency and be respected for their accomplishments and efforts. The program must become increasingly aligned with the school's educational goals, objectives, and outcomes, and school counselors must engage in a continuous, self-reflective process that will result in the adoption of effective interventions and practices and the discarding of ineffective interventions and practices.

Second, if the results are communicated accurately and well, the program will gain institutional legitimacy. The program will become increasingly regarded as indispensable to the school by the leading opinion and decision makers, and the staff of the program will be increasingly regarded as professionals who are capable of self-direction and self-correction. Next, the program will begin to attain political legitimacy. Increasingly, school counselors will have opportunities to participate in leadership activities that establish the school's policies, structure, and routines that define the role and work of school counselors.

Finally, the program and its personnel will be regarded as essential to the work of the school, and their value will be worth *far* more than their resource. The centrality of the program will be dependent on school counselors' capacity to document important results, use these results to improve practice, and effectively communicate these results (and the processes used to obtain the results) to the school community.

What is to become of the profession of school counseling? In the end, I believe it will depend on the actions of passionate professional school counselors and whether or not they *decide to act*.

◆ ◆ ◆

PART FOUR

Your Charge

Whether you are currently a practicing professional school counselor or you are learning about school counseling in your very first graduate-level course, this text was written to provide you with detailed technical support to become the best school counselor you can be for the students you currently serve or will serve each and every day. If you are an administrator, this text is written to assist you as you ensure the students in your school or district are provided the professional school counseling program they so deeply deserve and desperately need.

If you are a counselor educator, school counselor leader, legislator, or anyone else with political clout you can leverage, please utilize this text and the many resources shared within it and online to support and promote the profession of school counseling and hold each school counselor accountable.

Throughout this text I will share stories from my experience as a school counselor and administrator as well as examples from graduate students and practicing school counselors. I hope the content, stories, and strategies will assist, support, and motivate you to *take action*—to become a policy entrepreneur promoting the results of your program to your stakeholders. In the end, I hope each and every student has access to a professional school counselor, a safe climate in which to learn, and guaranteed equitable opportunities for a rigorous education leading to the post-secondary opportunity of his or her choice.

Will that take another miracle?

I hope not.

We can't wait any longer. The policy window is open. If school counselors are unable to become more efficient and effective, if they are unable or unwilling to measure their impact, if they are unable to therefore legitimize themselves with proof of their positive effects and data-driven outcomes, then sadly, I fear the window of opportunity may close, and the school counseling profession may run the risk of succumbing to the same demise as ships in the Bermuda Triangle—*it may disappear.*

I choose not to believe that.

Do NOT wait for another miracle—there is no time.
We need 1,000 miracles—we need one every day.
Go create one.

Now is the time
The streams have converged
And the impossible awaits
I believe—do you?

1

Implementing School Counselor Common Core Standards

Every Student Gets Every *THING*

This chapter will guide the school counselor in designing standards-based, schoolwide school counseling core curriculum and individual student planning to ensure every student receives the benefit of the school counseling program. Before beginning, it will be helpful to provide a brief contextual framework regarding the history and current movements in standards-based education and the school counselor's role in implementing the new Common Core State Standards.

STANDARDS-BASED EDUCATION

Since the release of *A Nation at Risk* (National Commission on Excellence in Education, 1983), standards-based education has been the motivation behind most educational reform policies at the federal, state, and local levels in the United States. Standards-based education emerged from a passionate perspective that student performance could and should be improved. In order for achievement to improve, it was critical to set specific goals for student performance. This meant all students should have access to a challenging, content-specific curriculum they could master at a proficient-to-high level. In 1996, federal law required all states receiving Title I funds (funds provided to high poverty schools) to develop academic standards. The No Child Left Behind Act (NCLB) created further pressure in 2001, forcing all states to implement standards in their schools. Based on these standards, schools are kept accountable for testing and other measures of adequate yearly progress (NCLB, 2001).

Educational standards provide clear goals for student learning to help teachers ensure their students gain the knowledge and skills necessary to be successful. In 2012, the National Governors Association Center for Best Practices (NGA Center) and the Council of Chief State School Officers (CCSSO) coordinated the Common Core State Standards (CCSS) Initiative. These new standards, developed in collaboration with teachers, school administrators, and other experts, provide a consistent framework of specific *knowledge* and *skills* necessary to ensure students are prepared for success in college and the workforce (National Governors Association Center for Best Practices and Council of Chief State School Officers, 2012).

IMPLEMENTING THE COMMON CORE: THE ROLE OF THE SCHOOL COUNSELOR

Successful implementation of the CCSS calls for school counselors to "create a sense of urgency" (Achieve, 2012a, p. 2). In a recently released Action Brief, the education organization Achieve charged school counselors with recognizing their responsibility to assist in the transformation of schools through the strong

---

COMMON CORE STATE STANDARDS (CCSS) INITIATIVE

"These standards define the knowledge and skills students should have within their K–12 education careers so they will graduate high school able to succeed in entry-level, credit-bearing academic college courses and in workforce training programs. The standards:

- Are aligned with college and work expectations;
- Are clear, understandable, and consistent;
- Include rigorous content *and* application of knowledge through high-order skills;
- Build upon strengths and lessons of current state standards;
- Are informed by other top-performing countries, so all students are prepared to succeed in this global economy and society; and
- Are evidence- and research-based." (NGA Center, 2012)

implementation of CCSS. Calling on school counselors to take an "active role" in working with school leaders to support shifts in cultural and instructional environments, the Action Brief offers recommendations as a starting point. School counselors need to increase awareness regarding their role in implementing CCSS, understand how schools must change, and understand how the new standards will affect the academic, career, and personal/social domains of school counseling. As uniquely positioned professionals, school counselors are further charged to support and take action on the new CCSS. Action steps for school counselors align with the American School Counselor Association's (ASCA's) National Model (2012a) and are recommended in eight specific areas, including those for instructional practice:

- Determine the impact of the CCSS on *systemic approaches* to help students develop appropriate education plans
- *Develop and continually update six-year individual student educational (learning) plans* for every student relating to college- and career-readiness
- *Develop college- and career-readiness lesson plans* that align with CCSS college- and career-ready anchor standards, and reinforce subject-specific standards
- Develop a calendar for when *lessons will be conducted and push into classrooms*
- Prepare to present and/or share the *action plan* for ensuring that all students have a completed and up-to-date Individualized Education Plan (Achieve, 2012a)

The Common Core State Standards Initiative provides an ambitious agenda requiring policies be created to support various needs: (a) establishment of high academic standards, (b) uniform standards-aligned curriculum and instruction, (c) assessment systems that measure and monitor students' needs and progress, (d) accountability systems that hold educators and policymakers responsible for student achievement, and (e) intervention systems of support for students who are struggling (EdSource, 2013). School counselors, as student advocates, are central to these efforts in many capacities. Consider the following questions:

- What standards or competencies should all students know and be able to do as a result of the school counseling program?
- How will the school counseling program ensure all children have access to individual learning plans with rigorous curriculum content?
- How will the school counseling program ensure all students learn content at proficient-to-high levels of performance?
- What policies will be created to support establishing and implementing school counseling core curriculum that is aligned with standards?
- What assessment system will be put into place for school counselors to measure and monitor students' needs and progress?

- What system of accountability will hold school counselors responsible for student achievement?
- What systems of interventions will be created to support struggling students or schools?

ASCA AND STANDARDS-BASED EDUCATION

The ASCA National Standards (Campbell and Dahir, 1997), now referred to as ASCA Student Standards (ASCA, 2004), were created to help ensure students have the knowledge and skills necessary to be successful by providing clear goals for student learning in the school counseling domains. To ensure all students get the core content they need for academic, career, and personal/social development, the ASCA National Model calls for school counseling programs to be comprehensive and an integral part of the total educational program (ASCA, 2003, 2005, 2012a). For this to occur, school counselors, like teachers, must also agree to provide school counselor common core activities, including individual learning plans and core curriculum to ensure students are receiving a consistent, high-quality education from school to school, district to district, and state to state.

INDIVIDUAL STUDENTS' LEARNING PLANS

Individual Student Learning Plans (SLPs) are student-focused planning and monitoring tools for exploring and identifying college and career goals and post secondary plans. In 2011, the Rennie Center for Education Research and Policy reported SLPs were required in 23 states plus the District of Columbia (Rennie Center, 2011). Fourteen states require students to enroll in default college- and career-ready curriculums (meaning all students start high school taking college preparatory courses) with parental opt-out waivers (Achieve, 2012b). Eighteen states are members of the American Diploma Project Network, which focuses on providing more challenging college- and career-ready standards and aligning individual Student Learning Plans with more rigorous graduation requirements. In these states, such as New Mexico, for example, Student Learning Plans (called Next Step Plans) are a requirement by law (NM Public Statute, Article 13, Section 22–13–1.1) School counselors or other school officials hold a yearly meeting with the parent and student, beginning in eighth grade, where plans for postsecondary options are reviewed, and a signed agreement is reached for the student's coursework in the upcoming year. School counselors are the appropriate school professionals to create and oversee systems to ensure that each student has an appropriate SLP that is reviewed and updated regularly. Readers are encouraged to visit the achieve.org website to discover whether their state requires all students to complete a college- and career-ready curriculum. An excellent sample of an entire toolkit for developing SLPs is provided by Hope High School from Providence Public Schools in the online appendix.

SCHOOL COUNSELOR CORE [GUIDANCE*] CURRICULUM

*Historically, *guidance curriculum* has been the most common term used to represent a planned instructional program that is presented to all students in all grade levels by school counselors and other educators (ASCA 2003, 2005; Gysbers, 2010). The third edition of the ASCA National Model renamed guidance curriculum as *school counseling core curriculum* (ASCA, 2012e). Renaming guidance curriculum aligns with the late-1960s position shift from *guidance counselor* to *school counselor* (Ligon and McDaniel, 1970) and with the ASCA governing board's unanimous vote in 1990 to "call the profession 'school counseling' and the program a 'school counseling program'" (ASCA, 2005, p. 9). The renaming of guidance curriculum as school counseling core curriculum in the third edition of the ASCA National Model (2012e) continues the national call for consistency of position, profession, program, and curriculum.

Every effort was made to replace the term *guidance curriculum* within this book and to utilize the term *school counseling core curriculum* or simply *curriculum* when possible and appropriate. However, several artifacts created, submitted, and permissioned for this book contain prior terminology. Readers are encouraged to consider the terms *guidance curriculum* and *school counseling core curriculum* interchangeable and to utilize the term *school counseling core curriculum* in their future work.

A graduate student asked, "How do you decide which students in fourth grade receive school counseling curriculum?" The response: "Which don't?" The purpose of a Schoolwide Core Curriculum Action Plan is to ensure "*every* student gets *every* THING!" By *virtue of breathing*, ALL students receive instruction from the school counseling program. The Schoolwide Core Curriculum Action Plan, used when creating and presenting the school counselor core curriculum, is similar to a teacher's scope and sequence. The District of Columbia Public Schools (DCPS) describes the scope and sequence document as used to "establish consistency of instruction throughout the district—in different grade levels and subject areas—by providing clear guidance on what your children's teachers should teach and when they should teach it" (2011). The district's website describes the rationale for creating a scope and sequence in language that mirrors the reasons school counselors create schoolwide curriculum action plans:

For example, first grade students throughout DCPS will learn about animals and their habitats in November (as part of "The Amazing Animal World" unit theme). This consistency will allow DCPS to provide targeted resources and support that all teachers can use and provide the opportunity for schools to share successful ideas with other schools across the district.

It also helps prevent interruptions or repetitions in the education of transient students. Consider the common case of a student at School A on one side of town who then transfers to School B on the other side of town during the school year.

With a common scope and sequence in place, that student can now easily transition to his or her new school without missing any important information about animals and their habitats. And because those lessons are taught across the district around the same time, that transfer student wouldn't repeat the "The Amazing Animal World" unit just because she changed schools (DCPS, 2011).

> Why is it so different for school counselors? I remember walking into my school counseling office on the first day and there was NOTHING in the office except a manila folder with the names of the "G.A.T.E." students listed in it. I realized I was truly on my own and would have to start from scratch. Can you imagine a teacher entering his or her classroom with no curriculum? How would the teacher know what to teach?

Just as teachers have collaborated to determine grade-level expectations, scope and sequence, and pacing charts for timely delivery of subject content, school counselors are called to collaborate and create similar documents ensuring all students are on target to receive common core instruction from school counseling programs. As parents come to know their third-grade students will be learning multiplication tables as their standard in math starting in January, so too will they understand the school counseling lesson for January is about problem-solving, which supports a school counseling competency. Teachers will meet to agree on "essential standards" or "power standards" for each grade level; similarly, school counselors will collaborate to determine which content is most appropriate for students at each grade level, based on developmental and site-specific, data-driven needs. Following the same standards-based education expectations created for teachers, school counselors coordinate standards across schools, districts, and even states to decide which standards will be prioritized and what curriculum they plan to deliver.

By What Criteria Should Counseling School Core Curriculum Be Determined?

School counselors are encouraged to review the CCSS recommendations when developing school counseling lesson content and Schoolwide Core Curriculum Action Plans (Achieve, 2012a). Additionally, it may be beneficial to explore how district and state initiatives with regard to the CCSS may complement, inform, or contribute to the school counseling program's standards.

- Will the school counseling core curriculum be aligned with and promote a college and career readiness agenda?
- Will curriculum include preparation and instruction for completing or reviewing yearly individual Student Learning Plans?
- Will college and career readiness and preparation be included in the K–12 curriculum scope and sequence?
- Will standards-based school counseling curriculum be consistent from classroom to classroom and school to school?

- Will the lessons be understandable, so school counselors, students, and parents know what they need to do to help students learn?
- Will the curriculum be uniform across schools, so students have similar expectations for rigor regardless of where they live?
- Will the curriculum include application of knowledge through higher order skills?
- Will the curriculum build upon the strengths and lessons in other core standard areas?
- Does the curriculum contain 21st century skills, so all students are prepared to succeed in this global economy and society?
- Will the curriculum be designed utilizing an evidence- and research-based approach?

What Does the Alignment With Common Core State Standards Mean for K–12 Students, School Counselors, and Schools?

Like standards for math and language arts, school counseling standards are intended to provide more consistency regarding expectations for student learning among schools and across districts and states. Until recently, every state determined its own set of academic standards. This meant students in different states in the same grade level have been expected to achieve at different levels (NGA Center, 2012). Since 2012, all but a few states, and 85% of the nation's public school systems, have adopted the Common Core State Standards (Achieve, 2013).

School counseling standards continue to vary from state to state. Some states have common expectations; many leave decisions about expectations up to individual districts and schools. Although CCSS for school counseling do not exist at press time, adopting common core standards for school counseling will not guarantee equitable levels of achievement among students. Rather, much like the common core standards for teaching, aligning standards for school counseling—whether the standards are new common core or existing state or ASCA Student Standards (ASCA, 2004)—within a core framework for a school or district will ensure only that each student receives consistent exposure to learning experiences and curriculum materials.

How Will Standards Be Delivered?

Standards do not prescribe how teachers or school counselors *deliver* their curriculum; rather, the standards help all educators determine the *knowledge, attitudes,* and *skills* their students deserve to receive to support their learning and achievement. Depending on the student-to-counselor ratio, school culture, or efficiency and effectiveness of other school staff, school counselors may implement standards-based core curriculum themselves, in collaboration with teachers, through overseeing an advisory program model, or through some combination of the above. The ASCA National Model calls for school counseling programs to establish and convene an advisory council to review program goals and results and to make recommendations for the school counseling program (ASCA, 2003, 2005, 2012a; Johnson & Johnson, 2001). Effective use of an advisory council can assist in determining which method of curriculum implementation best meets student and district needs.

Gunn High School in Palo Alto, California, convened the Gunn Guidance Advisory Committee to provide extensive review and recommendations for the school counseling program in alignment with the district's strategic plan goal to "improve guidance and counseling services that prepare students for college and other post-secondary opportunities" (Gunn Guidance Advisory Committee, 2013, p.1). Guiding questions included the following:

- How do we define and measure student success?
- What would be true for all Gunn students if they were successful in academic, social-emotional and post-secondary domains?
- Which student success outcomes are highest priorities for Gunn to support? (Gunn Guidance Advisory Committee, 2013, p. 7)

As different implementation methods of standards-based core curriculum and program delivery were being considered, Dr. Pope from the School of Education at Stanford University and the author of this text were asked to respond to the following guiding questions:

- What essential criteria and principles should guide the design of any student support approach or model?
- What do educational research and best professional practices suggest are guiding design principles for any highly effective student support delivery system? (Gunn Guidance Advisory Committee, 2013, p. 12)

Dr. Pope recommended the following (abbreviated):

- Community buy-in from all stakeholders (teachers, administrators, counselors, parents)
- Clarity of program purpose
- Professional development for school counselors and advisors to ensure clarity of respective roles and responsibilities
- Strong program and curriculum content and structure. (Gunn Guidance Advisory Committee, 2013)

Serving as a consultant to the district, the author of this text recommended the following guiding design principles:

- Comprehensive program model:
  o Developmental in nature (scaffold the learning content)
  o Preventative in design (not reactive)
  o Comprehensive in scope (academic, career, personal/social)

- Program goals and objectives are clearly stated and agreed upon and are related to student achievement and success for each and every student.
- Proactive model, not reactive model; every student receives the benefit of the program, not only those who know who the school counselor is or where his or her office is located, or those who are in the top 10% or most needy bottom 10%.
- All students receive standards-based core curriculum in academic, career, and personal/social development (agreed upon scope and sequence).

- All students receive an individual student plan regardless of post-secondary goals. Plans are reviewed, revised, and updated.
- Early warning responsive services systems are in place, which help identify students at risk of not meeting program goals. Mechanisms are in place, which trigger appropriate supports and interventions for identified students
- Evidenced-based model of program evaluation is implemented:
  o Problem Description: Knowing what needs to be addressed
  o Outcome Research Use: Knowing what is likely to work
  o Intervention Evaluation: Knowing if the intervention is making a difference

- Appropriately trained, licensed and credentialed educators (as per education code and national professional guidelines) provide services for students. (Gunn Guidance Advisory Committee, 2013, pp. 12–13)

Discussions focused on what outcomes the advisory committee wanted for students, regardless of delivery system; a review of data to determine whether they were already meeting those outcomes; and what support they felt they were not receiving. After months of meetings and school site visits, 17 members of the diverse advisory committee came to unanimous consensus, making detailed recommendations in the following areas: (a) support structures, (b) school environment and culture, (c) communication, (d) connection and curriculum, (e) improve outcomes for all, and (f) leadership.

Readers are encouraged to review *Supporting the Success of All Gunn High School Students: A Report by the Gunn Guidance Advisory Committee,* located online at http://www.gunngac.org/Gunn%20GAC%20Final%20Report%202013.pdf.

As school counseling teams begin to work on aligning with standards and creating core curriculum action plans, consider creating your own guiding principals. The ASCA National Model (2003, 2005) includes assumptions the school counseling team may want to consider as well. Standards will help students and parents by setting clear and realistic developmental goals and expectations for student success. Standards in all core subject areas, including school counseling, are the first step toward providing students with a high-quality education in preparation for college and career readiness for all students. *How* these standards will be *implemented,* however, matters as much as the content of the standards. Consider the following:

- What types of guaranteed programmatic services (curriculum, individual Student Learning Plans should each and every student receive?
- What data will trigger an appropriate guaranteed intervention?
- What data will we use to determine "success"?

SCHOOLWIDE CORE CURRICULUM ACTION PLANS

Figures 1.1, 1.2, and 1.3 provide examples of Schoolwide Core Curriculum Action Plans indicating the specific curriculum every student in the district will receive from the school counseling program in elementary, middle, and high school. Note that in each plan, the school counseling program has scheduled the lessons to be delivered at different points throughout the school year, and that the lessons are distributed equitably across a variety of different core subjects so as not to consistently occur in the same subject area classrooms. Some school counselors prioritize lesson delivery through collaboration with teachers of elective courses. While this may avoid interruption of teaching in core subjects, utilizing electives exclusively may also send a message to elective teachers that their instruction time is of less value. Also, if some students are not enrolled in the chosen elective, careful consideration must be made to ensure *all* students still receive the school counseling curriculum. Consulting with teachers and administration regarding the most efficient and effective manner for curriculum delivery reinforces professional and collegial faculty relationships.

Care is also taken to ensure school counseling standards are addressed in all three domains (academic, career, and personal/social), with attention to a minimum number of agreed-upon lessons for each grade level. The number of lessons delivered may vary depending on the student-to-counselor ratio or the extent to which the school counselors deliver all lessons or assist others in the delivery of the curriculum (such as when school counselors supervise advisories or when elementary teachers deliver *Second Step* violence prevention curriculum). Since school counseling curriculum is delivered to all students, the same numbers per grade level appear in each grade level under "Projected Number of Students Impacted." Some curriculum is school counselor generated, and other curriculum may come from prepackaged programs, but all include a method for evaluation that will be discussed later in this text.

While some lessons include immediate and/or long-term evaluation tools, this is not to imply the school counselor would measure every lesson in every way annually. Rather, the Schoolwide Core Curriculum Action Plan may provide a list of which outcome data might be reviewed or examined as significant data points that align with each curriculum lesson. The school counseling team selects a few lessons each year to evaluate and improve based on their alignment with schoolwide and/or program goals (discussed further in Chapter 4). Finally, in the last column on the right, note school counselors implement some lessons, while other lessons are taught in collaboration with colleagues such as the language arts teacher or an elective class teacher. At the bottom, note the principal's signature of approval and a date scheduled for the staff presentation. Ideally, a Schoolwide Core Curriculum Action Plan is reviewed and approved by administration in advance and shared each year at the first faculty meeting, accompanied by a calendar indicating when the lessons will be delivered, so teachers can prepare in advance. Additional discussion about the importance of utilizing planning calendars is presented in Chapter 9.

After reviewing the samples in this chapter (Figures 1.1., 1.2, and 1.3), start from scratch and create your own action plan (see template in Figure 1.4). Also, consider ways in which the samples provided might be improved. For instance, should more career development lessons be added to an elementary action plan (Figure 1.1)? Figure 1.5 provides a real example created by Danielle Duarte for her elementary school. Her evaluation measures align with the goals of the Elementary and Secondary School Counseling Grant (See Figure 3.8 in Chapter 3) she and her team were implementing. Do you agree with the evaluation methods selected? How might you revise them?

Figure 1.1 Elementary School Curriculum Action Plan

			XYZ School District—Elementary School Counseling Schoolwide Core Curriculum Action Plan 20xx–20xx					
Grade Level	Lesson Content	American School Counselor Association (ASCA) Domain/Standard	Curriculum and Materials	Number of Lessons	Projected Start/ Projected End	Projected Total Number of Students Impacted	Evaluation Methods How will the results be measured?	Implementation Contact Person
K	Social Skills	Personal/Social AB	Peace-Making Skills	5	September	120–140	Teacher Observation Feedback	Counselor A
1	Friendship Skills	Personal/Social AB	"Friends to the End"	1	February	120–140	Demonstration of Skill Observational Feedback	Counselor A
	School Resources	Academic A Personal/Social ABC	What is a school counselor? How do I ask for help?	1	August	120–140	Demonstration of Skill	Counselor B
2	Resolving Conflict	Personal/Social ABC	"Telling vs. Tattling"	1	November	120–140	Pre/Post Demonstration of Skill	Counselor A
	Communication	Personal/Social ABC	"I" Statements	1	February	120–140	Pre/Post Report Card Grades on Citizenship Habits	Counselor A
3	Peer Relations	Personal/Social AB	"Don't Laugh at Me"	2	October	120–140	Pre/Post Number of Conflict Mediation and Discipline Referrals	Counselor A
4	Anti-Bullying	Personal/Social ABC	Be Cool!	2	March	120–140	Pre/Post Number of Conflict Mediation and Discipline Referrals	Counselor A
	Academic Success	Academic ABC	"Organization Skills"	2	October	120–140	Pre/Post Report Card Marks on Work Skills and Study Habits	Counselor B
5	Academic Success	Academic ABC	"Study Skills"	1	September	120–140	Pre/Post Report Card Marks on Work Skills and Study Habits	Counselor B
	Conflict Resolution	Personal/Social ABC	Conflict Resolution Lessons	2	January	120–140	Pre/Post Number of Discipline Referrals Youth Risk Behavior Survey (YRBS)	Counselor A
	Academic Success	Academic ABC	"Test-Taking Skills"	2	March/April	120–140	Pre/Post Reported Use of Skills Scores on Tests	Counselor B
	Career Awareness	Academic ABC	"Career Key"	1	May	120–140	Pre/Post Completion of Career Assessment	Counselor B

Principal's Signature   Date   Date of Staff Presentation   Prepared By

Figure 1.2 Middle School Curriculum Action Plan

XYZ School District–Middle School Counseling Schoolwide Core Curriculum Action Plan 20xx–20xx

Grade Level	Lesson Content	American School Counselor Association (ASCA) Domain/Standard	Curriculum and Materials	Projected Start/ Projected End	Projected Number of Students Impacted	Class/Subject in Which Lesson Will Be Presented	Evaluation Methods How will the results be measured?	Implementation Contact Person
6	Study Skills	Academic ABC Personal/Social ABC	Counselor Generated from Materials in Student Agenda	October	369	Rotating Core Subjects	Pre/Post ASK (Attitude, Skills, Knowledge) Agenda Use Homework Marks Report Card Grades	Counselor A
	Cyber-Bullying and Harassment	Academic AC Personal/Social ABC	Compiled from Cyber-Bullying Training and District Harassment Policy	November	369	Rotating Core Subjects	Pre/Post (ASK) Number of Mediation/ Discipline Referrals School Climate e.g. Youth Risk Behavior Survey (YRBS)	Counselor A
	Respect and Conflict Resolution	Personal/Social ABC	Selected Lessons from "Steps to Respect"	January/ February	369	Rotating Core Subjects	Pre/Post (ASK) Number of Mediations/ Discipline Referrals School Climate: YRBS	Counselor A
	Introduction to College and Career Options	Academic ABC Career ABC	Counselor Created and Generated	February/March	369	Rotating Core Subjects	College Knowledge Survey Promotion Rate (> 2.0)	Counselor A
	Test-Taking Success and Motivation	Academic AB	Counselor Created and Generated	May	369	Rotating Core Subjects	Pre/Post (ASK) Reported Use of Strategies Test Scores	Counselor A
7	Goal Setting	Academic ABC Career B Personal/Social B	District SMART Goals Lesson	November	376	Rotating Core Subjects	Pre/Post Write SMART Goal (for Academics) % Attaining SMART Goal	Counselor B
	Ask for Help Suicide Prevention	Academic AC Personal/Social ABC	District Yellow Ribbon Curriculum	November/ December	376	Rotating Core Subjects	Yellowribbon.org. Survey Number of Concerned Person Referrals School Climate: YRBS	Counselor B
	Postsecondary Options	Academic AB Career B Personal/Social AB	Curriculum and Counselor Generated	January	376	Rotating Core Subjects	Pre/Post Scores on College Knowledge Survey Number Registering for College Prep Courses (Algebra, Spanish)	Counselor B

XYZ School District–Middle School Counseling Schoolwide Core Curriculum Action Plan 20xx–20xx

Grade Level	Lesson Content	American School Counselor Association (ASCA) Domain/Standard	Curriculum and Materials	Projected Start/ Projected End	Projected Number of Students Impacted	Class/Subject in Which Lesson Will Be Presented	Evaluation Methods How will the results be measured?	Implementation Contact Person
8	Naviance "Career Key"	Academic BC Personal/Social ABC Career ABC	Naviance Curriculum	February/March	376	Rotating Core Subjects	Pre/Post Numbers Creating Naviance Logins Career Assessment Completion Use of Naviance (number who log in)	Counselor B
	Academic Goal Setting	Academic AB Career B Personal/Social AB	Counselor Generated and Curriculum Materials	October/November	402	Rotating Core Subjects	Pre/Post SMART Goal (for Academics) % Attaining SMART Goal	Counselor C
	Getting Ready for High School	Academic BC Career ABC Personal/ Social AB	Counselor Generated and Curriculum Materials	November/December	402	Rotating Core Subjects	Pre/Post GPA Algebra Passage Rate Promotion Rates Ninth Grade on Track Q1	Counselor C
	College Knowledge	Academic ABC Career ABC	Counselor Generated and GEAR UP/ Curriculum Materials	January/February	402	Rotating Core Subjects	Pre/Post Assessment of College Requirements and Perceptions of Postsecondary Education Ninth Grade on Track Q1	Counselor C
	Making Healthy Choices	Academic ABC Personal/Social ABC	Counselor Created and Curriculum Material	February/March	402	Rotating Core Subjects	Pre/Post Scores on Healthy Choices Section of YRBS	Counselor C
	Naviance Careers	Academic C Personal/Social A	Naviance	May/June	402	Rotating Core Subjects	% Completing Naviance District Career Assessment Requirements Number With Four-Year Plans Number Using Naviance	Counselor C

Principal's Signature   Date   Date of Staff Presentation   Prepared By

Figure 1.3 High School Curriculum Action Plan

XYZ Unified School District—High School Counseling Schoolwide Core Curriculum Action Plan 20xx–20xx

Grade Level	Lesson Content	American School Counselor Association (ASCA) Domain/Standard	Curriculum and Materials	Projected Start/ Projected End	Projected Number of Students Impacted	Class/Subject in Which Lesson Will Be Presented	Evaluation Methods How will the results be measured?	Implementation Contact Person
9	Welcome to Ninth Grade: Credits COUNT!	Academic ABC	PowerPoint: GPA Game Lesson Plan	October 18–22	All Ninth-Grade Students	Earth Science/ Physics/ Advanced Physics	Pre/Post Survey Number of Ninth Graders on Target (not credit deficient)	Counselor A
	Introduction to Naviance	Academic ABC Career C	Naviance PowerPoint	December 13–17	All Ninth-Grade Students	English	Number Initially Logging in to Naviance Number of Times Using Naviance	Counselor C
	Course Planning in Naviance	Academic ABC	Naviance— Computer lab	January 30 to February 4	All Ninth-Grade Students	English	Number Completing Course Plan and Articulation (number using Naviance)	Counselor A
	Suicide Prevention	Personal/Social C	District Provided Yellow Ribbon	February	All Ninth-Grade Students	English	Pre/Post Survey Number of Concerned Person Referrals	Counselor A
	Academic Support and Intervention Options	Academic ABC	PowerPoint CAC Handouts	January 10–14	All Ninth-Grade Students	Earth Science/ Physics/ Advanced Physics	Pre/Post Survey Number of Ninth Graders on Target (not credit deficient)	Counselor A
	Post High School Options and Opportunities	Academic BC Career AB	PowerPoint Handouts	March 21–25	All Ninth-Grade Students	Earth Science/ Physics/ Advanced Physics	Pre/Post Survey Number Taking Advanced Courses	Counselor C
10	Introduction To Naviance	Academic ABC Career C	Naviance Computer Lab	November 29 to December 3	All 10th-Grade Students	World History	Number Initially Logging in to Naviance	Counselor C
	Tenth Grade Review/ Course Planning	Academic ABC Career ABC Personal/Social B	Naviance Computer Lab	January 18–21	All 10th-Grade Students	World History	Pre/Post 4 Year Plans on File % in College Prep	Counselor B
	College Knowledge Presentations	Academic B Career C Personal/Social B	Introduction to CAC	December 13–17	All 10th-Grade Students	English 3,4	Pre/Post Survey	Counselor B
	Career Assessment Naviance	Academic C Career ABC Personal/Social B	Naviance Computer Lab	April 18–22	All 10th-Grade Students	World History	Number Completing Career Assessment in Naviance Number Using Naviance	Counselor B
11	Class Assembly for Yellow Ribbon Week	Personal/Social C	PowerPoint/ Video	October 20–21	All 11th-Grade Students	American Literature	Completion of Post Survey	Counselor A

XYZ Unified School District—High School Counseling Schoolwide Core Curriculum Action Plan 20xx–20xx

Grade Level	Lesson Content	American School Counselor Association (ASCA) Domain/Standard	Curriculum and Materials	Projected Start/ Projected End	Projected Number of Students Impacted	Class/Subject in Which Lesson Will Be Presented	Evaluation Methods How will the results be measured?	Implementation Contact Person
	Naviance District 11th Grade	Academic ABC Career C	Naviance Computer Lab	November 15–19	All 11th-Grade Students	US History	Completion of Naviance Items Number Using Naviance	Counselor C
	Junior Time Line	Academic ABC Career C Personal/Social B	PowerPoint	November 1	All 11th-Grade Students	American Literature	Pre/Post Survey	Counselor B
	Course Planning	Academic ABC Personal/Social B	Naviance Computer Lab	January 3–7	All 11th-Grade Students	US History	Completed Course Plan— Naviance Report	Counselor C
	Post High School Plan	Academic ABC Career C Personal/Social B	Naviance Computer Lab	May 2–6 ???	All 11th-Grade Students	US History	Naviance Report of Use	Counselor B
	Early Academic Program Assessment	Academic A B Career C Personal/Social B	PowerPoint	Week of March 28 or April 11	All 11th-Grade Students	American Literature	Pre/Post Number Taking/ Passing EAP	Counselor B
12	Naviance	Academic ABC Career C	Naviance Computer Lab	October 11–15	All 12th-Grade Students	Government/ Economics	Completion of Naviance Required Items Number Using Naviance	Counselor C
	Senior Time Line	Academic ABC Career C Personal/Social B	PowerPoint Calendar	September 16	All 12th-Grade Students	Government/ Economics	Pre/Post Survey Number of Seniors on Target	Counselor B
	College Application or Post High School Plan	Academic ABC Career ABC Personal/Social B	Naviance Computer Lab	November 1–5	All 12th-Grade Students	Government/ Economics	Naviance Report Graduation Rates Number of College Applications	Counselor B
	FAFSA Presentation	Academic BC Career B Personal/Social B	FAFSA Power Point/ Handouts	December 1–2	All 12th-Grade Students	World Literature	Pre/Post Survey Number of FAFSAs Submitted	Counselor B
	Career Assessment/ FAFSA Pin Number	Academic BC Career ABC Personal/Social B	Naviance Computer Lab	December 6–10	All 12th-Grade Students	Government/ Economics	Naviance Report Number of FAFSAs Submitted Scholarship Money Awarded	Counselor B
	Resume Naviance	Academic ABC Career ABC Personal/Social B	Naviance Computer Lab	January 10–14	All 12th-Grade Students	Government/ Economics	Naviance Report Number of Resumes Completed	Counselor B
	College Life and Post High School Survey	Academic BC Personal/Social ABC	Naviance Computer Lab Senior Exit Survey	May 16–20	All 12th-Grade Students	Government/ Economics	Naviance Report % With Postsecondary Plan % Graduating With College Eligibility	Counselor C

Principal's Signature   Date   Date of Staff Presentation   Prepared By

Figure 1.4 Schoolwide Core Curriculum Action Plan

Blank Form

_____ Unified School District—
School Counseling Schoolwide Core Curriculum Action Plan 20___–20___

Grade Level	Lesson Content	American School Counselor Association (ASCA) Domain/Standard	Curriculum and Materials	Projected Start/ Projected End	Projected Number of Students Impacted	Class/Subject in Which Lesson Will Be Presented	Evaluation Methods How will the results be measured?	Implementation Contact Person
		Academic ABC Career ABC Personal/Social ABC						
		Academic ABC Career ABC Personal/Social ABC						
		Academic ABC Career ABC Personal/Social ABC						
		Academic ABC Career ABC Personal/Social ABC						
		Academic ABC Career ABC Personal/Social ABC						
		Academic ABC Career ABC Personal/Social ABC						
		Academic ABC Career ABC Personal/Social ABC						
		Academic ABC Career ABC Personal/Social ABC						
		Academic ABC Career ABC Personal/Social ABC						
		Academic ABC Career ABC Personal/Social ABC						
		Academic ABC Career ABC Personal/Social ABC						

_____   _____   _____
Principal's Signature   Date   Date of Staff Presentation   Prepared By

Figure 1.5 Alvin Dunn Elementary School Guidance Curriculum Action Plan 2011–2012

San Marcos Unified School District

Grade Level	Lesson Content	American School Counselor Association (ASCA) Domain/Standard	Curriculum and Materials	Projected Start/Projected End	Projected Number of Students Impacted	Time of Lesson	Evaluation Methods How will the results be measured?
K	Second Step: Empathy	Academic A Career A Personal/Social ABC	Second Step Violence Prevention Program	September–January	100	Every other week @ 12:15 Burkey: Mon Hernandez: Tues Wurster: Thurs	Teacher Feedback
	Second Step: Impulses and Problem Solving	Academic A Career A Personal/Social ABC	Second Step Violence Prevention Program	February–June			
1	Second Step: Empathy	Academic AB Career A Personal/Social ABC	Second Step Violence Prevention Program	September–January	110	Weekly Ray/Colburn: Mon @ 2:45 Kincaid: Thurs @ 2:20 Cruz: Tues @ 2:40 Cerda: Thurs @ 2:40 Reynolds: Thurs @ 11:35	Monitoring N's and U's on Report Cards (work skills and study habits) Teacher Feedback
	Second Step: Impulses and Problem Solving	Academic AB Career A Personal/Social ABC	Second Step Violence Prevention Program	February–April			
	Second Step: Anger Management	Academic AB Career A Personal/Social ABC	Second Step Violence Prevention Program	May–June			
	Appreciating Differences	Personal/Social ABC	Book: *It's Okay to Be Different*	September			
	College and Career Awareness	Career A	Books: *L M N O Peas* and *Look Out, College, Here I Come!*	January			
	Anti-Bullying	Personal/Social ABC	Book: *Stop Picking on Me*	March			
2	Second Step: Empathy	Academic AB Career A Personal/Social ABC	Second Step Violence Prevention Program	September–January	100	Every Other Week @ 11:05 DeMarco: Mon Nicolai: Tues Hernandez: Wed Navarro: Thurs	Monitoring N's and U's on Report Cards (work skills and study habits) Teacher Feedback
	Second Step: Impulses and Problem Solving	Academic AB Career A Personal/Social ABC	Second Step Violence Prevention Program	February–April			

(Continued)

Figure 1.5 (Continued)

			San Marcos Unified School District				
Grade Level	Lesson Content	American School Counselor Association (ASCA) Domain/Standard	Curriculum and Materials	Projected Start/Projected End	Projected Number of Students Impacted	Time of Lesson	Evaluation Methods How will the results be measured?
	Second Step: Anger Management	Academic AB Career A Personal/Social ABC	Second Step Violence Prevention Program	May–June			
	College and Career Awareness	Career ABC	Books: *L M N O Peas* and *Look Out, College, Here I Come!*	January			n/a
	Anti-Bullying	Personal/Social ABC	Book: *Stop Picking on Me*	March			Behavior Referral Rates
3	Second Step: Empathy	Personal/Social ABC	Second Step Violence Prevention Program	September–December	90	Every Other Week Vitiello/Martinson: Mon @ 2:00 Sanchez: Tues @ 2:00	Monitoring N's and U's on Report Cards (work skills and study habits)
	Second Step: Impulses and Problem Solving	Personal/Social BC	Second Step Violence Prevention Program	January–March			
	Second Step: Anger Management	Academic AB Career A Personal/Social ABC	Second Step Violence Prevention Program	April–June			
	Red Ribbon Week	Personal/Social ABC	Counselor-Generated Anti-Drug/Alcohol Lesson	October			n/a
	College and Career Readiness	Academic BC Career ABC Personal/Social AB	Counselor-Generated College Lesson; College and Career Presenters Day	January			Pre/Post Survey
	Stand UP to Bullying Month	Personal/Social ABC	Book: *My Secret Bully* 4 Corners Lesson Stand UP to Bullying Calendar	March			Behavior Referral Rates
4	Second Step: Empathy	Personal/Social ABC	Second Step Violence Prevention Program	September–December	100	Weekly Salmon: Mon @ 1:30 Walker: Tues @ 1:30 Miringoff: Wed @ 9:00	Monitoring N's and U's on Report Cards (work skills and study habits)
	Second Step: Impulses and Problem Solving	Personal/Social BC	Second Step Violence Prevention Program	January–March			

Grade Level	Lesson Content	American School Counselor Association (ASCA) Domain/Standard	Curriculum and Materials	Projected Start/Projected End	Projected Number of Students Impacted	Time of Lesson	Evaluation Methods How will the results be measured?
	Second Step: Anger Management	Academic AB Career A Personal/Social ABC	Second Step Violence Prevention Program	April–June		Vandervort: Tues @ 11:30	
	Red Ribbon Week	Personal/Social ABC	Counselor-Generated Anti-Drug/Alcohol Lesson	October			n/a
	College and Career Readiness	Academic BC Career ABC Personal/Social AB	Counselor-Generated College Lesson; College and Career Presenters Day	January			Pre/Post Survey
	Stand UP to Bullying Month	Personal/Social ABC	Book: My Secret Bully 4 Corners Lesson Stand UP to Bullying Calendar	March			Behavior Referral Rates
5	Second Step: Empathy	Personal/Social ABC	Second Step Violence Prevention Program	September–December	90	Weekly Hayashi: Mon @ 8:50 Falk: Thurs @ 1:30 Watters: Fri @ 12:20	Monitoring N's and U's on Report Cards (work skills and study habits) CA Healthy Kids Survey
	Second Step: Impulses and Problem Solving	Personal/Social BC	Second Step Violence Prevention Program	January–March			
	Second Step: Anger Management	Academic AB Career A Personal/Social ABC	Second Step Violence Prevention Program	April–June			
	Red Ribbon Week	Personal/Social ABC	Counselor-Generated Anti-Drug/Alcohol Lesson	October			CA Healthy Kids Survey
	College and Career Readiness	Academic BC Career ABC Personal/Social AB	Counselor-Generated College Lesson; College and Career Presenters Day	January			Pre/Post Survey
	Stand UP to Bullying Month	Personal/Social ABC	Book: My Secret Bully; 4 Corners Lesson; Daily Calendar	March			CA Healthy Kids Survey Pre/Post Survey
	Transition to Middle School	Academic ABC Career A Personal/Social A	Counselor Generated	April and May			Monitoring D's/F's in Q1 Middle School 2012/2013

San Marcos Unified School District

2

Intentional Guidance

Some Kids Need MORE

WHAT IS INTENTIONAL GUIDANCE?

According to an online dictionary, the term *intent* suggests "clearer formulation or greater deliberateness"; *intention* is defined as "what one has in mind to do or bring about"; and finally, *intentional* refers to "an action done deliberately, on purpose, and not by accident" (Intention, 2013; Intentionally, n.d.).

Guidance is defined as "the act or function of guiding; leadership; direction; advice or counseling, esp. that is provided for students choosing a course of study or preparing for a vocation" (Guidance, n.d.b) and as "counseling or advice on educational, vocational, or psychological matters" (Guidance, n.d.a).

While guidance is often provided for every student, the concept behind *intentional guidance* is "some kids need more." Determining which students need more is paramount in conceptualizing intentional guidance. Thus, when aligned to the work of a school counselor, a sample definition of intentional guidance might be, "A deliberate act by a school counselor to guide, lead, direct, or provide purposeful interventions for students in need academically, personally, or socially." As we discuss the reasons, research, and alignment of intentional guidance with other reform movements in education, this definition might be revised. But for now . . . let's start with this one.

Fundamentally, the philosophy behind intentional guidance activities is "not by accident." As mentioned above, "some kids need more," but which kids? Intentional guidance activities are purposeful, planned, data driven, and specific. Unlike the more traditional expectation that school counselors provide responsive interventions primarily for students who are referred or who refer themselves, the intentional guidance approach requires school counselors to determine, using data, which students require interventions and at what intervals. Then, predetermined interventions are provided to meet identified needs.

The life of a school counselor is hectic. School counselors often spend their days working with students, teachers, and parents who were not necessarily on their schedule the previous day. Student referrals are never ending, and many school counselors report feeling overwhelmed by the randomness of their referrals. "Counselor-student ratios are high, and there is never enough time to see all the students that have been assigned to a counselor or that the counselor would like to see" (Myrick, 2003, p. 177). School counselors often complain they feel as though they are spinning their wheels, unsure they are working with the right students. Others liken it to "gurgling at the water line," "running like a chicken with its head cut off," and "juggling a variety of responsibilities" (Field & Baker, 2004, p. 62). Thus, school counselors often end up performing what I often refer to as "random acts of guidance" instead of *intentional* acts of guidance. Consequentially, their days happen to them; they don't "happen to their days." The many acts of reactivity in the school counseling profession can wear on a professional counselor—likening the role to "putting fingers in the proverbial dike" and being no more than a firefighter running around with an extinguisher (Dooley, 2010).

Intentional guidance activities are not random. Rather, they are calendared in advance. They are data-driven, specific, time-sensitive interventions that occur as scheduled for students who qualify. For instance, after the first progress report or grading period, every ninth grader with two or more F's in core classes will be provided a specific intervention, as will every fourth grader with 10 or more absences and every sixth grader with three or more referrals for anger management. The intentional guidance philosophy considers that the core school counseling curriculum, for some students, has not resulted in the desired outcome and that more intervention is necessary. Before providing more detail, let's review a few important concepts from the ASCA National Model that align with the concept of intentional guidance (ASCA, 2005).

INTENTIONAL GUIDANCE AND THE ASCA NATIONAL MODEL

The *ASCA National Model: A Framework for School Counseling Programs* was introduced in 2002 in draft form (Bowers & Hatch), followed by the first edition (ASCA, 2003), a second edition in 2005, and a third edition in 2012. Since that time it has sold more than 200,250 copies (J. Cook, personal communication, January 24, 2013) and has become a seminal document for the profession.

> The *ASCA National Model: A Framework for School Counseling Programs* (2005), now in its second edition, continues to clearly call out to all school counselors to use data to drive important decisions and to evaluate those decisions against the level of impact on student success/achievement. This landmark document has paved the way for school counselors to navigate the chaotic landscape of education in more comprehensive, consistent, and systematic ways—a manner unprecedented in our profession's history. The ASCA National Model® provides a framework that helps school counselors practice with greater intention and increased clarity. (Sabella, 2006, p. 412)

Most school counseling graduate students are taught the ASCA National Model in their first introductory course, and it is used widely throughout school counselor education programs to provide the framework for building a comprehensive school counseling program.

When the ASCA National Model was being developed, the term *intentional guidance* was recommended during the original conversations held in Tucson, Arizona, in 2001 (Bowers, Hatch, & Schwallie-Giddis, 2001). As the national leaders met, several "model components" were agreed upon, including this one: "Comprehensive school counseling programs must include the concept of intentionality in the development of the program to ensure that underserved or underperforming populations achieve the required competencies" (Bowers et al., 2001, p. 18).

During the two-and-a-half-day summit, national leaders also agreed upon a list of assumptions and criteria that would be central to the development of the ASCA National Model. Statements regarding a need for intentionality and working with targeted groups were evident. Below are comments made regarding what should be included in the ASCA National Model as stated by the development team and archived by Lori Holland (Lori Holland, personal communication, June 1, 2000). who served as one of two scribes at the ASCA model meeting (speaker names removed):

- "intentionally focus on existing school data about kids who are not achieving or not attending"
- "targeted and intentional guidance for students who come to light in the data as having needs"
- " . . . intentional activities to bring about intended change. All students will receive these lessons . . . , but for these students we need to target certain areas: F students, attendance problems. . . ."
- "You don't see these kids unless you intentionally look to them."
- "program is for every student, with specific attention to the targeted population"
- "intentional guidance and every student guidance . . . advocacy and leadership are infused throughout . . . equity and access for all and for the targeted group"

The final summary in notes stated, "Improving achievement for every student includes targeted, intentional activities focusing on underserved and underperforming student populations" (Lori Holland, personal communication, June 1, 2000).

At the end of the summit, the eighth (of nineteen) assumptions agreed upon as the writing team moved forward was as follows:

A school counseling program should provide intentional guidance to specifically address the needs of every student, particularly students of culturally diverse, low socioeconomic status, and other underserved or underperforming populations (ASCA, 2003, p. 77).

As writing for the ASCA model began, and feedback on early drafts was shared with original team members, much discussion ensued, and in the end, the terminology agreed upon for the intervention action plan in the ASCA National Model (ASCA, 2003, 2005) was "Closing the Gap."

Within the ASCA National Model, school counselors are charged with developing a comprehensive school counseling program that contains four components: (a) foundation, (b) delivery, (c) management, and (d) accountability (ASCA, 2005). Each of these components aligns with the concept of intentional guidance.

Foundation

Beliefs do indeed drive behavior. If school counselors do not believe "some students need more" or that, as professional school counselors, they have an obligation to ensure underperforming or underrepresented students receive unsolicited academic and personal/social interventions, then results will be impacted. Success occurs when every member of the school counseling team works together with a common philosophy that includes proactive interventions. Mission statements envision future student success. Intentional guidance is designed to target those who are not attending, behaving, or achieving. Intentional guidance aligns with the ASCA National Standards. Academic Standard A states, "Students will acquire the attitudes, knowledge and skills that contribute to learning in school and across the lifespan" (ASCA, 2003, p. 81). The language says "students," not *some* students. This important distinction ensures school counselors work to support every student in achieving the national standards, and that requires intentionality.

Delivery

The term *intentional guidance* most closely aligns with responsive services, because, as the term indicates, school counselors respond to the students' needs as identified by data. Responsive services are not reserved for only personal/social issues, such as crisis intervention. Absences from school, failing classes, and being off target to promote to the next grade are also calls for immediate responsive interventions designed to meet the students' needs.

Additionally, when looking at the data, the school counseling team may determine a subgroup of students is underrepresented in classes with rigorous coursework. School counselors might encourage students to pursue more rigorous education when delivering curriculum in the classroom, facilitating small group pullout sessions, or during individual student planning time.

Management

Implementing intentional guidance requires an agreement with administration that counselors will intercede on students' behalf when the data indicate a need for intervention. Annual agreements ensure school counselors and principals are on the same page regarding the additional support students will receive and when they will receive it. Plans should be shared with the school site's advisory council so everyone is aware of the types of interventions school counselors are providing as well as the results when the intervention is completed. The use of data is central to this work and will be discussed in more detail in the upcoming chapters.

Action plans are instrumental to implementing intentional guidance. The ASCA National Model (ASCA, 2003, 2005) called for guidance curriculum and closing-the-gap action plans. As discussed in Chapter 1, the 2012 edition of the ASCA National Model revised the language to core curriculum action plans and added small group action plans to provide an increased focus on using data to design and evaluate small groups (ASCA, 2012a). Many samples of action plans will be shared in this text. The use of time and use of the school calendar are important in this work, as it might be tempting for school counselors to become so immersed in interventions (there are so many of them) that they find they are spending far too much time in responsive services and not enough time in prevention education. Spending 90% of the school counselor's time with 10% of the students is not the philosophy of intentional guidance.

Accountability

Collecting results is an integral part of demonstrating the impact school counselor activities and the program are having on students' attendance, behavior, and achievement. Additionally and most important, measuring the results of an intervention provides an opportunity to determine what worked and what didn't, and to answer the question, "What do we do differently in the future to get better results on improving students' attendance, behavior, or achievement?" Intentional guidance alignment with the school counseling performance standards will be discussed toward the end of this chapter.

Finally, in the Program Audit of the 2003 and 2005 versions of the ASCA National Model, the concept of intentional guidance is included in several areas (1.4, 1.5, 7.3, 7.4, 12.2, 12.4, 13.1, 13.9, 15.5, 16.7). In the 2012 edition, the audit was retitled Program Assessment. Intentional guidance is included in the Program Assessment in the following areas: mission (c), programs goals (c), delivery (c), action plans (a), calendars (b), and program results (b), (c). See Figure 2.1 for a comparison of these documents.

Figure 2.1 ASCA First and Second Edition Models Compared With 2012 Model

Component Area	ASCA Model 2003, 2005 Program Audit	Component Area	ASCA Model 2012 Program Assessment
Beliefs and Philosophy 1.4	Includes a plan of closing-the-gap activities for underserved student populations	**Mission** c.	Advocates for equity, access, and success of every student
1.5	Focus is on primary prevention, intervention, and student developmental needs	**Program Goals** c.	Address schoolwide data, policies, and practices to address closing-the-gap issues
Responsive Services 7.3	There is a systemic and consistent provision for the referral of students who exhibit barriers to learning.	**Delivery** c.	Provides individual and/or group counseling to identify students with identified concerns or needs

(Continued)

Figure 2.1 (Continued)

Component Area	ASCA Model 2003, 2005 Program Audit	Component Area	ASCA Model 2012 Program Assessment
7.4	A system is in place to ensure intervention for identified students.		
Use of Data and Closing the Gap 12.2	The data are systemically analyzed to determine where students are and where they ought to be.		
12.4	The identified needs become sources for the determination of closing-the-gap activities.		
Action Plans 13.1	Closing-the-gap plans are drafted by the counseling team at a planning meeting.	Action Plans a.	Data are used to develop curriculum, small group, and closing-the-gap plans.
13.9	Action plans and closing-the-gap plans are completed in the spring for the next year and signed by the counselor and principal.		
		Calendars b.	Reflect program goals and activities of school counseling curriculum, small group, and closing-the-gap action plans
Results Report 15.5	A results form for the collection of data from closing-the-gap activities is accepted by the administrators and the counselors.	Program Results b.	Small group results reports are analyzed and implications are considered.
Counselor Performance Evaluation 16.7	Is written to assess the school counselor's ability to be a leader, student advocate, and systems change agent.	c.	Closing-the-gap results reports are analyzed, and implications are considered.

Themes

The themes on the outside of the graphic in the ASCA National Model (ASCA, 2003, 2005, 2012) are like the blood in the veins of the professional school counselor (see Figure 2.2). Intentional guidance takes forward thinking and proactivity. The themes of leadership, advocacy, collaboration, and systemic change that are drawn from the work of the Education Trust (2009) are central to this work and will be infused throughout this text.

Figure 2.2   ASCA National Model 2003 Compared With ASCA National Model 2012

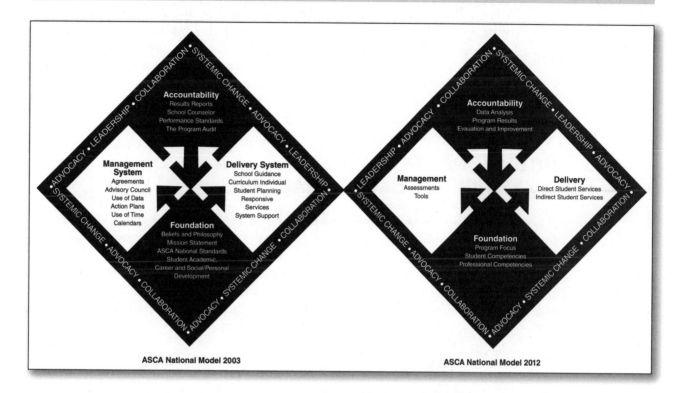

Figure 2.2   ASCA National Model 2003 Compared With ASCA National Model 2012

The third edition of the ASCA National Model (ASCA, 2012a) continues to strongly promote an intentional philosophy. Principle 13 from the theory behind the ASCA National Model reads, "Intentionally designing interventions targeting identified needs or specified goals and objectives as more efficient than interventions that are not intentionally designed" (Henderson, 2012, p. 139). The term *data-driven* is mentioned more than 21 times and *intervention* is mentioned 41 times throughout the third edition text (ASCA, 2012a).

INTENTIONAL GUIDANCE AND THE ASCA PROFESSIONAL COMPETENCIES

In 2008 the ASCA published *School Counselor Competencies* in an effort to continue to provide a unified vision for the profession. The competencies outline the knowledge, attitudes, and skills required of school counselors to meet the needs of preK–12 students and the rigorous demands of the school counseling profession (ASCA, 2008). The third edition of the ASCA Model (ASCA, 2012a) led to newly revised ASCA *School Counselor Competencies* (ASCA, 2012c). The school counselor competencies that align with the intentional guidance philosophy are listed below:

- I-A-9. The continuum of mental health services, including prevention and intervention strategies to enhance student success
- II-C-5. Is intentional in addressing the information, opportunity, and achievement gaps
- III-B-3a. Reviews and disaggregates student achievement, attendance, and behavior data to identify and implement interventions as needed

- IV-B-3a. Lists and describes interventions used in responsive services, such as individual/small group counseling and crisis response
- III-B-6a. Uses appropriate academic and behavioral data to develop school counseling core curriculum, small group and closing-the-gap action plans, and determines appropriate students for the target group or interventions
- V-B-1d. Uses student data to support decision-making in designing effective school counseling programs and interventions
- V-B-1e. Measures and analyzes results attained from school counseling core curriculum, small group, and closing-the-gap activities

INTENTIONAL GUIDANCE AND EVIDENCE-BASED PRACTICES

School counselors are increasingly encouraged to use evidence-based approaches to improve effectiveness with students. In Dimmitt, Carey, and Hatch (2007), school counselors are charged to use evidence-based school counseling practice by determining: (a) what needs to be done (the problem description), (b) which interventions or practices should be implemented (outcome research use), and (c) whether the implemented interventions or practices were effective (intervention evaluation). Intentional

Figure 2.3 A Model of Evidence-Based School Practice (EBP) in Counseling Practice

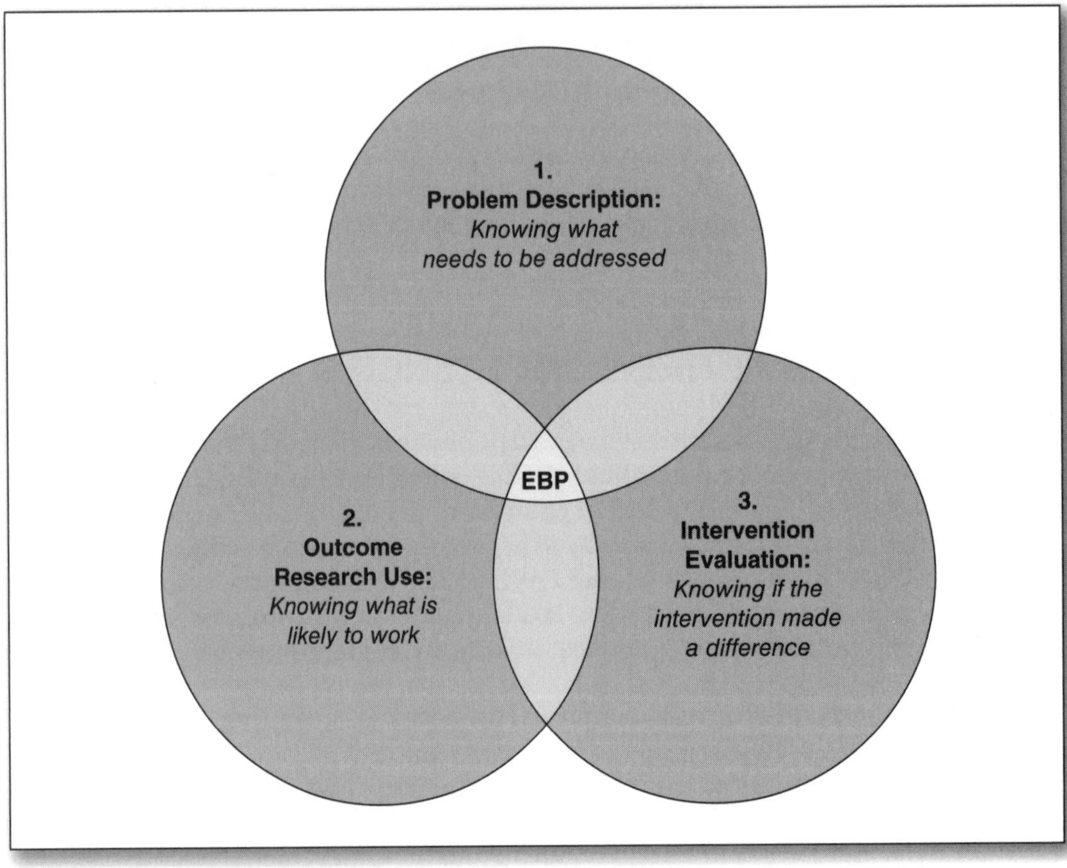

Source: Dimmit et al. (2007, p. 4).

guidance aligns with evidence-based practices in that data will inform the school counselors' practice in determining which students need interventions. Research will support the school counselor in determining which type of intervention is appropriate to implement, and finally, evaluation will be required to determine if the intervention was impactful with students (Figure 2.3).

INTENTIONAL GUIDANCE AND RESPONSE TO INTERVENTION (RTI) AND POSITIVE BEHAVIOR INTERVENTIONS AND SUPPORTS (PBIS)

In the late 1990s, response to intervention (RTI) came into the national forefront in education as a new approach to identifying students with disabilities. RTI recommended that a broad system of early intervention and support be in place, one aspect of which was evaluating a student for suspected learning disabilities. More recently, RTI has grown beyond special education identification and has become a comprehensive, data-based prevention model for helping students who are struggling to achieve (Kennelly & Monrad, 2007). The school counselor's role with regard to RTI is also clearly aligned with the ASCA National Model. "Once you get to know the RTI process, you realize it is highly consistent with all of the components of a comprehensive school counseling program as espoused by the ASCA National Model" (Sabella, 2012, p.73).

Similar to RTI, positive behavior interventions and supports (PBIS) is a model of support utilizing differentiated instruction. PBIS is a problem-solving model designed to employ a continuum of proactive, positive, multitiered behavioral interventions. Both RTI and PBIS promote universal instruction in Tier 1, targeted interventions in Tier 2, and individual interventions in Tier 3. Schoolwide PBIS involves all members of the school community in parallel endeavors, thereby helping students learn positive behaviors consistently across various settings. Research demonstrates significant increases in student respectfulness, motivation, and responsibility for schools that implement PBIS. Reduced referrals, suspensions, and tardy rates support increased attendance and connectedness as well as achievement (Brown, D'Emidio-Caston, & Benard, 2001; Garfat & Van Bockern, 2010; Horner et al., 2009).

Figure 2.5 is a representation of an integration of the ASCA National Model and the "Pyramid of Interventions," or RTI model. It was codeveloped by the author in collaboration with the Georgia Department of Education and was adapted for this text. Figure 2.4 shows the pyramids of interventions from which this integration has been developed.

Tier 1: A standards- and competency-based curriculum (referred to as the School Counseling Core Curriculum in the third edition of the ASCA National Model [ASCA, 2012a]) comprises the core curriculum lessons that are in place in all classrooms for all students. The standards for these lessons are based on the ASCA National Standards in the areas of academic, career, and personal/social development, and they are the foundation for the content delivered to students. This type of instruction focuses on the delivery of standards and competencies and is designed to be developmental in nature, preventative in design, and comprehensive in scope (ASCA, 2003, 2005, 2012a). School counselors monitor the knowledge, attitudes, and skills students learn as a result of these lessons to guide and adjust their instruction. Tier 1 also includes individual planning, so every student receives an individual (four- or six-year) plan. In a perfect world, all students would attend, behave, achieve, and graduate with the preparations to choose from a wide variety of postsecondary options, including college. When this is not the case, Tier 2 is implemented.

Figure 2.4 RTI Pyramid of Interventions Compared With School Counseling Pyramid of Interventions

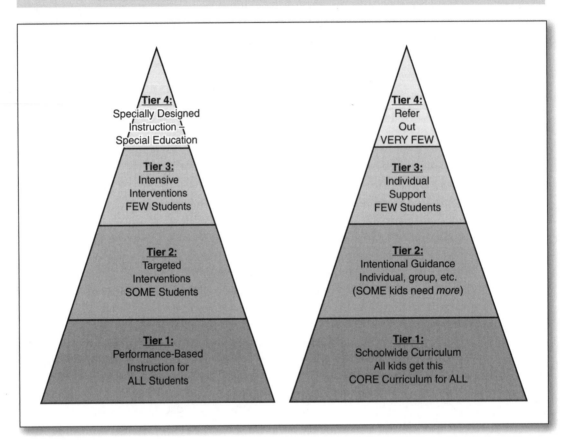

Tier 2: Intentional guidance answers the question, "What are we prepared to do when students do not learn?" Tier 2 describes preplanned interventions that should already be in place for students who are not being sufficiently successful or adequately challenged with Tier 1 curriculum activities. Targeted students participate in specific intentional guidance activities that address the identified concerns. The identified concerns come from relevant data and include attendance, behavior, failing grades, or equity and access issues. Interventions may include individual or small group interactions, referrals to schoolwide intervention programs, or services through a menu of services or systemic interventions. These preplanned interventions are predeveloped and supported at the administrative level, thereby becoming "standard intervention protocols" that are proactively in place for students. Working collaboratively, school counselors and school leaders design, develop, implement, and evaluate the impact of appropriate interventions for students in need.

Tier 3: Intensive intervention is the next layer of intervention or responsive services to a temporary crisis event or severe intervention need. The student support team (or student assistance team, or RTI team) may meet to discuss students who are still not attending, behaving, or achieving at the expected rate. During this process, the team analyzes the specific needs of the individual student. While in Tier 2 standard interventions are put in place, Tier 3 becomes much more individualized, as the student's teachers, school counselor, and parents systematically determine the concerns that need to be addressed for the student. Interventions are then strategically

Figure 2.5   Integration of the ASCA National Model and the RTI Model

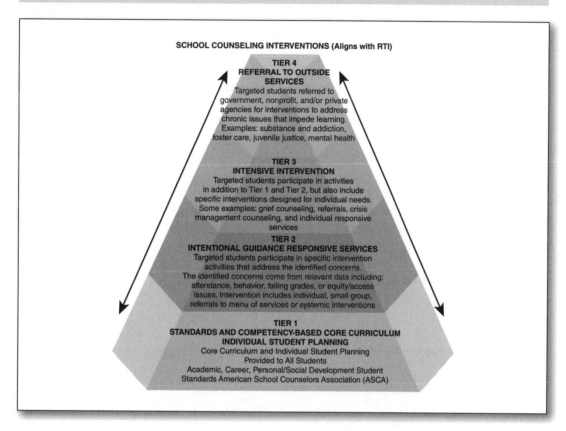

put in place. Monitoring student progress becomes more formal in nature. Tier 3 also includes individual counseling for short-term crises or for students who are waiting for outside referrals. Group counseling or individual counseling may occur in Tier 3.

Tier 4: Referral to outside resources is designed to serve students with severe or acute needs. This would include students who have been identified with needs that exceed the training of the school counselor or the capacity of the school counseling program. It would be appropriate to provide a referral to community services in these cases, as they exceed the scope of the school counseling role. Concerns may include severe emotional disturbance or special education and related services for eligible students provided in the general education classroom, or in some cases, in a resource, pullout, self-contained, or offsite facility. Students with mental health issues such as cutting, suicidal ideation, depression, and so forth would also fall into this category (ASCA, 2010b; 2012b).

DROPOUT PREVENTION EDUCATION AND INTENTIONAL GUIDANCE

Although the overall graduation rate has increased nationally from 71.5% in 2002 to 75% in 2009, 12 states accounted for the majority of the gains, while 10 states reported lower graduation rates (Balfanz, Bridgeland, Bruce, & Fox, 2012). On average, one in four students will fail to graduate high school in four years. When minority graduation rates are analyzed, the dropout rate increases to 40%. Solving the dropout issue is a national educational emergency. By the time a student reaches ninth grade, the chance that she or he will drop out can be predicted with 85% accuracy (Bridgeland, Dilulio, & Balfanz, 2009).

Balfanz, Bridgeland, Moore, and Fox (2010) contend that with greater intentionality and accountability, more accurate measures, and better tools and strategies, we could improve the rate at which students graduate from high school. Dropout prevention experts recommend that schools develop early warning systems to help identify students at risk of dropping out, and they encourage schools to develop the mechanisms that trigger appropriate supports for these students (Balfanz, Herzog, & Mac Iver, 2007; Balfanz et al., 2010). Intentional guidance is the mechanism designed to trigger the appropriate interventions and support to prevent student dropout.

Dropping out of school does not begin in high school—it begins in elementary school. The primary indicators are poor attendance, behavioral problems, and course failure (Bridgeland et al., 2009; Neild, Balfanz, & Herzog, 2007; Rumberger, 1995). The dropout prevention recommendations align seamlessly with intentional guidance activities coordinated and/or performed by school counselors. Who better than school counselors to lead the design of support service interventions for students at risk of dropout? The school counselor is perfectly positioned to be the provider of these most vital services.

Intentional Guidance? Or Intentional School Counseling?

As mentioned in Chapter 1, the renaming of guidance curriculum aligns with the late 1960s position shift from "guidance counselor" to "school counselor" (Ligon & McDaniel, 1970) and with the ASCA governing board's unanimous vote in 1990 to "call the profession 'school counseling' and the program a 'school counseling program'" (ASCA, 2005, p. 9). The renaming of guidance curriculum as school counseling core curriculum in the third edition of the ASCA National Model (ASCA, 2012a) and in this text align consistently with the move to a common core curriculum and the national call for consistency of position, profession, program, and curriculum.

In this chapter, however, and in the remainder of this text, the term *intentional guidance* is used, when perhaps the term *intentional school counseling* may be more appropriate. Consideration was given to revising the *intentional guidance* terminology to *intentional school counseling;* however, the author remains undecided regarding this particular change, because the decision requires more thoughtfulness with respect to the unforeseen impact this type of shift might have. Guidance definitions include counseling or advice on educational, vocational, or psychological matters. The term *intentional school counseling* could suggest to some that the position of the school counselor is solely as an interventionist. Additionally, the number of artifacts created, submitted, and permissioned in this text containing *intentional guidance* terminology precluded a revision of this magnitude without strong justification.

Readers are invited to utilize the terms *intentional guidance* and *intentional school counseling* to consider the philosophy behind the terms, the meanings each term implies, and the possible impact of shifting terminologies. They are also asked to provide the author feedback for future editions.

LET'S GET STARTED!

Before learning more about how to design, develop, implement, and evaluate intentional guidance action plans, we will review the important components of data analysis. Understanding why data are so important in the work of a school counselor and which data are most important to disaggregate, monitor, and evaluate will assist the school counselor in designing better action plans. The remainder of this text will answer the following questions:

What types of data are most important to collect and measure?

Where/how do I get the data?

What do I do with them once I find them?

How do I design intentional guidance action plans?

What types of surveys will help me determine interventions?

How do I create pre/post assessments?

How do I implement intentional guidance for systems issues?

How will I find the time to do intentional guidance?

How do I report my results using the Flashlight approach?

3

The Use of Data to Drive Interventions

A school counseling graduate student has just completed her final examination and is ready to go out for her first interview. When she arrives, she feels confident because she is well trained in developmental counseling, social justice, ethical standards, systems change, group counseling, and counseling theories. As the interview begins, she is answering questions about how to report child abuse and how to handle a suicidal referral. And then it comes, the question:

"Imagine the district is facing budget cuts and school counselors are mentioned as one of the programs at risk of being cut. Board members are wondering how school counselors are contributing in a meaningful way to the overall academic achievement of students. The superintendent (or principal) calls you in and asks the following questions:

> What is the purpose of your program?
> What are your desired outcomes?
> What is being done to achieve the outcomes you desire?
> What data or evidence is there that the objectives are being met?
> Is your program making a difference for students?
> Can you prove it?"

How would YOU respond?

Comprehensive school counseling programs in the 21st century are data driven (ASCA, 2012a, 2012e; Dimmit, Carey, & Hatch, 2007). Using data to drive decisions ensures *every* student receives the benefit of a school counseling program that is preventative in design, developmental in nature, and comprehensive in scope. School counselors use data to ensure *every* student receives the instruction that our professional standards require in academic, career, and personal/social development. School counselors use data elements to monitor the progress of their students and to alert them when students are in need of an intervention. School counselors use data to measure the impact of their interventions and activities. They seek to determine what result, if any, may be aligned with or attributed to their intervention. School counselors use data to share what they learn about the impact of their interventions with other educators. Finally, and most important, school counselors use data to improve their programs and services for students.

SCHOOL COUNSELOR DATA PROFICIENCY

In order for school counselors to utilize data, they must be proficient in understanding how to collect data. Getting access to site and district data is *a necessary first step*. Sometimes the data are provided to the principal who then shares it with school counselors. Some districts are fortunate enough to have central office personnel who can work directly with school counselors to collect and disaggregate data. School counselors in these circumstances must let others know they are interested in utilizing the data for program improvement. By attending committee meetings where data are reviewed (such as meetings of accreditation teams or school leadership teams), counselors can be part of the team that collects, interprets, and analyzes data.

If you do not have direct access to your district data, check your state department websites, as most have easily accessible databases. In California, for instance, these websites provide excellent school data:

- http://data1.cde.ca.gov/dataquest provides a disaggregated database of enrollment patterns, course-taking patterns, staffing, credentialing, and statewide testing data.
- http://www.cpec.ca.gov/OnLineData/OnLineData.asp provides disaggregated data on high school and college-going rates.
- http://nces.ed.gov/surveys/sdds/index.aspx provides US Census data of school districts.

Using statewide data allows school counselors to analyze their school or district performance in relationship to that of other districts. Please see the online appendix for links to state databases.

High-quality state-of-the-art student database systems provide cross-platform web portals allowing for real-time access to student data and information on the school counselor's desktop. School counselors can use these data tools to monitor trends in student behavior, attendance, and achievement. Data can be disaggregated into smaller groupings, allowing school counselors to query targeted data and easily identify students on their dashboards (and in their caseloads) who are falling behind. School counselors with access to real-time data can regularly and immediately target students in need and provide them with intentional guidance interventions long before others might notice.

States have been encouraged to create student identifiers to track students across grade levels, schools, and districts. The Data Quality Campaign is currently underway to help states build integrated, longitudinal data systems with unique statewide student identifiers that allow student-level data to be linked across databases and across years. (For more information, see http://www.dataqualitycampaign.org.)

Having immediate access to student data is a powerful and time-saving asset for the school counselor. However, once collected, what do the data mean? Professional school counselors must be adept at interpreting the data, as mistakes in data interpretation could lead to the development of new programs or activities that take time, cost money, and may be unnecessary. Knowing how to explain standardized test scores (understanding norms, percentages, stanines, and grade equivalency) is essential when interpreting test data for parents or program improvement. Understanding how data elements impact one another and how to look for upward and downward trends is essential to designing interventions.

School counselors must be proficient in the analysis of data. To fully utilize data, counselors must interpret them within the context of the larger picture for students and the school system. A thorough and thoughtful analysis of the data may uncover patterns, trends, or discrepancies that may reveal a schoolwide need, rather than a specific student's need. Analyzing the larger picture may lead to opportunities to recognize and advocate for systems change. Finally, data have multiple diagnostic and intentional uses and are therefore categorized in several different ways. In the next section, three aspects of data will be examined: (a) types of data, (b) ways to evaluate data, and (c) data changes over time. Before we begin, please take the following pretest.

Pretest—Use of Data

For items 1–8, please select the answer that best represents what type of data is listed.

1. Standardized Test Scores
   a. Standards and competency data
   b. Achievement-related data
   c. Achievement data
   d. Process data
   e. Perception data

2. Percent of Students Graduating College-Eligible
   a. Standards and competency data
   b. Achievement-related data
   c. Achievement data
   d. Process data
   e. Perception data

(Continued)

(Continued)

3. Percentage of Students who demonstrate Conflict Resolution Skills
   a. Achievement-related data
   b. Achievement data
   c. Process data
   d. Perception data
   e. Results data

4. Number of Discipline Referrals
   a. Standards and competency data
   b. Achievement-related data
   c. Achievement data
   d. Process data
   e. Perception data

5. Student Grade Point Average
   a. Standards and competency data
   b. Achievement-related data
   c. Achievement data
   d. Process data
   e. Perception data

6. Suspension Rate
   a. Standards and competency data
   b. Achievement-related data
   c. Achievement data
   d. Process data
   e. Perception data

7. Number of Students Seen in Group Counseling
   a. Standards and competency data
   b. Achievement-related data
   c. Achievement data
   d. Process data
   e. Perception data

8. Attendance Rate
   a. Standards and competency data
   b. Achievement-related data
   c. Achievement data
   d. Process data
   e. Perception data

For items 9–14, please select the correct answer.

9. "What others think, know, or demonstrate" as a result of curriculum lessons is considered what kind of data?
   a. Process
   b. Perception
   c. Results

10. "What you did for whom," or evidence that an event occurred, is considered what kind of data?
    a. Process
    b. Perception
    c. Results

11. "So what" data measuring whether the activity has impacted student behavior is considered what kind of data?

    a. Process

    b. Perception

    c. Results

12. Pre- and posttests are typically an example of what kind of data?

    a. Immediate

    b. Intermediate

    c. Long range

13. Dropout rate is an example of what kind of data?

    a. Immediate

    b. Intermediate

    c. Long range

14. Data-driven action plans that focus on closing the gap are called

    a. Schoolwide counseling curriculum

    b. Intentional guidance

For items 15 and 16, please select the answer that best reflects your attitude about data.

15. I am excited about using data to effect change:

    a. Strongly agree   d. Disagree

    b. Agree   e. Strongly Disagree

    c. Neutral

16. Data is a "Four-Letter-Word" to me:

    a. Strongly agree   d. Disagree

    b. Agree   e. Strongly Disagree

    c. Neutral

TYPES OF DATA

Data have multiple intentional and diagnostic uses and are categorized in several different ways. Three *types of data* will be presented below: student achievement data, achievement-related data, and standards and competency–related data. Each one is important to the other two. We will start with what many consider the most important type of data in schools.

Student Achievement Data

Student achievement data are often referred to as the "big ticket item" (Dimmitt, Carey, & Hatch, 2007, p. 29). The No Child Left Behind Act (2001) requires districts to publish student achievement data. These data are often looked to as the measure of success in schools. Parents and others look at achievement data when comparing their child's school to another school. Student achievement data can impact property values and can lead to administrative or superintendent reappointments or reassignments. They measure students' academic progress and include but are not limited to the following:

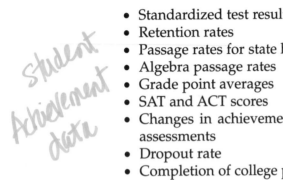

- Standardized test results
- Retention rates
- Passage rates for state high school exit exams
- Algebra passage rates
- Grade point averages
- SAT and ACT scores
- Changes in achievement levels (math, reading) as measured by benchmark assessments
- Dropout rate
- Completion of college preparation requirements
- College freshman remediation rates

School counselors sometimes find it hard to draw direct correlations from their programs to some of these specific student achievement elements. For example, everyone is working on improving standardized test scores. There is no way for counselors to show, definitively, that their activities were a direct reason these scores went up (or did not). Certainly, other variables will always contribute. However, while school counselors can never take all the credit for improvements, they cannot be denied a piece of the action, either. If the entire school team is working toward this goal, and counseling is integral to the total educational process, then it is appropriate for school counselors to take their fair share of credit. Achievement data alone, however, are not enough to prove the linkage between the activity and results. Achievement-related data can provide those links.

Achievement-Related Data

Students' achievement-related data are the data elements that psychological and educational research has identified as impacting students' achievement. Studies have shown that when students behave, attend, do homework, and enroll in rigorous courses, they perform better (Dimmit et al., 2007). The third edition of the ASCA National Model refers to achievement-related data as "behavioral data," defining them as "those fields the literature has shown to be correlated to academic achievement" (ASCA, 2012a, p. 50). The following are examples of research that shows how achievement-related data impact students' achievement data (Additional examples are found in the Appendix).

Discipline referrals and suspension rates

- Students who behave better achieve better (e.g., Van Horn, 2003).
- There is a strong relationship between social behavior and academic success. Social skills (getting along with peers, teamwork) positively predict academic achievement (e.g., Malecki & Elliott, 2002).
- Disruptive behavior (including hitting others) can affect academic achievement. (e.g., Gibson, 2006).
- Students who are suspended are less likely to be high academic achievers (e.g., Williams & McGee, 1994).

Attendance rates

- A statistically significant relationship exists between student attendance and student achievement (e.g., Roby, 2003).
- Student achievement is affected in a negative way by absenteeism (e.g., DeKalb, 1999).
- Students who attend school perform better than those who do not (e.g., Easton & Englehard, 1982).

Course enrollment patterns

- Students who take more rigorous coursework do better on standardized tests (e.g., Smith & Niemi, 2001).

Homework completion rates

- Students who complete and turn in homework do better in school (e.g., Cooper, Lindsay, Nye, & Greathouse, 1998).

Parental involvement

- The influence of parental involvement is significant for secondary students (e.g., Jeynes, 2007).
- Students benefit from both formal (i.e., school based) and informal (i.e., home based) parent involvement (e.g., LeFevre & Shaw, 2011).
- A small to moderate and practically meaningful relationship exists between parental involvement and academic achievement (e.g., Fan & Chen, 2001).

As Figure 3.1 depicts, improvement in achievement-related data can lead to improvements in achievement data. Students who are enrolled in rigorous coursework are more likely to complete college prep requirements (Smith & Niemi, 2001); students who complete homework are more likely to perform better in school (Cooper et al., 1998). The same is true for students who improve their attendance or who have fewer disciplinary problems.

Figure 3.1 Relationship Between Achievement-Related Data and Achievement Data

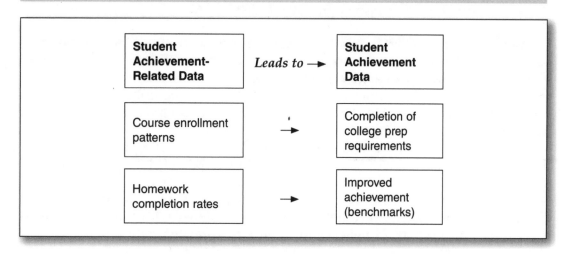

Many school counselors were teachers before becoming school counselors.

What did they do on many a Friday morning?

Many assessed students by giving quizzes, benchmarks, tests, et cetera. So what happened once they earned their master's degrees?

Did they leave their responsibilities to assess students' knowledge and skills at the door of the counseling office?

Achievement-*related* data can provide valuable information about how to improve achievement data. Achievement-related data may be more easily accessible to school counselors, may appear to align or correlate with their activities or services more directly, and may be more closely linked to school counseling program results than students' achievement data. However, both types are important to collect and share. Monitoring achievement-related data provides an opportunity to show how counselors are contributing to achievement results. School counselors who can show their programs and services contribute to improving the data in any one of these areas have cause for celebration.

Standards- and Competency–Related Data

Standards and competency–related data serve as indicators of whether or not the students have *learned* what they were *taught*. Just as teachers have standards and competencies, so too do school counselors. Likewise, just as teachers assess the impact of their lessons, so too should school counselors. Standards and competencies for school counselors measure what students have learned as a result of the lesson they were taught or the activity that was conducted. Ideally, as a result of the school counselor's activity or lesson, students are able to improve or shift their *attitudes,* obtain more *knowledge,* or demonstrate a *skill.* Examples of competencies measured may come from the ASCA Student Standards (ASCA, 2012a; Campbell & Dahir, 1997), the National Career Development Guidelines (National Career Development Association, 2013), accreditation standards and competencies, or state school counseling competencies. Ideally each district or school will have an agreed-upon set of measureable student competencies. It is important to remember that not all competencies and indicators are measurable. Careful consideration should be given to selecting and collecting data from indicators that are measurable, such as the percentage of students who

- *Know* the required courses for admission to a college or university (knowledge)
- *Believe* it is important to come to school (attitude)
- *Demonstrate* conflict resolution skills (skills)

Linking standards and competency data to achievement-related data and then to achievement data creates the conceptual linkage necessary to define the influence of the school counseling program. While this represents a correlation and not a causal relationship, school counselors can demonstrate how they contribute in a meaningful way to the overall goal of academic achievement. A visual representation of this contribution is shown in Figure 3.2.

One of the areas of weakness within the school counseling profession is the lack of empirical research connecting these three types of data in a *causal* way (Dimmit et al., 2007). Imagine the power of indicating that when a school counselor ensures students achieve certain competencies in time management, goal setting, decision making, or other competencies aligned with the goal of attendance, they also report an increase in achievement-related data (attendance), as

Figure 3.2 Linking Competency Attainment, Achievement-Related Data, and Achievement Data

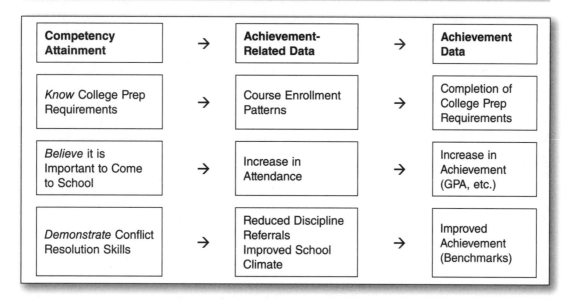

well as an increase in achievement data (test scores). Imagine the impact on the profession if there were overwhelming research indicating that, when a school counselor or school counseling program ensured *every* student received and mastered specific agreed upon standards and competencies, achievement-related data improved, and then, also, student achievement data improved (see Figure 3.3).

Figure 3.3 Linkages Between Standards and Competency Data, Achievement-Related Data, and Achievement Data

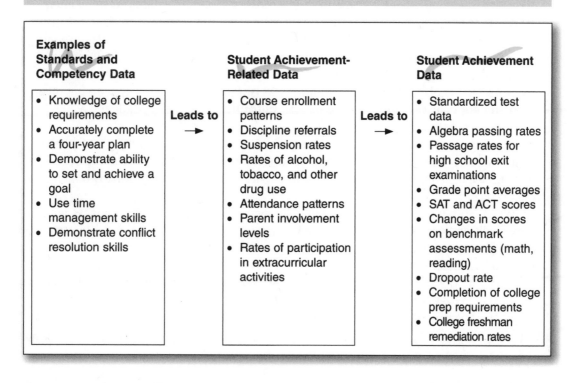

While most school counselors are not involved with researching whether an activity designed to assist students in the attainment of student competencies actually *caused* student improvement, much can still be gained by (a) using the conceptual frameworks shared in this chapter to describe the rationale for their work and (b) looking at data to see if the activity is, indeed, a factor in moving in the right direction. Later, in Chapter 4 (Program Evaluation), we will address the ways school counselors can immediately begin to collect and report program evaluation and action research data to (a) share with others the impact of their school counseling curriculum or interventions and (b) improve their counseling programs. School counselors can begin to measure the impact of their activities by selecting one thing to measure each year. Instead of measuring everything school counselors do, counselors can create the conceptual framework (link the concepts) and select one thing to measure (as will be discussed in Chapter 5) and use the results to advocate for their program and to inform their practice. In this way they can answer the question of how school counselors are contributing in a meaningful way to the overall academic achievement of students. By conceptualizing the linkages for the purpose of the activities in the school counseling program, important questions can begin to be answered.

Interviewing Our Potential New School Counselor

In the beginning of this chapter, the interviewee was asked several questions. Let's answer the first two:

> What is the purpose of your program?
> What are your desired outcomes?

Our interviewee answers as follows:

"The purpose of my program is to ensure all students attain the *standards and competencies* (academic, career, and personal/social) necessary to improve student *achievement-related* data, which in turn improve student *achievement* data. School counseling programs are responsible to ensure students receive the instruction, curriculum, activities, and services necessary to improve the *achievement-related* data items (which measure factors often referred to as barriers to learning) such that they then improve their student *achievement* data. The desired outcome is improving academic achievement for every student.

"So when I teach students to create four-year plans, for example, it is my goal that students will enroll and succeed in the appropriate courses (preferably rigorous coursework) and become more likely to graduate prepared to participate in the postsecondary option of their choice.

"When I teach conflict resolution skills, for example, my goal is that students learn these skills and become less likely to engage in violence in school; then discipline referrals decline and climate is improved. As research tells us, students who behave do better in school, and students at schools that have a positive climate achieve at a higher rate. By improving the school climate, the school counseling program contributes in a meaningful way to overall academic achievement of students. Here let me show you"—and she draws the following chart.

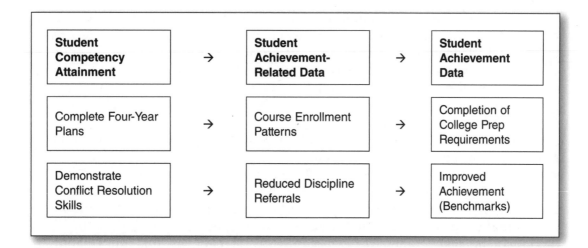

In summary, as seen in the chart our counseling candidate drew, whenever school counselors seek to assist students in obtaining a standard or competency, it is with the expectation that this will contribute to improvement in students' achievement-related data and ultimately improve achievement data. In this way, school counselors are contributing in a meaningful way to the overall goal of academic achievement.

DISAGGREGATION OF DATA

"This is a great plan," the interviewer states. "I appreciate that you know your purpose and desired outcomes, but tell me, how do you know what standards and competencies our students need? There are so many data (achievement-related and achievement) to look at, how do you make decisions regarding what programs and services you provide? What are your data sources?"

Each of the types of data previously mentioned (achievement, achievement-related, and competency-related data) can also be disaggregated. To *disaggregate* means to separate or break up into smaller, more defined groupings. Disaggregation can be done by

- Gender
- Race/ethnicity
- Socioeconomic status
- Language
- Special education identification
- Grade level

Disaggregating data allows school counselors to focus attention where resources are needed most. Perhaps there is a 92% attendance rate in a middle school, but when disaggregated, the data indicate that eighth graders' attendance rate is 85%, while sixth graders have a 98% attendance rate. Rather than do a schoolwide activity to improve attendance, the school counselor could focus interventions on only the eighth grade, with potentially greater overall impact. To ensure that even more specific attention is given to those in need, the school counselor could further disaggregate the data by gender, ethnicity, et cetera. Detailed discussion of disaggregating data will be provided in Chapter 8.

Perhaps the school counselor wants to know more about the 50% student failure rate in the science department, because she plans to provide a series of support activities in all the science classes (e.g., study skills lessons, tutoring referrals). Before assuming every student needs services, the school counselor can disaggregate the data to ensure interventions are designed to address specific actual needs. Suppose she decides to disaggregate by teacher. Care must obviously be taken when disaggregating by teacher, as this information is extremely sensitive and should be delicately managed. The purpose of disaggregating by teacher might be to determine if one teacher's failure rate might be skewing the entire department's data, rather than inferring that every teacher in the department has a high failure rate. If this were true, and one teacher's rate were significantly higher than the rest, then the counselor may want to provide a support activity in this one room (perhaps on the importance of homework) as well as share this information with the administrator, who could then work to mentor or support that particular teacher. Utilizing disaggregated data allows the school counselor to use time wisely by providing an intervention only for the specific area of need.

SETTING REASONABLE, MEASUREABLE OUTCOME GOALS

In some schools, data-based decision-making (DBDM) teams provide a group process for defining problems, setting goals, targeting interventions, and evaluating outcomes for students (Dimmit et al., 2007). School site data teams may include administrators, teachers, and representatives from the school counseling department. The purpose of the data teams is to analyze school data and discuss ways in which educators can work together to uncover and address student needs. As you conduct data conversations, consider including other educators who are equally committed to leadership and data-driven decision making. Further discussion on how to determine which outcomes are reasonable will be presented in Chapter 8.

Once needs are identified, it is time to create and prioritize data-driven goals. Begin by examining the school's data profile to identify areas of strength and need. Look for racial/ethnicity, gender, age or grade-level gaps and needs in attendance, behavior, and achievement (ASCA, 2012a; Dimmitt et al. 2007). Consult with the principal with the intent to align the school counseling program goals with the overarching goals of the school. In what way can the school counseling program contribute in a meaningful way to the overall academic achievement of every student? What data-driven challenges are reasonable and appropriate to invest time, talent, and resources in? If the goals selected are important only to the school counseling program, the impact of success on the quest for legitimacy and efforts to garner additional social capital are lost. Finally, be careful to limit goals to what might actually be accomplished.

As described in the third edition of the ASCA National Model (ASCA, 2012a) and in ASCA's Recognized ASCA Model Program (RAMP) application, school counseling program goals

1. Promote achievement, attendance, behavior, and/or school safety

2. Are based on school data

3. May address schoolwide data, policies, and practices or address closing-the-gap issues

4. Address academic, career, and/or personal/social development

5. Are SMART: specific, measurable, attainable, results-oriented, and time-bound (ASCA, 2012a)

FEDERAL SCHOOL COUNSELING GRANTS CALL FOR MORE DATA-DRIVEN DECISION MAKING

Each year, federal Elementary and Secondary School Counseling (ESSC) program grants are funded to establish or expand school counseling programs with the goal of improving the quality of counseling services (US Department of Education, 2011a). These competitive grants are awarded to districts that demonstrate need. The primary goals of the program are to reduce student-to-school-counselor (or mental health provider) ratios and to reduce incidences of violence in schools, as measured by numbers of student referrals. While the amount of federal dollars available each year varies, approximately 40 to 60 grants (of about $400,000 per year for three years) are awarded nationally. Although grant requirements have been relatively consistent, they were recently revised.

In an effort to enable more data-driven decision making, *priority* was given to 2012 grant applications designed to collect (or obtain), analyze, and use high-quality and timely data, including data on program participant outcomes, in the following priority areas: (a) instructional practices, (b) policies, and (c) student outcomes in elementary or secondary schools. Applicants who failed to meet these absolute priorities were considered ineligible for funding.

The author created the following planning charts (Figures 3.4–3.7) to assist grant writers in focusing on the specific data-driven requirements necessary to gain *priority*. The charts provide a structure for ensuring specific grant-required data elements are addressed when writing the text of the grant. The final chart, Figure 3.8, indicates goals, objectives, intervention strategies, and outcome measures for the ESSC program. Note schoolwide core curriculum for all students (Goal #2) and intentional guidance interventions for students with identified needs (Goal #3). Whether or not school counselors are planning to write grants, creating these types of visual charts can assist them in organizing and designing the overall plans of their programs.

Figure 3.4   Planning Chart to Gain Priority: Collect, Analyze, and Use High-Quality and Timely Data

Data to Collect and Analyze	High-Quality Source	Data Must Reflect This Time Period
✓ Demographic Data (Ethnic/Language/Socioeconomic)	Site Database System	2012
✓ Attendance (# Days Absent)	Site Database System	2010–2011
✓ Discipline	SIMS	2010–2011
✓ Report Card (Social Skills and Study Habits, Number of N and U Grades)	Report Card	Each Quarter or Trimester
✓ Standardized Test Results (Math and ELA)	State Reported	2011
✓ CHKS (California Healthy Kids Survey)	West Ed	2011

Figure 3.5   Planning Chart to Address the Requirement to Use Data to Improve Instructional Practices

Instructional Practice (Activity) Data	Program Participant Outcome (Data Element)	Data to be Collected at These Times
✓ Classroom Lessons (Violence Prevention, Study Skills)	Perception Data (Pre/Post)	Before/After Lesson
✓ Group Counseling (Social Skills and Study Habits)	Perception Data (Pre/Post)	Before/After Group
✓ Parent Training and Evening Events	Survey Evaluation	At End of Each Event
✓ Staff Development (Teacher Instruction on Coteaching Violence Prevention Curriculum)	Survey Evaluation	At End of Training
✓ Staff Development (Teacher Instruction on Schoolwide Positive Behavioral Support Program)	Survey Evaluation	At End of Training
✓ Inservice Training of Paraprofessionals	Survey Evaluation	At End of Training

Figure 3.6 Planning Chart to Address the Requirement to Use Data to Improve Policy

Policy Problem (Concerns?)	Policy Solution	Policy Outcome Data	Time Period to Implement Solution
1. Lack of data element to identify students in need of social skills or study habits interventions	—Faculty trained in positive behavior expectations (PBIS) —Faculty create social skills and study habits indicators on student report cards	Student report cards contain consistent social skills/study habits indicators at all grant sites	Year 1
2. Lack of consistent classroom expectations, rules, and procedures	—Faculty trained in positive behavior expectations (PBIS) —Faculty create common rules and procedures	Common classroom behavior expectations, rules, and procedures	Year 1
3. Lack of consistent schoolwide discipline plan class to class	—Faculty trained in coordinated administrative interventions —Faculty create schoolwide discipline plan	Schoolwide discipline plan, policies, and procedures	Year 2
4. Lack of consistent districtwide discipline policies school to school	Collaborate to create consistent discipline policies in all grant schools	Consistent districtwide discipline plans, policies, and procedures for all grant schools	Year 2

Figure 3.7 Planning Chart to Improve Student Outcomes at the Elementary Level

Student Outcome Data			
Outcome	Measure	High-Quality Source	Intervals at Which Data Are Collected
✓ Discipline Referrals	✓ −10%	SIMS (SDBS)	Monthly/Yearly
✓ Protective Factors (CHKS)	✓ +10%	West Ed	Yearly
✓ N's and U's on Report Cards in Social Skills and Study Habits	✓ −10%	Electronic Report Cards	Q1, Q2, Q3, Q4
✓ State Test Scores (Math/ELA)	✓ +10%	State testing	Yearly
✓ Truancy Rates (Absences)	✓ −10%	Student Database System	Monthly/Yearly

Figure 3.8   ESSC Grant Program Goals, Objectives, Intervention Strategies, and Outcome Measures

Program Goals	Objectives	Intervention Strategies	Outcome Measures
GOAL 1 Implement a comprehensive elementary school counseling program that is data driven, standards-based, and accountable for results and that serves as a catalyst for expansion throughout the district, as well as influences and supports efforts in other districts.	1. Hire highly qualified elementary school counselors to reduce counselor-to-student ratio to bring it closer to national average of 1:250. 2. Provide extensive training and support from the project director and principal investigator to the new counselors, as well as to the staff at all grant school sites, to ensure the creation and delivery of a comprehensive counseling program that addresses the developmental needs of all students, and systematically screens, assesses, and provides appropriate preventative and intervention services for students with various risk factors.	• LEA will extensively recruit highly qualified applicants with extra efforts to seek out bilingual/bicultural candidates. • New counselors will receive extensive training in selected SAMHSA approved violence prevention curriculum, effective teaching pedagogy, and classroom practice. • School counselors will receive instruction in the ASCA National Model, results-based counseling, data collection, and evaluation. • Project director will meet with school counselors and school staff monthly. • The principal investigator will meet regularly with program staff.	Employment records Calendars/agendas of trainings and meetings Staff surveys and evaluations
GOAL 2 All students will develop the personal/social knowledge, attitudes, and skills that will lead to improvements in behaviors that support increased academic achievement.	1. 10% decrease in discipline referrals 2. 10% increase in protective factors and feeling of safety on campus utilizing the California Healthy Kids Survey (CHKS) 3. 10% increase in number of students receiving positive evaluations on citizenship and study habits measures on their report cards 4. 5% increase in students who score proficient and above on California Standards Test (CST)	*School counselors will* • Create Core Curriculum action plans to ensure delivery and evaluation of violence prevention education. • Ensure all teachers and counselors receive instruction on implementing the SAMHSA approved violence prevention curriculum. • Train student conflict managers and implement patrols (peace patrol). • Provide training for parents and paraprofessionals.	Discipline records CHKS results Report cards CST scores Training and in-service records

Program Goals	Objectives	Intervention Strategies	Outcome Measures
GOAL 3 Identify and provide systematic interventions for students experiencing barriers to academic success.	1. 10% decrease in discipline referrals at grant sites 2. 10% decrease in truancy rates at grant sites 3. 10% decrease in number of students receiving negative evaluations on study habits and citizenship measures on report cards.	*School counselors will* • Create intentional guidance (closing-the-gap) intervention action plans for all students referred for discipline, receiving low citizenship or study habits marks, or identified as having attendance problems • Work individually and/or create small groups to provide intervention to meet identified needs (barriers to learning) • Work with parents of all students receiving individual or group interventions, making outside referrals as needed • Participate in SSTs and other intervention meetings as necessary.	Discipline records Attendance records Report cards

Sample Schoowide and Targeted Goals for an Elementary School

Figures 3.9 and 3.10 show sample goals at the elementary level in attendance, achievement, behavior, and school safety. They are divided into schoolwide goals for all students (Figure 3.9) and targeted goals for intentional guidance (Figure 3.10) for students who are identified by the data as needing additional intervention. As recommended above, school counselors work with administrators to select the few most important goals to focus on each year.

Figure 3.9 Schoolwide Goals for All Students

Schoolwide Goal (All Students)		
Measureable Objectives	**Outcome Data (High Quality, Specific, and Measureable)**	**Intervals at Which Data Are Collected**
10% increase in prosocial behaviors	% of fifth grade students reporting HIGH in prosocial behaviors on California Healthy Kids Survey (CHKS; West Ed)	Yearly Each Spring
10% increase in feelings of safety	% of fifth grade students reporting HIGH on feelings of safety on CHKS (West Ed)	Yearly Each Spring
10% increase in protective factors	% of fifth grade students reporting HIGH on protective factors on CHKS (West Ed)	Yearly Each Spring
10% decrease in discipline referrals	Discipline records for grades 3–5 as reported on Aeries Student Database	Q1, Q2, Q3, Q4
10% decrease in suspensions	Suspension records for grades 3–5 as reported on Aeries Student Database	Yearly End of Q4
10% decrease in number of N's and U's on study habits measures on report cards	Number of N's and U's for study habits on students' report cards in grades 3–5	Q1, Q2, Q3, Q4
10% decrease in number of N's and U's on social skills measures on report cards	Number of N's and U's for social skills on students' report cards in grades 3–5	Q1, Q2, Q3, Q4
10% increase in number of students scoring proficient and above in ELA on state standardized test	% proficient in grades 2–5 on ELA portion of state standardized test	Yearly Each Spring
10% increase in number of students scoring proficient and above in math on state standardized test	% proficient in grades 2–5 on math portion of state standardized test	Yearly Each Spring
5% increase in attendance	Attendance records for identified students on Aeries Student Database	Yearly End of Q4

Figure 3.10 Targeted Goals for Intentional Guidance

Targeted Goal for Intentional Guidance (Some Students)		
Measureable Objectives	**Outcome Data (High Quality, Specific, and Measureable)**	**Intervals at Which Data Are Collected**
50% decrease in discipline referrals for identified students	Discipline records for identified students on Aeries Student Database	Q1, Q2, Q3, Q4
30% decrease in N's and U's in social skills for identified students	Number of N's and U's for citizenship on students' report cards in grades 3–5	Q1, Q2, Q3, Q4

Targeted Goal for Intentional Guidance (Some Students)		
Measureable Objectives	**Outcome Data (High Quality, Specific, and Measureable)**	**Intervals at Which Data Are Collected**
30% decrease in N's and U's in study habits for identified students	Number of N's and U's for study skills on students' report cards in grades 3–5	Q1, Q2, Q3, Q4
50% decrease in truancy rates (truancy is defined as three or more unexcused absences)	Attendance records for identified students on Aeries Student Database	Q1, Q2, Q3, Q4
50% decrease in total number of unexcused absences for identified students	Attendance records for identified students on Aeries Student Database	Q1, Q2, Q3, Q4

Activity #1

Consider the program goals in the following list. These were created to increase the number of students who graduate from high school both college- and career-ready and to increase college-going and college-completion rates. Discuss priorities and consider which goals your school counseling team might select to focus on. Use the templates in Figures 3.11 and 3.12 to create specific, measurable, attainable, results-oriented, timely (S.M.A.R.T.) goals.

1. Increase college knowledge for students in grades K–12
2. Increase ninth grade credit efficiency rate (number of credits each student has earned)
3. Increase high school graduation rate
4. Increase college-prep course completion rate
5. Increase college-going rate (four-year, community college, trade school, etc.)
6. Increase Advanced Placement (AP) course completion and passage rate
7. Reduce need for postsecondary remedial courses
8. Increase scholarships and financial aid dollars

Figure 3.11 Template for Schoolwide Goals for All Students

Schoolwide Goal (All Students)		
Measureable Objectives	**Outcome Data (High Quality, Specific, and Measureable)**	**Intervals at Which Data Are Collected**

Figure 3.12   Template for Targeted Goals for Intentional Guidance

Targeted Goal (Some Students)		
Measureable Objectives	Outcome Data (High Quality, Specific, and Measureable)	Intervals at Which Data Are Collected

Activity #2

Consider the sample of districtwide goals provided in Figure 3.13. How might you recommend addressing each of these goals? Through schoolwide core curriculum? Intentional guidance interventions? Both?

Figure 3.13   Sample of XYZ's Districtwide Goals

XYZ District Goals			
Goal Areas	Elementary	Middle	High
Attendance	50% reduction in the number of absences for students identified truant (six or more unexcused absences) Q1–Q3	25% reduction in the number of full-day unexcused absences (three or more) for all students Q1–Q3	
Behavior	30% reduction in schoolwide discipline referrals for conflict; grades 3, 4, 5 Q1–Q3	20% reduction in the number of repeat offences by students with multiple (more than 5) behavioral referrals	
Behavior	25% decrease in discipline referrals for at-risk students (five or more referrals or one or more suspension) who participate in social skills groups Q1–Q3		
Study Skills/ Homework	20% increase in positive report card marks in areas of homework completion, motivation, and study skills Q1–Q3		

Figure 3.13 (Continued)

XYZ District Goals			
Goal Areas	**Elementary**	**Middle**	**High**
Credits Earned		20% reduction in the number of students academically at risk (below 2.0 GPA) Q1–Q3	20% reduction in the number of ninth grade students academically at risk (below 2.0 GPA) Q1–Q3
Graduation			50% reduction in the number of seniors who are NOT on target to graduate Q1–Q3
Financial Aid			10% increase in the percentage of students who complete the FAFSA (compare 2013 to 2014)
% of Students Graduating College-Eligible			10% increase in the percentage of students eligible for and who apply for college (compare 2013 to 2014)

4

Program Evaluation

Using Data to Evaluate Interventions

What is the purpose of your program?
What are your desired outcomes?
What is being done to achieve the outcomes you desire?
What data or evidence is there to show the objectives are being met?
Is your program making a difference for students?
Can you prove it?

Program evaluation data are used to measure the impact or effectiveness of a school counseling program's activities and to gain information that can be used for program improvement. Program evaluation data show how school counselors are contributing in a meaningful way toward the goal of student achievement. When designing core curriculum or intentional guidance action plans and preparing results reports, program evaluation data are used to measure the effectiveness of the counseling activities.

Three different types of program evaluation data—process, perception, and results—will be presented.

PROCESS DATA: WHAT YOU DID FOR WHOM

Process data provide evidence that an event occurred. They tell what was actually going on (Weiss, 1988). They answer the question: "What did the school counselor *do*, and *for whom* did the counselor do it?" Process data can almost be thought of as "selfish" data, because they tell only what the school counselor has done; they tell nothing about what students have learned. Process data supply the "who," "what," "when," "where" and "how often." They do not address the question of "so what?"

Who (received services): Which students? All students? Only eighth-grade boys? How many of them were there?

What (did they receive): What standard/competency or need is this activity addressing? What is the curriculum? Is it being implemented as prescribed? This is important if researched-based curriculum is being used, as it is only validated for use as designed.

When (did they receive it): When did they receive this activity or service? All year? Once? Twice? For 15 minutes?

Where (did they receive it)/How (was it provided): Was the lesson delivered to 30 students in their classroom or to 300 in the multipurpose room? This is important, because the results may indicate the lesson was more effective when given in the classroom than in the multipurpose room.

Examples of process data include the following:

Who: Three groups of ten seventh-grade students

What: Eight-week group counseling sessions for students with low motivation, utilizing the "Why Try" curriculum

When: Once a week over an eight-week period (rotating periods so as not to take students out of the same class each day)

Where/How: In the school counseling office

Putting it all together:

- Three groups of ten (30 total) seventh-grade students met once a week (rotating class periods) for eight weeks in the school counseling group room to learn motivational skills utilizing the "Why Try" curriculum.
- All high school students (2,700) were seen at least one time individually by their school counselor during the 20xx–20xx school year to prepare their four-year academic plan utilizing the Naviance online program.
- Two-hundred-fifty parents or guardians attended a two-hour evening event about identifying career goals and career pathways at XYZ high school.

While some might be impressed with a school counselor who presented these process data, others might say, "So what? Did the student learn anything? Is he or she more or less likely to attend school, graduate, or behave in class?" Process data do not tell us *anything* about whether or not the student is *different* as a *result* of this activity. We know only the school counselor *did* the activity.

However, in some ways, process data are still valuable. For example, suppose two school counselors at different schools each implemented a bully prevention curriculum. Each counselor's program was successful in reducing the number of suspensions or referrals for bullying. However, when comparing process data, the two colleagues discover that although the programs were equally successful, there were differences in design. At the first school, five groups of 12 students each met a total of four times for 30 minutes each time. In other words, the school counselor spent a combined total of 10 hours serving 60 students. At the second school, eight groups of eight students each met six times for 45 minutes. The total amount of group time at the second school was 36 hours, significantly more than the total time at the first school. Analyzing data in this way can enable a school counselor to save huge amounts of valuable time. It can also inform counselors about how altering certain variables, such as group size, may lead to more efficacious results.

PERCEPTION DATA: DID YOU ASK?

Whereas process data are about what the school counselor did, perception data address what the student learned. Perception data tell what a student thinks, knows, or can demonstrate as a result of a lesson or activity. Standards-based education encourages educators to measure knowledge, attitudes, and skills (Darling-Hammond, 1998). When school counselors teach core curriculum in the classroom, hold group counseling sessions, provide an evening parent presentation, or perform another school counseling function, they are delivering (or aligning with delivery of) the American School Counselor Association (ASCA) National Standards and Competencies (Campbell & Dahir, 1997).

When the classroom lesson is completed, why not "ASK" students what they learned? By shifting around the words *knowledge, attitudes,* and *skills,* the acronym ASK (**a**ttitudes, **s**kills, **k**nowledge) is created to remind counselors to measure what students gained or learned from a lesson or activity. Perception data, therefore, measure whether (a) students' attitudes or beliefs changed or shifted as a result of an activity or intervention, (b) students learned the skill (attained the competency), or (c) students' knowledge increased. School counselors can demonstrate that students have benefited from an activity or presentation by collecting ASK data before and/or after the completion of an activity. Whereas process data measure *what the counselor did,* perception data tell what the student *got* from it.

Attitudes or Beliefs

Students' attitudes or beliefs can be measured utilizing pre/post tests or surveys. For example,

- Before receiving a classroom lesson, 52% of fourth-grade students *believed* using their planner could help them get better grades. After the lesson, 79% *believed* using their planner could help them get better grades.

- Before receiving a classroom lesson, 22% of students *believed* taking career technical education (CTE) courses could benefit them after high school. After the lesson, 74% of students *believed* taking CTE courses would be beneficial.
- Before receiving a classroom lesson, 53% of African American females *believed* they could afford to attend college. After the lesson, this increased to 78%.
- Before receiving a classroom lesson, 30% of students *believed* taking college prep courses was important. This increased to 80% after the lesson.
- Before receiving a classroom lesson, 19% of seventh-grade students *agreed* or *strongly agreed* reporting cyber-bullying was every student's responsibility. After the lesson, 64% agreed or strongly agreed reporting cyber-bullying was every student's responsibility (see Figure 4.1).

Skills (Competency Attainment)

School counselors can collect data to indicate a student has achieved the competency desired through watching a role-play or completing an activity, a document, a survey, a pre/post test, or other task. Sometimes skills are best assessed through pre/post testing; other times, only post assessment is required. (More details on this will be provided in Chapter 7).

For example,

- Every seventh-grade student *completed* an interest inventory.
- 85% of fifth graders could accurately *role-play* the conflict resolution process.
- 97% of students in Grades 9–12 *completed* a four-year plan.
- 100% of students demonstrated the ability to accurately organize a binder.
- 30% of students could identify missing pieces of a planner prior to lessons; afterward, 35% could. More work is needed here (see Figure 4.2).

Figure 4.1 Seventh Graders Reporting Cyber-Bullying Is Every Student's Responsibility

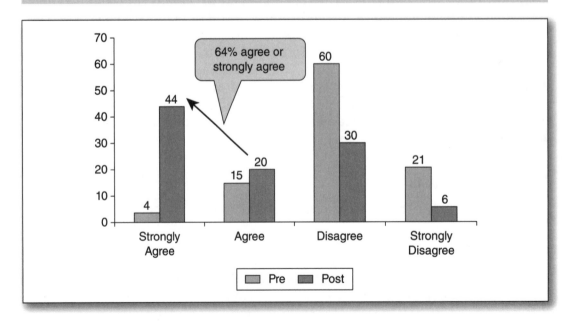

Figure 4.2 What Skills Did Sixth Graders Learn?

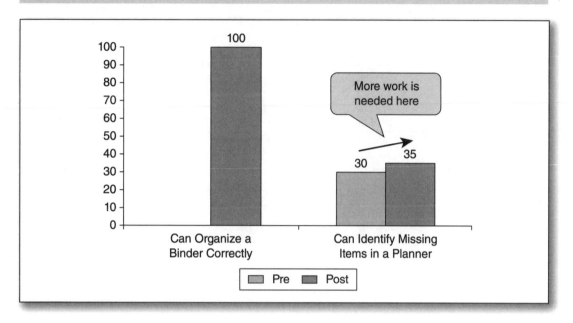

Knowledge

Pre/post test items addressing knowledge provide an indication that the students learned the information presented in the lesson. For example,

- Prior to receiving classroom lessons, 15% of students in the seventh grade demonstrated *knowledge* of promotion retention criteria; after the lesson, 89% of students demonstrated *knowledge* of such criteria.
- Before a series of group counseling sessions, 56% of fifth-grade males referred for anger management support *knew* three ways to divert anger in a healthy way; after the sessions, this increased to 92%.
- Before individual counseling sessions, 53% of tenth-grade students *knew* the number of English credits needed to graduate from high school; after the session, the number jumped to 100% (see Figure 4.3).

Putting it All Together: ASK

Attitudes, skills, and knowledge (ASK) work together to influence behavior change. When school counselors design activities and lessons that both address and measure all three of the ASK perception data areas, behavior change is more likely to follow. It is this behavior change that leads to results (see Figure 4.4).

Many school counselors can tell a story about a group of students who seem to know fighting is against school rules, know that there are consequences for fighting, and even know alternative strategies for expressing angry feelings, yet a great deal of fighting is still occurring in the classroom. A school counselor might be asked to collect information regarding how the issue of fighting is being addressed as part of the department's effort to collect accountability data. *Process* data could show that the school counselor taught anger management or conflict resolution lessons in a classroom three times in a month, or that a certain number of identified students received

Figure 4.3 Percentages of 10th Graders Who Know Credits Needed in Subject Areas to Graduate

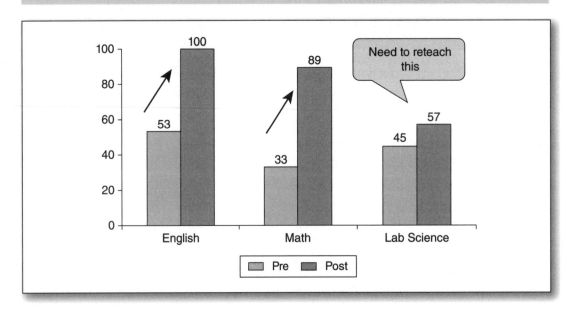

Figure 4.4 Addressing All Three of the ASK Areas to Create Behavior Change

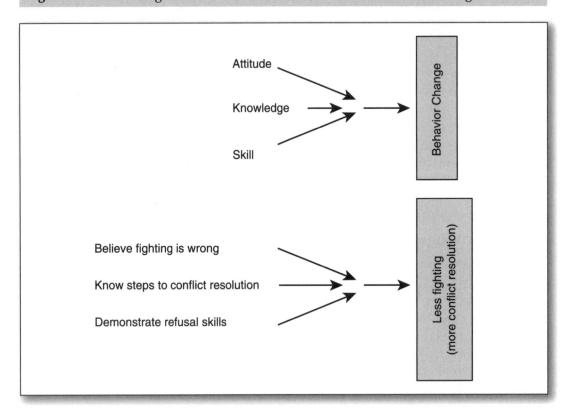

additional small group intervention. *Perception* data might indicate that students *know* fighting is wrong. The students may *know* how to handle the situation differently and may even be able to demonstrate conflict resolution *skills*. Yet, the data could reveal that behavior has not changed. What might be the missing piece? Perhaps it is *attitude*. If students don't *believe* fighting is wrong, they are less likely to stop their fighting behavior. As a result, overall incidences of fighting might not decrease.

Stakeholders want to know school counseling activities and interventions make a real difference. They want to see that the number of fighting incidences, referrals, detentions, or suspensions has decreased. If the data do not show improvement, the lessons may have been only partially effective. By assessing the ASK, the school counselor can determine where additional motivation, skills development, or education is needed. When all three areas are improved, the likelihood of behavior change is much greater. And behavior change leads to the next level of program evaluation data: Results.

When I was a school counselor, a third-grade boy named Joey would come to my office to calm down after a fight.

"Joey, do you know that fighting is wrong?"
"Oh, yes, I know fighting is wrong."
"What happens to you when you fight, Joey?"
"I get in trouble; sometimes I get detention."
"Joey, do you believe it is wrong to fight in school?"
He nods, "Yes."
*"What can you do differently, Joey, when you are
angry and want to hit someone?"*
"Well, I could draw a picture, tell the teacher, or
go to the conflict resolution corner in the classroom."

As the school counselor, my *process* data indicate I have gone in Joey's classroom three times this year to teach anger management lessons. *Perception* data tell us Joey understands that fighting is wrong, believes it to be wrong, and knows what to do if he is angry enough to fight, but it is not enough, is it? Joey has not changed his *behavior*. Is it really enough for stakeholders to know I delivered a lesson and can show only process data? No, it is not. Teachers, principals, and others want to know our programs have made a *real* difference. If the incidences of fighting have not decreased since I began these lessons, and if there is not improvement in the data on referrals, detentions, or suspensions, then was my lesson really effective? Well, partially, but not with the type of data stakeholders want to see, unless Joey's behavior has changed.

RESULTS DATA: SO WHAT?

Results are the "so what?" data, the hard data, the application data. Results are the proof the activity or intervention either has or has not positively influenced the students' ability to utilize attitudes, skills, and knowledge to change their behavior. The counselor taught the curriculum (anger management), students reported learning (techniques of conflict resolution), but do students now fight less? Do climate surveys indicate students feel safer in school? Results data provide feedback as to whether students' overall behavior has changed as well.

The three most important results school counselors and student support services personnel can measure are attendance, behavior, and achievement. Improved average daily attendance (ADA) increases financial resources to the district, leading to more revenue and hopefully more resources (e.g., supplies, professional development, programs) to support learning. In addition, research shows better attendance improves academic achievement (Easton & Englehard, 1982). Behavior is important because research confirms students who behave better in school are more likely to achieve (Van Horn, 2003). Behavior changes and their consequences may be measured with two types of data: achievement or achievement-related. Earlier, it was discussed how competency attainment leads to achievement–related data, and research shows achievement-related data supports student achievement data. When school counselors measure results and find improvement in student achievement-related data, it is good practice to see if academic achievement is improving also. While such findings do not demonstrate a causal relationship, achievement-related results are often able to show school counselors are contributing in a meaningful way to the overall academic achievement of students.

Some examples of achievement-related results include the following:

- Attendance of Latino students in seventh and eighth grades has improved by 12% this year.
- The number of referrals for incidences of bullying in fourth and fifth grades has decreased 51% from the first semester to the second.
- Attendance improved from 74% to 83% following the intervention.
- Over three trimesters (T1, T2, T3), the number of N's and U's on the Study Skills section of the report card significantly decreased in third and fourth grade, but it did not significantly alter in fifth grade (see Figure 4.5).

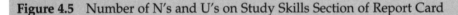

Figure 4.5 Number of N's and U's on Study Skills Section of Report Card

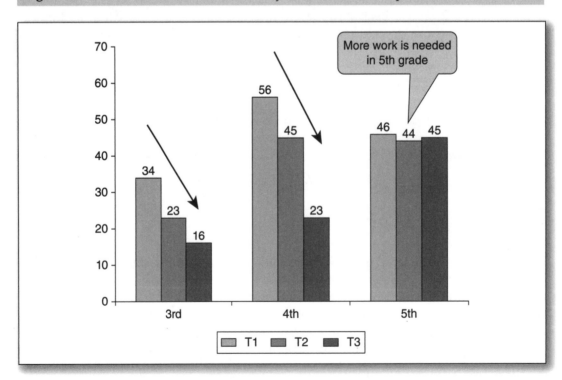

Some examples of achievement results include the following:

- 85% of students who earned below a 2.0 overall GPA in the first trimester (T1) improved by earning a 2.0 GPA or better by the third trimester (T3).
- Graduation rates for African American females improved 16% over the last three years.
- Benchmark exam scores for third- and fourth-grade students participating in academies have improved each trimester. (Students selected to participate in the academy program were identified as "at-risk.") (See Figure 4.6).

Figure 4.6 Percentages of Students Scoring Proficient or Better on Benchmark Exam

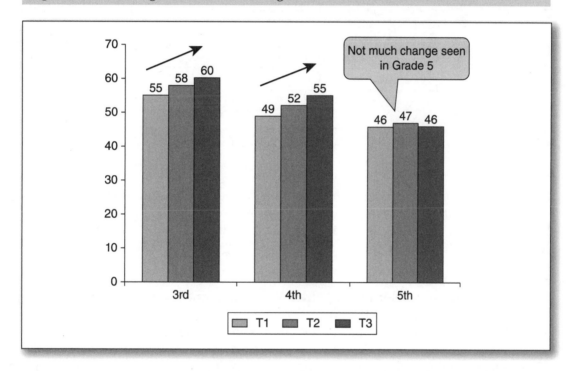

In summary, when school counselors collect process data for the activities they conduct within the school counseling program, important questions about what is "being done" are answered. When they measure competency attainment data (perception data), they are collecting evidence that their objectives (improving student attitudes, knowledge, and skills) are being met. This leads to behavior change, which will be measured by achievement-related and achievement data as school counselors look for validation that the activity is contributing to student achievement.

HATCHING RESULTS CONCEPTUAL DIAGRAMS

The Hatching Results Conceptual Diagram (see Figure 4.7) visually represents this explanation of how school counseling activities (and ultimately, the entire program) can contribute to students' achievement. Review the conceptual diagram as you read

Figure 4.7 Hatching Results Conceptual Diagram

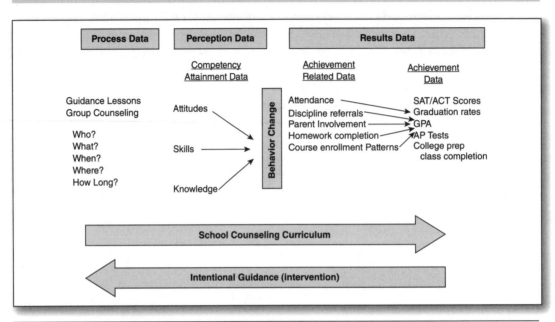

Source: Hatch (2005b).

the application of this scenario in the following bullet list, and align the written explanation with the visual representation. Note the headings: Process Data, Perception Data, and Results Data. Competency attainment falls under Perception Data, and Results Data is an umbrella over achievement-related data and achievement data.

- The school counselor teaches students a classroom lesson on conflict resolution skills (process data).
- The school counselor measures competency attainment (ASK perception data).
- Students believe fighting is wrong (*attitude* shift).
- Students demonstrate conflict resolution skills through role-play (*skills* learned).
- Students answer knowledge questions regarding steps to conflict resolution (*knowledge* gained).
- Students use their ASK to change their behavior and avoid fighting.
- The number of fights decrease (that's *results!*—achievement-related data).
- The improvement in school climate contributes to better grades and test scores (that's also *results!*—achievement data).

Conceptual Diagram for a School Counseling Curriculum

The conceptual diagram for a school counseling curriculum (Figure 4.7) provides a practical model school counselors can use to guide their wide use of data by visually laying out the relationship between the types of data (standards and competency, achievement-related, and achievement), and the ways to evaluate data (process, perception and results) (Dimmitt, Carey, & Hatch, 2007; Hatch, 2005a). The diagram visual, included in the Iowa Department of Education's School Counseling Program Framework, helps describe and show how "school counseling programs contribute to student achievement" (Iowa Department of Education, 2008, p. 13). Figure 4.7 reads left to right and represents an action framework connecting what counselors do (measured with process data) to the attainment of specific student competencies (measured with perception data) and behavior change, leading to an improvement in results (reflected in achievement-related data and subsequently in achievement data). For example, when a school counselor teaches a classroom lesson on conflict resolution, he or she might assess whether students acquire (1) the *attitude* that it is important to solve problems peacefully, (2) the *skill* of role-playing steps to conflict resolution, and (3) the *knowledge* of where and when to seek help when needed to avoid a conflict. In this scenario, the goal of the lesson would be to support the reduction of discipline referrals and suspensions, which can lead to improved school climate (achievement-related), which in turn supports improved student academic performance (achievement).

Conceptual Diagram for Intentional Guidance

Conversely, the conceptual diagram for intentional guidance (Figure 4.8) reads right to left. When students (or groups of students) are not performing to expectations on achievement data elements, it would be appropriate to inquire about what achievement-related data elements are lacking (attendance, behavior, course enrollment, homework completion, etc.). School counselors would "fishnet" the students to identify and focus on those who met certain criteria. For instance: *students with multiple failures, who are not on target to graduate, who are in danger of retention.* Using a "fishnet" approach, the school counselors disaggregate the data to determine which students need additional intervention.

Once identified, the next inquiry (moving left in the diagram) would be to look at the perception data to discover what is needed. Knowledge? Attitudes? Skills? Once determined, moving left again to the process data, an intervention could be designed to address the specific need. When students struggle academically, they are routinely assigned remedial courses or tutoring, when in fact the barrier may be motivation. Alternatively, perhaps students are placed in a counseling group to improve motivation when the issue may be that they need tutoring. Furthermore, perhaps the students do not need tutoring or counseling for motivation, but instead, have irregular attendance, or do not feel safe at or connected to school. All too often, the intervention is decided for students before the specific barrier is identified. Struggling students, who come to school counselors from many diverse backgrounds and experiences, are often provided interventions without taking time to consider the particular needs emerging from each student's unique world. By using the conceptual diagram, school counselors can thoughtfully consider systemic interventions that target students' needs.

Conceptual Diagram for Systems Change

Imagine working with a student who is not taking college preparatory courses and is not on target to graduate college-eligible. In looking at the data, it becomes

Figure 4.8 Conceptual Diagram for Intentional Guidance

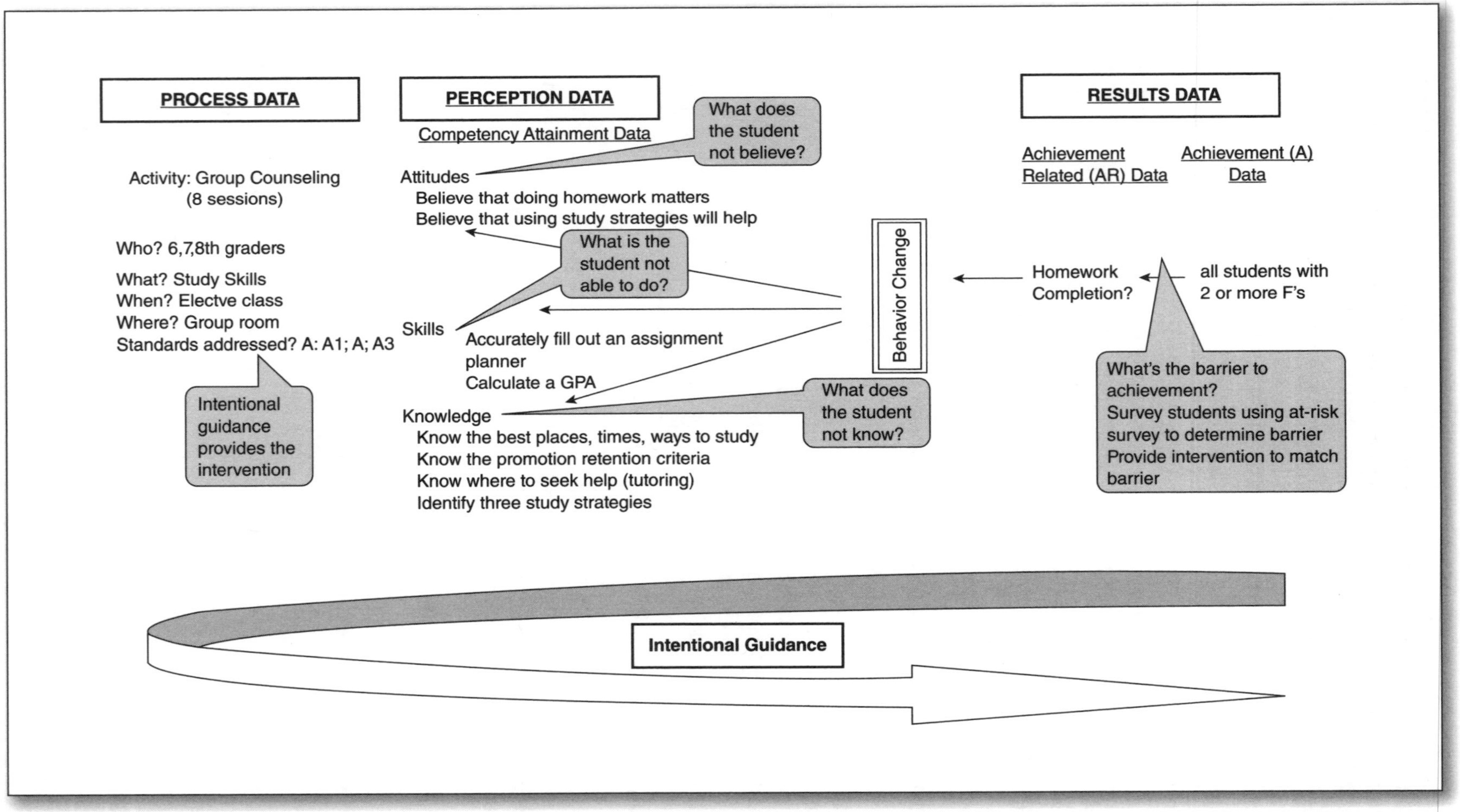

Source: Hatch (2010b).

apparent the student has the knowledge, attitudes, and skills (desire, awareness, and ability) to enroll in the right courses. However, the school is not allowing her to enroll in these courses, because she has not achieved a 3.0 or better in the required prerequisite courses. This is an example of a systems issue, and the intervention would need to take place on a systems level, not just a student level (see Figure 4.9).

Sometimes, the intervention required is outside of the students themselves. When 80% of students are failing a particular teacher's physics course, this may not be a student issue, but a systems issue. When first graders are absent or late to school, it might not have anything to do with the students' attitude, knowledge, or skills, but rather the parents may be responsible for the student missing school. Consequently, when decisions are made regarding interventions, care must be taken to consider whether the intervention required is best focused on the student, the parent, or the school system. Chapter 8 will provide more detail on intentional guidance for systems issues.

Figure 4.9 Conceptual Diagram for Systems Change

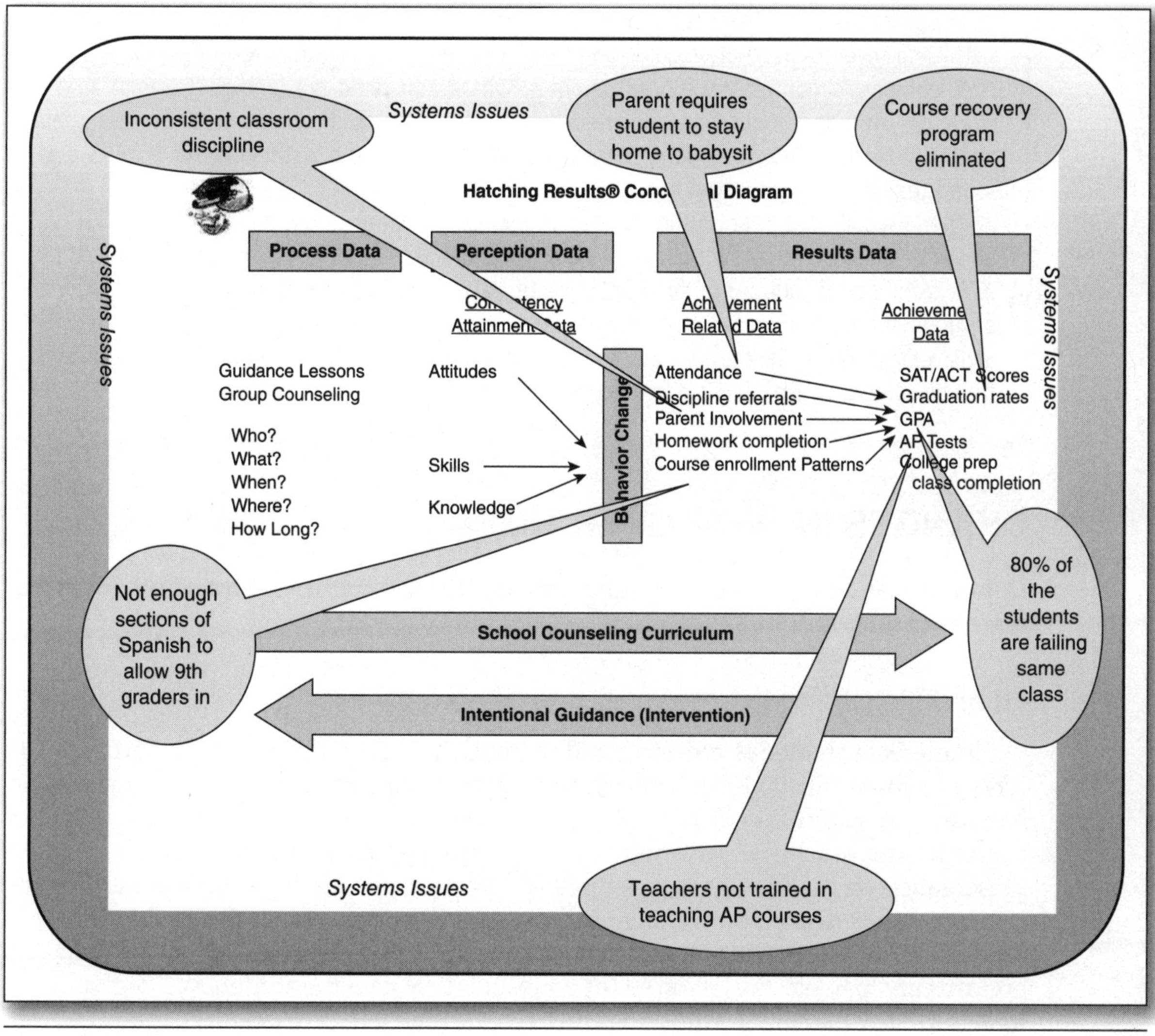

Hatch, T (2006)

Referring back to the interview with our potential new school counselor in Chapter 3, recall the following example she shared of how her purpose (goals/objectives) and outcomes are linked to the activities she performs:

"When I teach conflict resolution skills, for example, my goal is that . . . discipline referrals decline, and climate is improved. . . . By improving the school climate, the school counseling program contributes in a meaningful way to overall academic achievement of students."

Next, she is asked the following questions:

> What is being done to achieve the outcomes you desire?
> What data or evidence is there that the objectives are being met?
> Is your program making a difference for students?
> Can you prove it?

She responds, "Yes, I can. Last year, as a graduate student, the school counselor supervisor and I reviewed data indicating discipline referrals had steadily increased in the past few years at the school site. I worked collaboratively with my school counselor colleagues to go into sixth- and seventh-grade classrooms and teach two lessons on conflict resolution skills using 'XYZ Company's' conflict resolution materials. We administered pre- and posttests to assess students' attitudes about fighting, their knowledge of conflict resolution skills, and their ability to demonstrate (role-play) these skills. We analyzed the data from these tests and found that students improved in every area!

Then we collected data on the number of discipline referrals in the quarters before, during, and after the lesson to see if there was any change. Indeed, we found referrals were reduced by 37% from the first quarter to the third. In addition, the teachers reported the student learning environment was improved, and as we know, when school climate improves, so too does achievement. While we know we can't take credit for all of this change, I do believe we proved that our program is making a difference for students."

CHANGES IN DATA OVER TIME

Data can also be reviewed over time utilizing three categories: immediate, intermediate, and long-range change.

Immediate Change

Immediate change is reflected in data that are collected right away and give the school counselor instant feedback about whether the activity, lesson, or group session had any impact on knowledge, attitudes, or beliefs. Using a pre/post test, a school counselor can quickly learn whether his or her newly created hot-to-trot PowerPoint presentation on graduation requirements is effective (see Figure 4.10). It certainly provides greater benefits than waiting until the end of the year and realizing that students report hearing the lesson but never understanding it. Immediate feedback provides an opportunity to revise the lesson so the counselor is certain the students understand the material. See Chapter 7 for tips on how to create effective pre/post tests.

Figure 4.10   10th-Grade Curriculum: Pre/Post Test Results

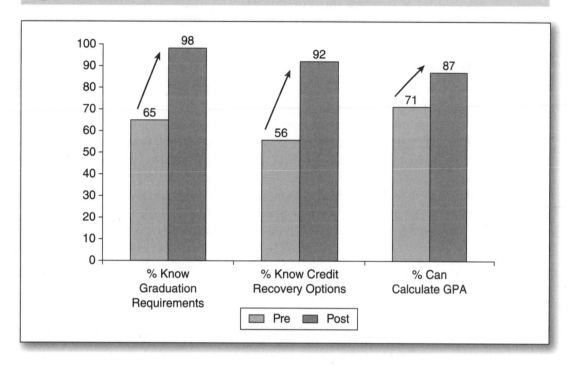

An elementary counselor, Monique, had a favorite lesson on consequences she presented each year to first-grade students. When it was suggested that she begin to collect data on the effectiveness of the lesson, she resisted, at first. "But Trish," she said, "the teachers and the students LOVE this lesson." Indeed, they did. In fact, students and teachers loved Monique because she was a caring, playful, nurturing, animated, warm individual who hugged kids and made lessons FUN! Students sang songs, played with puppets, and listened to stories. She was persuaded, however, to try giving a pre/post test in just one classroom. She developed a pre/post test that covered the content of her lesson—those things she believed students should "know and be able to do" because of her lesson. Not long afterward, Monique came to the office with a smile. "Guess what?" she said, "The students may love me, but they didn't learn a THING in my lesson." Monique, however, did learn something. She discovered that the term "consequence" was a little too advanced for first-grade students. So Monique revised her lesson content until the results of her pre/post test aligned with the intent of her lesson.

Intermediate Change

Intermediate change is reflected in data collected after a quarter, trimester, or semester. It is hard to wait an entire year to see if a program is working. Worse yet, if it is not working, valuable time has been lost when revisions could have been made in an attempt to improve the activity or lesson. Using many state-of-the-art database systems, school counselors can query students and create a dataset of those who are not performing well and who may be at risk of not being promoted to the next grade. For instance, they can query students with two or more F's on their first progress report, or when they receive the first quarter report card, or at the end of the first semester. Then, after providing the intentional guidance intervention, the school counselor can query the dataset for overall changes to the group (see Figure 4.11).

Long-Range Change

Changes in data over a longer period are important, because they can reveal patterns, trends, and discrepancies. School districts often collect long-term data or year-to-year data, disaggregate the information, and make it available for school counselors' use. Long-range data can uncover trends that show the impact over time of specific programs. A high school that provided instruction and intervention for students at risk would monitor the number of students each year who are credit deficient and thus not on target to graduate (see Figure 4.12). This would become informational data for the school as it monitors other long-term data, such as graduation rates. Impact-over-time data are best presented in charts and graphs, so trends are easily identifiable.

DISAGGREGATING DATA

Disaggregating data by gender and ethnicity provides a more accurate perspective than is available in whole datasets. For example, a high school graduation rate may have increased 2% in the last three years, but when disaggregated, the data may indicate graduation rates have increased 2% among White students and 6% among African American students, but have decreased 3% for Latino students (see Figure 4.13). If they did not disaggregate the data by ethnicity, the counseling team might believe their guidance curriculum and interventions alone were successful, when further analysis uncovers a concern that needs addressing.

Figure 4.11 Number of Students With Two or More F's

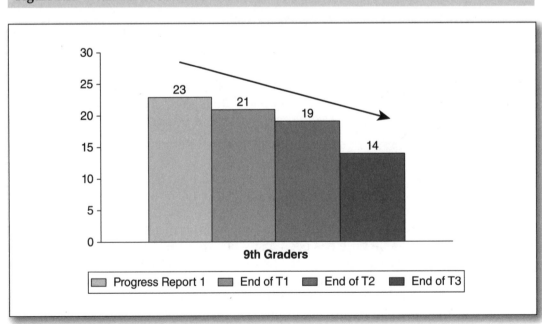

Figure 4.12   Ninth-Grade Credit Deficiency Data

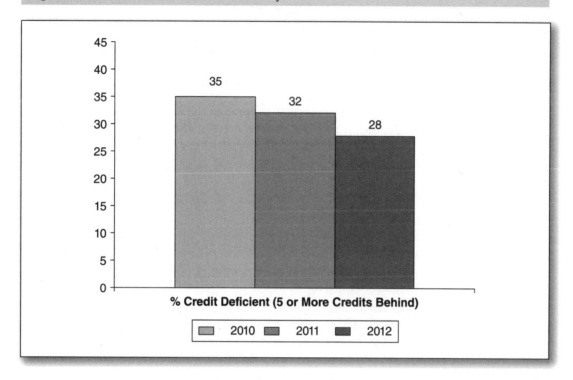

Figure 4.13   Graduation Rates

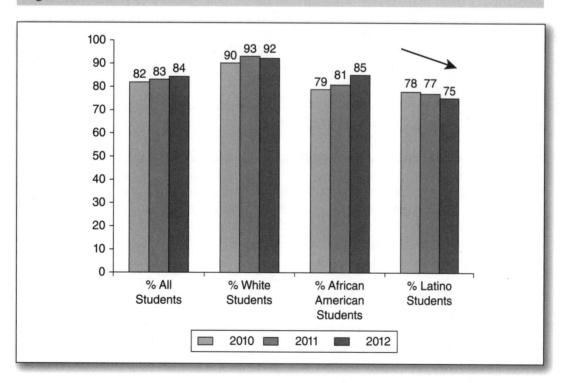

WHERE DO I START? WHAT DATA SHOULD WE LOOK AT EVERY YEAR?

Imagine you were selling your home and you were interviewing real estate agents regarding their credentials. Would you expect that when they came to the interview, they would know the prices of comparable homes for the area? Would you want them to know the average amount of time homes in the area stay on the market? Would you expect they could quote you the current approximate rates for loans? Would it not seem reasonable for the professional real estate agent to *know* these data points? Should a loan officer know today's loan rate? How about an investment broker? Should they know the Dow Jones Industrial Average? The S&P 500? What it was yesterday, or a year ago, and in what direction it is headed? You would *expect* them to know this information, because knowing it is their profession, and you are relying on them for your financial future.

Parents should expect no less from school counselors. Parents consider school counselors (with master's degrees) to be the experts in their field. Therefore it is the school counselors' professional responsibility to review certain data points every year at each level, to ascertain what the current data indicate, and to compare them to (a) the state average, (b) like schools (schools with similar demographics), and (c) over time.

Parents of elementary school students have the right to know the likelihood that, based on data from the past several years, their child will graduate from the feeder high school eligible to enter college. Further, they have a right to know whether this likelihood is any different for their female child than their male child, or for their African American child compared to their neighbor's Filipino child. *What do all parents deserve to know?* What data should all school counselors become "experts" in? It is important for school counselors at each level to determine the data points they will review consistently leach year. The ASCA National Model provides a School Data Profile Analysis that can be used for summary purposes (2012a). Figure 4.14 is a list of the types of districtwide data school counselors should have knowledge of at each grade level and should review each year. Do you agree? Disagree? Is there any other data you would like to add to the list?

A WORD ABOUT DATA ADDICTION

School counselors cannot, and should not, collect data to measure the impact on everything they do—they would lose their minds! We cannot have that; counselors are supposed to be some of the sanest people on campus! Collecting process, perception, and results data on everything you do puts too much data on your desk, more than you can manage in a meaningful way. So choose wisely—start with just one activity you want to measure, such as the effectiveness of a core curriculum lesson and/or an intentional guidance activity.

SUMMARY

School counselors can use multiple types of data to effect change for the students they serve. By becoming proficient in data collection, interpretation, and analysis, counselors can validate existing programs and focus additional recourses where they are

Figure 4.14 Types of Districtwide Data

	DATA	Elementary School	Middle/Junior High School	High School	Alternative Education
Achievement-Related Data	Attendance	X	X	X	X
	Tardies/Truancies	X	X	X	X
	Discipline/Suspensions	X	X	X	X
	Youth Risk Behavior Survey (Violence, Drug Use, etc.)	X	X	X	X
	Scholarship Dollars Earned		X	X	X
	Course Enrollment Patterns (Honors, AP, Remedial)		X	X	X
	Number of Applications to College		X	X	X
Achievement Data	Post-Secondary/College-Going Rates	X	X	X	X
	University Admission Rates		X	X	X
	Exit Exam Passage Rate		X	X	X
	SAT/ACT—Average Scores and Who Takes It		X	X	X
	Credits Earned (Percentage Credit Deficient)			X	X
	Return to College Rate			X	X
	Dropout Rate	X	X	X	X
	Standardized Test Scores	X	X	X	X
	Graduation Rates	X	X	X	X

most needed. School counselors collect data to ensure standards and competencies are met and to link the results of their programs to achievement-related data and achievement data. In the evaluation of program effectiveness, school counselors collect process, perception, and results data, which provide immediate, intermediate, and long-range feedback. When conceptualizing their work, utilizing the two-pronged approach (schoolwide curriculum and intentional guidance) will help school counselors focus on measuring only a few things, so they do not drown in the data (Hatch, 2004b). Finally, school counselors use data to advocate for systems change, ensuring equity and access to a rigorous education for every student.

DATA POSTTEST

Now that you have completed reading Chapter 3 about the types of data and Chapter 4 about program evaluation data, please return to the data pretest in

Chapter 3 and check your answers. How did you do? *Where is the answer key?* The answer key lives within Chapters 3 and 4. With regard to items 15 and 16, if you do not already "strongly agree," keep reading. Hopefully by the time you reach the end of this text, *data* will no longer merely be a four-letter word to you.

5

Action Plans

A Two-Pronged Approach

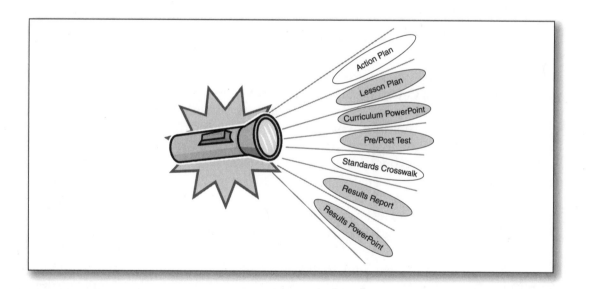

The original *ASCA National Model: A Framework for School Counseling Programs* (ASCA, 2003, 2005), presented two types of action plans, the "Guidance Curriculum" action plan and the "Closing the Gap" action plan, or what this text refers to as the intentional guidance action plan (see Chapter 2). These two types of actions plans represent a two-pronged approach (prevention and intervention) to implementing effective school counseling programs.

In the third edition of the ASCA National Model (2012a, 2012e), "Guidance Curriculum" action plans were retitled: "School Counseling Core Curriculum" action plans. In this chapter, school counseling core curriculum action plans will be referred to as *curriculum action plans*.

Curriculum action plans are standards driven and ensure *every* student gets *every* **thing** (Hatch, 2008). What content will *every* student receive, because he or she came through the schoolroom door? What can each parent and student be told each student will receive from the school counseling program as a third grader, sixth grader, or ninth grader?

Intentional guidance action plans use data to drive decision making and are created because *some students need more*. Although the curriculum is designed for every student, intentional guidance activities address the discrepancies that exist in meeting students' needs and their achievements. What do the data tell about who needs additional support or assistance? What data drive the need for the activity? Is this a student need or a systems need? In 2012 "Small Group" action plan was added to the third edition of the ASCA National Model (ASCA, 2012a; 2012e). Intentional guidance activities can include small group interventions, schoolwide interventions, and/or interventions addressing policy, programs, practices, or procedures.

SCHOOL COUNSELING CORE CURRICULUM: *EVERY* STUDENT GETS *EVERY THING*

The first prong of the two-pronged approach for providing prevention and intervention within the school counseling program is school counseling curriculum. By virtue of breathing, every student in the school receives school counseling curriculum. The curriculum is developmental in design, preventative in nature, and comprehensive in scope, and parents, students, teachers, and other stakeholders know exactly what curriculum their student(s) will receive. The curriculum, much like math or science, is competency driven, created by school counselors and student service professionals to address the standards and competencies of the ASCA Student Standards (ASCA, 2012a, 2012e; Campbell & Dahir, 1997).

The school counselors, in collaboration with site administrators (or in some cases, district coordinators), determine what content will be covered in each lesson and align it with the standards. School counselors create an action plan, calendar these lessons, and collect process data, perception data, and results data. Lessons are designed by school counselors and become consistent from school to school to ensure that when students transfer within a district, they will receive the same curriculum from the school counseling program. For example, just as all third graders are taught multiplication tables, so too are all sixth graders taught the "Time to Tell" violence prevention lesson.

In Chapter 1, examples were provided for schoolwide curriculum action plans. School counselors won't have time to measure every lesson, but they are encouraged to select a few to measure each year to inform their practice. The samples below provide a detailed description for completing the curriculum action plan when measuring the impact of a lesson or unit of lessons.

Curriculum action plans consider the following:

- Lesson content
- Domain and standard to be addressed: academic, career, personal/social
- Description of actual curriculum the school counselor or counseling team will provide
- Assurance that the curriculum is provided for *every* student
- Title of any packaged or created curriculum that will be used
- Timeline for completion of activity
- Name of individual responsible for delivery
- Means of evaluating students' attitudes, skills, and knowledge (ASK) using pre/post tests or demonstration of competency or product

- Expected achievement and achievement-related results for students, stated in terms of what will be demonstrated by the student
- Indication that the plan has been reviewed and signed by the administrator

GUIDELINES FOR USING CURRICULUM ACTION PLANS

Samples of curriculum action plans for elementary, middle, and high schools are shown in Figures 5.1., 5.2, and 5.3. The sections below explain the content of the columns of each of these plans.

Lesson Content

When deciding which content you will provide to every student, it will be helpful to review your developmental crosswalk of the ASCA National Standards. Which domains do you want to be certain to address? Ideally, and with a low ratio, you would want to address every domain, but this may not be possible. Consider your priorities, and begin in these domains. Priorities might include areas the data indicate need attention. Perhaps your Youth Risk Behavior Survey (YRBS) or school climate survey indicates you have a high number of students who are feeling unsafe at school, who have been victims of bullying, and so on. Based on these data, you might prioritize this lesson. Then add a few lessons each year until all domains are addressed.

ASCA Domain/Standard

You will note on the blank schoolwide action plan in Chapter 1 (Figure 1.4), that all the standards are listed. Circle or underline which standard each lesson is addressing, or delete the standards not addressed, leaving those that are. Then, once a specific lesson is selected to measure, provide more detail as seen in Figures 5.1–5.3.

Curriculum and Materials

This column asks you to identify the specific content to be taught in the lesson. For example, the competency might be study skills, but the content will vary by grade level and student population. Fourth-grade students may receive the study/test-taking skills curriculum from the "Sunburst" video, seventh graders may use the SIMS study skills techniques, and high school students may use techniques from the College Board. By tracking the different curricula being used (especially in the same grade level) and measuring and comparing the results of lessons, school counseling teams can determine which curriculum is most effective, thereby improving the program and avoiding the cost of purchasing ineffective curriculum.

Projected Start/End

Knowing when an activity will occur and when it will be completed are essential to team planning. This facilitates intelligent planning of when events will take place in the school system. For example, teaching test-taking strategies is most effective when done just prior to statewide standardized test administration. Doing it months before or after students have been tested would miss the critical teaching moment. Similarly, teaching conflict resolution skills would be more appropriate in the beginning of the school year than at the end, as the skills might be forgotten during the summer.

Projected Number of Students Impacted

This column asks school counselors to provide the number of students projected to receive the school counseling core curriculum. Ensuring every student is accounted for sends a clear message of equity and access for all.

Class/Subject in Which Lesson Will Be Presented

When counselors are deciding in which subject area to deliver their lessons, it is important to recognize and appreciate the standards and competencies that the classroom teachers are required to address. Effort should be made to implement the curriculum in several subject areas as opposed to impacting only one academic area. Perhaps checking to see which of the subject content areas the curriculum also addresses would be helpful. For instance, a lesson on calculating GPA might be well suited for a math course, writing a resume in language arts, violence prevention in social studies, and drug prevention in science.

Evaluation Methods

Before the delivery of services, it is important to consider the criteria by which success will be measured. First, is it necessary for 100% of the students to demonstrate the skill, or is improvement in the number of students successfully demonstrating the skill acceptable in some situations? For example, demonstrating an understanding of promotion/retention criteria or developing an educational plan may be appropriate for all students at every level, while identifying five early warning signs of violence or demonstrating the ability to resolve conflict may be presented to only one grade level or group of students. What type of data will be collected? Will a pre/post test be designed to measure knowledge, attitude, or skills? Will the completion of a competency (such as filling out an interest inventory) be measured? What results data will be measured: attendance, behavior, or academic?

Implementation Contact Person

In this column, specific names are important. Who will be the individual responsible for ensuring the action plan is carried out? Several educators may be involved in an activity; however, it may be helpful for one person to have the primary responsibility.

The Administrator's Signature

The signature of the administrator ensures collaboration in and agreement with the proposed activities of the school counseling program.

Prepared By

While the entire school counseling team is responsible for the programmatic implementation, one person (typically the lead counselor) takes responsibility for preparing the document and keeping the files.

SAMPLE CURRICULUM ACTION PLANS

Figure 5.1   Sample Elementary School Curriculum Action Plan

XYZ Unified School District
XYZ Elementary School Counseling Curriculum Action Plan for 20XX–20XX

Grade Level	Lesson Content (Topic Area)	ASCA National Standard	Curriculum and Materials	Projected Start/ Projected End	Projected Number of Students Impacted	Class/ Subject in Which Lesson Will Be Presented	Evaluation Methods How will the results be measured?		Implementation Contact Person
							Perception Data: (ASK Examples)	Results Data:	
4, 5	Anti-bullying Violence Prevention	Personal/Social Competency: PS: A2 Acquire Interpersonal Skills PS: C1 Acquire Personal Safety Skills	XYZ Violence Presentation Prepackaged Programs or Anti-bullying Programs	In January During National School Safety Week	300: ALL Fourth and Fifth Graders in School [All students—remember every one receives curriculum, because it has been determined that this is a lesson all students should know]	To Be Arranged With Each Teacher	*Attitude:* 1. ___% who believe that calling people names hurts them 2. ___% who believe it's okay to hit someone if that person hits you first *Skills:* 1. ___% who can role play conflict resolution skills 2. ___% who can verbalize an "I statement" *Knowledge:* 1. ___% who know the steps to conflict resolution 2. ___% who know the consequences of bullying in schools 3. ___% who know who to go to if they need to ask for help	*Achievement Related (AR):* Number of students who are referred for discipline Number of students suspended Statewide youth survey (Title IV) data on bullying items *Achievement (A):* Achievement improvements in classes with improved climate	Elementary School Counselor

_____   _____   _____

Principal's Signature   Date   Date of Staff Presentation

_____

Prepared By

Figure 5.2 Sample Middle School Curriculum Action Plan

XYZ Unified School District

XYZ Middle School Counseling Curriculum Action Plan for 20XX–20XX

Grade Level	Lesson Content (Topic Area)	ASCA National Standard	Curriculum and Materials	Projected Start/ Projected End	Projected Number of Students Impacted	Class/Subject in Which Lesson Will Be Presented	Evaluation Methods How will the results be measured?		Implementation Contact Person
							Perception Data: (ASK Examples)	Results Data:	
6, 7, 8	Promotion / Retention Guidelines Study Skills Importance of Homework	Academic *Competency:* A: A1 Improve Self-Concept A: A3 Achieve School Success	Counselor-Generated PowerPoint	October–November	1,500 [All students—remember every one receives curriculum, because it has been determined that this is a lesson all students should know]	English (language arts)	*Attitude:* 1. ___ % who believe that doing homework matters 2. ___ % who believe that using study strategies will help them do better in school *Skills:* 1. ___ % who can accurately fill out an assignment planner 2. ___ % who can calculate a GPA *Knowledge:* 1. ___ % who demonstrate knowledge of best places, times, ways to study 2. ___ % who know promotion retention criteria 3. ___ % who know where to seek help (tutoring) 4. ___ % who can identify three study strategies	*Achievement Related (AR):* Homework completion rate *Achievement (A):* Compare academic improvement: GPA from Trimester 1 to Trimester 2 and/ or Trimester 1 to Trimester 3.	School Counselors Melon (6) Peach (7) Berry (8)

_____   _____   _____

Principal's Signature   **Date**   **Date of Staff Presentation**

_____

Prepared By

Figure 5.3   Sample High School Curriculum Action Plan

XYZ Unified School District
XYZ High School Counseling Curriculum Action Plan for 20XX–20XX

Grade Level	Lesson Content (Topic Area)	ASCA National Standard	Curriculum and Materials	Projected Start/ Projected End	Projected Number of Students Impacted	Class/Subject in Which Lesson Will Be Presented	Evaluation Methods How will the results be measured?		Implementation Contact Person
							Perception Data: (ASK Examples)	Results Data:	
9	Transcript Review	Academic *Competency:* A: A3 Achieve School Success A: B2 Plan to Achieve Goals	Counselor- Generated PowerPoint Using District Graduation Requirements and State and CSU/UC Requirements Each Student's Own Transcript Four Year Plan	October (right after first quarter grades)	2,400: ALL in District [All students— remember every one receives curriculum, because it has been determined that this is a lesson all students should know]	English or PE Site Specific or Tech Class?	*Attitude:* 1. ___ % who believe that grades earned in ninth grade matter 2. ___ % who believe taking college prep courses is important *Skills:* 1. ___ % who can accurately fill out a four year academic plan 2. ___ % who can calculate a GPA *Knowledge:* 1. ___ % who know the graduation requirements 2. ___ % who can identify difference between types of GPAs 3. ___ % who know college prep requirements	*Achievement Related* (AR): Homework completion rate Course enrollment patterns (college prep and advanced math and science coursework— honors, AP, etc.) *Achievement (A):* Course completion rates (ninth grade credit deficiency rates) College prep graduation rates (data over time)	All High School Counselors

_____   _____   _____   _____
Principal's Signature   **Date**   **Date of Staff Presentation**   **Prepared By**

99

INTENTIONAL GUIDANCE: SOME KIDS NEED *MORE*

The second prong of the two-pronged approach to providing prevention and intervention within a school counseling program is referred to as *intentional guidance*. While receiving standards-based curriculum may be adequate for many students, the intentional guidance philosophy is "some students need *more.*" Intentional guidance action plans can be directed toward *students* or *systems* (see Chapter 8). When these plans are directed toward *students*, school counselors design data-driven (as opposed to standards-driven) activities. School counselors monitor student progress individually and schoolwide at regularly scheduled reporting times each year. After analyzing the data, school counselors determine which students need which type of additional intervention support. The specific areas of data-driven needs are focused on attendance, behavior, and achievement. Monitoring these types of data regularly and over time can lead school counseling programs to make decisions for when and how to provide services based on real (not perceived) needs. Programs and services are planned and directly linked to the statistical patterns, trends, and discrepancies that consistently emerge and are evaluated over time.

Students do not all learn at the same pace. Disaggregating the data drives the focus to where additional help is needed, for example, to students with two or more F's on first quarter grade reports, students with ten or more absences in the first quarter, or students with five or more days of suspension. The data show these students need additional assistance. Rather than waiting for students to be referred (reactive model), school counselors query the student database and create intentional guidance action plans detailing specific school counseling activities designed to address the specific student need.

As will be discussed in Chapter 6, because not all students will require or benefit from the same intervention, utilizing an at-risk survey is helpful in determining each student's appropriate intervention. In some cases the appropriate intervention may be small group counseling for social skills, study skills, student engagement or empowerment, and so on. In these instances, school counselors can use intentional guidance action plan forms comparable to those shown in Figures 5.4 through 5.10 or the Small Group Action Plans in the third edition of the ASCA National Model (2012a). Both are designed for targeted student interventions and ask for similar information.

For some students, however, a more comprehensive approach to interventions may be required. When looking at the data, the school counselor may realize the "more" students need is not a small group counseling activity but rather a referral to tutoring, mentoring, or credit deficiency programs; to the SST or RTI team; to the counselor for a few individual, brief, solution-focused counseling sessions (Sklare, 2004); or to an outside agency (social worker, therapist) for family assistance. Intentional guidance action plans in this chapter can also be used for these circumstances. In these cases, the school counselor may also want to consider using the Closing the Gap Action Plan in the ASCA National Model (2012a). The distinction between the Small Group Action Plan and the Closing the Gap Action Plan in the ASCA National Model is that the Closing the Gap Action Plan is designed to address equity issues or discrepancies in behavior or academic data between students of different *demographic* groups. In this case, it would be discrepancies between groups who are attending, behaving, or performing and those that are not.

Still other students may need the counselor's advocacy to work within the system to change an existing policy or practice that may be denying some students access to or equitable participation in rigorous educational opportunities. These may include social justice issues, parity issues, or issues that stir a moral imperative for counselors to act on students' behalf (Hatch, 2012a; Holcomb-McCoy, 2007). An example might be advocating for changes in the curriculum guide when counselors recognize that prerequisite requirements are holding students back rather than moving them forward to more rigorous education. The work of the Education Trust and MetLife Foundation National School Counselor Training Initiative (2002) aligns with this view of intentional guidance for systems change. When the data reveal that the discrepancies between groups stem from systems issues outside of the students' control, interventions are designed and directed toward systemic change. Intentional guidance action plans for systems change will be presented and discussed in Chapter 8.

Intentional Guidance Action Plans Consider the Following:

- What is the target group?
- Why was this group topic or intervention chosen?
- What are the specific *data that drive the decision* to provide this particular intentional guidance activity?
- Domain and standard to be addressed: academic, career, personal/social
- Student competency addressed
- Description of actual activity the school counselor or support services team will ensure occurs
- Resources needed to implement intervention activity
- Projected number of students
- Timeline for completion of activity
- Name of individual responsible for delivery
- Means of evaluating student success (what data will be used to show improvement?)
- Expected result for students, stated in terms of what will be demonstrated by students
- Indication that the intentional guidance action plan has been reviewed and signed by the administrator

GUIDELINES FOR USING INTENTIONAL GUIDANCE ACTION PLANS

Intentional guidance action plans are very similar in design to curriculum action plans. Samples of these plans are shown in Figures 5.4 through 5.10. Note that samples shown in Figures 5.4–5.7 were designed to align with the strategies identified in Goal 3 of Figure 3.8 in Chapter 3. However, they could easily be revised to address attendance, behavior, or study-skill needs at the middle or high school level. The sections below explain the different content provided in the columns of each of these plans. (Additional Action Plans are available in the on-line appendix.)

Target Group

Focus on an overarching topic for a targeted group of students who are identified because of a data-driven need. Who will you intervene with? What is the principal concern? Poor attendance? Credit deficiency? Lack of homework completion? State the grade level and title of target group here.

Target Group Selection Is Based Upon the Following Data

On this line, indicate the specific data element or reason these particular students are being targeted for intervention. What data were used to select these students? As a reminder, indicating "all students referred for group by teachers" would not be appropriate for this action plan. This plan is for data-driven, not teacher-referral-driven, interventions. If this intervention is related to a program goal or SMART goal (as described in Chapter 3), it might also be appropriate to indicate that here so as to show alignment between this action plan and the program goals.

School Counselor and Other Student Services Professionals

Sometimes interventions are best provided through a collaborative relationship with other support service providers, such as the school psychologist or social worker. Indicate all stakeholders participating in this intervention, and then, in the Type of Activity column, indicate their role.

Intended Effects

Indicate the impact the action plan intends to make on attendance, behavior, or academic achievement.

Type of Activity to Be Delivered in What Manner?

Determining what intervention to provide will require understanding the barrier to learning. Interviewing or surveying the students prior to determining the intervention activity may accomplish this. Perhaps an attendance "hot list" should be created for students who are habitually truant, or an anger management group should be started for those identified as having five or more suspension days for fighting. Indicate what will be done and the intended curriculum (if any).

Often school counselors just indicate they met with the students individually a few times, or they referred them to tutoring or assigned them to a group. As will be discussed in Chapter 6, determining which intervention is appropriate is an important part of the intentional guidance process. Additionally, sharing the multiple activities involved in the entire process provides a more comprehensive picture of what school counselors do than just indicating "small group."

Resources Needed

What resources will be required to ensure the intervention occurs? Will the intervention require funds to purchase curriculum? Will it require a larger space to hold a group meeting? Identify the resources needed here.

Projected Number of Students Impacted

When implementing the intentional guidance action plan, it is important to ensure there are a significant numbers of students impacted. At least 30 to 40 students are recommended. Understandably, there are small schools and rural schools where there may be fewer students who qualify. However, speaking from a global perspective, it is difficult to sell the results of the program if only a few students participate, because the impact on the entire school is minimal. This is not to say school counselors shouldn't service smaller groups of students; it is to say, however, that very small groups of students with similar needs would not be recommended as appropriate for intentional guidance action plans and evaluation. Additionally, when only a few students on a counselor's caseload are provided ongoing weekly sessions, there may be a tendency to assume these are intensive services for students at the "top of the pyramid." Intentional guidance is not therapy. It is not designed for a few students. It is designed primarily as a Tier 2, not a Tier 3, intervention. (Refer to Chapter 2 for definitions of these tiers.)

SAMPLE INTENTIONAL GUIDANCE ACTION PLANS

Figure 5.4   Sample Intentional Guidance Action Plan for Students Struggling With Behavior Management Concerns

Target Group: *All third, fourth, and fifth graders struggling with behavior management concerns*

Target Group selection is based upon the following data: *Any student in third, fourth, or fifth grade with three or more discipline referrals in Q1; Q2; Q3. Address program goal to reduce discipline referrals for repeat offenders.*

XYZ Unified School District
XYZ Elementary School Intentional Guidance (Small Group) Action Plan 20XX–20XX

School Counselor or Other Student Services Professional	ASCA National Standards	Type of Activity to Be Delivered in What Manner?	Resources Needed	Projected Start/End	Projected Number of Students Impacted	Evaluation Method (How will you measure results?)		Intended Effect on Academics, Behavior, or Attendance?
						Perception Data (ASK Examples)	Results Data	
Counselor Name Social Worker Name	*Personal/Social* PS:A1 Acquire Self-Knowledge PS:A1.8 Understand the Need for Self-Control and How to Practice It PS: A2 Acquire Interpersonal Skill PS:A2.6 Use Effective Communications Skills PS:B1.6 Know How to Apply Conflict Resolution Skills PS: C1 Acquire Personal Safety Skills	Letter home to parents about group intervention Interview student to ensure group as appropriate intervention Group counseling for anger management and conflict resolution Refer students who are not appropriate for group counseling to alternative interventions (e.g. social worker) Contract with students Reward system	Purchase curriculum ($125.00) Time at staff meeting to explain program and intervention Disaggregated data from first quarter discipline referrals Group counseling facility (room) Clerical assistance for letters home to parents	November to March	60 students	*Attitude:* 1. ___% who believe that it's ok to hit someone if student is hit first 2. ___% who believe fighting is okay if someone calls you a bad name *Skills:* 1. ___% who can accurately demonstrate conflict resolution skills 2. ___% who identify alternatives to fighting in a scenario *Knowledge:* 1. ___% who demonstrate knowledge of conflict resolution process 2. ___% who know what discipline occurs if they fight	*Achievement Related (AR):* ___% improvement in number of discipline referrals from Q1 to Q2; Q2 to Q3; Q3 to Q4. *Achievement (A):* Compare grades for targeted students to see if behavior is impacting achievement: Compare GPA from Q1 to Q2, Q2 to Q3, and Q3 to Q4	Students will improve their behavior Students will improve academically (GPA)

_____   _____   _____   _____

Principal's Signature   **Date**   **Date of Staff Presentation**   **Prepared By**

Figure 5.5 Sample Intentional Guidance Action Plan for Students for Whom There Are Attendance Concerns

Target Group: *All third, fourth, and fifth graders for whom there are attendance concerns*

Target Group selection is based upon the following data: *Any student in third, fourth, or fifth grade with five or more absences in the first quarter*

XYZ Unified School District

XYZ Elementary School Intentional Guidance (Small Group) Action Plan 20XX–20XX

School Counselor or Other Student Services Professional	ASCA National Standard	Type of Activity to Be Delivered in What Manner?	Resources Needed	Projected Start/End	Projected Number of Students Impacted	Evaluation Method (How will you measure results?)		Intended Effect on Academics, Behavior, or Attendance?
						Perception Data (ASK Examples)	**Results Data**	
Counselor A	*Academic:* A: A2 Acquire Skills for Improved Learning A: A3 Achieve School Success PS: B1 Self Knowledge Application	Letter home to parents Group counseling on importance of attendance and time management skills Parents meeting Contract with students Reward system	Purchase curriculum ($125.00) Time on staff agenda to explain program Disaggregated data from first month's attendance data Group counseling facility (room) Clerical assistance for letters home	November to March	40 students	*Attitude:* 1. ___ % who believe that coming to school everyday is important *Skills:* 2. ___ % who can accurately set an alarm clock 3. ___ % who can demonstrate time management skills *Knowledge:* 1. ___ % who demonstrate knowledge of time school starts 2. ___ % who know what discipline might occur if student is truant from school	*Achievement Related (AR):* ___ % improvement in attendance and decrease in tardies *Achievement (A):* Compare academic improvement: GPA from Q1 to Q2	Student will improve attendance Students will improve academically (GPA)

Principal's Signature   Date   Date of Staff Presentation   **Prepared By**

Figure 5.6 Sample Intentional Guidance Action Plan for Elementary Students Exhibiting Poor Study Habits

Target Group: *All fourth-grade students exhibiting poor study habits*

Target Group selection is based upon the following data: *Any fourth grader with an N or U in Work Skills and/or Study Habits on academic-related categories as reported on the first trimester fourth grade report card.*

XYZ Unified School District
XYZ Elementary School Intentional Guidance (Small Group) Action Plan 20XX–20XX

School Counselor or Other Student Services Professional	ASCA National Standard	Type of Activity to Be Delivered in What Manner?	Resources Needed	Projected Start/End	Projected Number of Students Impacted	Evaluation Method (How will you measure results?)		Intended Effect on Academics, Behavior, or Attendance?
						Perception Data (ASK Examples)	**Results Data**	
School Counselors	*Academic:* A: A2 Acquire Skills for Improved Learning A:A3 Achieve School Success PS: B1 Self Knowledge Application	Notification letter home to parents Group counseling on study skills, use of lesson planner, homework strategies, etc. Contract with students Reward system Support services (to help gather data)	Review curriculum and expectations with school staff Disaggregated data from first trimester report card data Group counseling Review/purchase study skills curriculum and/or supplies and materials Reward system	November to May	30 to 50 students per school site	*Attitude:* 1. % who believe that homework is important 2. % who believe it is important to use time wisely *Skills:* 1. % who can demonstrate how to use a planner 2. Increase in % who complete classroom work *Knowledge:* 1. % who demonstrate knowledge of organizational skills 2. % who have knowledge of time management skills	*Achievement Related (AR):* % improvement in homework and class work completion Decreased number of N's and U's on Work Skills and Study Habits on student report card *Achievement (A):* Improvement in performance level status in ELA and math	Students will improve rate and accuracy of homework and class work Students will show improvement in academic-related categories on fourth grade report to parents

Principal's Signature   Date   Date of Staff Presentation   Prepared By

Figure 5.7   Actual Example of Intentional Guidance Action Plan for Students Who Need Assistance With Life Skills and Study Habits

Target Group: *Third-, fourth-, and fifth-grade students with N's and U's on Life Skills and/or Work Habits section of first trimester report card*

(observes school/playground rules, observes classroom rules, demonstrates self-control, behaves with courtesy and respect, works cooperatively with others, works without disturbing others, works independently, follows verbal and written directions, demonstrates organizational skills, completes neat and careful work, completes and returns homework on time, communicates ideas clearly, participates and contributes to discussions)

Target Group selection is based upon the following data: *Students with 5 or more N's and U's in the Life Skills and/or Work Habits section of their report card (sections as listed above)*

San Marcos Unified School District
Alvin Dunn Elementary School Intentional Guidance Action Plan 2011–2012

School Counselor or Other Student Services Professional	ASCA Standards	Type of Activity to Be Delivered in What Manner?	Resources Needed	Projected Start/End	Projected Number of Students Impacted	Evaluation Method (How will you measure results?)		Intended Effect on Academics, Behavior, or Attendance?
						Perception Data (ASK Examples)	Results Data	
Ms. Duarte, School Counselor	*Academic:* A: A1.5 Identify Attitudes and Behaviors Which Lead to Successful Learning A: A2.2 Demonstrate How Effort and Persistence Positively Affect Learning PS: A1.6 Distinguish Between Appropriate and Inappropriate Behavior A: B1.7 Become a Self-Directed and Independent Learner	Meet with students individually prior to group starting and administer pretest Eight-week intentional guidance lessons in small groups (beginning in January) Parent and teacher notification Additional support and referrals to outside resources as needed	Disaggregated data from report reports Counselor-generated curriculum Student incentives Collaboration with teachers (present to staff and attend PLC meetings) Pre/post tests Collaboration with teachers to coordinate group times	December 2011 to March 2012 Repeated third trimester (starting mid-March)	Third grade: 20 Fourth grade: 20 Fifth grade: 15	*Attitude:* % who think setting goals/ checking progress helps them do better in school % who believe there is an adult at school who cares about them *Skills:* % who can write a school-related goal and explain ways they can achieve their goal *Knowledge:* % who can list one thing they can do to practice self-control in the classroom % who try to work out problems by talking or writing	*Achievement Related (AR):* Decrease in the number of N's and U's on this group of students' second and third trimester report cards Decrease in the number of behavior referrals *Achievement (A):* Increase in number of 3s and 4s on second and third trimester report cards Increase in scores of proficient and above on CST	Students will have a better attitude toward school, peers, and teachers, which will decrease the number of referrals and decrease the number of N's and U's on report cards. Improved student behavior will contribute to increased academic achievement.

Whitney DeSantis 　　　 *October 15, 2011* 　　　 *To be presented at February 2012 Staff Mtg.* 　　　 *Danielle Duarte, School Counselor*

Principal's Signature 　　　 **Date** 　　　 **Date of Staff Presentation** 　　　 **Prepared By**

Figure 5.8 Sample Intentional Guidance Action Plan for Middle School Students in Danger of Failing

Target Group: *All sixth-, seventh-, and eighth-grade students in danger of failing*

Target Group selection is based upon the following data: *Any student with a GPA below 1.3 at the end of first trimester*

XYZ Unified School District
XYZ Middle School Intentional Guidance (Small Group) Action Plan 20XX–20XX

School Counselor or Other Student Services Professional	ASCA National Standard	Type of Activity to Be Delivered in What Manner?	Resources Needed	Projected Start/End	Projected Number of Students Impacted	Evaluation Method (How will you measure results?)		Intended Effect on Academics, Behavior, or Attendance?
						Perception Data (ASK Examples)	**Results Data**	
Counselor (6th) Counselor (7th) Counselor (8th)	*Academic Standard A:* Students will acquire the knowledge, skills, and attitudes that will contribute to effective learning in school and across the lifespan.	Create multiple counseling groups to address students identified barrier to homework completion Student success skills (SSS) curriculum 8 to 10 weeks of curriculum 45-minute sessions Alternating classes (so that students miss less class time)	Purchase curriculum ($125.00) Time on staff agenda to explain program Disaggregated data from first trimester report cards Group counseling facility (room)	November to March	100 students	*Attitude:* ___ % who believe that doing homework matters *Skills:* ___ % who can accurately fill out an assignment planner *Knowledge:* ___ % who demonstrate knowledge of best places, times, ways to study OR ___ % who know where to seek help (tutoring)	*Achievement Related (AR):* Homework completion rate *Achievement (A):* Compare academic improvement: GPA change from Trimester 1 to Trimester 2 AND/OR Trimester 1 to Trimester 3	Students will improve their rate and accuracy of homework completion Students will improve academically (GPA)

_____   _____   _____

Principal's Signature   **Date**   **Date of Staff Presentation**   **Prepared By**

Figure 5.9 Sample Intentional Guidance Action Plan for Ninth-Grade Students at Risk of Failure

Target Group: *Ninth-grade students at risk of failure*

Target Group selection is based upon the following data: *All ninth-grade students who have two or more F's at first quarter grade reporting*

XYZ Unified School District
XYZ High School Intentional Guidance Action Plan 20XX–20XX

School Counselor or Other Student Services Professional	ASCA Standards and Competency	Type of Activity to Be Delivered in What Manner?	Resources Needed	Projected Start/End	Projected Number of Students Impacted	Evaluation Method (How will you measure results?)		Intended Effect on Academics, Behavior, or Attendance?
						Perception Data (ASK Examples)	Results Data	
Counselor A Counselor B Counselor C	*Academic Standard A:* Students will acquire the knowledge, skills, and attitudes that will contribute to effective learning in school and across the lifespan.	Letter/phone call home to parent includes referral opportunities for tutoring and offer to place in students groups Referral to staff mentor Individual counseling session Group counseling for motivation and / or study skill issues that are barriers to learning Alternating classes (so that students miss less class time)	Disaggregated data from first quarter report cards Purchase or create curriculum for groups Time on staff agenda to explain program Group counseling facility (room) Clerical help for letters home and scheduling of meetings and groups	November to March	120 students	*Attitude:* 1. ____ % who believe that passing classes in ninth grade matters 2. ____ % who indicate they will ask for help when they need it *Skills:* 1. ____ % who can identify resources for tutorial help 2. ____ % who can identify their barrier to learning 3. ____ % who can identify where and when to seek help *Knowledge:* 1. ____ % who know credits necessary to graduate 2. ____ % who know where and when to seek help for tutoring	*Achievement Related (AR):* Homework completion rate *Achievement (A):* Compare academic improvement: Classes passed at quarter to classes passed at semester	Students will improve their rate and accuracy of homework completion Students will improve academically (GPA)

Principal's Signature   Date   Date of Staff Presentation   Prepared By

Figure 5.10 Sample Intentional Guidance Action Plan for High School Students Who Lack Needed Credits

Target Group: *Credit-deficient students in Grades 10–12*

Target Group selection is based upon the following data: *All students in Grades 10–12 who have less than 20 credits*

XYZ Unified School District
High School Intentional Guidance Action Plan 20XX–20XX

School Counselors or Other Student Service Personnel	ASCA National Standard	Type of Activity to Be Delivered in What Manner?	Resource Needed	Projected Start/End	Projected Number of Students Impacted	Evaluation Method (How will you measure results?)		Intended Effect on Academics, Behavior, or Attendance?
						Perception Data (ASK Examples)	Results Data	
School Counselors Administration Clerical Support Central Office Administration	*Academic Standard B:* Students will complete school with the academic preparation essential to choose from a wide variety of postsecondary options.	Counselors query the list of students with 20 or fewer credits at the end of each final grading period Letter sent home to parents informing them of credit deficiency; letter includes counselor contact information and referral information for tutoring and credit recovery courses (including online CR) Counselors call in each student for individual counseling session to discuss alternatives, resources, and options Referrals offered for group counseling (motivation, study skills) Referrals also made to the following as appropriate: alternative education, SARB, or SSTs Counselors document actions/ contacts on behavior screen of discipline file in SIS Administrators inform counselors if/when parents are scheduled for meetings on issues regarding these students	Ensure that credits are accurate—need to ensure registrar enters credits in a timely manner (currently four months behind) Need support (full time secretary was cut) students / parents not being assisted in timely manner—missing scheduling support for parents/students meetings Ensure all school counselors have training in querying student data and in logging of contact and intervention data Clerical help for letters home and scheduling of meetings Credit recovery classes to offer students Room in alternative education (many students qualify—currently no room for them—need to free space for them and determine as a district that criteria ensure placement in alternative education). Need meeting time with alternative education principal to address issues of placement	Ongoing and querying at each final grade reporting	60 (30 per high school) At XYZ High School, 15 students have 0 credits—two failed all their classes; others have no paper trail or are awaiting data entry	*Attitude:* % who indicate they will ask for help when they need it *Skills:* % who can identify resources for credit recovery tutorial help % who can identify on transcript how to get additional credits needed *Knowledge:* % who know credits necessary to graduate % who know where and when to seek help for tutoring % who know number of credits they have	*Achievement Related (AR):* Number of students enrolled in courses to make up for credit deficiency Number of students referred to alternative education Number of students on waiting list for alternative education *Achievement (A):* Year-to-year comparison of number of students who have less than 20 credits, OR Year-to-year comparison of number of credits earned per student Credits earned at each grading period Graduation rates	Student will gain credits towards graduation Students will improve academically (GPA)

_____   _____   _____

Principal's Signature   Date   Date of Staff Presentation

_____

Prepared By

6

Determining Curriculum and Interventions

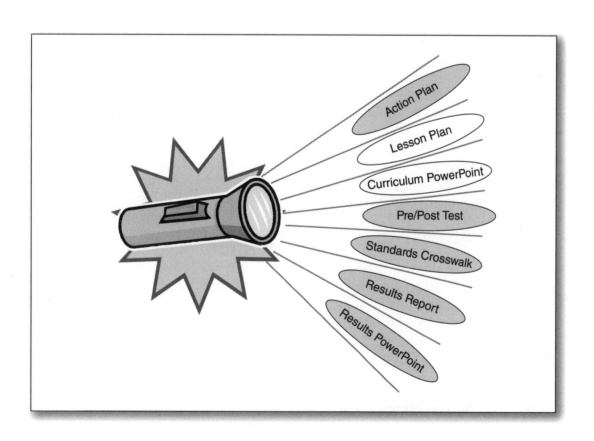

DATA-DRIVEN CURRICULUM DECISIONS

School counselors often ask, "How do I decide which curriculum to deliver? There is only so much time and there are so many needs." When designing school counseling core curriculum for every student, the ASCA National Model recommends school counselors review both the ASCA Student Standards (ASCA, 2012a, 2012e) and other student standards (e.g. common core, state standards, 21st Century) and make decisions based on the developmental needs of the students. Additionally, school counselors draw upon their professional wisdom to determine (in consultation with others) the minimum number of lessons they would recommend all students receive in the school. Sometimes school counselors find there are more lesson topics to deliver than time to deliver them. When this occurs, they must make decisions about which lessons will take priority. There are several ways to determine which curriculum is appropriate.

Analyzing schoolwide data is the first step in selecting the curriculum when topics are overwhelming and time is limited. In one school district, counselors delivered a variety of lessons; two of which were tobacco use prevention education (TUPE) lessons (e.g., Smokey Joe, Tar Jar) to students in tenth grade. To meet Safe and Drug Free School's requirements, the California Healthy Kids Survey (CHKS), a schoolwide needs assessment, was administered to students. Analysis of the survey data revealed few ninth-grade students in the district smoked. In fact, the smoking rate was half the state average. The TUPE lessons had been delivered every year to tenth-grade students, so certainly the data did not reflect instruction. Survey results also revealed students in the ninth grade were drinking alcohol at *twice the state average* and those in the seventh grade were *three times as likely* as other seventh graders in the state to be using inhalants. At the time, there were no lessons taught addressing the areas of alcohol or inhalants in middle or high school. In this particular circumstance, the data served as a catalyst that focused attention on a data-driven need and resulted in the allocation of additional resources necessary to provide a data-driven curriculum.

In an urban high school, data revealed few students were taking college entrance examinations (e.g., SAT or ACT). Despite evening presentations and posted advertisements for these college preparation tests, few students registered. School counselors utilized the data to leverage additional classroom instruction time to teach lessons addressing the different types of tests available to students, as well as funding to cover the cost of exams for students who qualified. At a different high school in the same district, taking the SAT and ACT was common practice for more than 90% of the students. At this school, teaching specific lessons about the differences in college prep tests are neither a necessity nor an efficient use of time. Instead, school counselors included a few slides in the comprehensive "college knowledge" lesson delivered to all tenth graders and then disaggregated registration data to determine which students needed additional support, encouragement, or assistance to register.

CURRICULUM NEEDS ASSESSMENT SURVEYS

In one moderately affluent middle school, counselors traditionally had a 300:1 student-to-counselor ratio. When budget cuts hit, ratios increased to 500:1, and

RETHINKING THE PURPOSE OF FACULTY NEEDS ASSESSMENTS

I recently read a blog post that told the story of a school counselor who admitted needing thick skin after receiving faculty feedback on a needs assessment (Fuller, 2012). The blogger stated the assessment gave her a great picture of what the teachers *thought* her counseling role *should* be as well as what they thought was missing. The blogger said the feedback was extremely helpful in directing her purpose for the year. The struggle she openly shared was the impact of the constructive criticism on her perfectionist nature; she personalized it.

I can totally relate. As a first-year school counselor in 1987, I was charged with giving my faculty needs assessments in the fall and spring for two reasons: (a) to determine priorities about how I should spend my time that year as a school counselor, and (b) to identify how faculty thought I was performing each of these responsibilities. It basically read, "How important is this activity?" and "How well is it being done?" As a masters-degreed professional, I was confused as to why I, the "expert," would *need* or even *want* to ask my faculty to determine what services I should provide or what they thought my priorities ought to be. I mean, if I didn't *know* what I was supposed to do, and I had to ask them, what did I need my degree for? I also wondered, as teachers, how they would even know how well I was performing my duties. Last, I wanted to know when I was going to get to fill out a form that allowed me to tell teachers how *they* should spend their time.

The assessment made no sense to me and I stopped doing it. Instead, I surveyed teachers to assess their priorities regarding equally important developmentally appropriate standards-based school counseling curriculum, as well as prioritizing which of the many data-driven interventions they felt deserved the most urgent attention in their classroom and schoolwide. I wanted their feedback, because given very limited resources (one school counselor at two schools with a caseload of more than 1,000 students), important decisions had to be made. The curriculum and intervention surveys in this chapter are examples of the types of surveys that allow teachers and parents to provide valuable input into the school counseling program without allowing those not training in school counseling to determine how their day is spent or how well they are spending it. Evaluation is best accomplished from assessing the difference interventions make in the students' attendance, behavior, or achievement. Sharing results of both the assessments and interventions will inform faculty of students' needs and the impact of the school counseling program on the lives of the students they serve.

counselors needed to determine how to meet all student needs with fewer resources. They generated a list of the curriculum lessons they currently delivered at each grade level and surveyed the parents and teachers on back-to-school night to gather feedback on the priorities of their stakeholders. The survey served as a mechanism to market the curriculum, inform parents about the reduction of services, and provide counselors with valuable feedback on which topics were perceived to be most helpful to parents and teachers. Garnering stakeholder feedback provided important information for school counselors as they entered their decision-making process. Contrary to the school counselor's beliefs that parents might want more curriculum content on high school and

Figure 6.1 School Counseling Lesson Topics Survey #1

Dear Teachers and Parents:

At XYZ Middle School, school counselors delivered eight lessons in each classroom last year. The topics provided last year are listed below. Due to a reduction in resources, school counselors will be able to provide only four to five lessons this year. To assist us in meeting the needs of your students, please RANK the lessons in ORDER of your preference for your students. This information will be useful to us (along with schoolwide academic and climate survey data) as we make important curriculum decisions. Thank you for your assistance.

Sixth Grade:

_____ Promotion Requirements

_____ Career Interest Inventory

_____ Study Skills/Organizational Strategies

_____ Test-Taking Skills

_____ Bullying and Bystanders

_____ Conflict Resolution Skills

_____ Friendship Skills

_____ Making Healthy Choices (Drugs, Alcohol, etc.)

_____ High School Graduation Requirements

Seventh Grade:

_____ Promotion Requirements

_____ Career Pathways

_____ Study Skills/Organizational Strategies

_____ Test-Taking Skills

_____ Sexual Harassment

_____ Conflict Resolution

_____ Making Healthy Choices (Drugs, Alcohol, etc.)

_____ Taking Responsibility for My Education

Eighth Grade:

_____ Promotion Requirements

_____ Preparing for High School

_____ College Preparation Requirements

_____ Careers of Tomorrow

_____ Study Skills/Organizational Strategies

_____ Test-Taking Skills

_____ Sexual Harassment

_____ Conflict Resolution

Comments: _____

college entrance requirements, the survey results revealed lessons in organizational skills and peer relationships were most requested by parents. In another district, school counselors were just beginning to discuss content for lessons. Seeking staff input, they designed the survey shown in Figure 6.1 and used the feedback, in conjunction with the data and developmental student standards, to discuss with their administrator which lessons to deliver at each grade level. A second sample survey is shown in Figure 6.2.

Figure 6.2   School Counseling Lesson Topics Survey #2

Name: _____

Title: _____

School Site: _____

SCHOOL COUNSELING CORE CURRICULUM

School counselors deliver core curriculum in the classroom at each grade level across the district. Below is a list of common lesson topics. Please rate the importance of the topics. If you have a grade level preference for the lesson, please indicate that as well.

Rate: 1 = Very   2 = Important;   3 = Moderately   4 = Less   5 = Unimportant
Important;   Important;   Important;

_____ Promotion/Graduation Requirements   Grade Level: (_____)

_____ College Prep Requirements   Grade Level: (_____)

_____ Financial Aid/Scholarships   Grade Level: (_____)

_____ Study Skills   Grade Level: (_____)

_____ Test-Taking Skills   Grade Level: (_____)

_____ Organizational Strategies   Grade Level: (_____)

_____ Attendance   Grade Level: (_____)

_____ Bully Prevention   Grade Level: (_____)

_____ Friendship Skills   Grade Level: (_____)

_____ Conflict Resolution   Grade Level: (_____)

_____ Drug/Alcohol/Tobacco Prevention   Grade Level: (_____)

_____ Sexual Harassment   Grade Level: (_____)

_____ Career Interest Inventories   Grade Level: (_____)

_____ Other _____   Grade Level: (_____)

A very important clarification to make prior to reviewing the sample survey is to ensure school counselors are *not* asking teachers, "What should I teach?" Instead, school counselors, who are professionals in their field, determine which lesson content is appropriate to consider and then ask for feedback on what priority teachers give different topics. In this way, school counselors include teachers and garner their mutual investment but are not looking to them for direction—a very important difference.

Finally, it is important to ensure non–English-speaking parents are provided an equitable opportunity to contribute to their child's curriculum content. Translating surveys into parents' native languages ensures all stakeholders have an opportunity to have their voices represented (Spanish versions of the surveys in this chapter are provided in the online appendix).

DATA-DRIVEN INTENTIONAL GUIDANCE DECISIONS

Which Interventions Are Best for Each Grade Level?

As mentioned in Chapter 3, school counselors use data to drive interventions. The most common interventions recommended are in areas of attendance, behavior, and achievement. Attendance is crucial, because research states that students with minimal absences have better academic performance (Easton & Englehard, 1982). Also, those students with positive behavior are likely to have better grades than those who misbehave and get suspended (Williams & McGee, 1994; Van Horn, 2003). Attendance collects revenue for the school, funding programs and services on site. The more absences, the less funding the institution receives. Therefore, both attendance and behavior contribute to student achievement. Promotion rates, scores on state exams, and credits earned are examples of student achievement performance.

When determining which interventions to offer to students, school counselors are encouraged to collect and analyze consistent data elements each year to determine the greatest area of need. The ASCA National Model, third edition, includes a data profile tool with recommendations for the types of data you may want to consider (ASCA, 2012a). Figure 6.3 provides another way to document this information. Depending on resources and greatest need, school counselors decide where best to intervene.

As seen in Figure 6.3, the use of achievement-related data is suggested for intervention at the lower grade levels, and achievement data at secondary. In the lower grades, attendance, behaviors, citizenship marks, and study habits represent early warning signs of students at risk (Balfanz, Bridgeland, Moore, & Fox, 2010). Students begin exhibiting behaviors that lead to dropping out as early as elementary school. Recognizing the early warning signs of dropout behavior, and intervening to teach the knowledge, attitudes, and skills students need, helps prevent future student failure. Successful student habits developed in the formative years build the foundation for academic success in later years. The transitions from elementary to middle school and then to high school are challenging for many students, as with each change they enter a new system that requires them to adapt to new standards and procedures, longer-range assignments, greater teacher expectations, and more responsibilities in order to be successful (Perkins & Gelfer, 1995; Schumacher, 1998; Weldy, 1991). Rather than limiting elementary interventions to students with poor grades, school counselors are encouraged to consider students who receive moderate grades but may struggle in adapting to these new challenges because they lack sufficient study and organizational skills. Such decisions will help the students gain the skills they need to succeed as the academic curriculum increases in its rigor.

Figure 6.3 Sample Data Profile Tool

	DATA	Elementary School	Middle/Junior High School	High School
Achievement-Related Data	**Attendance (Unexcused)**	X	X	
	Students with X or more absences (truancies)			
	Tardies	X	X	
	Students with X or more tardies			
	Discipline Referrals	X	X	
	Students with X or more discipline referrals			
	Report Card Citizenship	X	X	
	Students with N's and/or U's			
	Report Card Study Habits	X	X	
	Students with N's and/or U's			
	Homework Completion Rates	X	X	X
	Students with three or more zeros			
	Students with 25% or more zeros			
Achievement Data	**Promotion/Retention**		X	
	Students not on target to promote			
	Exit Exam Passage Rate			X
	Students who have not passed exit exam			
	F's			X
	Ninth graders with two or more F's on first progress report (or quarter grade report)			
	Credit Deficiency			X
	Ninth graders with fewer than X credits			
	Tenth graders with fewer than X credits			
	Eleventh graders with fewer than X credits			
	Twelfth graders with fewer than X credits			

Once a student is in high school, attendance and behavior, while highly correlated with dropout rates (Railsback, 2004), are not always the most accurate indicators of poor achievement. A student at a high school I worked at boasted upon graduation that she and her friends competed with each other to see how many days of school they could miss and still get A's in their classes. *Amazing.* In high school, failing classes in freshman year is an urgent call for immediate attention and intervention, because an F results in credit deficiency; grades and success in courses is the single greatest predictor of graduation (Allensworth & Easton, 2007). This is a very different outcome than in elementary or middle school. If students do not earn enough credits, they will not graduate. High school at-risk indicators as cited by Pinkus (2009) include the following:

(a) Freshmen with less than a C average are more likely to drop out than to graduate (Allensworth & Easton, 2007).

(b) Three-fourths of the students who dropped out of high school failed English or math in eighth grade and had attendance below 80% (Neild & Balfanz, 2006).

(c) Students on track with credits earned at the end of ninth grade are four times more likely to graduate than students with insufficient credits at the end of ninth grade (Miller, Allensworth, & Kochanek, 2002).

Research advocates for providing intensive interventions at high schools beginning in freshman year for students who have two or more F's during the first grade-reporting period, because first semester failure is the single indicator most aligned with failing to graduate (Allensworth & Easton, 2005, 2007; Heppen & Therriault, 2008). The sooner interventions are provided, the greater the possibility of getting the student back on track for graduation. Counselors can provide earlier intervention by collaborating with the ninth-grade core subject teachers to set up a system whereby they are notified at the end of each semester or quarter with the names of students who have received F's in any academic courses and the number of F's students have received in core academic courses (Heppen & Therriault, 2008). If the school has an online grading tool, counselors can query this information and begin providing an intervention even sooner. The National High School Center (2012) recommends charting at-risk indicators and monitoring time as seen in Figure 6.4.

Figure 6.4   National High School Center At-Risk Indicators

Early Warning Indicators Middle Grades Tool (EWIMS) Indicators and Monitoring Time Frame		
Indicators	**Time Frame**	**Middle Grades Benchmark (Flagged at-Risk)**
Incoming Indicator	• Before school begins	• Local indicator of risk
Attendance	• First 20 or 30 days • Each grading period • End of the year	• Missed 20% or more instructional time (absences)
Course Failures	• Each grading period • End of the year	• Failure grade in ELA or Math
Behavior	• Each grading period • End of the year	• Local thresholds

Early Warning Indicators High School Tool (EWIHS) Indicators and Monitoring Time Frame		
Indicators	**Time Frame**	**High School Benchmark (Flagged at-Risk)**
Incoming Indicator	• Before school begins	• EWIMS Middle Grades Tool
Attendance	• First 20 or 30 days • Each grading period • End of the year	• Missed 10% or more instructional time (absences)
Course Failures	• Each grading period • End of the year	• Failure one or more semester courses (any subject)
Grade Point Average	• Each grading period • End of year	• Earned 2.0 or lower (on a 4.0 scale)
Behavior	• Each grading period • End of year	• Local thresholds
On-Track Indicator	• End of year	• Failed two or more core courses, or accumulated fewer credits than required for promotion to next grade.

Source: National High School Center (2012).

When school counselors have low counselor-to-student ratios and ample resources, providing intervention for all students who qualify is recommended. When resources are limited, and counselors are unsure about which intentional guidance intervention(s) to prioritize, it may be helpful to engage members of the site's data-based decision-making (DBDM) team (Dimmitt, Carey, & Hatch, 2007), the leadership team, or the entire faculty to assist in decision making. Figure 6.5 is an example of a high school survey that could be adapted to meet site needs. By surveying staff and administration, school counselors will garner support for the program and educate the staff about the important services provided by school counselors. A survey also serves as a notice to alert staff that counselors will be intervening. Finally, by sharing that counselors would like to intervene in many ways (but due to time constraints must be selective), staff will be informed as to why school counselors cannot meet the intervention needs of every student, although they would like to.

Figure 6.5 National High School Center At-Risk Indicators

Sample Intentional Guidance Intervention Survey

School counselors use data to determine which students will be screened and targeted for interventions. The following data will be reviewed by the school counselors and members of the DBDM team. Given time constraints for interventions, school counselors will select only three targeted areas for intensive intervention and evaluation this year. Which of the following areas do you consider the greatest area of need? Please prioritize the following interventions by RANK ORDER: 1st, 2nd, and 3rd.

____ Students with multiple *absences*

____ Students with multiple *behavior referrals*

____ Students with multiple *missing assignments*

____ *Ninth grade* students who are *credit deficient*

____ *Tenth grade* students who are *credit deficient*

____ *Eleventh grade* students who are *credit deficient*

____ *Twelfth grade* students who are *not on target to graduate*

____ Other _____

Any additional comments:

_____

_____

Thank you for your assistance!

©2009 Phillip Martin. All Rights Reserved.

THE FISHNET APPROACH

Once the team has determined which intervention(s) it will provide during the year, decisions must be made to finalize whether counselors will see students as they "qualify" (as soon as they meet the specific criteria, such as missing three assignments or being absent five times) or will use a "fishnet" approach to gather names at regular and specific intervals in time of the students who qualify for interventions. Determining when to fishnet students ensures every student who qualifies is referred. The fishnet approach does not rely on teacher referral but rather on the timing of the counselors' query of data. Perhaps school counselors want to intervene with students who have five or more absences. Will the counselors get new students who qualify day by day? This might prove a bit chaotic. A more efficient way might be to determine a point in time (30 days into the school year for example) when counselors will fishnet all those students who have five or more absences. In this way, the counselors schedule time-certain intervention points to gather data. Setting aside a specific time to look at the number of students in need ensures a system is in place to manage the data and put interventions into motion.

Student database systems such as those created by betterhighschools.org provide immediate access to data on the school counselor's desktop, so the counselor can identify students at risk (Figure 6.6), target and record interventions (Figure 6.7); and provide detailed reports (Therriault, O'Cummings, Heppen, Yerhot, & Scala, 2012).

Figure 6.6 Database Screen for Identifying Students at Risk

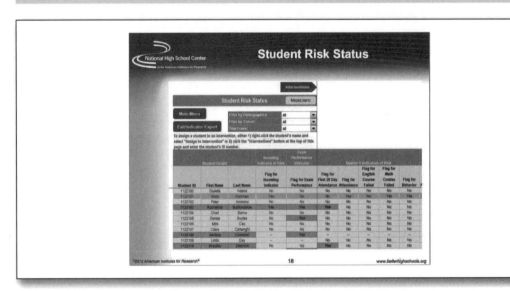

Figure 6.7 Database Screen for Targeting and Recording Interventions

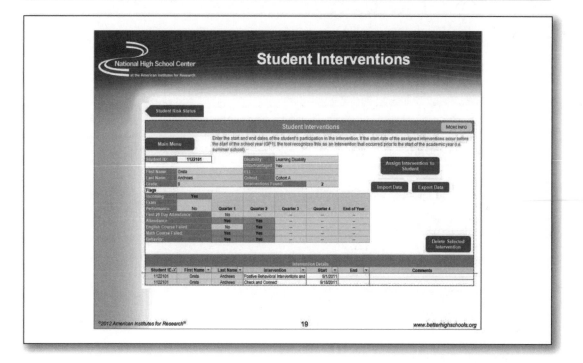

AT-RISK STUDENT SURVEYS

Once data have been disaggregated, and counselors have identified the students who qualify for interventions, it's time to determine which intervention is best for each student. Providing the appropriate intervention for a student requires collecting and considering all data, including the student's perspective. One way to obtain this information is to talk with the student and ask him or her: "Why are you late to school every day?" or "Why do you think you are failing three classes?"

Figures 6.8 and 6.9 are samples of at-risk student surveys developed to assist school counselors in seeking students' perspectives when placing them in appropriate interventions. School counselors met to design the survey in Figure 6.8 for ninth-grade students, surveyed the students, worked together to determine appropriate interventions, and then placed them in the appropriate intervention. The survey in Figure 6.9 was designed for middle school students and is followed by a sample survey for attendance (Figure 6.10). School counselors also meet with parents when students are at risk; a sample parent survey is shown in Figure 6.11.

Once the survey is completed, the student and the counselor can compare the student's responses with information in the student database. For instance, an at-risk student may indicate, "the work is too hard" but might not check the box on "my attendance is poor." The school counselor may notice, when looking at the data, that the student has

Figure 6.8   Ninth-Grade Preconference Survey—Student

Name: _____ Grade _____ Male _____ Female _____

Circle the best answer for each question below.

1. I have been asked to this conference because

    a. I have two or more F's
    b. I am behind in credits
    c. Both of the above
    d. I am not sure why I am here

2. I believe I am on target to graduate with my class.

    a. Strongly agree
    b Agree
    c. Disagree
    d. Strongly disagree

3. I want to graduate with my class.

    a. Strongly agree
    b. Agree
    c. Disagree
    d. Strongly disagree

School counselors work with many students who struggle to succeed in school. Listed below are some of the *most common reasons* students tell us they fall behind. Please tell us the *top three* reasons you believe you are struggling in school.

Mark #1, # 2, and #3 on the list below.

____ My attendance is poor.

____ My behavior in and/or out of class gets in my way.

____ I don't care about school; I lack motivation.

____ The work is too hard. (I try, but it is too hard.)

____ The work is too hard. (I have stopped trying.)

____ I need better study skills or test-taking strategies.

____ My family or personal problems get in my way.

____ Other (please explain): _____

Please give this to your school counselor.

Thank you! ☺

Figure 6.9 Middle School Preconference Student Survey

Name: _____ Grade _____ Male _____ Female _____

Circle the best answer for each item below.

1. I have been asked to this conference because (circle all that apply)

   a. I have less than a 2.0 GPA
   b. I have been suspended
   c. I have one or more U's
   d. I have more than three tardies/truancies
   e. I have missed three or more days of school
   f. All of the above
   g. I am not sure why I am here

2. I believe I have the grades and behavior needed to move on to the next grade.

   a. Strongly agree
   b. Agree
   c. Disagree
   d. Strongly disagree

3. I need help with my academics, behavior, or attendance.

   a. Strongly agree
   b. Agree
   c. Disagree
   d. Strongly disagree

School counselors work with many students who struggle to succeed in school. Listed below are some of the *most common reasons* students tell us they fall behind. Please tell us the *top three* reasons you believe you are struggling in school.

Mark #1, #2, and #3 on the list below.

____ My attendance is poor.

____ My behavior in and/or out of class gets in my way.

____ I do not care about school.

____ The work is too hard. (I try, but it is too hard.)

____ The work is too hard. (I have stopped trying.)

____ I need better study skills or test-taking strategies.

____ My family or personal problems get in my way.

____ Other (please explain): _____

Please give this to your school counselor.

Thank you! ☺

Figure 6.10   Preconference Attendance Survey—Student

Name: _____ Grade _____ Male _____ Female _____

Circle the best answer for each item below.

1. I have been asked to this conference because (circle all that apply)

    a. I have two or more F's.
    b. My behavior is poor.
    c. I am not attending school.
    d. I am often late to school.
    e. I am not sure why I am here.

2. I want to attend school.

    a. Strongly agree
    b. Agree
    c. Disagree
    d. Strongly disagree

3. I believe it is important to be at school on time every day.

    a. Strongly agree
    b. Agree
    c. Disagree
    d. Strongly disagree

School counselors work with many students who are struggling to succeed in school. You have been asked here today because you are not attending school. Listed below are some of the *most common reasons* students tell us they are absent or late to school. Please check the boxes next to all of the reasons you are late to school or are absent.

❏ I get up too late.
❏ My teacher does not like me.
❏ I did not want to get in a fight.
❏ I do not have any clean clothes.
❏ I missed the bus and had no ride.
❏ The work is too hard.
❏ I have to assist with siblings at home.
❏ I have no friends.
❏ Someone is bothering me (bully).
❏ I can't find my book bag.
❏ My family had car trouble.
❏ I hate school. (Can you tell us why?) _____
❏ I got home late last night.
❏ I had to go to church.
❏ Other (please explain): _____

Please give this to your school counselor.

Thank you!

Figure 6.11 Preconference Survey—Parent

Student's Name: _____ Grade _____

Circle the correct answer for each item below.

1. I have been asked to this conference because my child

    a. Has not passed the high school exit exam
    b. Is behind in credits
    c. Is not attending school
    d. All of the above
    e. I am not sure why I am here.

2. I believe my child is on target to graduate on time with his/her class.

    a. Strongly agree
    b. Agree
    c. Unsure
    d. Disagree
    e. Strongly disagree

3. I want my student to graduate with his/her class.

    a. Strongly agree
    b. Agree
    c. Unsure
    d. Disagree
    e. Strongly disagree

School counselors work with many students who are struggling to succeed in school. Listed below are the *most common reasons* students tell us they fall behind. Please tell us the *top three reasons* you believe your child is struggling.

Mark #1, #2, and #3 on the list below.

____ Student's attendance is poor.

____ Student's behavior in class gets in the way.

____ Student does not care about school, lacks motivation.

____ The work is too hard. (Student tries, but it is too hard.)

____ The work is too hard. (Student has stopped trying.)

____ Student needs better study skills or test-taking strategies.

____ Student's family or personal problems get in the way.

____ Other (please explain): _____

Please give this to the school counselor.

Thank you! ☺

a rather serious attendance problem. The counselor now has an opportunity to utilize his or her counseling skills to help the student recognize the impact poor attendance may be having on academic performance and to assist the student in selecting an appropriate intervention to address this concern. Comparing the parent's survey with the student's survey might provide another opportunity for a counseling conversation.

Preconference Survey Results

At Paramount High School, counselors surveyed each of their at-risk students to determine their barriers to learning. There were 274 10th-grade students with three or more NP (no passing) grades. As seen in Figure 6.12, the data revealed most students identified their greatest barrier to learning was the need to improve their study skills. Although some faculty assumed lack of parental support was the reason for student failures, this factor was identified as a concern for only four students (out of 274). The data collected were shared with faculty, along with schedules for planned interventions. At the next grading report, counselors reported an 18% reduction in NP's.

Postconference Survey Forms

Following the counseling conference, postconference surveys for students and parents (Figures 6.13 and 6.14) collect data on the student's understanding of why the conference was held and the benefit of the conference to the student and parent, and it provides an opportunity for the student to commit to a targeted school-counseling

Figure 6.12   PHS Students Reported Their Barriers to Learning

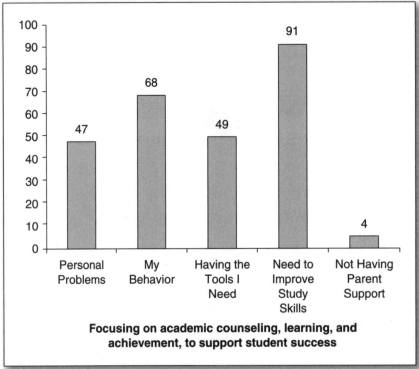

Focusing on academic counseling, learning, and achievement, to support student success

Figure 6.13   Postconference Survey—Student

Name: _____ Grade _____ Male _____ Female _____

Circle the correct answer for you below each item.

1. I was asked to this conference because I

   a. Have not passed one or both parts of the high school exit exam
   b. Am behind in credits
   c. Both a and b
   d. I am not sure why I am here.

2. I understand what I will need to do to graduate high school on time with my class.

   (a) Strongly Disagree   (b) Disagree   (c) Agree   (d) Strongly Agree

3. I want to graduate on time with my class.

   (a) Strongly Disagree   (b) Disagree   (c) Agree   (d) Strongly Agree

4. I believe I will graduate on time with my class.

   (a) Strongly Disagree   (b) Disagree   (c) Agree   (d) Strongly Agree

5. This intervention conference was helpful to me.

   (a) Strongly Disagree   (b) Disagree   (c) Agree   (d) Strongly Agree

6. I feel comfortable talking with my school counselor.

   (a) Strongly Disagree   (b) Disagree   (c) Agree   (d) Strongly Agree

7. I agree to participate in the following intervention(s). Check all that apply.

   _____ Group Counseling for Study Skills

   _____ Group Counseling for Motivation

   _____ Individual Counseling for Personal Issues

   _____ Tutoring in Math

   _____ Tutoring in Reading/Writing

   _____ Mentoring Program

   _____ Credit Recovery

   _____ Other: _____

Please put this in the YELLOW BOX on your way out!

Thank you! ☺

Figure 6.14 Postconference Survey—Parent

Name: _____ Grade _____

Circle the correct answer for you for each item below.

1. I was asked to this conference because my child
   a. Has not passed one or both parts of the required High School Exit Exam
   b. Is behind in credits
   c. Has frequent absences
   d. All of the above
   e. I am not sure why I was asked to come

2. I understand what my student needs to do to graduate from high school on time with his/her peers.

   (a) Strongly Disagree   (b) Disagree   (c) Agree   (d) Strongly Agree

3. I want my student to graduate on time with his/her class.

   (a) Strongly Disagree   (b) Disagree   (c) Agree   (d) Strongly Agree

4. I believe my student will graduate on time with his/her class.

   (a) Strongly Disagree   (b) Disagree   (c) Agree   (d) Strongly Agree

5. This conference was helpful to me.

   (a) Strongly Disagree   (b) Disagree   (c) Agree   (d) Strongly Agree

6. This conference was helpful to my student.

   (a) Strongly Disagree   (b) Disagree   (c) Agree   (d) Strongly Agree

7. I feel comfortable talking with my student's school counselor.

   (a) Strongly Disagree   (b) Disagree   (c) Agree   (d) Strongly Agree

8. I would like my child to participate in the following intervention(s):

   _____ Group Counseling for Study Skills

   _____ Group Counseling for Motivation

   _____ Individual Counseling for Personal Issues

   _____ Tutoring in Math

   _____ Tutoring in Reading/Writing

   _____ Mentoring Program

   _____ Credit Recovery

   _____ Other: _____

Please put this in the YELLOW BOX on your way out!

Thank you! ☺

intervention (Figure 6.15). These data can be shared with stakeholders. The student's "commitment to intervention" form may also be provided to the students separately from the postconference survey to ensure anonymity with feedback regarding the benefits of the meeting to the student and parent. A sample student agreement form is provided below.

Figure 6.15 Sample Middle School Counselor/Student Agreement

I, _____, agree to participate in the following intervention(s) (check all that apply):

_____ Group Counseling for Study Skills

_____ Group Counseling for Motivation

_____ Individual Short-Term Counseling for Personal Concerns

I also agree to

_____ Afterschool Tutoring

_____ Weekly Grade Check (Progress Report)

_____ Student Organization Participation

_____ Mentoring Program

_____ Other: _____

Student Name (Print): _____ Date: _____

Signature: _____

School Counselor Name: _____

FOR OFFICIAL USE ONLY

	October	November	December	January	February	March
Attendance						
Behavior						
GPA						

SCHOOL COUNSELOR REFERRAL FORMS

Using a fishnet approach to implementing intentional guidance interventions does not eliminate teacher referrals, but it should reduce them. If a system is in place to ensure that students who have a data-driven need receive the interventions they require, teachers can reserve referrals for students who demonstrate changes in typical behavior or experience personal or family crisis.

The referral form in Figure 6.16 has unique characteristics that will prove helpful to school counselors. First, the teacher is required to contact the parent before referring the student to school counseling (unless the issue is abuse related or of a sensitive or personal nature to the student, e.g. puppy love distraction in class, etc.). It is absolutely appropriate for the teacher to make contact with the parent prior to referring a student to the school counselor. In this way, the teacher and parent have an opportunity to resolve the problem prior to a counseling referral, or if the problem is not resolvable, then at least the parent is alerted to the call he or she may receive from the school counselor. Every effort should be made to refrain from seeing students whose families have not first received this form. A form serves as an accountability tool everyone will appreciate having if or when an incident occurs.

The referral form is divided into attendance, behavior, and achievement categories to remind teachers of the areas in which school counselors deliver services. Note that the teacher is asked to indicate the level of severity of the problem. Just as an emergency room intake worker must decide which patients need immediate attention and which must wait longer to be seen, school counselors must "triage" their referrals to determine which students require immediate interventions.

Because some teachers are more inclined to refer students for assistance than others, one of the problems with referral forms is that some teachers refer many students, while others refer few or none. Having a systemic data-driven intervention program in place, with guaranteed data-driven fishnet approaches to identifying students in need of interventions, will cut down on frivolous referrals and ensure those who have needs receive the support they require.

Additionally, a distinction must be made between the "discipline" referral and the "school counseling" referral. These are fundamentally different forms used for different purposes. If a student is misbehaving and a teacher is concerned and wants help to find out what might be going on personally for the student that is contributing to the behavior, then it is appropriate to refer the student for school counseling. If, however, the teacher has exhausted the classroom discipline plan and is now referring the student to receive a consequence, a discipline referral is appropriate. Simply stated, does the teacher want the student to receive assistance or a consequence? There may be times when a follow-up conversation with the student is appropriate after the consequence is delivered (e.g., a postsuspension conference). School counselors are encouraged to work with their administrators to put systems in place to ensure postsuspension conferences occur in a timely manner.

Finally, it is recommended school counselors collaborate with their administrators to provide in-service training for staff explaining the purposes of the different referrals. These conversations often occur during schoolwide positive intervention behavior support (PBIS) training, where faculty agree on first-, second- and

Figure 6.16 Sample Counseling Referral Form

School Counseling Referral Form

Please complete as many details as possible and return to the School Counselor's box

STUDENT'S NAME: _____ GRADE: _____ TEACHER: _____

REFERRED BY: _____ Date: _____

REASON FOR REFERRAL:
**Reminder: Students with chronic attendance, behavior, social skills or work habits concerns will be targeted for counseling interventions on a regular basis through data-driven methods. Please use this referral for students experiencing sudden or concerning changes in the above, personal problems, or a family crisis.

☐ Change in Attendance ☐ Change in Behavior ☐ Change in Social Skills ☐ Change in Work Habits ☐ Personal/Family Concern

Please describe your reason(s) for this referral and any additional concerns or information:
_____
_____
_____

Steps taken to address concern:

What interventions are in place? ☐ Parent Conference ☐ Outside Counseling ☐ SST/RTI ☐ IEP

☐ Behavior Support Plan ☐ Discipline Referral ☐ Behavior Contract ☐ Other: _____

How long have you had this concern? ____ Today ____ A Few Days ____ One Week ____ Two Weeks or More ____

Has this issue been discussed with the students' parent/guardian? ___ Y ___ N Last date of contact: _____
(Required unless this of a personal nature or related to possible abuse/violence/safety)

Outcome of Parent /Guardian Contact (Parent Response or Action):
_____
_____
_____

Please rate the severity of this referral.

On a scale of 1-10, please circle how serious (immediate) this problem is:									
Less Serious				**Moderately Serious**				***Very* Serious**	
1	2	3	4	5	6	7	8	9	10

Please note: This referral will be screened immediately and responded to utilizing a triage approach. The school counselor will provide acknowledgement of receipt and status of referral within 3 working days.

CONFIDENTIAL

third-level classroom and playground behavior infractions and responses. School counselors are encouraged to share several examples of typical referral scenarios and, along with their staff, agree on both the action the teacher should take, the most appropriate referral form to use, and the level of severity the situation might suggest. For example, "student does not bring pencil to class" is likely not a 7 on a severity scale where 7 is the severest infraction; it is much less serious. Likewise, a normally energetic student who suddenly appears distant and resistant to talking is not a 3 but rather a much more urgent concern. The severity scale assists the counselor in prioritizing which students are seen first, much as the emergency room worker does—the heart attacks are seen before the broken fingers.

An excellent comprehensive referral process guide with many sample templates has been developed by school counselors in Missouri and is available online at http://www.missouricareereducation.org/doc/referral/ReferralProcess.pdf. Other excellent examples of PBIS referrals for low-level incidents are available at http://www.modelprogram.com/resources/DraftLLR.pdf.

Feedback Following Referral

Providing timely feedback to faculty after seeing a student is a professional responsibility. After receiving the referral and providing counseling for a student, it is helpful to provide feedback to the teacher on the status of the referral. The form in Figure 6.17 serves as a record of request for intervention and an important and timely accountability document for both the teacher and school counselor.

MENU OF SERVICES

When school counselors meet with at-risk students and/or their parents to review needs and options for interventions, it is helpful to have a list of services available at the school. Figure 6.18 is a sample of a menu of available services. Note the school counselor's interventions are only some of the options available to the students. It is not the school counselor's responsibility to provide all of the interventions. Rather, it is the school counselor's responsibility to know when and where to refer the student to the appropriate interventions (some of which may be provided by the school counselors). It may also be possible for students to come up with effective solutions for themselves. These personal solutions may be more valuable to them. The menu of services includes (a) assessment services, (b) intervention processes, (c) disciplinary options, (d) educational skills training available, (e) integrated support services, and (f) positive activity options.

SOLUTION-FOCUSED INTERVENTIONS

Some at-risk students benefit most from a few individual sessions with a school counselor skilled in solution-focused brief counseling. School counselors do not have the training or the time to provide therapy in schools (Sklare, 2004). While it's important to understand the underpinnings of various theoretical

Figure 6.17 Sample Counseling Feedback Form

SCHOOL COUNSELING PROGRAM FOLLOW UP/FEEDBACK

Date: Today's Date

To: Name of Teacher

From: Name of School Counselor

RE: School Counseling Referral

On (date), (name of student) was referred for school counseling services.

The student has meet with me in individual and/or group counseling on the following dates: (List dates. _____, _____, _____, _____, etc.)

The goal(s) for this counseling intervention were:

a) _____

b) _____

At this time I am:

_____Requesting an update on the student's progress

_____Dismissing the student from regular weekly sessions

_____Requesting the student sign in to see me in the front office (when necessary)

_____Providing the student (family) with a referral to outside counseling or other services

_____Other: _____

School Counselor Comments:

_____

_____

_____

Please contact me if problems recur, become more severe, or if there is a significant change in the student's attendance, behavior, or achievement.

Thank you for supporting the school counseling program.

Figure 6.18 Sample Menu of Services

XYZ Unified School District

Student Assistance Program
Menu of Services for Referral

Assessment Services

- SAP referrals
- School services
  Psychological
  Emotional
  Intellectual
- Health screening
- English language
  proficiency
- Outside referrals
- Academic
- Personal/Social
- Career
- Alcoholism and other
  addictions
- Psychological
- Speech

Intervention Process

- Health services
- Student Study Team
  (SST)
- School Attendance
  Review Board (SARB)
- Conflict management
- Student Assistance Team
- Individual Education Plan
- Section 504
- Alternative Education
  Committee (AEC)

Disciplinary Options

- Partial schedules
- Alternative scheduling
- Behavioral contracts
- In school suspension
- Suspension
- Law enforcement
- Suspended expulsion
- Expulsion
- Detentions
- Independent Study
- Progress reports
  Daily
  Weekly

**Educational (Skills)
Component**

- Guidance lessons
- Insight class
  Anger
  Chemical Use
- Conflict Management
  Program
- Tobacco education
- English language
  proficiency courses
- Special Education
  support
- Alternative education
  placement
- Success Academy (MS)
- Intersession (YRMS)
- Summer school
- Tutoring

**Integrated Support
Services**

- School counseling
  Individual
  Group
- Mentoring
- Parent education
- Health services
- Support groups
  ATOD
  Anger
  Student Issues
- School Resource Officer
  (SRO)
- Crisis intervention
- Conflict mediation

Positive Activity Options

- Friday Night Live (HS)
- Club Live (MS)
- Sports
- School clubs
- School dances
- Field trips
- Site specific activities and
  opportunities
- Community sponsored
  sports and activities
- GSA (MS/HS)

Legend:

MS =   Middle School
HS =   High School
YRMS=   Year round middle school
ATOD = Alcohol, tobacco, and other drugs

perspectives, it is unrealistic and inappropriate to expect a school counselor to apply them in a school setting (ASCA, 2010b; Sklare, 2004). Sklare's solution-focused approach asks students to imagine how the present and future will look if they are successful in avoiding problems. Sklare's "Brief Counseling That Works" focuses on students' strengths and resources, encouraging them to take action. Successful action leads to improved confidence (attitudes) and to additional successful actions. Although deficit data may have determined the need for an intervention, Sklare's approach does not focus on the etiology or history of the problem. Past events are utilized only as a way to locate the times of exceptions to problems.

EVIDENCED-BASED APPROACHES TO CURRICULUM

Second Step: Skills for Social and Academic Success (Committee for Children, 2010) and *Student Success Skills Classroom Guidance Curriculum* (Brigman & Webb, 2004) are two examples of evidenced-based classroom curriculum materials. Outcome research coding protocol and evaluation was conducted on both Student Success Skills and Second Step by the National Panel for Evidence-Based School Counseling Practice (Carey, Dimmitt, Hatch, Lapan, & Whiston, 2008). Both curriculums have multiple empirical studies supporting effects on students' behavior and achievement (Webb, Brigman, & Campbell, 2005).

Student Success Skills Group Counseling Curriculum (SSS) is the most heavily researched school counseling intervention curriculum (Brigman, Campbell, & Webb, 2004). Similar to Sklare's (2004) solution-focused individual counseling skills, mentioned previously, SSS provides a strength-building approach rather than a deficit-reduction approach. SSS teaches the knowledge, attitudes, and skills to help low-performing students improve academic achievement.

Few other evidenced-based interventions have been researched. Therefore, school counselors need to use the evidence-based practice approach to determine what curriculum to use with students (Dimmitt et al., 2007). After looking at the data to determine what needs to be done, school counselors explore outcome research (what is likely to work) and finally evaluate the intervention (to determine impact and effectiveness).

OUTCOME RESEARCH ON NONCOGNITIVE FACTORS IMPACTING ACHIEVEMENT

Throughout this text, reference has been made to utilizing the work skills and study habits components of the report card as a method for gathering data to determine which students need interventions and to measure the impact of the interventions. As early as kindergarten, some schools add work habits to report cards (see Figure 6.19). Utilizing teacher ratings of students' work habits serves as a measure for pre- and postassessment for interventions. (See additional sample report cards in the online appendix.)

Figure 6.19 Sample Work Habits Section of Report Card

	PERSONAL BEHAVIOR			
SOCIAL AND EMOTIONAL	Establishes positive social relationships			
	Demonstrates appropriate behavior			
	Follows classroom rules			
	Follows daily classroom routines			
	Interacts cooperatively with adults and peers			
	Takes care of personal needs			
WORK HABIT	Works cooperatively in groups			
	Follows directions			
	Exhibits appropriate attention span			
	Works independently on classroom tasks			
	Completes activities in a reasonable time			
	Takes pride in work			

The behaviors, skills, attitudes, beliefs, and ways in which students perceive themselves in relationship to their learning, or academic mindset, are referred to as "noncognitive factors." The University of Chicago Consortium on Chicago School Research released a literature review entitled *Teaching Adolescents to Become Learners*, which explored noncognitive factors, including social skills and learning strategies (e.g., study skills, time management, goal setting), and their impact on school performance (Farrington et al., 2012).

Aligning with the experience of many school counselors, the review validated the importance of students developing the attitudes, knowledge, and skills vital to the success of academic performance in their classes—those often not reflected in cognitive test scores (see Figures 6.20 and 6.21). Studies show the way students interact within the context of the educational environment impacts their attitudes, motivation, and performance (Farrington et al., 2012). While some consider noncognitive

Figure 6.20 Relationship of Noncognitive Skills to Academic Performance

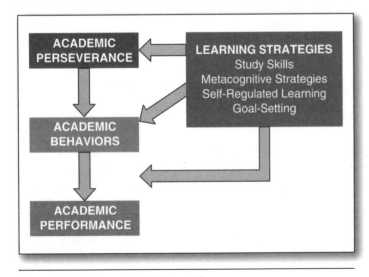

Source: Farrington et al. (2012, p. 10).

skills "fluffy" and "soft" skills, research tells us students' beliefs can influence academic mindsets related to persistence on academic tasks, impacting educational outcomes and reducing racial/ethnic and gender achievement gaps (Farrington et al., 2012). Interventions are also currently being designed and evaluated for their impact on reducing stereotype threat and improving the performance of racial/ethnic minority students.

Learning strategies have important relationships with other noncognitive factors. Utilizing appropriate learning strategies can make students' academic behaviors more productive and effective, contributing to improved academic performance. As a result, learning strategies tend to increase students' self-efficacy (the *I can succeed at this* mindset), which in turn is related to increased academic perseverance when schoolwork becomes challenging. There is also clear evidence that students with higher self-efficacy or who place a high value on the work they are doing are much more likely to use metacognitive and self-regulatory strategies to engage in learning. Positive academic mindsets drive strategy use, which makes students' academic behaviors more persistent and effective, leading to improved performance. Successful academic performance, in turn, reinforces positive mindsets.

Conversely, a lack of effective learning strategies can contribute to poor academic behaviors and poor performance. Students are less likely to complete homework if they do not know how to organize themselves to get it done, and they are less likely to study for tests if they do not have study strategies that help them review effectively. Not completing homework and not studying have a depressive effect on students' grades. Poor grades in turn undermine positive student mindsets, which can then diminish students' academic perseverance. Likewise, students with low self-efficacy or who place a low value on the work they are asked to do are much less likely to use metacognitive strategies or to self-regulate their learning; their academic behaviors are less likely to produce learning and quality work, even when students do complete the work. Thus, learning strategies are an important component in a chain of noncognitive factors that shape students' academic performance. (Farrington et al., 2012, p. 39)

When designing curriculum for study skills interventions, school counselors would be wise to locate and utilize, revise, or design curriculum that addresses critical factors leading to academic performance, such as the students' knowledge of and ability to use learning strategies, their attitudes about learning, their beliefs in their own ability to learn, their self-control and persistence, and the quality of their relationships with peers and adults. Four specific academic mindsets found to contribute to academic success are the following:

1. I believe in this academic community;

2. My ability and competence grow with my effort;

3. I can succeed at this; and

4. This work has value for me. (Farrington et al., 2012 p. 28)

Figure 6.21   A Hypothesized Model of How Five Noncognitive Factors Affect Academic Performance Within a Classroom/School and Larger Sociocultural Context

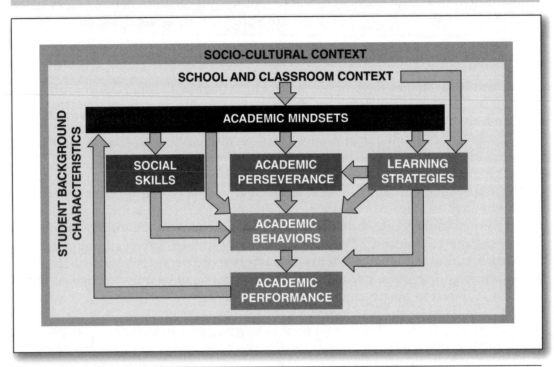

Source: Farrington et al. (2012, p. 12).

LESSON PLAN SAMPLES AND RESOURCES

Resources for creating your own curriculum lesson plans are abundant. A simple search of "school counselor lesson plans" provides more than a counselor could deliver in a lifetime just on Pinterest.com! Most do not contain assessments. In Chapter 7 you will learn to create your own.

Felipe Zanartu (a former student) created an online school counselor lesson plan template that is optimized for use within Microsoft Word (http://digitalcounselor.com/lesson-plans.html). Counselors can write a lesson plan within 7 to 15 minutes using the developer feature of Word which allows you to use text boxes, drop downs, and check boxes to streamline some of the more tedious aspects of creating a lesson plan.

Free Curriculum and Group Counseling Materials:

- The West Virginia Department of Education has posted guidance curriculum lessons and group lessons for school counselors for Grades K–2, 3–5, 6–8, and 9–12. The guidance curriculum lessons are at http://wvde.state.wv.us/counselors/guidance-curriculum.html (click and scroll down to Elementary). Topics include anger management, self-control, study skills, test-taking strategies, and more. Follow this link for group lesson materials and more: http://wvde.state.wv.us/counselors/group-lessons.html.

- "I Have a Plan Iowa" at ihaveaplaniowa.gov contains many resources for curriculum lessons about goal-setting and study skills that can be modified for groups. Enter the webpage by clicking on the Educator link at the bottom and see the many wonderful materials provided free of charge.

- The Missouri Center for Career Education's eLearning Center contains hundreds of valuable resources for school counseling, including extensive curriculum for classroom and small groups: http://www.missouricareereducation.org/for/content/guidance/.

- LiveBinders provides an exhaustive compilation of free resources on study skills available at: livebinders.com/play/play?present=true&tab_layout=top&id=60155

- YouTube has 12 fun videos on test-taking strategies (such as eliminating wrong answers and staying relaxed) provided in a twelve-part series (http://www.youtube.com/user/pauldevoto?feature=watch). YouTube is also an excellent source of inspirational, motivating videos that can be incorporated into curriculum.

- Additional resources are available at this book's website online.

7

Creating Pre/Post Tests

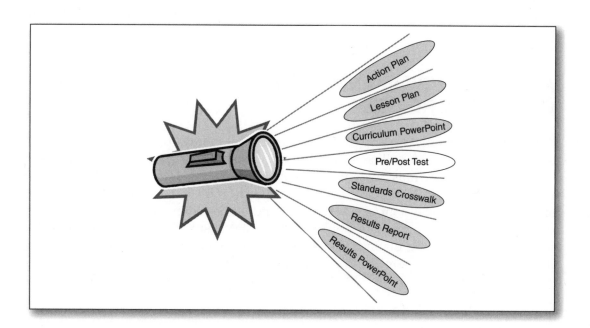

WHY ASSESSMENT? "WE ARE TEACHERS, TOO"

While it is not required in most states, many school counselors were once teachers. What did teachers do after teaching a unit to students? They assessed whether or not students learned the content of the lesson. When school counselors teach their curriculum in the classroom, or provide skills-based group counseling sessions, it is also appropriate for them to assess whether students have learned what was taught. It answers the questions: Was this a good use of instructional learning time? Was this a valuable use of school counselor time or students' time? In order to determine this, assessments must be provided immediately following the lesson. Although school counselors provide counseling in their offices, when they are in front of a group of students providing instruction, they are teaching. Therefore, as professional educators, it is appropriate for school counselors to also assess the impact of their teaching in much the same way teachers do.

A-S-K (ASK THEM WHAT THEY LEARNED)

When school counselors are developing pre/post tests, they are encouraged to assess the three areas called for in the ASCA Student Standards: knowledge, attitudes, and skills. The acronym ASK is a reminder that when the school counselor is finished teaching a lesson, he or she should ASK the students what they learned. ASK stands for *Attitudes, Skills,* and *Knowledge.* This reminds us to measure all three areas; however, when constructing the actual pre/post tests, arranging questions in the following order: attitudes, knowledge, and skills is suggested.

Imagine a school counselor who would like to create a pre/post test for a proposed lesson plan. What students believe (attitude), what they know (content learned), and what they can demonstrate (skill) as a result of the lesson are the outcomes to be measured. Attitude and knowledge should be first, and then move to measuring skill.

ATTITUDE: HOW IS AN ATTITUDE QUESTION CREATED?

Attitude questions measure opinions or beliefs. This is most often done by creating a question using a scale, called a Likert scale (Likert, 1932). The Likert (pronounced "lick-ert") scale is the most widely used scale in survey research. When respondents answer these scaled items, they are responding to their level of agreement to the statement. The typical item is a statement, and students are asked to indicate the degree to which they agree or disagree with the statement. Usually, the item is written in a bipolar scaling manner (measuring a positive or negative response to the item). Typically, a five-point scale is used. For example:

1. Strongly agree

2. Agree

3. Neither agree nor disagree

4. Disagree

5. Strongly disagree

While this scale includes a middle value representing a neutral position or an undecided position, it is also possible to use a *forced choice* scale by removing that option. In this way, the respondents are forced to decide whether to lean more toward the "agree" or "disagree" end of the spectrum. This can be helpful when it appears a student may not take the survey seriously and choose to opt out via the middle ground rather than commit to an opinion.

Now that we know the school counselor will ask a Likert scale question let's look at the areas the school counselor plans to assess (refer to Figure 5.2):

- Believe doing homework matters
- Believe using study strategies will help students do better in school

Scaled items might read as such:

Attitude Questions	Strongly Disagree	Disagree	Neither Agree nor Disagree	Agree	Strongly Agree
I believe doing homework is an important part of achieving in school.	a	b	c	d	e
I believe using study skills will help me get better grades in school.	a	b	c	d	e

When creating scale questions, it is not always necessary to use (a) strongly agree, (b) agree, (c) neither agree nor disagree, (d) disagree, and (e) strongly disagree. Attitude questions can be scaled in different ways, depending on what it is being assessed. The University of Connecticut has created the chart shown in Figure 7.1 with the most common Likert questions in areas of agreement, frequency, importance, quality, and likelihood (Siegle, 2010).

Figure 7.1   Most Common Likert Questions

Agreement	• Strongly Agree • Agree • Undecided • Disagree • Strongly Disagree		
Importance	• Very Important • Important • Moderately Important • Of Little Importance • Unimportant		
Quality	• Excellent • Above Average • Average • Below Average • Extremely Poor		

(Continued)

Figure 7.1 (Continued)

Frequency	• Very Frequent • Frequently • Occasionally • Rarely • Very Rarely • Never	• Always • Very Frequently • Occasionally • Rarely • Very Rarely • Never	
Likelihood	• Like Me • Unlike Me	• Definitely • Very Probably • Probably • Possibly • Probably Not • Very Probably Not	• Almost Always True • Usually True • Often True • Occasionally True • Sometimes But Infrequently True • Usually Not True • Almost Never True

Source: Siegle (2010).

Another way to assess beliefs is to use a survey with a continuum, such as the one below:

> On a scale of 1–10 (with 1 being the lowest and 10 being the highest), circle the number that best indicates how confident you are that you will graduate high school:
>
> Not Confident   Very Confident
>
> 1   2   3   4   5   6   7   8   9   10

Granted, this type of scaling will require additional support in hand tallying and analyzing, but it provides an opportunity to respond on a visual continuum and may be necessary for some learners.

Questions can be written to garner different beliefs or feelings. On a Likert scale, it is important to create the question in a bipolar manner and have an equal number of responses on each side of the neutral choice. Below are some sample questions for high school seniors from a curriculum lesson designed to prepare them for college.

- Compared to high school classes, I think college classes will be _____.
  a) A lot harder
  b) A little harder
  c) About the same
  d) A little easier
  e) A lot easier

- In college I think I will _____.
  a) Study a lot more
  b) Study a little more

   c) Study the same amount

   d) Study a little less

   e) Study a lot less

- Which of these reflects your feelings about going away to college?

   a) Not nervous at all

   b) A little nervous

   c) Nervous

   d) Very nervous

- If you did decide to go to college, do you think you will have the money you need?

   a) Yes, definitely

   b) Probably

   c) Not sure

   d) Probably not

   e) No, absolutely not

- Do you think you will involve yourself in a club or group activity in college?

   a) Yes, definitely

   b) Probably

   c) Not sure

   d) Probably not

   e) No, absolutely not

- Which of these best reflects your thoughts about making friends in college?

   a) It will be very easy

   b) It might be easy

   c) Not sure how it will be

   d) It might be hard

   e) It will be very hard

KNOWLEDGE: HOW IS A KNOWLEDGE QUESTION CREATED?

The school counselor now wants to create a knowledge question to measure what students know prior to the lesson and, after the lesson, what they have learned. How will she know what to ask? One method is to ask herself, "What do I want my students to know that I think they don't already know?" If the school counselor thinks students already know the content, then it should not be part of the lesson. If the counselor is not sure, then it is a good idea to find out before going into the classroom. Take a look at one of the knowledge areas the school counselor plans to cover in a sample curriculum lesson on promotion/retention guidelines (see Figure 5.2):

- Know the promotion/retention (exit) criteria

Several questions could be asked to assess students' learning in this area. Where will the school counselor get the ideas for the questions to ask? *From the lesson.* In the lesson, the school counselor will teach students that in their middle school, a 2.0 overall GPA is required to promote to the next grade. This is a factual question, not an attitude question. Unlike an attitude question, a scale *will not work* for a knowledge question. Fact questions are either *right* or *wrong*, whereas attitude questions have a *degree of agreement.* There is no degree of agreement in a knowledge question, because its answer is not an opinion; it is a fact.

In another example, imagine planning to teach elementary school students the steps to conflict resolution, and some of the content is learning the following four rules: (1) no name calling, (2) tell the truth, (3) agree to solve the problem, and (4) do not interrupt. Imagine the following question:

- One of the four rules in conflict resolution is "no name calling."

    a) Strongly agree
    b) Agree
    c) Disagree
    d) Strongly disagree

The scaled attitude response doesn't make sense or fit the question, because there is no degree of agreement when the answer to the question is a fact. In this scenario, the answer would be either *true* or *false.*

Multiple Choice Versus True/False

The best way to ask a knowledge or information question is by asking it in a multiple-choice or true/false format. Which format is better? Multiple-choice questions with five responses (a, b, c, d, e) are often better, because each answer presents a 20% guess factor, while the true/false format has a 50% guess factor. More improvement due to actual learning (and not chance) can be demonstrated with a multiple-choice answer. Below are a few examples of how to change true/false questions to multiple-choice questions.

True or False:

___ To be promoted to the next grade, you must have an *overall* grade point average of 2.5.

___ To be promoted to the next grade, you must receive a C or better in both math and language arts.

___ One of the rules in conflict resolution is "no name calling."

Multiple Choice:

- To be promoted to the next grade, you must have an *overall* grade point average of

    a) 1.0   b) 1.5   c) 2.0   d) 2.5   e) 3.0

- Which of the following two classes *must be passed* with a C or better to be promoted to the next grade?
  - a) Math and language arts
  - b) Language arts and science
  - c) Science and social studies
  - d) PE and elective
  - e) Math and science
- Which of the following is a rule you must agree to in conflict resolution?
  - a) Agree to tell the teacher
  - b) No yelling
  - c) Agree to take only 10 minutes to talk
  - d) Girls always talk first
  - e) No name calling

Sometimes it is difficult to think of more than three responses. In these situations, the counselor may decide to add an "all of the above" or "none of the above" category. Sometimes providing the response: "both 'a' and 'b' are correct" is utilized, but typically only for older students.

Content Validity

Content validity is concerned with whether or not the pre/post test given is accurate in providing the information needed. Content validity measures the degree to which the test items are representative of the content area (Weiss, 1998). In other words, does the question measure what it is intended to measure? For example, there are many pre/post tests available on the CESCaL website (cescal. org). However, if the school counselor uses a pre/post test on bullying and the curriculum being taught is about violence prevention, then it may not align, and the pre/post will not be valid. A reminder in alignment is this: *If you don't teach it, you don't test it. If you teach it, you test it.*

SKILLS: HOW IS A SKILLS QUESTION CREATED?

Once students' attitudes and knowledge have been assessed, the next step is to determine whether they have learned the skill the lesson was intended to teach them. Creating skills questions is more complex than creating knowledge questions, because it requires a different level of understanding: knowledge, comprehension, and application (Bloom, Englehart, Furst, Hill, & Krathwohl, 1956). Students have to think about what they learned, identify the knowledge necessary to answer the questions, and then apply the knowledge to a new situation or scenario (Dimmit, Carey, & Hatch, 2007). When assessing skills, the respondent might be asked to apply the knowledge learned and his or her personal attitude to a situation in a "What would you do?" scenario. Respondents might also be asked to

- Demonstrate conflict resolution skills through role-play
- Fill out a four-year plan
- Complete a career assessment
- Complete a job application
- Fill out a financial aid form
- Identify the location of their classes on a school map
- Locate a missing part of an assignment planner
- Write a short-term or long-term goal

Skills can be assessed through pre/post tests, but if a pre/post is used, it may require the scenario approach. A scenario approach provides an opportunity to utilize the knowledge in an example to determine the response. In a math equation, for example, "$2 + 6 - 3 = \_$" is a knowledge question, which assesses the students' knowledge of addition and subtraction. A skills question is more like a word problem in math: "Mario has two apples, Jaime gave him six more, and Laurie ate three of them. How many apples does Mario have left?" This requires the respondent to put the word problem into a math formula to solve. Similarly, if students were asked to identify the second step in the conflict resolution process, it would be utilizing a knowledge question. A skills question might ask the respondent to read a conflict resolution scenario and identify which step of conflict resolution was missed, which requires knowing the steps and applying them to a particular situation.

The school counselor wants to be certain the students not only have the knowledge of what GPA is necessary to promote, but have also learned the skill of calculating their GPAs. The school counselor creates the following pre/post test question (see Figure 5.2):

- In the sample report card below, what is the student's overall GPA?

Class	Grade
Social Studies	A
Science	F
PE	B
Language Arts	B
Math	C
Elective	B

a) 3.5   b) 3.0   c) 2.5   d) 2.0   e) 1.75

Sometimes Skills Are Post-Only

Note the new school counselor also wants to be certain that students understand how to accurately fill out a planner. In this case, she might wonder how to give a pretest. Would she have them fill it out incorrectly? Instead, she may want to consider having all students fill out a planning sheet as part of the lesson, and then report that X number of students performed this task accurately. If this was done during a lesson, it is possible for 100% of students to be successful.

Alternatively, the school counselor could provide a sample of an assignment planner sheet with errors on it. In the assignment space, the school counselor might write, "Math due Tuesday." The goal would be for the students to identify what is missing or inaccurate in the planner. For instance, missing or inaccurate items might include the math book page number, the number of problems to complete, whether students are to complete odd or even problems, and so on. Because completing an assignment sheet as part of a pre/post test might be time-intensive to grade, this skill could be assessed through peer review as part of the lesson. Again, the results could be that X% of the students were able to accurately identify errors in an assignment planner.

BEGINNING IDEAS

When first creating pre/post tests, it might be helpful to identify the type of question being asked (attitude, skill, or knowledge) as a method of reviewing what has been asked, and determining whether each type of question was asked in the best way. The pre/post test in Figure 7.2 was created for a "Get Real About Violence" lesson. The letter in parentheses at the end of each question indicates whether it assesses attitude (A), skill (S), or knowledge (K). Note that in this pre/post test, the skill questions are presented in the form of a scenario. The students use the knowledge gained to problem-solve what they would do in a situation. In this way, they are demonstrating the skill of application.

Figure 7.2   "Get Real About Violence" Pre/Post Test (Sample)

Directions: Circle the best response to each statement.

1. I believe watching fights is a lot of fun. (A)
   a. Strongly agree
   b. Agree
   c. Disagree
   d. Strongly disagree

2. My attitude affects my risk of being involved in violence. (A)
   a. Strongly agree
   b. Agree
   c. Disagree
   d. Strongly disagree

3. Which of the following is a way to resist violence? (K)
   a. Conflict management
   b. Moving to a safe area
   c. Both a and b
   d. None of the above

(Continued)

Figure 7.2 (Continued)

4. Which of the following influence teenagers' views about violence? (K)
   a. Music
   b. Home
   c. School
   d. Television
   e. All of the above

5. Conflict management is best defined as (K)
   a. Ignoring the person until the problem goes away
   b. Working out your problem by talking it out
   c. Physically fighting
   d. Yelling at each other

6. Some students come up to you at lunch and start calling your mom names and want you to fight. Which of the following is a good way to resist violence? (S)
   a. Tell them you will see them after school
   b. Get friends to back you up
   c. Push one of them and run
   d. Tell them you do not want to get suspended because of them

7. Which of the following is the best thing to say if you want to use a refusal skill? (S)
   a. "I will fight you after school."
   b. "I'm going to get my friends to help me fight."
   c. "I'm not dealing with this right now."
   d. "I refuse to let you call my mom names."
   e. "I am not getting suspended because of you."

COMMON QUESTIONS ABOUT PRE/POST TESTS

What Are the Differences Between Survey Questions and Pre/Post Tests?

Pre/post tests assess knowledge, attitudes, and skills. Surveys can be utilized to measure self-reported student behavior. Pre/post tests are typically given prior to and following classroom lessons or interventions to assess what students learned as a result of the lesson or activity. Survey questions may not be as helpful as a pre/post test, because more time is required to assess changes in behavior. Imagine giving a pretest prior to a lesson on the importance of doing homework and a posttest afterward, where the desired outcome is to know how many hours per night students report studying. The answer to this question would not be expected to change as a result of the lesson alone. This question is not whether students have learned a new attitude, knowledge, or skill. Instead it asks for a student's self-report of his or her behavior, and the answer would not change from the pretest to the posttest. Therefore, it is not a pre/post test question.

It still might be an important piece of information for the counselors to have, however. Therefore, it might be an added survey question at the beginning or end of a pretest to assess current behavior. In this situation, the school counselors would *not* put the survey question on the posttest, but would (perhaps) use the data collected in the pretest on the students' reported homework time as part of the lesson. The counselor might share that (for example) the average student reports spending 30 minutes a day on homework, and studies show that in ninth grade, the appropriate amount of time spent on homework is one hour per day (for example), thereby encouraging students to devote more time each day to completing homework. Subsequently, the counselor would teach the lesson; give the posttest for knowledge, attitudes, and skills; and then, perhaps a few weeks later, return to survey the students regarding the number of hours now spent on homework to see if it shifted. Additionally, the school counselors could compare the percentage of homework completion by individual student or class and then check grade improvement. This would complete the conceptual link from the activity performed (classroom lesson), to the attitudes, knowledge, and skills gained (pre/post), to self-reported behavior change via time spent doing homework and homework completion rates (achievement related) and finally to improved grades (student achievement).

Sometimes it's a good idea to give a survey question before the lesson to determine if the behavioral concern or problem the lesson is designed to address really is a problem. Imagine a lesson is planned on cyberbullying, because concerns exist regarding this issue. It may be helpful to find out if cyberbullying really is an issue for students at the school. Next, imagine the survey is administered to students prior to the lesson, and the counselor learns the students do not consider cyberbulling a problem. Does that mean it is not a problem? Perhaps the students do not understand the accurate definition of cyberbullying. For instance, what if the survey question asks, "How many times have you been cyberbullied in the last month?" If students do not understand what cyberbullying is, they may respond inaccurately. Surveying students again after the lesson defining cyberbullying would ensure students are responding to the question more accurately. Further, with the goal of decreasing the behavior, school counselors may want to survey the students a month or two later to determine if the level of now accurately reported cyberbullying has diminished.

Why Give a Pretest? Why Not Just a Posttest?

There are many benefits of the pretest. It provides baseline data for what students already know and a way to discover whether there is a difference of knowledge between classes. It also provides the counselor an opportunity to focus limited instructional time on the areas students really need to understand. It is not efficient to spend an entire lesson on college entrance requirements if 90% of the students already know the information. It might be best in this case to add content about financial aid or scholarship opportunities. Once the pretest provides the baseline data, the lesson is finalized to design the content in the most efficient and effective way for students' learning. Counselors then provide engaging lessons with the goal of seeing improvement on the posttest assessment.

Should the Posttest Be Given Immediately After the Lesson, or a Few Weeks or Months Later?

One reason to measure immediately after the conclusion of the lesson is to determine whether the students learned what the school counselor intended them to learn. In the same way that teachers assess knowledge and skills at the end of a chapter before moving on, so too it is appropriate for school counselors to determine if the content of the lesson was learned before proceeding to the next level of material or a different topic.

To equal degrees, the posttest measures the students' knowledge gained and the school counselor's competency in delivering an effective lesson. It is essential for the school counselor to revise instructional strategies to meet the students' needs and ensure competency attainment. The risk of waiting weeks or months to deliver a posttest is the school counselor may never know whether students learned the content initially and subsequently forgot, or they never understood the information to begin with. In this way, the posttest also serves as feedback for the school counselor to improve his or her practice.

If there is concern about the students retaining the information, the school counselor may consider delivering a *second* posttest a few weeks or months after the lesson was delivered. In other cases, it may be helpful to deliver a second posttest after an extended break. For example, a school counselor may have taught lessons about enrolling in college prep courses at the end of the students' ninth-grade year, and may be interested to see if those same students retained the information at the start of their tenth-grade year. However, when resources and instructional time are less available for school counselors, it is often most effective to deliver one posttest immediately following the lesson, and utilize intermediate and long-range data from other sources to assess the impact over time.

WHAT TO DO IF A PRETEST IS FORGOTTEN

In the event no pretest was given, counselors can still ask follow-up questions to address responses that may have been influenced by participation in the lesson or intervention. Post-test items such as those in the examples in Figure 7.3 still provide the school counselor with valuable feedback about the perceived impact of the lesson or intervention.

Figure 7.3   Sample Questions for Use Without a Pretest

For students

1. Attending the counseling group has helped me learn about optimism and encouragement.

   a) Strongly agree   b) Agree   c) Disagree   d) Strongly disagree

2. Attending the counseling group has helped me learn strategies to deal with pressure and stress.

   a) Strongly agree   b) Agree   c) Disagree   d) Strongly disagree

3. Since attending group, I have used the study strategies I learned.

   a) Strongly agree   b) Agree   c) Disagree   d) Strongly disagree

4. I believe participation in group has been helpful to me in school.

   a) Strongly agree   b) Agree   c) Disagree   d) Strongly disagree

5. Since attending group I have seen improvement in my schoolwork.

   a) Strongly agree   b) Agree   c) Disagree   d) Strongly disagree

6. I would recommend participating in group to other students who need help in school.

   a) Strongly agree   b) Agree   c) Disagree   d) Strongly disagree

List at least three Student Success Strategies:

1.

2.

3.

What was the most helpful part of group for you?

For teachers:

1. Since attending the counseling group, my students have demonstrated more optimism.

   a) Strongly agree   b) Agree   c) Disagree   d) Strongly disagree

2. Since attending group, my students have more strategies to cope with pressure and stress.

   a) Strongly agree   b) Agree   c) Disagree   d) Strongly disagree

3. Since attending group, my students have used the study strategies they learned.

   a) Strongly agree   b) Agree   c) Disagree   d) Strongly disagree

4. I believe participation in group has been helpful to my students.

   a) Strongly agree   b) Agree   c) Disagree   d) Strongly disagree

5. Since attending group, I have seen improvement in my students' academic achievement.

   a) Strongly agree   b) Agree   c) Disagree   d) Strongly disagree

6. I would recommend participating in group to students who need additional academic support.

   a) Strongly agree   b) Agree   c) Disagree   d) Strongly disagree

Please comment on improvements seen:

Other comments:

HINTS FOR CREATING AND ADMINISTERING PRE/POST TESTS

Avoid Essay and Fill-in-the-Blank Questions

It is recommended school counselors create pre/post tests that are quick and easy to administer and complete. Essay tests should be avoided, as school counselors do not have time to correct them. The same is true for fill-in-the-blank questions. School counselors are busy people with little time to grade these types of tests, as such tests inherently require analyzing. If a school has Scantron machines, these are great for quick scoring. Scantrons come in 10-item sheets, and 10 questions can be enough to assess whether the students are learning what the lesson intends. Perhaps "clickers" are utilized at the school, which allow students to use a handheld device to report their answers, which show up on a PowerPoint slide for all to see. Remember, measuring every part of every lesson in the curriculum is not advised. Rather, test for the main points. Try to tease out the 10 or 15 most important things students should know, believe, and do.

Forced Choice Options

Decide when and where to include a forced choice option. When deciding whether to include or remove the neutral option, the general rule of thumb is this: If it is possible for a person to have no opinion about something, leave it in. Or, if it is possible for a person not to understand the concept being assessed, leave it in as well. For instance, a question might state, "I believe filling out financial aid forms is important." It is possible that a student does not know what "financial aid" means and therefore has no opinion. Or if the question states, "I believe I will have enough money for college," a student might not know, because she or he has no idea what college costs. However, the statement, "Having enough money for college is important to me," is something the student either agrees with or does not. Another consideration is that students often select the "no opinion" option as a response when they are disengaged in the lesson. By forcing a choice, the test requires these students to identify an opinion one way or another.

Try It Out First!

Try giving the pre/post test a week before the lesson to assess what students already know. If it turns out the students know half of the material already, the presentation can be revised. Also, it is not necessary to survey every student if you are seeking a general idea of what knowledge all students currently possess. About 100 responses will do, so long as it is a representative group, considering the size of the school's population.

Eliminate Double Negatives

Try not to use double negatives. Imagine the knowledge question: "Which of the following is not true about homework?" with one of the responses: "No credit is given for later work." Or imagine the attitude question: "It is not acceptable to turn in late work." Since "disagree," is one of the responses, this becomes a double negative. Double negatives in survey questions are difficult even for adults! If students answer incorrectly, it should be because they do not know the information, not because they did not understand what was being asked. Reducing the cognitive thought process will help students answer questions more quickly and accurately.

One Question at a Time

Sometimes items ask too much, such as in the following example: "I believe going to bed at 8:00 p.m., getting a good night's sleep, and eating a good breakfast are important if I want to do well on the state test." The problem with this question is, if the student believes bedtime should be 7:30 or 8:30, but agrees with the other two recommendations, the student will not know how to respond. Instead, ask one thing clearly: "I think it is important to eat a good breakfast on the day of the test."

Watch Your Language

If English language learners are being assessed, have the pre/post test translated for them. When the test is presented in their language, it is ensured they understand what is being asked. Also, pay attention to using language that is developmentally appropriate. Asking middle school students if they believe their class is "rigorous" might lead to incorrect responses, because they do not understand the question's vocabulary. If you are unsure whether the developmental reading level is accurate, ask the teacher to preview the questions. This can help ensure the students' pre/post answers are connected to knowledge of the content, not the reading level. Also, using common language is important. In a recent lesson on transitioning to middle school, a school counselor wanted to ask if the students knew where the *facilities* were. When it was suggested to use a more common term, several were thought of, including *washroom, lavatory,* and *men's room.* Finally, *bathroom* was selected as the most common term.

Little Ones

With younger children, symbols can be used. The following is an example of a continuum some school counselors use for very young children:

Giving a pre/post test to kindergarten students presents a special developmental challenge. But just as teachers in kindergarten classrooms are able to assess students' knowledge of letters and numbers through assessment in "centers," so too can school counselors. Just "become a center" in the classroom, and use that small group time to ask students the questions. Alternate options are to show pictures, do matching activities, or create a role-play. Get creative! Having said that, if measuring only one or two things each year, consider measuring at an older grade level.

You Don't *Know* What They *Know* Until You *Know* What They *Know*

School counselors often ask students, "Do you know the number of credits you need to graduate?" Students might say they do, but how do you *know* they *really know?* Caution should be taken when writing knowledge questions that ask only what students *believe* they know. For instance, what if a middle school counselor asked students if they knew the overall grade point average (GPA) needed to pass to the next grade? How would the counselor know if the students really knew? Instead, the counselor should ask students to choose the answer from a multiple-choice selection. By requiring students to identify the exact GPA required, the school counselor can determine whether they know it. So instead of asking, "Do you know the GPA required for promotion to the eighth grade," the question becomes the following:

1. To be promoted to eighth grade, I need a GPA of

    a. 2.0 overall (total average of all classes)

    b. 2.0 or better in math and language arts only

  c. 2.0 or better overall and 2.0 in math and language arts

  d. 2.0 or better in every class

  e. None of these is the right answer

By asking the question with a multiple-choice response, the school counselor knows exactly what percentage of students really know the promotion requirements.

ONLINE PRODUCTS

Zoomerang (zoomerang.com) and Survey Monkey (surveymonkey.com) are two helpful computer-generated survey software systems that can assist a school counselor in designing, collecting, and analyzing data from pre/post tests. Both offer a limited amount of free services as well as more advanced features that are reasonably cost efficient for school systems to afford. The challenge is ensuring students have access to computers to take the surveys.

DataDirector is an example of a set of tools school counselors can use to measure the impact of their lessons on students utilizing pre/post assessments. Teachers commonly use DataDirector to assess students' performance on benchmark assessments. DataDirector is a web-based data assessment management system that uses plain paper scanning and high-speed optical mark reading (OMR) to allow educators immediate access to detailed results (DataDirector, 2012). It is especially helpful because student identifiers allow specific detailed score sheets indicating who did well and who needs further assistance.

The Online Assessment Reporting System (OARS) also uses high-speed scanning to collect, report, and analyze student progress in curricular areas before and after instruction. Figure 7.4 shows the results of an OARS pretest given to high school students on graduation requirements. While most students answered item #7 correctly, many other knowledge questions were answered incorrectly, validating the necessity of delivering curriculum content. Note the attitude questions mark "agree" and "strongly agree" (D and E) as correct.

Utilizing a tool or system like OARS allows counselors to identify which students score less than 70% overall. School counselors can target these students for additional instruction. Pre/post assessments can also be aligned with the ASCA Student Standards to determine which specific standards and competencies students have met and on which students need additional instruction. If those students who did not meet competency receive additional instruction, school counselors can potentially state that 100% of students have achieved standards (and they will be able to prove it!). It might be that some students are less likely to answer honestly regarding their beliefs if the students know they might be identified; therefore school counselors are wise to use their professional wisdom when deciding which pre/post tests should employ the student's personal identifier.

Finally, many schools use "clickers," or remote personal response systems, that resemble TV remote control units (Turning Technologies, 2013). These devices work by transmitting individual responses to a projector, allowing all participants to see the results when in a group setting.

Figure 7.4 Results of a Pretest Using OARS

⬆ Drill Up to District | ⬇ Drill Down to Class

🅜 Filter by Department

Question Number	Assessment Area	Responses					Blanks & Mult. Marks	Percent Answered Correctly
		A	B	C	D	E		
1.	Attitude	5	14	120	255	207	0	76.9 %
2.	Attitude	14	18	16	226	327	0	92 %
3.	Attitude	23	73	41	268	195	1	77 %
4.	Attitude	112	69	9	60	347	4	67.7 %
5.	Knowledge	61	63	91	197	186	3	32.8 %
6.	Knowledge	97	156	56	198	93	1	15.5 %
7.	Knowledge	4	13	30	21	531	2	88.4 %
8.	Knowledge	53	21	387	27	113	0	64.4 %
9.	Knowledge	167	61	13	128	230	2	21.3 %
10.	Knowledge	25	5	89	17	460	5	76.5 %
11.	Knowledge	149	117	204	51	80	0	8.5 %
12.	Knowledge	37	185	60	143	173	3	23.8%
13.	Knowledge	38	78	146	200	137	2	24.3%
14.	Skills	139	301	126	21	10	4	50.1%
15.	Skills	116	71	353	37	20	4	58.7 %
16.	Skills	98	34	203	43	217	6	33.8 %
17.	Skills	26	175	309	49	35	7	29.1 %

Summary

Average Percent Correct	49.5
Percent of Students at or above 70 %	8.7

Source: Red Schoolhouse Software.

Silva's Story

Liliana Silva wondered why, even though her school district offered guaranteed admission for students meeting college prep requirements to the local university, few students completed high school having met college prep requirements. Using ASK to guide her assessment of the impact of a series of classroom lessons, Silva (2005) found that on the pretest, most of the students (64%) knew the subject requirements (math for instance), and 74% knew that in order to go to college they had to complete the college prep requirements, yet only 30% of the students believed taking college prep courses was important.

(Continued)

(Continued)

As a result, she revised the curriculum to specifically address the "belief" concern. Silva divided the students into cultural and gender groupings and included activities designed to address the cultural beliefs students had about attending college and the barriers that students perceived to exist for them institutionally; thereby addressing the "attitude" component regarding completing college preparation courses and the pathways to overcome barriers. Silva's (2005) results showed after the classroom lessons, 80% of the students knew the subject requirements, 92% knew that in order to go to college they had to complete the college prep requirements, and 82% believed taking college prep courses was important.

Silva then collected data on how many students elected to enroll in college prep courses. Her goal as a school counselor was to increase the number of students who selected to take more rigorous coursework, with the intention of increasing the percentage of students graduating college-eligible. Subsequently, of the 108 students on this counselor's caseload, 106 enrolled in college prep courses, and of those, 56 enrolled in AP/honors classes (Hatch & Lewis, 2011).

ANALYZING AND IMPROVING PRE/POST TESTS

As you are learning to create pre/post tests, it is expected you will make mistakes. Let's take a look at a pre/post test created by a school counselor for her lesson on bullying. Read the items below, and note that next to each item, she has indicated whether she thought each question was an attitude (A), knowledge (K), or skill (S) question. How do you think she did? Are these good questions? Is she correct in her assignment of ASK questions? How might the questions be improved? When you have finished, read the detailed analysis and suggestions that follow.

Bullying Pre/Post Test Sample and Analysis

1. Do you know at least one thing you can do if you see/experience bullying? (S)

    ___Yes   ___No

2. Have you ever reported or would you ever report bullying? (A)

    ___Yes   ___No

3. Have you ever tried or would you ever try to stop someone from bullying? (A)

    ___Yes   ___No

4. Do you consider spreading rumors to be bullying? (K)

    ___Yes   ___No

5. Are there other types of bullying besides physical? (K)

    ___Yes   ___No

6. As long as you are left out of it, it is okay for someone to bully another person. (A)

   ___Yes   ___No

7. Someone who reports bullying is a snitch. (A)

   ___Yes   ___No

8. It is fun/funny to watch someone being bullied. (A)

   ___Yes   ___No

9. It is scary to watch someone being bullied. (A)

   ___Yes   ___No

10. You can write an anonymous note to report bullying. (S)

    ___Yes   ___No

11. A parent can call and report bullying. (S)

    ___Yes   ___No

12. You do not have to be identified as the victim/witness to report bullying. (K)

    ___Yes   ___No

Analysis of Bullying Pre/Post Test

Now that you have read through the questions, review the analysis below for each one. Were you able to find these flaws? The suggestions following each question may help this school counselor to improve her pre/post test. Perhaps you can suggest additional improvements.

1. **Do you know at least one thing you can do if you see/experience bullying? (S)**

   This question (and many of the questions below) asks two different questions that might result in different responses. It's possible that students know what to do if they *see* bullying but not if they *experience* bullying. However, even if students answer yes, how do you know if they know?

   Although the counselor listed this as a skill (S) question, this is a knowledge question (K) that can be answered by asking the students to list one thing they can do (although then the school counselor still has to grade it for accuracy). The counselor could also create a multiple-choice format. Another option is to ask if students feel "ready with good ideas" for what to do if they see a bully. In this way, the counselor can assess the student's confidence (A).

   Finally, *experience* is an advanced word—check for reading level and revise if necessary.

2. **Have you ever reported or would you ever report bullying? (A)**

   This attitude (A) question is asking two things ("have you" and "would you"). Asking "have you" is a survey question about previous behavior, not an attitude question. Further, it requests a yes/no response (but requires a scaled response). Instead, try the following attitude question:

2. If I saw someone being bullied I would report it.

   a. Definitely yes

   b. Probably yes

   c. Probably no

   d. Definitely no

3. **Have you ever tried or would you ever try to stop someone from bullying? (A)**

The school counselor must decide what she wants to ask: past behavior questions or possible future behavior questions? It is best for the school counselor to decide whether he or she wants data on behavior students have participated in, or behavior students believe they "would" perform. Questions inquiring about what students believe they "would do" are attitude (A) questions requiring a scaled response. Items asking what students "have done" are factual information statements reporting past behaviors, and the response is either yes or no. Further, historical fact responses are more appropriate as needs assessment or survey questions, because answers will not change after the lesson. The information could, however, be used to inform lesson planning.

4. **Do you consider spreading rumors to be bullying? (K)**

This question is tough to decipher—is it a knowledge (K) or attitude (A) question? If it is a knowledge (K) question, then it can be asked differently (multiple choice) by including "spreading rumors" as one of the options (see below). Also, as written, the answer would be yes or no, giving students a 50% guess percentage. By changing the item to multiple choice (a, b, c, d, e), respondents have only a 20% guess percentage.

4. Which of the following is an example of bullying?

   a. Hitting someone

   b. Calling someone names

   c. Spreading rumors

   d. All of these

   e. All of these except c

If the question is designed to assess the respondent's attitude (A), then it could be asked in this manner:

4. I believe kids who spread rumors are bullies.

   a. Strongly agree

   b. Agree

   c. Disagree

   d. Strongly disagree

5. **Are there other types of bullying besides physical? (K)**

This knowledge (K) question leads to a simple yes/no response. As in a prior question, it is suggested the question be reworded into a multiple-choice format such as, "Which of the following is a type of bullying?" [Then list multiple-choice responses.]

6. **As long as you are left out of it, it is okay for someone to bully another person. (A)**

This attitude (A) question is improved by using a Likert scale. As referred to previously, the choice of "neutral or "I don't know" is not necessary, as these items are more appropriate as forced choice items (strongly agree, agree, disagree, strongly disagree).

7. **Someone who reports bullying is a snitch. (A)**

Is the school counselor trying to ascertain whether the student believes (A) people who report bullying are snitches? Or does he or she want to know if the student understands (K), from the lesson, that adults do not consider it snitching to tell on a bully? This must be clarified before the question can be created correctly. And in this case, that is difficult. The students may learn from the counselor that reporting is not snitching but might still believe that it is. A knowledge question is more difficult to create, because the word *snitch* is loaded emotionally. If this item is designed to assess beliefs, a scale is in order.

7. I believe kids who report bullies are snitches.

    a. Strongly agree

    b. Agree

    c. Disagree

    d. Strongly disagree

8. **It is fun/funny to watch someone being bullied. (A)**

The question assumes everyone has seen someone being bullied, which might be presumptuous. In addition, the school counselor must decide which word he or she wants the students to respond to. The words *fun* and *funny* are different words with different meanings, and it is possible to think something is fun, but not funny. Also, in this case, it might be appropriate to provide a different type of scaled response to capture the attitude (A) or feeling; this can be done by including the feeling word in the answer.

8. Watching someone being bullied is:

    a. Always fun

    b. Usually fun

    c. Sometimes fun

    d. Usually not fun

    e. Never fun

9. **It is scary to watch someone being bullied. (A)**

This attitude (A) item presumes the student has watched someone being bullied. In addition, this question, similar to one earlier, is eliciting information from the student to learn whether the student feels scared. It is unlikely a classroom lesson will shift this response. This is therefore a needs assessment item and not a good pre/post test item.

10. **You can write an anonymous note to report bullying. (S)**

   This question is listed as a skill (S) question; however, it is written in such a way that it appears to be a knowledge (K) question. If the counselor wants to see whether students possess the skill to fill out the referral, then providing a blank referral form and asking the students to fill it out is an acceptable way to measure whether they possess the skill (S) to write a referral. If, however, the goal of the question is to see whether the students understand they are "allowed to turn someone in anonymously," then the question needs to be reworded in an age-appropriate way. Try this:

   10. The school rule says, "If I write a note to report (to tell on) a bully, I must sign my name."

       a. True
       b. False

   In this case, true/false may be the best choice to ensure clarity.

11. **A parent can call and report bullying. (S)**

   This is a knowledge (K) question, not a skill (S) question, unless the skill of calling is to be demonstrated. Again, if possible, multiple choice is preferred over true/false.

   11. Who is allowed to report bullying?

       a. Students
       b. Teachers
       c. Parents
       d. All of the above
       e. Everyone except parents

12. **You do not have to be identified as the victim/witness to report bullying. (K)**

   First, the questioner needs to decide whether he or she wants to ask about the witness or about the victim, as the students might think the answer is true for one but not the other. The use of "do not" would lead to a double negative in a true/false question. Instead, turn the negative statement into a positive statement. For example: I can report being a witness to bullying anonymously. Finally, it is important that the reading level match the students' needs. In this case, the word *identified* is tough to rewrite, but a sample of more kid-friendly language is attempted below. See if you can make it even better!

   12. If you tell the principal you saw someone getting bullied, the principal will

       a. Tell your parents
       b. Tell other kids
       c. Tell your teacher
       d. Tell the bully
       e. Not tell the bully

Parenting Pre/Post Test Sample, Analysis, and Revision

The following is an example of a pre/post test that was submitted for feedback by a school counselor regarding a parenting class she planned to teach on issues affecting preadolescents. Note the comments and suggestions under each question.

1. **Your preadolescent's attitudes, bodies, and relationships will change.**

    a. Strongly Agree

    b. Agree

    c. Disagree

    d. Strongly Disagree

This question has three concerns. First, this is a knowledge question, not an attitude question. Therefore, a scale is *not* appropriate. Knowledge questions require true/false or multiple-choice responses. Second, it is not reasonable for parents to actually "disagree" with this statement. Of course they know their preadolescents' bodies will change. Finally, it is possible a parent believes the child's body will change but disagrees with the idea that attitudes will change. However, the question has lumped three answers into one, and therefore respondents could find they are conflicted as to how to answer.

2. **I believe families provide an opportunity for a child to grow and change in a safe environment.**

    a. Strongly agree

    b. Agree

    c. Disagree

    d. Strongly disagree

When selecting questions for a pre/post test, it is important to choose items that have the possibility of shifting as a result of the training. What is the likelihood that this response will change after the training? This question is more of a barometer question (to learn about what parents think, know, or believe) than a question that might be impacted by the training, and it should be eliminated or used in a needs assessment.

3. **When my child begins to argue, *nevertheless* and *regardless* are key words that restate your position.**

    a. True

    b. False

The trouble with this question is it is too easy to guess the right answer. In addition, the counselor writes "my child" and later refers to "your position." If you pay attention to correcting grammatical mistakes, your survey will read more clearly. Also, this question is better asked in a multiple-choice format.

4. **When my child starts to argue, listening should happen ____.**

    a. First

    b. Second

    c. Third

    d. Last

Again, it is hard to get this wrong, because the correct answer is easy to guess. Because the important concept is listening (not when to listen, but how important listening is as opposed to other options parents have), try asking it in a different way.

5. Your child is unaffected by and unaware of world issues.

    a. True

    b. False

This statement has a negative tone. It might be better written as, "Most preadolescents are more aware of and more affected by world issues than most parents realize."

6. You may help your child with the problem of forgetting by

    a. Keeping a daily list

    b. Using their planner

    c. Checking ABI

    d. All of the above

Be certain the person taking the pretest knows what the acronym ABI stands for. It is not a fair pre/post test if it includes an acronym that has not been introduced yet, because this makes it more likely respondents will answer incorrectly.

7. When parents increase involvement in schools, students actually achieve more, enjoy school more, and have better family relationships.

    a. True

    b. False

In addition to the question being written awkwardly, the answer requires the respondent to accept all three claims of parental involvement as true. It might be better as a multiple-choice question: Studies show when parents increase their involvement in schools, students

    a. Achieve more

    b. Enjoy school more

    c. Have better family relationships

    d. Have better peer relationships

    e. All of the above

Parenting Pre/Post Test Revised

The questions from the parenting test were rewritten after review of the first version. Note each question includes an indicator to shown whether it is an attitude (A) or a knowledge (K) question. Do you think these are improved? Can you offer suggestions for improving them even more? Note that the test still lacks skills questions. Can you think of any?

Directions: Circle the best response to each statement.

1. I feel prepared for my child's preadolescence. (A)

    a. Strongly agree

    b. Agree

    c. Disagree

    d. Strongly disagree

2. Preadolescence will impact my child's (K)

    a. Attitudes

    b. Body image

    c. Peer relationships

    d. Academic confidence

    e. Family relationships

    f. All of the above

3. It is considered a normal part of development for a preadolescent to challenge household rules. (K)

    a. True

    b. False

4. I feel confident when handling my child's resistance to my requests. (A)

    a. Strongly agree

    b. Agree

    c. Disagree

    d. Strongly disagree

5. When a preadolescent starts to argue, what should parents do first? (K)

    a. Tell the child to calm down

    b. Listen for understanding

    c. Walk away

    d. Argue back

    e. Calmly tell the child why she or he is wrong

    f. Remind the child you are the parent

6. When my preadolescent wants to argue with me about the house rules, which words are key to restating my position? (K)

    a. *perhaps* and *maybe*

    b. *nevertheless* and *regardless*

    c. *impossible* and *possible*

    d. *never* and *unlikely*

    e. *circumvent* and *irrational*

7. Parents can help their children with the problem of forgetting by teaching them how to (K)

    a. Keep a daily list

    b. Use their planner

    c. Check their assignments online

    d. All of the above

8. Parents can help their children when they have problems with their preadolescent friends by (K)

    a. Staying out of it

    b. Being the negotiator/mediator

    c. Telling the friend to leave

    d. Listening and offering suggestions only as requested

    e. All of the above

NOW YOU TRY!

Figure 7.5 is an example of a pre/post test from an anger management lesson. See whether you can identify which questions are related to attitudes (A), which to skills (S), and which to knowledge (K). In addition, try to make your own improvements to the questions.

Figure 7.5   Anger Management Pre/Post Test

This pretest is a sample that needs improvement; it is provided as a practice activity.

Name _____ Date_____ School_____

CIRCLE THE BEST ANSWER:

1. **It is normal to be angry.**

    a. True

    b. False

2. **Anger is a bad feeling.**

    a. True

    b. False

3. **I am able to calm myself down when I feel angry.**

    a. Yes, usually I can

    b. Sometimes I can

    c. No, usually I can't

4. **When anger is held inside (bottled up), it is *good* because no one gets hurt.**

    a. True

    b. False

5. **Which of these is a good idea for me to try when I am angry?**

    a. Think of a happy place

    b. Talk to an adult

    c. Play a sport

    d. Write or draw my feelings

    e. All of these are good ideas

6. **I am able to control my angry feelings.**

    a. Always

    b. Usually

    c. Sometimes

    d. Usually not

    e. Never

7. **Which of the following is a good way to control anger?**

    a. Throw something

    b. Take deep breaths

    c. Hit somebody

    d. Yell at someone

8. **I believe learning how to control my anger is a good idea.**

    a. Yes

    b. No

    c. I'm not sure

9. **You can tell people are angry when they are**

    a. Relaxing their muscles

    b. Having a calm expression

    c. Clenching their fists

    d. Laughing

10. **Sometimes people act angry when they are really sad or afraid.**

    a. True

    b. False

11. **Being angry helps me solve problems.**

    a. Yes

    b. No

    c. I'm not sure

12. **Angry feelings can cause**

    a. My heart to beat faster

    b. Me to breathe faster

    c. My fists to tighten

    d. All of the above

13. **Joe is feeling angry because he didn't get to go to recess. Which of the following is the best way for him to calm down?**

    a. Hold the feelings inside

    b. Yell at his teacher

    c. Take a few deep breaths

    d. Kick a desk

(Continued)

Figure 7.2 (Continued)

14. **I believe anger is not good for my health.**

   a. Yes

   b. No

   c. I'm not sure

15. **List three safe ways to get angry:**

   1 _____

   2 _____

   3 _____

16. **List three safe things to do when you get angry:**

   1 _____

   2 _____

   3 _____

FINAL THOUGHTS ON PRE/POST TESTS

Pre/post assessments are wonderful tools for evaluating the impact of the lessons taught on students' knowledge, attitudes, and skills. The results of pre/post tests can validate the use of instructional time and be used to focus instruction where more work is needed. They can also be used to compare the impacts of lessons taught by different presenters or in different settings. Were classroom lessons more impactful—in terms of the knowledge, attitudes, and skills students learned—than presentations in the multipurpose room? Were the lessons on college knowledge delivered by teachers, parent volunteers, and graduate students as effective as the lessons delivered by the school counselor? Ultimately, the goal is to improve instruction, programs, and practices for the benefit of the students served. Additional pre/post assessments are available online.

8

Intentional Guidance for Systems Change

I n Chapter 2, the definition of intentional guidance was suggested as "a deliberate act by a school counselor to guide, lead, direct, or provide purposeful interventions for students in need academically, personally, or socially." In Chapter 6, a "fishnet" approach was used to identify, survey, and ensure intentional interventions were provided for students who were struggling to attend, behave, or achieve. While individual counseling, group counseling, or referrals to outside agencies may be appropriate for many students as interventions, other students' data-driven needs may trigger a call for a schoolwide or systems approach.

SCHOOL COUNSELORS AS SOCIAL JUSTICE ADVOCATES

School counselors are social justice advocates who embody the themes on the outside of the American School Counselor Association (ASCA) National Model diamond (Figure 2.2) as leaders, advocates, collaborators, and systems change agents (ASCA, 2003, 2005, 2012a). School counselors promote equity and access to rigor and opportunity so all students can reach their full potential in K–12 schools and beyond. Professional Ethical Standards (ASCA, 2010b) call on school counselors to advocate for, lead, and create equity-based school counseling programs that will help close achievement, opportunity, and attainment gaps—all of which may deny students the opportunity to pursue future career and college goals (Holcomb-McCoy & Chen-Hayes, 2011).

ASCA's school counselors' ethical guidelines include the following:

A.3.b. Ensure equitable academic, career, post-secondary access and personal/social opportunities for all students through the use of data to help close achievement gaps and opportunity gaps. (ASCA, 2010b)

E.2.g. Work as advocates and leaders in the school to create equity-based school counseling programs that help close any achievement, opportunity and attainment gaps that deny all students the chance to pursue their educational goals. (ASCA, 2010b)

Ethical school counselors have high expectations for every student and are social justice advocates who ensure access to rigorous college- and career-readiness curriculums (Education Trust, 2009; Hines & Lemon, 2011; NOSCA, 2011). Utilizing tools for cultural proficiency, school counselors juxtapose barriers against guiding principles, ethics, and professional frameworks for effective communication and problem solving in diverse communities (Stephens & Lindsey, 2011). As agents of change, highly motivated and culturally competent school counselors utilize data to remove institutional and environmental barriers that may deny students rigorous academic, college/career, and personal/social opportunities (ASCA, 2010b; Hatch, 2012a, 2012b; Holcomb-McCoy & Chen-Hayes, 2011). School counselors are social justice advocates when they

- Disaggregate attendance, behavior, grade, and course-taking patterns with a special focus on diverse populations (ASCA, 2010b)
- Contribute to schoolwide systemic change and educational reform, including parent and guardian engagement with school-family-community partnerships (Bryan & Holcomb-McCoy, 2004)
- Promote career and college access and readiness for all students in K–12 schools (NOSCA, 2011)
- Intentionally address inequitable social, political, and economic conditions that impede the academic, career, college-access, and personal/social development of students (Ratts, 2009)
- Develop cultural competence as leaders who acknowledge issues of power, privilege, and oppression (Fouad, Gerstein, & Toporek, 2006; Holcomb-McCoy & Chen-Hayes, 2011; Stephens & Lindsey, 2011)
- Research the educational experiences of traditionally marginalized youth (e.g., young men of color) and commit to transforming their opportunities and experiences (Lee & Ransom, 2011; NOSCA, 2012).
- Commit to serving as social justice advocates for underrepresented, underserved, and underperforming students (ASCA, 2010b; Education Trust, 2009; Holcomb-McCoy & Chen-Hayes, 2011).
- Assess and change school policies, practices, and behaviors in culturally proficient ways that serve students, schools, communities, and society (Stephens & Lindsey, 2011)

PROGRAMS AND ACTIVITIES

When reviewing data, school counselors may realize/discover gaps for groups of students who are underrepresented, underserved, or underperforming academically, personally/socially, or in college/career readiness. Intentional guidance for systems change may call on the counselor to perform deliberate acts to guide, lead, direct, or provide *additional purposeful schoolwide program and activities* to address gaps in achievement or performance between or among race, social class, gender, or other groups within the larger system. Schoolwide intentional guidance requires school counselors to utilize leadership, collaboration, and advocacy skills to design opportunities for additional instruction, support, and assistance.

For example, an underrepresentation of students of color in honors and Advanced Placement (AP) courses could lead a counseling team to create multiple new schoolwide programs and activities designed to encourage enrollment of underrepresented students in rigorous courses.

Some of the many ideas may include the following:

- Additional focus on promoting honors and AP during counselors' classroom lessons and during the registration process
- Utilizing the College Board's "AP Potential" data tool to identify students who might not have considered taking an AP course
- Creating a panel of diverse alumni to share their experiences taking honors and AP courses and the impact on college readiness
- Creating an evening event for students and parents to promote the AP program and honors courses, presented in the families' native languages
- Encouraging teachers to attend the AP conferences to improve classroom experiences
- Promoting honors and AP study groups within the school

POLICIES AND PRACTICES

Schoolwide programs and activities may serve to support additional enrollment in AP, however, further investigation may also uncover access or opportunity concerns reflecting gatekeeping policies, practices, or procedures that may also be contributing to low enrollment (Hart & Jacobi, 1992; Hines & Lemon, 2011; Holcomb-McCoy, 2007). When analyzing the school's data, the school counselor may also realize the intervention students need is not a school counseling activity (group counseling, individual counseling, etc.) but rather the school counselor's advocacy to work within the school system to *change an existing policy or practice* that may be denying some students access to rigorous educational opportunities. These may include social justice issues, parity issues, or issues that stir a moral imperative for counselors to act on students' behalf (Hatch, 2004b). Access and opportunity data are often represented in artifacts relating to a student's rights, or the accessibility or availability of admission into a course, activity, or program. It is incumbent on the school counselor to inquire about the following:

- What are the prerequisites for access to an honors or AP course?
- Are students required to have a 3.0 GPA in order to enroll in honors or AP courses?
- Are students required to have the approval of the honors or AP teacher to enroll?

- What is a *reasonable* prerequisite for students to take honors and AP courses?
- Can *any* student take an AP course?
- What control is appropriate for teachers to have over which students will sit in their classrooms?
- What role is appropriate for the professional school counselor?
- Who makes the final decision about course enrollment?

Intentional guidance for systems change also calls the school counselors to perform deliberate acts to guide, lead, or direct *reform efforts to initiate, revise, or eliminate policies or practices* that serve as barriers to access or opportunity and that contribute to achievement gaps for underrepresented, underserved, or underperforming students.

ACCESS AND OPPORTUNITY

Disaggregating and analyzing access data may shed light on the ways in which the institution is contributing to the creation of achievement gaps. As social justice advocates, school counselors use their voices to address institutional oppressions and systems that have historically disenfranchised certain students (ASCA, 2010b; Hatch, 2012a; Holcomb-McCoy & Chen-Hayes, 2011). Access data can be used to advocate for the right of every student to graduate college-ready (Hatch, 2012a; House & Martin, 1998; Johnson, 2002; Lee & Goodnough, 2011).

Examples of access and opportunity data include the following:

- College-prep courses: Are classes open to all students or some students? If not all, why not all?
- Honors courses: Are there enough honors courses for all students who want to take honors? What are the requirements to access honors courses?
- AP courses: How many are offered? What are the requirements to take AP courses?
- Dual-enrollment opportunities: Are these courses open to all students?
- College assessment (SAT, ACT, PSAT, PLAN): Is funding available for all students to take these tests? Are they offered locally?
- College-going school counseling curriculum: Do all students receive information? How often? In class? How is equitable receipt of the curriculum (e.g., the items in the bulleted list below) ensured?

  o College eligibility requirements
  o College application process
  o Financial aid literacy

- College/career exploration programs, inventory assessments, and so on: Who has access? When is the career center open?
- Parent/guardian college/career readiness events: When are these offered? Are they provided in various languages? Is childcare provided?
- Articulation opportunities between middle and high school: Who participates?
- Articulation between high school and university or community college: Who participates?

- College-planning opportunities: Are these guaranteed for all or some students?
- Four-year plans: How often do students receive a review? Do students have to ask to have their plan reviewed, or will the counselor call them in?
- College visits: Who is invited? What is the cost?
- TRIO, STEM, GEAR UP, Bridge programs: Who can participate?
- Financial aid/scholarship-planning nights: Who is invited? Students? Parents? Are materials available in the students' native languages?
- Cocurricular activities such as clubs and sports: Can everyone participate? What can be done for the students who cannot afford them?
- Enrichment activities: Can everyone participate? Are there fees associated?
- Intervention programs: How are students invited to participate?

In addition to advocating for access, monitoring course enrollment and extracurricular participation allows counselors to discover why some students who have open access to opportunities still choose not to participate. Conducting student and parent focus groups focusing on their perceptions and experiences can provide rich qualitative information. Data gleaned from these conversations may result in a call for new policies or interventions.

TAKING ACTION

Lack of Access Example at the High School Level

Maria, a junior, understood all the college-prep requirements she needed to take at her school in order to attend her local university. She had a strong desire to attend college, because she knew she would be the first in her family to do so. She filled out her registration form for Spanish and prepared her schedule of courses for junior year. She knew she needed advanced math and a foreign language (Spanish). Unfortunately for Maria, her high school counselor informed her of the school's policy that did not allow Maria to take Spanish unless she met the prerequisite of a B average overall or received approval from the teacher. At Maria's school, only 15% of Latinos graduated college eligible (although they made up 55% of the school's population). Maria wondered why she had to have a B average overall before she could take Spanish (her native language). Maria was anxious, because she didn't know the teacher and worried she might not get approval. She wondered why her friend, who had a different counselor, was able to take Spanish without the teacher's approval, even though she had a C average.

SPANISH 1				
Grade	☒ 9	☒ 10	☒ 11	☒ 12
Length		☐ Semester	☒ Year	
Prerequisite				
"B" average or better overall or teacher approval.				

So what do school counselors do when they uncover an access and equity issue (like that of Maria above)? When a course is an integral piece of an educational program for student success, is it ethical practice for a school counselor to (a) tell Maria she can't take the class unless she has the teacher's permission, (b) place Maria in a teacher's class against school policy and hope the teacher doesn't notice, (c) ask the teacher to take "just this one student I promise" as a favor, (d) suggest Maria take Spanish at the local university, (e) complain to the Spanish department that the current prerequisites are discouraging some students from enrolling and hope they will change them? School counselors as social justice advocates must work *within* the system to *reform* the system's policies, practices, and procedures for the benefit of all students.

Lack of Opportunity Example: Transitioning From Middle School

In a large high school district, eighth-grade teachers from surrounding districts send placement cards for incoming freshmen with their recommendations for students' placement into one of four tracks: (a) honors college prep, (b) college prep, (c) high school graduate, and (d) completion (for some, special education). Students are subsequently placed into courses per recommendations of middle school teachers. Imagine now, as the school counselor, it's a student's junior year, and the parents of a student with A's and B's have just discovered their child is not on target to attend college, because the track the child had been placed in from middle school was a non–college prep track. It is far too late to restart on a different track. What is the counselor's responsibility?

- If teachers from a previous school predetermine student placement, what is the responsibility of the school counselor when the student comes to high school?
- What schoolwide program or activity might a school counselor implement?
- What systems change might a school counselor lead?
- What policy or practice might require reform?
- What responsibility does the ethical school counselor have to guide, lead, or direct *reform efforts to initiate, revise, or eliminate policies or practices* that serve as barriers to access or opportunity and that contribute to achievement gaps for underrepresented, underserved, or underperforming students?

Intentional guidance for systems change aligns with the preamble of ASCA's ethical code: "Professional school counselors are advocates, leaders, collaborators and consultants who *create* opportunities for equity in access and success in educational opportunities" (ASCA, 2010a). The ethical code empowers school counselors to employ the same advocacy paradigm they use to advocate for a victim of child abuse as they voice the need for necessary change. By using data to tell their story, counselors can advocate for policies and practices that promote academic achievement and success for *all* students. They can challenge the status quo and existing belief systems and begin to promote a climate of advocacy for every student. School counselors can address achievement barriers created by inconsistent district policies, past practices, and outdated belief systems and work to remove the obstacles that impede student progress.

Systems Change Example at the Elementary Level

Danny, a third grader, was withdrawn. His mother had been killed in a car accident. Danny's school counselor noticed he spent a great deal of time in detention due to incomplete homework assignments. She counseled Danny to address his grief issues but realized there was also a systems issue. Students who needed extra help with homework were put in a punitive detention environment. The counselor decided to look at the data and found the detention room had an 84% increase in detentions within the last year caused by a lack of homework among students, not behavior concerns. In response, the counselor helped design a homework club to meet the growing need. As a result, instead of punishing students for missing homework, they received the academic interventions and support they needed. Detentions were reduced, and academics were improved (and Danny improved too!).

DATA TEAMS

When school counselors conduct data conversations, they should consider including other educators who are equally committed to leadership in addressing equity and access issues and data-driven decision making (Dimmitt, Carey, & Hatch, 2007). Reviewing data will help stir important conversations needed to dispelling myths about students of color and students who live in poverty, ultimately preventing any attempt to predetermine the potential of students from certain groups (Holcomb-McCoy & Chen-Hayes, 2011; House & Martin, 1998). It may be challenging when team members are first learning how to talk with one another about difficult data-driven issues. This can be especially sensitive, because counselors come from diverse backgrounds and exhibit different levels of passion and compulsion when advocating for students. Johnson (2002) discusses four ways team members often talk about data:

- *Raw debate:* Members hold strong to their position while listening only as a matter of personal strategy.
- *Polite discussion:* Members mask their positions through politeness and never reveal what they are really thinking. This is the most dysfunctional/deceptive form of conversation.
- *Skillful discussion:* A productive way of conversing that incorporates a balance of inquiry and advocacy for one's own position.
- *Dialogue:* Members suspend their positions and participate in inquiry so that everyone has a thorough understanding of the issue(s); assumptions are probed, and new discoveries are made.

Throughout data conversations, counselors are encouraged to maintain a culture of inquiry, exploring perceptions regarding why things are the way they are, and engaging in candid conversations about how to improve the academic and college/career-readiness culture of the school (Johnson, 2002). Looking at data over time reveals patterns and identifies student needs and opportunities for advocacy. Disaggregating and cross-tabulating the data using tools like the ASCA National Model's Data Profile allow school counselors to see student trends over time (ASCA, 2012a). In this way, school counselors can monitor student progress and look for inequities in access, attainment, and achievement (ASCA, 2010b; Lee & Goodnough, 2011). Analyzing the disaggregated data over time can surface equity and access issues and call on school counselors to act on their ethical responsibility to address barriers and gaps. These may be student issues, policy issues, systems issues, or social justice issues. School counselors serve students best when they collaborate with other implementers of change to identify data-driven and equity-based priorities, determine measures of progress, and seek to implement activities or necessary reforms to support success for every student (Johnson, 2002).

Each year students in my CSP 769 course complete "The Data Project." For this assignment, which is typically referred to by students as the most challenging project and research paper in the program, students disaggregate multiple data sets from their fieldwork site and prepare a comprehensive PowerPoint presentation, which is presented to their school counselor and often to their administrators. This year, due in part to the advocacy of their vice principal, Ricardo Cooke, two students, Bryant and Andrew, were invited to share their presentation with the entire high school faculty the same week I was turning in the first draft of this text and sharing it with students. Below is the email I received the next day from Andrew sharing his story, complete with his thoughts on where it might be added to the text! Andrew and Bryant's PowerPoint is available in the online appendix.

Dr. Hatch,

I was reading through chapter 8 and found a space that this amazing story might fit in! I am thinking on page 180 (of the draft), after the conclusion of the "Data Teams" section and before the "Activity: Who Falls Through the Cracks" [He even advocated for where it goes!☺]

- I am pleased to say that our data presentation to the staff went very well! I am very satisfied with the way we presented our data and for the way we represented ourselves and the SDSU School Counseling Program. I am very proud of the fact that we conducted ourselves with class and professionalism throughout the presentation.
- The data presentation had to be shared with sensitivity and awareness. Some of it reflected very well of the school while some of the data showed areas for improvement. Some of the data highlighted achievement and gender gaps. There was the possibility that members of the staff may take the data as a personal reflection of themselves and/or their department and may not agree with the idea of an achievement gap. For this reason, it was very important that Bryant and I relay the data as it was and to not add any personal judgment.
- Before the start of the presentation, we circulated a sheet of paper for each faculty member in the room. At the top of the sheet of paper was the mission statement. We displayed this here so that faculty could think about the mission statement throughout our presentation. Next, we asked them to consider the following question: In terms of student data (demographics, graduation rates, A-G completion rates, college going rate, CAHSEE testing, AP, SAT/ACT), how do you think Steele Canyon compares to Valhalla High School, Grossmont Union High School District, and the State?
- At the beginning of our presentation, the VP at our high school and strong student and school counseling advocate gave us an introduction. He described the school's goal of moving toward data driven practices and policies, and that the school counseling program was taking the lead on this. He then stated that Bryant and I would be presenting data about the school as a way to show how the school counseling program is working towards being data driven.
- As an introduction before we presented the data, I addressed the following points to the staff:
  - Who we are: Interns from the SDSU School Counseling program and that we are very excited about the opportunity to share with you some data from students at Steele Canyon.
  - Thanked them for their time, we know that it is valuable.
  - Because we would only have 20 minutes, we respectfully request that they hold their questions until the end.
  - Why we are here today: To present a picture of student data at Steele Canyon. It is important to understand where we stand as a school and how we are performing.

- ○ Data comes from California Department of Ed. Taken from the Dataquest website, and it was reported by Steele Canyon High School.
- ○ We will compare various data pieces to Valhalla (because it is a similar school), the district, and the state and will be comparing three years: 2008–2011. This is the most recent available data. We do this because it can be beneficial to examine trends over time.
- ○ Not about teachers, admin, or school counselors, it's not a personal reflection on the school. It is just data . . . numbers

- After talking about these points in the introduction, we addressed the various data at the school. First, we talked about some of the staff perceptions at the school. To do this, we displayed various quotes from staff members about how they perceived their school was performing in relation to a like school, the district, and the state. Next, we addressed the demographics of the school and compared them to a like school, the district, and the state. From there, we addressed graduation rates, college-going rates, A-G completion rates, CAHSEE testing, AP/SAT/ACT testing data. To conclude the presentation, we highlighted strengths of the school as well as areas to target for growth. In addition, we described potential recommendations to improve the data.

- Concluding the presentation, there were several thoughtful questions and comments such as, "I think we should begin to talk about this gender gap. As you guys have shown, there is a large gender gap at this school and I think it is important to begin addressing it." There were also questions about finding out additional data for the school. Unfortunately, we could not get to all of the questions and comments because of the time sensitivity. However, it was promising to see the staff having so many questions and comments.

- Before we sat back down in our seats, the VP gave us a strong word again. This time, talking about all the hard work we had put into this presentation and how we did a lot of good things in beginning these types of conversations. He also talked to the staff about some of the things we have been doing for students and the difference we have been making at the school.

- After the meeting was over, Bryant and I both had several staff members congratulate us on our presentation. They had nothing but positive things to say about us and the data that we showed. Many of them wanted to know if we could send them the slides, and we assured them that we would send it out to the entire faculty. Overall, they appeared very impressed at what we had accomplished. Two of the other VPs also gave me a strong review. They each complimented us on our presentation and praised our professionalism and the way we conducted ourselves. They even asked questions and began to think out loud about other additional data that would be important to explore. At the end of the day, I ran into one of the teachers. This teacher is one of the department chairs and is a major power/political figure on campus. This person also congratulated me and told me that the presentation was 'very well done' and 'very polished.' Better yet, this teacher told me how they had a great conversation during lunch about some of the data that came up during the presentation!

- Overall, this was a tremendous experience. Here we were, as school counseling fieldwork students, capitalizing on the opportunity to present NECESSARY, IMPORTANT, and MEANINGFUL data to the staff. This was something that had never been done before at the school. This data was being seen by the staff for the very first time, so we understood the importance of what was taking place. As a result of the data presentation, we look forward to courageous conversations that will begin to take place.

Table 8.1   Who Falls Through the Cracks?

State Standardized Test Data

Activity Sheet

Grade Level →	Reading			Language			Spelling			Math		
	3	**7**	**10**	**3**	**7**	**10**	**3**	**7**	**10**	**3**	**7**	**10**
Asian	+10											
	52	50	40	56	54	46	60	54	X*	64	57	53
White	+8											
	50	48	43	51	51	45	48	47	X	56	48	47
African American	−5											
	37	36	31	39	39	33	42	39	X	43	35	36
Latino												
	37	35	33	41	40	34	42	37	X	47	37	38
Low SES												
	35	33	30	39	38	32	41	36	X	45	35	37
District Average	**42**	**43**	**39**	**45**	**46**	**41**	**45**	**43**	X	**50**	**43**	**44**

*There was no spelling test given in the 10th grade.

Source: author unknown; adapted for text.

ACTIVITY: WHO FALLS THROUGH THE CRACKS?

Disaggregating data is necessary when looking more closely at access, attainment, and achievement gaps in a school (NOSCA, 2011). Well-meaning educators are often involved in various kinds of data analysis and activities. Table 8.1 could depict many types of data: attendance rates, discipline, SAT scores, college-going rates, and so on. This table contains state standardized test data provided during professional development training. Note how the first disaggregated score was determined. The district average reading score in Grade 3 is 42%. Asian students scored 52% proficient in reading. Therefore, the "difference" is +10. For the White students, the difference is +8, and for the African American students, a −5. In the activity, professional development attendees were asked to fill out the rest of the chart and to respond to the questions below the chart within their small table groups. Note takers collected the comments for subsequent reporting. As you look at the data table, answer the questions for yourself before reading further. If possible, break into groups with others and share your thoughts before reading more. This will provide a helpful self-analysis during the activity.

Questions to Consider:

1. What trends do you notice about the data?
2. What might be some possible explanations for these data trends?
3. What steps should be taken to improve the data?
4. Who else needs to be engaged in this conversation?

[Answers to the disaggregation of data are provided below for convenience.]

State Standardized Test Data
Completed Activity Sheet

Grade Level →	Reading			Language			Spelling			Math		
	3	7	10	3	7	10	3	7	10	3	7	10
Asian	+10	+7	+1	+11	+8	+5	+15	+11		+14	+14	+9
	52	50	40	56	54	46	60	54	X	64	57	53
White	+8	+5	+4	+6	+5	+4	+3	+4		+6	+8	+3
	50	48	43	51	51	45	48	47	X	56	48	47
African American	−5	−7	−8	−6	−7	−8	−3	−4		−7	−8	−8
	37	36	31	39	39	33	42	39	X	43	35	36
Latino	−5	−8	−6	−4	−6	−7	−3	−6		−3	−6	−6
	37	35	33	41	40	34	42	37	X	47	37	38
Low SES	−7	−10	−9	−6	−8	−9	−4	−7		−5	−8	−7
	35	33	30	39	38	32	41	36	X	45	35	37
District Average	42	43	39	45	46	41	45	43	X	50	43	44

After each small group completed the data analysis and their table conversation, table reporters shared the table comments with the entire group. Listed below are samples of statements from responses shared with the entire group. As you read through the responses, imagine yourself as a school counselor in attendance at this meeting or training. What reactions do you have to these statements? Do you agree with the other faculty members' analyses of the data? Did you see these trends? What other trends did you see?

1. What trends do you notice about the data?

   - African American students' and Latino students' scores are far below those of other groups.
   - As students get older, scores are lower, and students fall farther behind.
   - Asian and White students are above average over time.
   - District average goes down as grade goes up.
   - Deviation from district average increases for African American students in higher grades.
   - There is a 22-point discrepancy in seventh-grade math between the scores of Asian students and those of low SES.
   - White and Asian students score above average, and other groups score below average.
   - Spelling scores are closer to district average for all groups.
   - Low-SES students have the lowest scores in all areas except math.
   - African American students score lowest of all groups in math.
   - Asian students in third grade have higher scores in spelling than in any other subject area.

- Asians score considerably higher than Whites in all subjects.
- Although Asian students enter the district with higher scores, it appears they lose ground over time as well.
- Regardless of race, all students lose ground over time.
- Third graders are performing the best.

Now, read the comments provided in answer to Question 2, below. These responses are reproduced with few edits. What is your reaction to these possible explanations? Do you agree or disagree they are reasonable explanations in relationship to the data provided? Are these the types of responses you would have expected to read? Are educators from your school more or less likely to respond as these educators did? Do any of these comments trouble you? Do any align with your thinking? What thoughts or feelings do you have as you read these responses? How might you have responded if you had been present at this meeting and heard these responses? What additional explanations did you think of that are not included below?

2. What might be some possible explanations for these data trends?

- Kids don't value education.
- The older kids get, the less they care.
- This is a bad year; it is a bad class.
- Kids come with lots of baggage; we cannot help them all.
- Some students (Asian, White) are better at test taking than others (African American, Latino).
- Middle school teachers are not preparing students well enough.
- Elementary teachers need to prepare students with better success skills.
- High school teachers do not care and do not promote the importance of tests.
- Educators lack cultural competency.
- Maybe Asian and White students are more dedicated.
- Questions on these tests are not culturally relative or relevant.
- We need more rigor.
- We pass kids along and we shouldn't; they need to be held back.
- Students with low SES do not have access to resources like computers.
- Students with low SES have less help at home.
- Lack of parental involvement.
- Low expectations from teachers.
- Latinos and African Americans are more likely to have low SES and are therefore more disadvantaged.
- Some cultures value education—some do not.
- Self-fulfilling prophecy.
- Latinos score lower because of their language issues.
- Latinos are English learners.
- Asians perform higher because of their culture.
- Environmental factors contribute.
- Curriculum is watered down (for some groups).
- Lack of cultural role models in schools.
- Students lose interest in school as they get older.
- Students in high school don't care about tests.

- Parents have to be more involved.
- Teachers only teach the smart students (cultural preference?).
- Kids do not care, so they don't try.
- Teachers are not doing their jobs, and the union protects them.
- Students did not attend preschool.
- We need new textbooks. (Our textbooks are outdated and don't meet standards.)

After listing all the suggestions, table groups discussed ideas for next steps. Below are the responses provided. Do you agree or disagree with these suggestions? Can you think of any other steps you might have suggested they take to improve the data?

3. What steps should be taken to improve the data?

- Make more ESL classes
- Teach to test
- Buy new textbooks
- Longer school day
- Eliminate PE and give more core courses
- Mandate preschool
- Smaller class sizes
- Tutoring mandatory for anyone failing a class
- Eliminate D grades and give A's, B's, C's, and F's
- Hire more school counselors
- Offer more supports to teachers in core classes
- Fire teachers whose students have repeatedly poor test scores
- Switch teachers around and place "better teachers" where needed
- Increase placement in advanced classes
- Put school in program improvement
- Response to Intervention (RTI)
- Collaborate and discuss data
- Hire curriculum coordinators
- Hire data coaches
- Tutoring
- Increase rigor and homework
- Reinstate summer school

4. Who else needs to be engaged in this conversation?

Responses to Question 4 included parents, teachers, administrators, counselors, community members, and anyone who wanted to participate in these conversations.

Time to Debrief: What Was Missing?

When analyzing school data, well-meaning educators may be quick to make program decisions based on immediate, shoot-from-the-hip responses such as those provided above to Question 3. At the end of the conversation above, members in one group agreed the best choice was to purchase new textbooks. What is your reaction to that decision? *The ways in which decisions are made using data are as important as what data are collected, when they are collected, how they are collected, and how they are presented.*

In this example, what type of data conversations can you imagine were occurring from the responses provided? Raw debate, polite discussion, skillful discussion, or dialogue? Dialogue involves members suspending their positions and participating in inquiry in order to remove assumptions and make new discoveries. What new discoveries might have been made if members were involved in inquiry? Rather than asking questions about contributing factors or possible solutions, members could have asked additional questions. *What question do you have about this data? What other data might be considered?* The following are questions that were not considered but should have been.

Questions of Inquiry

- How many schools and students do these data represent?
- How many students are in each group?
- How do these scores compare to the statewide data?
- How do these scores compare to last year's scores?
- How do these scores compare to the district average?
- How do these scores compare to schools with similar demographics?
- What role does language play in the data?
- Do we know the gender breakdown? Might there be a gender gap?
- Are the scores of special education students included in the data?
- What other populations should we be concerned with?
- We do not know the test scale; what scores constitute proficiency?
- Is there a combination of factors or an underlying dominant variable?
- What percentage of each ethnic group is categorized low SES?
- Is this a score or percentage rank?
- Are these scores from testing the same group of students in different years (cohort data)? Or a snapshot of different students in the same testing year? What percentage of the students in this district are English learners?
- What are the ethnic percentages of students in each demographic?
- What is the ethnic representation in the low-SES group?
- What is the school's transiency rate?
- Who is performing at an average level?
- How do these scores compare to benchmark assessments?
- What is the curriculum currently in use? Are teachers happy with it?
- What is the school doing to improve test scores?
- Have there been any recent school or districtwide interventions?
- Is there any improvement since new programs were started?
- Can we see the grades for these students? Do they align with the students' test scores?
- What is the college-going rate?

In the activity above, decisions were made based on reactions by faculty and staff utilizing one set of incomplete data. Participants had no reference to historical data, trend data, comparison data, or demographic data prior to being asked their opinions on contributing factors. As can occur when well-meaning people gather to address students' needs, beliefs impacted behaviors. Imagine sitting in the meeting as presented above and hearing some of the oppressive statements made regarding marginalized groups. As a school counselor, what would you do? What response would you have? Challenging colleagues in public spaces can be uncomfortable if passions overtake rational decision making and quickly steer a group away from dialogue into raw debate.

When engaged in challenging conversations, every attempt must be made to focus on the data and not the assumptions made by participants about the data. If the data are incomplete, suggest members hold their thoughts or opinions about what conclusions should be drawn or what next steps to take until more data are provided. Offer inquiries regarding the data as presented above. Suggest a subgroup of educators particularly interested in data-driven decision making gather the additional data to present at a future meeting. Creating a PowerPoint to provide a visual representation of the data with clearly labeled slides disaggregating historical, trend, and comparison data (see Figures 8.1, 8.2, and 8.3). If multiple data sets reveal consistent and compelling gaps, consider policies, practices, or procedures that may be contributing to or impeding student success. Then, provide information, research, or professional development directed at dispelling myths regarding the ability of all students to achieve (Education Trust, 2009.) Share research about evidenced-based intervention programs and interventions. Finally, continue to advocate for access- and opportunity-aligned shifts in policies, practices, and procedures.

USING DATA TO TELL YOUR STORY— ACHIEVEMENT GAP HIGH SCHOOL

As an introduction to using data to tell your story, refer to the data in Figure 8.1, from the fictitious XYZ High School, which reveal that all students attending XYZ HS are graduating at a relatively high rate. If these were the only data a team reviewed, potential achievement gaps might not be found. When looking at the trend in the data over time for XYZ HS (Figure 8.2), it appears that although the percentage of

Figure 8.1   Graduation Rates by Ethnicity: A Look at XYZ HS 2011–2012

	# of Seniors	# of Graduates	% Graduating
Asian	98	98	100%
Filipino	41	41	100%
Latino	52	49	94%
African American	32	32	100%
White	269	257	96%

XYZ HS for the most recent school year, yielded **high rates of graduates in all ethnic groups**

students graduating college eligible is greater at XYZ HS than the state and school district averages, when compared to a school with similar demographics, within the same district, XYZ HS's percentage of students graduating college eligible has decreased over time, while the percentage of students graduating college eligible at the fictitious ABC HS has increased (Figure 8.2).

Figure 8.2   Seniors Graduating College-Eligible: A Comparative Look Through Time

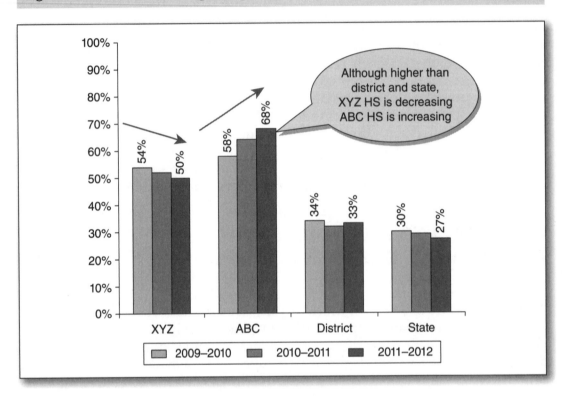

Now consider this distinction when referring to Figure 8.3, which shows percentages of students graduating college-eligible at the real (but fictitiously named) Achievement Gap High School. They appear similar to those of Another High School, the state, and the district. However, when disaggregated by ethnicity, clear achievement gaps emerge. At Achievement Gap HS, Latino students, who represent 88% of the population, are graduating at a rate of 66%, and only 24% graduate college eligible (Figure 8.4). The data also reveal gaps between Filipino, African American, and White students, although the text box does not specifically address that. Care must be taken when presenting data to equitably represent any and all achievement gaps to ensure interventions at a program or policy level are provided for all.

Imagine a data team was reviewing the college-eligibility rates and requested statewide test data. Figure 8.5 represents the state testing data for Achievement Gap HS. What trend might the data team notice? What additional data might the data team want to review?

After reviewing Figure 8.5, the team requests data on which students are enrolled in math at Achievement Gap HS. Figure 8.6 reveals the data for Achievement Gap HS indicating an achievement gap between Asian and Filipino students and Latino, African American, and White students. Data from Figure 8.6 might spur additional questions regarding policies and practices for how students access advanced math courses.

Figure 8.3 College Eligible Completion Rates: Achievement Gap School Comparison to Similar School, District and State

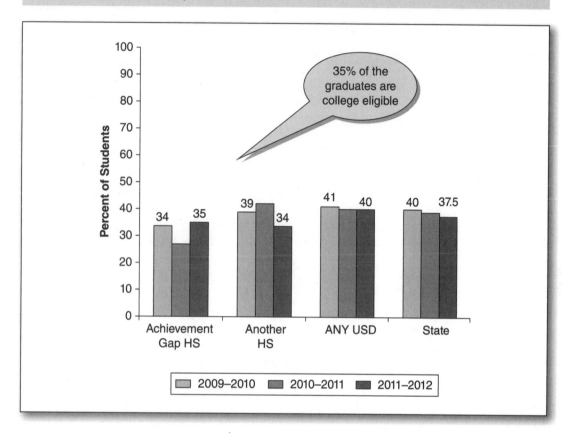

Figure 8.4 College Eligible Completion Rates: Trends Over Three Years for Different Student Groups at Achievement Gap HS

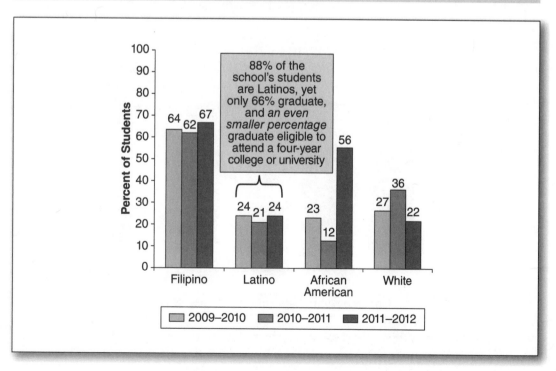

Figure 8.5 Standardized Test T Scores: Algebra 1 and English Language Arts

Achievement Gap HS students performing proficient and above in **Algebra 1**

	2009–2010	2010–2011	2011–2012
9th grade	39%	14%	8%
10th grade	6%	11%	6%
11th grade	5%	1%	7%

Achievement Gap HS students performing proficient and above in **English Language Arts**

	2009–2010	2010–2011	2011–2012
9th grade	39%	31%	8%
10th grade	25%	29%	6%
11th grade	24%	25%	7%

At this rate, in a few years, % of proficient students may be ~0%

* Every year the % of students performing proficient DECREASES!!!!

Figure 8.6 Students Enrolled in Advanced Math and Science

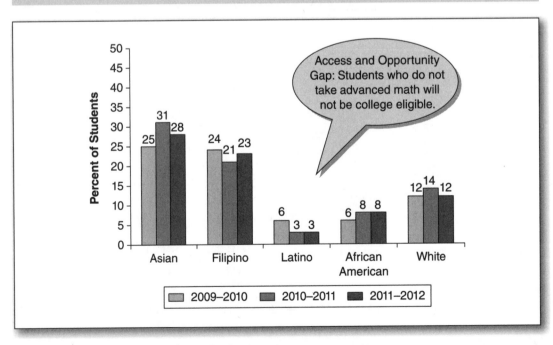

Access and Opportunity Gap: Students who do not take advanced math will not be college eligible.

In a different district, faculty at LMN HS requested the data team provide information on the numbers of students receiving free and reduced-price lunch. Faculty wondered if there was a shift in these numbers, and if the shift may have contributed in some way to a leveling of test scores despite best efforts to improve them. As seen in Figure 8.7, the percentage of students receiving free and reduced-price lunch increased from 45% to 71%. In this circumstance, the data provide the faculty additional insight into the challenges that may be impacting test scores and validated the teachers' inquiry, which suggests more resources may be needed than previously predicted.

Figure 8.7 Percentage of Students Receiving Free and Reduced-Price Lunch

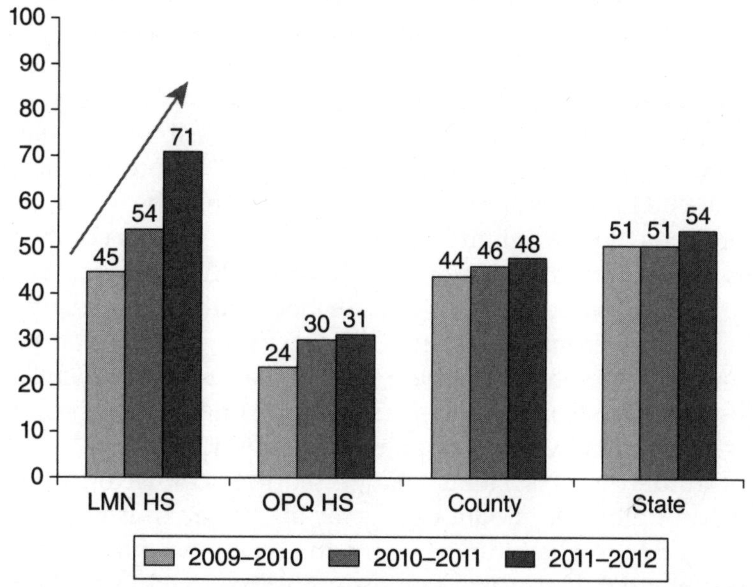

Below are examples of the types of policies, practices, and procedures that might be uncovered once data are presented and inquiry is made regarding potential contributing factors to achievements gaps. What types of systems change action plans might be created to address these policy needs?

- Students who are late to class are locked out until the next period.
- Students who are tardy three times are suspended from school.
- Students with ten days of absence receive an F in the class.
- Students are required to get a C in algebra to take geometry. Seniors are credit deficient because they are taking algebra repeatedly for no credit.
- Teachers give counselors lists of students to remove from their classes, because they have identified these students as "non–college prep."
- Students are not allowed to participate in middle school graduation if they owe money to the library.

ADVOCATING FOR SYSTEMS CHANGE

Many of the systems issues presented result in *gatekeeping,* or keeping particular students out of specific classes and programs (Hart & Jacobi, 1992). Response requires the school counselors to utilize a politically appropriate advocacy voice, prepared with a thorough analysis of the data, a strong understanding of the issues at hand, a thoughtful recommendation for equitable stress-free solutions, and opportunities to consider new ways of providing access to students without blaming past practice. When conversations regarding the data begin, strong beliefs about students, families, and opportunities may emerge.

School counselors are encouraged to support their recommendations with research and to ask others to do the same. When engaged in discussions, counselors should repeat any demeaning statements they hear to help others recognize these statements' inappropriateness. Sometimes people don't realize what they've said until they hear it repeated back. School counselors serve as social justice agents of change when they work to challenge low expectations. Be prepared for some to dislike your suggestions or advocacy and for them to shift their focus to personal attacks. Remind yourself you are advocating for students; disagreements may be addressed to you but are more likely addressing the possibility of change.

If teams come to agreements on challenging decisions, ensure minutes are taken and disseminated. Decide for yourself what you are willing to be on TV or in print for. Can you live with it? Then, do the right thing for students, even if it's not the popular thing to do. Students will be advantaged or disadvantaged by the voices and actions of school counselors and other educators. Adults in the school setting make daily decisions that impact students' future economic potential. Each and every decision to speak or not speak, to act or not act, demonstrates the potential to impact students' future career options and life opportunities. Bystander behavior is similarly problematic in these circumstances, as it is with bully behavior on the playground.

Intentional guidance for systems change requires counselors to use data, dialogue, passion, and ethics to model caring for all students. It requires a conscious commitment each day to all students' rights to access and opportunity in fulfilling their academic potential. It requires school counselors to educate themselves about what is and is not working in the system for first–generation immigrant youth, youth of color, and youth of poverty and to design and implement systemic closing-the-gap activities to support opportunities for all youth (Lee & Ransom, 2011; NOSCA, 2012). This commitment must carry the same urgency, value, and importance as caring about any other type of crisis in our students' lives.

Risk taking in these circumstances is no longer optional behavior.

Reese House was my dear friend, my advocate, and my hero. Reese urged school counselors to become more involved in school reform as leaders and advocates of student success. Reese served as director of the National Center for Transforming School Counseling at the Education Trust. Reese advocated for school counselors to play a greater role in closing the achievement gap between disadvantaged students and their more privileged peers. The following are quotes attributed to Reese House and collected by Peggy Hines, director of the Education Trust National Center for Transforming School Counseling (January, 2010).

Advocacy Thoughts From Reese House

1. You can advocate in different ways—softly, noisily, and so on.

2. There are different kinds of advocates; not everyone is the same.

3. Perhaps your idea of an advocate is based on a stereotype.

4. Data are very useful for advocates, because data speak for change, taking the onus off of you, the person.

5. Being an advocate is not easy. People take potshots at you, you become a target, it is not safe, and it is not always nice.

6. When you question policies, systems, plans, people will question you; expect the same kind of response as you give to others.

7. The best way to create change is to take action.

8. Taking action involves some risks—be aware of the risks.

9. Develop allies to help you with your work; who can make a difference and help?

10. Ask the person you think may be a blocker to help you with the project.

11. Find common ground for change.

12. Let your passion drive your work.

13. Know the power base of the school and community.

14. Trust yourself and that you are doing the right thing.

15. Believe in what you do, and do what you believe.

16. Realize that you cannot be an advocate 24 hours a day, especially alone—you will burn yourself out.

17. Collaborate with others.

18. Set realistic goals.

19. Take realistic steps.

20. Have a plan, be willing to change your plan, evaluate your plan, change your plan, create a new plan, evaluate your plan, create a new plan, change your plan, evaluate your plan, and so on.

Advocacy Questions

1. Is the system designed to serve the students or the adults?

2. Is sitting back and watching bad policy hurt students what you want to do?

3. What is my responsibility to students who are underserved, get the short end of the stick, and are discriminated against?

4. Is the issue at hand important enough to take the necessary risk?

5. Who benefits from the status quo?

6. Who benefits from change?

7. Who are the power brokers in the community?

8. What is the risk of inaction?

9. What happens if I do nothing?

10. Who gains/loses by your actions as a counselor?

11. How much power do I/you have?

12. How do you get enough power to make change in the system?

13. Who readily gives up power?

(Continued)

(Continued)

14. How do I know that I work for the good of all children?

15. Am I resilient? How do I get back up to fight another day?

16. Who/what helps me to be a strong advocate for others? (beliefs, etc.)

17. How do I get others to help me?

18. What do I fear most about advocating for my students?

INTENTIONAL GUIDANCE ACTION PLANS FOR SYSTEMS CHANGE

Intentional guidance for systems change action plans are designed to specifically address policies, practices, and procedures the data reveal may be contributing to discrepancies among student groups in areas of attendance, behavior, or academic achievement outcomes. Through leadership, advocacy, and collaboration, the school counselor works with others to promote additional purposeful schoolwide programs and activities and to create new or revised ineffective policies, practices and procedures. As mentioned in Chapter 5, the ASCA National Model recommends utilizing the Closing the Gap Action Plan for planned activities and resources leveraged to close academic and behavioral gaps when analysis of the data reveals discrepancies among student groups (2012a). A primary distinction between the intentional guidance for systems change action plan and the ASCA plan is that a counselor implementing ASCA's plan may focus on providing additional direct services (small group, etc.) and may or may not address systems change (policy, practice, procedure) issues.

Figure 8.8 addresses the lack of systemic processes or procedures for student referrals to the office, which resulted in the school counselor at the XYZ Elementary School providing various and inconsistent "random acts of discipline intervention." Some teachers sent students to the office after a few minor infractions, while others exhausted their extensive classroom management procedures prior to referral. Consequently, a disproportionate and inequitable number of students received discipline and interventions in some classes as compared to others. This gap in referrals, discipline, suspensions, and opportunities for data-driven interventions led to this action plan for systems change.

The systems changes may also be designed through the lens of access and opportunity. In the second action plan for systemic change (Figure 8.9), the activities are designed to address the opportunity and attainment gaps for Latinos at XYZ High School. Note that both plans add a research quote (helpful for Flashlight PowerPoint creation, which will be described in Chapter 10). Also, note these both utilize ASCA ethical guidelines as opposed to student standards, as the systemic change issues presented here call for the school counselor to draw from her or his ethical responsibilities to address multicultural and social justice advocacy and leadership and to "share results and best practices in assessing, implementing and annually evaluating the outcomes of data-driven school counseling programs with measurable academic, career/college and personal/social competencies for every student" (ASCA, 2010b).

Additional systemic change action plans are available in the online appendix.

Figure 8.8 XYZ Elementary School Intentional Guidance for Systems Change

Goal: Decrease suspensions by 30%. Improve school climate (reduce violence on campus).

Data-Identified Need: 20% increase in suspensions from 20XX–20XX.

Systems Concerns: (1) Lack of consistent classroom rules and expectations, (2) lack of consistent schoolwide discipline plan, (3) lack of referral form for use when students are sent from classroom to office for discipline, (4) lack of data entry into student database of referrals, (5) lack of ability to query students with multiple offences for intervention

Research: There is a strong relationship between social behavior and academic success. Social skills (getting along with peers, teamwork) positively predict academic achievement (Malecki & Elliott, 2002). Students who behave better achieve better (e.g., Van Horn, 2003).

Person Who Will Coordinate/ Participate in Systemic Change Action Plan?	ASCA Student Standards/State Standards or Ethical Guidelines	Activities That Will Occur to Create Systems Change	Policies, Practices, Procedures, and Documents to Review /Revise or Create	Project Start/ End	Evaluation Method (How will you measure results?)		Intended Effect on Academics, Behavior, or Attendance?
					Perception Data (ASK Examples)	Results Data	
Coordinator: X [Name] School Counselor	*ASCA Ethical Guidelines: C. 3.* a. Share the role of the school counseling program in ensuring data-driven academic, career/college and personal/social success competencies for every student, resulting in specific	(1) Review district policies/ practices for discipline	Education Code / District Board Policies	Fall 20xx through Spring 20xx	*Attitude:* % faculty who believe in creating common classroom behavior expectations	*Achievement Related (AR):* Decrease in discipline referrals to the office	Students will experience increased consistency in behavior management in classroom.
Team Members: X [Name] Administrator(s)		(2) Review education code	PBIS Training Course			Decrease in suspensions	Classroom climate will improve.
X [Name] School Counselor(s)		(3) Create common classroom expectations, rules, and procedures	Referral Forms		% faculty who believe in providing positive behavior supports prior to discipline	Increase in school climate data (CHKS)	As classroom climate improves, learning is impacted.
X [Name] Teacher(s)			SWIS or Other Student Database System				
X [Name(s)] Other(s)		(4) Create schoolwide discipline (positive behavior/ intervention support plan	Discipline Policies		*Skills:* % faculty who can accurately complete a discipline and counseling referral (use correct form)	*Achievement (A):* Monitor academic achievement (benchmarks and state test scores)	

(Continued)

Figure 8.8 (Continued)

Person Who Will Coordinate/ Participate in Systemic Change Action Plan?	ASCA Student Standards/State Standards or Ethical Guidelines	Activities That Will Occur to Create Systems Change	Policies, Practices, Procedures, and Documents to Review /Revise or Create	Project Start/ End	Evaluation Method (How will you measure results?)		Intended Effect on Academics, Behavior, or Attendance?
					Perception Data (ASK Examples)	Results Data	
	outcomes/indicators with all stakeholders (ASCA, 2010b). [Preamble] Each person has the right to feel safe in school environments that school counselors help create, free from abuse, bullying, neglect, harassment or other forms of violence (ASCA, 2010b).	(5) Create schoolwide consistent discipline referral form for use when students are sent from classroom to office

(6) Create school counseling referral form

(7) Ensure data entry of referral form into SWIS (or Aeries)

(8) Query behavior data each month to identify students in greatest need of intervention | | | *Knowledge:*

% faculty who know differences among Level 1, 2, and 3 behaviors (PBIS model)

% faculty who properly define zero tolerance | | |

Principal's Signature   Date   Date of Staff Presentation   Prepared By

Figure 8.9 XYZ High School Intentional Guidance for Systems Change

Goal: Increase percentage of Latino students graduating college eligible by 15% over next three years.

Data–Identified Need: Site rates for all students graduating college eligible increased 11% over two years, but there was a 2% decline in the rate for Latinos. Latino students are disproportionately underenrolled in college-prep courses (37% as compared to 22% White and 30% Asian). Few sections of Spanish are offered to students—over 100 more students signed up than there was room for in courses; students were given non–college-prep alternatives.

Systems Concern: Opportunity/access concerns are impacting ability to graduate college eligible. (1) Prerequisites require B or better for some college-going courses and honors courses. (2) AP courses require B or better GPA and teacher recommendation. (3) Master schedule does not have enough sections of Spanish. (4) Students/parents are confused about college requirements. (5) School counselors have been inconsistent regarding course placement policies. (6) Latinos are disproportionately underenrolled in honors/AP courses.

Research: "When students value the work they are doing, they feel a sense of belonging in the classroom context in which they are working, feel capable of succeeding, and believe they will master challenging material with effort, they are much more likely to engage in difficult work and see it through to completion (Farrington et al., 2012).

Person Who Will Coordinate/ Participate in Systemic Change Action Plan?	ASCA Student Standards/State Standards or Ethical Guidelines	Activities That Will Occur to Create Systems Change	Policies, Practices, Procedures Documents to Review/Revise or Create	Project Start/ End	Evaluation Method (How will you measure results?)		Intended Effect on Academics, Behavior, or Attendance?
					Perception Data (ASK Examples)	Results Data	
Coordinator: X [Name] School Counselor	ASCA Ethical Guidelines:	(1) Team reviews data with faculty revealing decline in eligibility in subgroups (especially Latino).	Course Enrollment Data	Fall 2013 through Spring 2016	*Attitude:* % faculty who believe students have the right to take honors and AP courses	*Achievement Related:* Increase in number of sections offered in college-prep courses	All students will have access to rigorous courses.
Team Members:	A.3.b. Ensure equitable academic, career, post-secondary access and personal/social opportunities for all students through the use of data to help close achievement gaps and opportunity gaps (ASCA, 2010b).	(2) Team reviews policies/ practices for student placement and creates consistent protocols.	Course Curriculum Guide				More Latino students believe they are expected to achieve.
X [Name] Administrator(s)			Education Code / District Board Policies		% faculty who believe the teacher has the right to choose which students are in their classes	Increase in number of students enrolled in college-prep courses	
X [Name] School Counselor(s)		(3) School counselors/team create new course registration forms promoting rigor.	Course Registration Form				More Latino students take rigorous college-prep courses.
X [Name] Teacher(s)			Curriculum Materials for College/Career Lessons (in English and Spanish)		*Skills:* % faculty who can analyze student transcripts	Increase in number of students taking honors/AP courses (and passing AP exams)	
X [Name] Other(s)		(4) Team revises curriculum guide to remove gatekeeping barriers to and prerequisites for honors/AP courses.					More Latino students graduate college eligible.

(Continued)

Figure 8.9 (Continued)

Person Who Will Coordinate/ Participate in Systemic Change Action Plan?	ASCA Student Standards/State Standards or Ethical Guidelines	Activities That Will Occur to Create Systems Change	Policies, Practices, Procedures Documents to Review/Revise or Create	Project Start/ End	Evaluation Method (How will you measure results?)		Intended Effect on Academics, Behavior, or Attendance?
					Perception Data (ASK Examples)	Results Data	
	E.2. g. Work as advocates and leaders in the school to create equity-based school counseling programs that help close any achievement, opportunity, and attainment gaps that deny all students the chance to pursue their educational goals (ASCA, 2010b).	(5) Administration/team provide faculty with professional development to dispel myths about college access/opportunity. (6) Administration/team promote/create "student-driven" master schedule. (7) School counselors utilize College Board's AP Potential tool to identify students with likelihood of success in AP courses. (8) Parent presentations are provided in Spanish on college-going culture. (9) Latino graduates now in college return to mentor students and encourage college-going culture.	Assessment Tools Master Schedule/ Timelines Policies AP Potential Data		% faculty who understand what a "student-driven" master schedule means *Knowledge:* % faculty to know the college entrance requirements % faculty who know statistics on success rates for students who take rigorous courses compared to those that don't	Increase in number of students taking PSAT *Achievement (A):* % students graduating college eligible % students passing AP courses and tests % students who apply to, are accepted at, and matriculate past one year of college	More students will apply to and be accepted into college.

Principal's Signature   Date   Date of Staff Presentation   Prepared By

ACTIVITY: SCENARIOS TO DISCUSS

Below are issues that came up at a recent high school counselor meeting. What thoughts or ideas do you have for how you might address these needs at your school? Which scenarios might call for utilizing an action plan for systemic change?

1. A student states he wants to get into sixth-period PE, because he wants to play football or basketball. However, if you remove the student from the sixth-period grant-funded "academy class," he may no longer receive his "academy" certification upon graduation. Further, removing the student from sixth-period PE will impact the number of students enrolled in the academy, which could affect his or her eligibility for grant funding. One idea is for the student to take the academy class in another period. Oh no! The only other time the course is offered is fifth period. Unfortunately, there are already 38 kids enrolled in the fifth-period class, and 34 kids are in the sixth-period class. (The union states classes may have a maximum of 36 students.) The student still wants to play sports (and now the basketball coach is pressuring the counselor to make it happen as well, because the student needs to "lift" e.g. work out in the weight room).

2. The Spanish teacher calls a counselor and wants a student taken out of her Spanish 1/2 class. She tells the counselor in the third week of school, "This kid won't make it" and asks to have the student rescheduled. The student also has mild behavioral concerns. The next day, a different teacher calls and wants the school counselor to take a student out of his AP Spanish class. He is certain the student "won't make it" and recommends the student drop the course. This student does not have behavioral concerns. (Would it matter?)

3. The high school and the middle school have an articulation agreement regarding placement of students taking eighth-grade algebra. If a student gets a D or an F in eighth grade, he or she is to repeat algebra in ninth grade, regardless of state testing scores for proficiency. Several students have a D or an F in Algebra I (from eighth grade) and performed at the proficient or advanced level on statewide assessment tests. They are now in ninth grade, and their algebra teachers claim the students have met competency requirements and are already bored in class. They want the students moved to geometry. The counselor is wondering about the impact of moving the students from algebra to geometry, given that they have not passed algebra with a C or better (which many colleges require). At the same time, 15 different students earned a C or D in the first semester of eighth grade in their algebra course but then received an A, B, or C in second semester. Since they tested below proficient on the state assessment, they were also placed in ninth grade algebra. These students are asking to test out of algebra to move to geometry. The counselor is wondering if advocating for this option is in the students' best interest.

4. Newly implemented night school requirements state students may not take night school if they have a D and that night school is only for remediation for F's. However, passing the night school course with C or better earns college-prep credit. A student comes to the counselor right before finals week with a D in a difficult course. The student is concerned she might not score well enough on the final to get a C. She's wondering if she should "fail" her final to get an F so she can retake the course in night school.

5. At one school, counselors meet to support and approve each other's students' independent study (IS) contracts before the head counselor approves. A student wants to have an IS contract. She is a 12th grader who is classified as an 11th grader because she is missing five credits. The student has already talked to several teachers, who agree to do an IS in geometry (F), algebra II (D), and art (F). She also wants to do an IS for Algebra I, because she can't go to night school (because she got a D, and night school is only allowed for F's). She prefers IS because she also has a job, and that would make it hard to attend night school. Would you recommend the counselors approve? The IS courses are not given all at once but are sequential, and students must pass one before enrolling in the next. She has a 1.84 GPA, and she needs a 2.0 to graduate.

Finding (Making) Time: Setting Priorities

> It's all about time.
> How DO you spend your time?
> How WOULD you like to spend your time?
> Who or what CONTROLS your time?
> How can you find MORE time?

TIME AND CHOICES

School counselors often share they have little control over their time. Many complain they are at the mercy of their administrators, who do not understand what they do (Louis, Jones, & Barajas, 2001). Yet, school counselors often do make choices about how they spend their time. Consider the following scenario: The school counselor is about to run a group or teach a lesson in a classroom, and the office clerk says, "Mrs. Smith [a parent] is on the phone for you." At this moment, the school counselor has many choices. She might stop and take the call right there and be a bit late to group or class. Or she might politely ask the clerk to

- Take a message
- Route the call to her answering machine at her desk
- Inform Mrs. Smith she is out for the day
- Inform Mrs. Smith she will call her back later in the day

- Remind Mrs. Smith about drop-in time, as the counselor is running groups for the remainder of the day
- Schedule Mrs. Smith for an appointment
- Find out why Mrs. Smith is calling, and, depending on what the concern is, ask the clerk to

  o Respond to the inquiry (e.g., what day is her parent-teacher conference?)
  o Inform Mrs. Smith that the answer is in a PowerPoint tutorial on the school counselor website (e.g., how do I read my child's transcript?)
  o Refer Mrs. Smith to the administrator (e.g., my child had his wallet stolen!), the teacher (e.g., what is my child's homework?), the attendance clerk (e.g., my child was out sick), or another appropriate service provider

School counselors make choices every day about how their time is spent, so whether a parent is calling or dropping in, what is the best choice? Does the school counselor stop and provide immediate service or delegate the first line of problem solving to someone else? Is there a system in place to support the professional school counselor's role in providing services by appointment through the use of a calendar? Does the administrator support this system? Administrator support is essential, because if a parent cannot see a counselor immediately, the administrator may be the parent's next stop. It is important that the administrator supports the collaboratively created and mutually agreed upon system for providing both scheduled and unscheduled counseling services.

Similar situations might occur if teachers stopped by the school counselors' room and peeked in to say hello. At that moment there are many options, ranging from a quick, "Hi" to "Hey, how is your daughter liking college?" either of which could lead to a 10- to 15-minute conversation. Of course no one is encouraging the school counselor to be antisocial; rather, the introduction to this chapter on time management is intentionally sharing scenarios to serve as a reminder that the efficient use of time is essential when implementing an effective school counseling program. With so many students on the caseload, important decisions must be made regarding how school counselors will use their time.

> We have consistently been impressed with the dedication and hard work of virtually all of the individuals with whom we have been involved. And yet, we are concerned that a great deal of energy, enthusiasm and resources are being expended in ineffective ways."
> —The Center for Higher Education Policy Analysis (Tierney & Hagedorn, 2001)

Administrators often share concerns regarding school counselors' use of time. For example, a high school counselor left a message complaining that the administrator asked the counselors to proctor the state tests. When asked about the rationale for his decision, the administrator explained he was on his way to order substitutes after a meeting concerning state test protocols. When he walked by the counseling office he saw that the counselors' schedules were open; so he filled them. He explained that because they weren't scheduled to do anything anyway, they might as well proctor tests. The counselors later confessed they were not in the habit of keeping a calendar; they called students in order of referral and had hoped to see their seniors that week. An empty calendar is problematic, as administrators (and others) may come to believe counselors are not busy and therefore can spend their time helping with noncounseling activities, or administrators may simply expect counselors to be available for students or parents in an on-call capacity whenever students or parents want to drop in.

Busy Professionals? Or Always Available?

Sending the message of "always available" is counterproductive to the role of any professional, including the school counselor. Imagine for a moment you wanted to see your dentist, and when you called to make an appointment, they said: "Come right down! We are available right now and ready to see you!" What if you could walk into the dentist's office and the dentist was able to see you without a scheduled appointment? How confident would you be that this particular dentist could properly fill your cavity? When school counselors are expected (or believe they are expected) to be in their offices waiting for parents or students to call or stop by to ask for their help, they send a message of availability that is counterproductive to the professional role of the counselor. School counselors who are always available to see parents or students are actually *not* performing the role of a professional school counselor.

Professionals are not sitting around ready to jump up and assist whoever walks through the door. A professional sets appointments. A professional is busy. A professional has a secretary or clerk who provides triage, answers frontline questions, manages a calendar, and makes appointments. Professionals have a plan of action. They know what they are doing, when, where, and why. They are accountable for the outcomes they seek for themselves within the organization. They have agreements with their administrators regarding their roles and responsibilities, which are appropriately aligned with and suitable for their training, salary, and experience in the institution.

In collaboration with the administrator, school counselors can work with classified staff to create a list of responsibilities, so clerks, secretaries, and other staff can support the school counselors in accomplishing the roles they are trained to perform. One helpful tip is to create a laminated page that explains the following:

1. Which student, teacher, or parent information questions are most appropriately answered by the frontline support staff (clerks, etc.)?

2. Which problems or questions should be referred to

   a. Administrators?
   b. Teachers?
   c. Others?

3. Which problems or questions are appropriate for an appointment within a week or two with a student's assigned school counselor?

4. Which problems or questions require an appointment today or tomorrow with a student's assigned school counselor?

5. Which problems or questions require an immediate intervention with any available school counselor? (See counselor-of-the-day discussion later in this chapter.)

6. Which problems are urgent enough to necessitate interrupting the assigned school counselor in any activity on campus (or calling the counselor back from a training off campus)?

School counselors are encouraged to work with their staff and administration to create this system and share it with staff and parents via newsletters and websites.

Successful planning and consistency of implementation will contribute to improved efficiency and customer satisfaction.

Are School Counselors Starters or Utility Players?

Coaching or playing on a sports team likely provides familiarity with the terms *starter* and *utility player*. A starter is a player who actively participates in the event and is often considered the best player at his or her respective position. There is often an element of prestige associated with being a starter (Starting Lineup, n.d.). A utility player is a player capable of playing consistently and in any of several positions (Utility Player, n.d.). Utility players may also be considered substitutes or bench players. Some are content serving as utility players simply because they are part of a team. Others might do anything they are asked (such as substitute for first base even though they usually play catcher), because they want to please the coach and show allegiance to the team. Utility players may also have other responsibilities, such as keeping score, gathering equipment, and supporting the needs of the starters.

> How do you think the school counselors are viewed at your school?
> Are they considered starters?
> Do they act like starters?
> Are they treated like utility players?
> Do they act like utility players?

Fair-share responsibilities are those everyone in the school contributes to (ASCA, 2012a; Gysbers & Henderson, 2012). If all educators are counting state tests or taking a turn supervising afterschool sports, it is appropriate for school counselors to take a turn also. If school counselors are the only people in school counting tests or supervising sports, then it is no longer considered a fair-share responsibility. The school counselor may have become a utility player in the school. School counselors, just like every other professional in the school, are asked at times to contribute to the overall operation of the school by assisting with activities that are beyond their training and expertise. Consider how much of the school counselors' time is spent in ways that are outside the role and training of the school counselor and whether the tasks are appropriate and necessary in light of the school counselors' training, the exact urgency of this need to the running of the school, and why the school counselor has been specifically selected to perform these tasks instead of others. In some small or rural schools with very limited school personnel, there is possibly more fair-share time expected from everyone than in larger schools. It is important to consider the amount of time spent in fair-share responsibilities compared to other professionals in schools and in comparison to other use of time measures for school counselors.

ASCA's latest edition of the National Model provides a "Use of Time Assessment," a helpful tool in considering how a school counselor's time is spent (ASCA, 2012a). While monitoring counselor time every 15 minutes seems excessive, it is appropriate for school counselors to consider, on a regular basis, how much of their overall time is spent in direct services, indirect services, program management (which includes the appropriate use of time in fair-share responsibilities) and nonschool counseling tasks (ASCA, 2012a).

Is This a Good Use of a Master's Degree?

Another way to determine whether a task or activity is appropriate should be to consider, "Is this activity a good use of a master's degree?" Most school counselors have the equivalent of a master's degree. This implies they are a "master" of something, presumably school counseling. At times during my trainings, I stand up on a chair as I say, "You have a master's degree!" in an effort to create a visual portrayal of a school counselor's position as elevated. Is a master's degree required to count state tests? Create the awards banquet program? Enter student registration numbers in the computer? Tell parents

when the SAT dates are? Organize a career day? Schedule SSTs or IEPs? Monitor lunch detention? Employees with master's degrees are expensive. If school counselors are spending valuable time performing these activities, whether by choice or because they are required to, it is probably time to rethink the purpose of the role of the credentialed school counselor. One of the best ways to begin this process is by working with the administrator to create an Annual Agreement (ASCA, 2012a) formerly called the Management Agreement (ASCA, 2003, 2005).

THE ANNUAL AGREEMENT

The Annual Agreement between the school counseling program team and the administration is an appropriate and necessary component of an efficient and effective school counseling program (ASCA, 2012a). The ASCA National Model includes a space in the Annual Agreement template for the mission statement and program goals. These serve as important reminders for everyone signing the agreement that the focus for all activities should be on the outcome goals of students. The recommendations for use of time and for when the advisory council meet are included in the template. One important shift in the Annual Agreement is referencing the previous years' results report when developing the annual calendar and action plan. Space is provided for assignments of professional collaborations and responsibilities, budget requirements, office organization (including hours of operation), and clarity for roles of other support service providers (ASCA, 2012a).

Completing an Annual Agreement can be a very powerful advocacy tool for the school counseling profession districtwide. It can also be a challenging experience if school counselors at a school site or in a district are not all on the same page. This can be especially problematic, because administrators may not be clear on appropriate roles. When one school counselor sends the message that it is reasonable or appropriate to spend 50% of her time performing nonschool counselor activities, it impacts the rest of the school counselors. In larger districts, administrators discuss what their school counselors are doing. Consider the impact on the entire district's counseling program when the school counseling team at one school site agrees to take major responsibility for the master schedule or meting out discipline. As your team completes the Annual Agreement, consider the following ideas and suggestions.

Student Assignment

When making decisions about student assignments, consider the pros and cons of assignment by alphabet versus assignment by grade level. While little research exists on this topic, school counselors report advantages and disadvantages to each (Akos, Schuldt, & Walendin, 2009). If school counselors are in a large high school with ratios that allow two or more counselors at each grade level, then grade-level counselor assignments can provide the advantage of a team approach to focus on the particular needs of the grade level. There are benefits to having a job-alike partner for each school counselor. For example, it can be very helpful when designing and implementing core curriculum and data-driven interventions for an entire grade level (ninth graders with two or more F's; juniors with less than 120 credits).

When there is only one school counselor at each grade level, there is no one to consult with regarding job-alike needs. In addition, if a high school counselor were to leave prior to senior year, the impact on students would be tremendous. The new school counselor would likely have no history of the students in their most important year and no counselor in the same grade level to consult. Grade-level assignments at the high school level tend to result in silo programs, as responsibilities vary greatly. Counselors deliver what "their" students need in "their" grade level, and not necessarily what the counselor who had that grade level provided the year before. This is problematic for teachers and parents who find the delivery of services inconsistent year to year. When consistency suffers, the school counseling program loses credibility. Grade-level counselors also report serious burnout after serving in ninth and twelfth grades, caused by the many needs of those students (Akos et al., 2009).

Counselors at high schools that assign students to counselors according to the first letter of the student's last name have the benefit of family connectedness with prior siblings and staying current about what is expected in all grades for students, but they often find it challenging to provide equitable and comprehensive services throughout the four grade levels, due to the transition needs of incoming ninth graders and the college application assistance necessary for seniors. Also, if school counselors aren't in agreement about service delivery, teachers find it confusing when the A–F counselor pulls their tenth-grade students out of class for individual student planning, but the G–M counselor does not. Consistency is vital to the reputation of the school counseling program.

Alphabetical or grade-level decisions tend to impact elementary and middle schools less than they do high schools. Many middle school counselors report finding it helpful to have grade-level assignments and prefer to follow their students from sixth through eighth grade. Regardless of the student assignment method school counselors select, the most important variable for students' success is the ability of the entire team to work together as a collective unit when designing the programs and services students will receive. Whether they are assigned students by grade level or alphabetically, school counselors are strongly encouraged to participate in the design and implementation of a consistent program of schoolwide core curriculum, individual student plans, and agreed-upon data-driven interventions for all students.

Counselor of the Day

One helpful way to manage efficiency in the school counseling office is to assign one school counselor to serve as the "counselor of the day" (Johnson & Johnson, 2001). This is most helpful in large schools with many school counselors rotating in this role; the counselor of the day responds to students in crisis or with immediate or urgent needs, while others in the department maintain their calendared activities, providing curriculum, attending SST meetings, and running groups without interruption. As previously discussed, it is necessary to ensure classified personnel are provided clear instructions for which types of situations necessitate seeing the counselor of the day. Most counselors state that changing student schedules is not a good reason to see the counselor of the day, while counseling a student reporting he was threatened or working with a crying student in crisis is most appropriate. One way to consider this role is much like that of a doctor in an urgent care clinic who provides necessary and timely intervention but not long-term heath care.

School Counselor Availability (Office Hours)

When is the school counseling office open for students, teachers, and parents? While doing a recent site visit, a sign on the door to the school counseling office read, "Closed for Lunch." It happened to be during the students' lunchtime. If students wanted to see a school counselor, they would have to come before or after school. Upon further investigation, it became apparent that the school counselors' entire schedule mirrored the students' schedules. Counselors arrived when students did and left at the students' last bell. This meant the only time to see students was during class time. Clearly this was not in the best interest of the students.

Always a School Counselor—Even on Supervision

At an overcrowded school in a growing community, administrators were concerned because of the sheer number of students on the grounds at lunchtime, and they requested assistance from the school counselors for additional supervision. School counselors resisted, because they wanted to be available to students during that time in their offices, and they considered lunch supervision a noncounselor activity. Although "lunch supervision" was one of their "noncounselor functions" in previous agreements with their administrator, everyone agreed it was a safety issue. Administrators simply needed more eyes and ears. After some brainstorming of ideas, these creative counselors decided to set up a college/career information table in the quad for students to visit, and rotated which counselors would provide supervision from this table while the others remained available in their offices for walk-ins. In this way, the administration received the supervision support needed and counselors performed an appropriate activity while assisting with school safety.

When completing the Annual Agreement with supervisors, school counselors are encouraged to consult their administrators and discuss the possibility of providing flexible arrival times, lunchtimes, and afterschool times, to ensure student needs are met. Having an open, honest conversation with coworkers about messages the school counseling team sends is important. The team of school counselors suffers when it does not manage itself well within the political nature of the school system.

Other Programs and Services

What types of programs and services will school counselors provide at the school? Will elementary and middle school counselors provide parenting classes? Will high school counselors be required to provide evening college planning and career readiness presentations? What can the students, parents, and administration expect from their school counselor and from the district's school counseling program? When considering equity and access to evening events and opportunities so all families can participate, what compromises can be made to ensure events occur? Annual Agreements can provide the vehicle for discussion and negotiated services for students and families. One school counselor may look forward to providing evening parenting classes, while another may prefer holding them during the day. By utilizing the agreement to negotiate offering classes at both times, all families can be served.

Another negotiation may result in a decision that an evening presentation time is a fair-share responsibility, and therefore another fair-share activity, such as football game supervision, may be removed from the counselors' schedule. These simple yet potentially problematic concerns can be addressed by working together to accommodate the students, families, and school counselors' needs. Ultimately, it comes down to communication, fair share, respect for the appropriate role and function of the school counselor, and the needs of the school and community.

Student Referral Forms

How do students "see" the school counselor? Do students have a referral form to fill out? Is there a clerk or receptionist in the school counseling center to provide a form or appointment for students or parents who want to see their school counselor? What level of severity do the school counselors, faculty, and administrator consider appropriate to justify allowing students to leave a classroom to see the school counselor or school counselor of the day? These conversations and agreements will assist in efficiency and effectiveness.

How does a teacher refer a student to the school counselor? Less than half of the school counselors at a statewide conference reported having and/or using referral forms. Many said they accept e-mails or texts from students and teachers. While this is technologically convenient and uses social media expediently, the challenge is that some students will gain greater access to counselors because of the method of seeking assistance, while others will not be referred at all. Chapters 2 and 6 discuss utilizing data to drive decisions and provide samples and instructions for using forms to drive student interventions.

There are times, however, when a teacher may notice a sudden change in a student's behavior or need assistance with a student the data did not identify due to

personal or family situations that may impact the student's ability to learn. For these students, referral forms are necessary. Samples of referral and feedback forms are provided in Chapter 6. School counselors who take on random "fly by" referrals can feel very overwhelmed. In this chapter on time management, counselors are reminded that without referral forms, teachers, parents and others will assume the counselor will remember to call in a student, when in fact, their referral is probably written on one of a dozen sticky notes somewhere, very easily misplaced or forgotten.

An excellent comprehensive referral process guide with many sample templates has been developed by school counselors in Missouri and is available online at http://www.missouricareereducation.org/doc/referral/ReferralProcess.pdf.

CALENDARS

The ASCA National Model calls for school counselors to keep and post annual and weekly calendars of the activities within their school counseling programs (2003, 2005, 2012a). School counselors develop and publish a master calendar to ensure students, parents or guardians, teachers, and administrators know what activities are scheduled along with the time and location of each. Calendars assist school counselors in gaining control of their days, so they are less likely to be swept up into noncounseling activities. School counselors who collaborate to create and live by their calendars are more likely to "happen to their day" rather than having "their day happen to them." Rather than performing "random acts of school counseling," they will implement prescheduled "intentional acts of school counseling."

A well-developed calendar is a powerful public relations tool. Published calendars provide tangible documentation that the activities necessary to meet the mission, vision, and goals of the school counseling program are actually scheduled to occur. The use of an annual calendar as part of the Annual Agreement promotes programmatic legitimacy, because it represents administrative support for scheduled school counseling activities to all. A calendar validates the school counseling program's importance to all students, parents or guardians, teachers, and administrators (ASCA, 2012a). A well-planned and filled-out calendar also supports the protection of the school counselors' time for school counselor-related activities. An "open" calendar lends itself to being filled with non-counseling responsibilities, as it may appear there is nothing more valuable scheduled. Suggestions for creating a calendar are provided in Figure 9.1.

Each spring, the school counseling team is encouraged to spend one entire day designing the next year's calendar. Early planning ensures conflicts are avoided, necessary arrangements are made for facilities use, and administrators, staff, parents, and students know the school counseling programs' plans before the beginning of the year.

The first step in creating a successful calendar is to indicate all of the *required activities or events with nonnegotiable and/or predetermined dates* that must be included in the school's planning calendar. Consider yearly events that are prescheduled by the state, district, local colleges, or community. These may include standardized testing dates, college application deadlines, SAT/ACT/AP testing dates, open house, progress reports and report cards, graduation, and events such as Red Ribbon Week or prom.

Next, add the *required activities and events that have negotiable or flexible dates*. Review the checklist provided to identify and prioritize activities that fall into this category, including annual activities such as visitations to feeder schools, evening presentations for parents, and class visits for course registration. When calendaring schoolwide curriculum, determine the best time to deliver specific lessons. Are certain topics best delivered at the same time each year (violence prevention in October, test taking in the spring)? Once grades are in, when will the team meet to review the disaggregated data, survey student needs, and determine intentional (data-driven) interventions? When and on what days of the week will small groups be held? Scheduling these events in advance

Figure 9.1 School Counseling Program Calendar Checklist

Annual School Counseling Program Calendars

- ❑ Are designed for the entire year in advance (typically in spring of the prior year)
- ❑ Utilize and reflect the school's master list of important dates for the upcoming year
- ❑ Include all scheduled activities provided in the school counseling program
- ❑ Reserve dates for use of the facility hosting the events or activities
- ❑ Identify prescheduled blocks of dates for schoolwide core curriculum lessons
- ❑ Identify prescheduled dates for gathering or "fish-netting" intervention data
- ❑ Identify prescheduled blocks of dates for planned group interventions
- ❑ Include prescheduled blocks of time for individual student planning meetings
- ❑ Include prescheduled blocks of time for student preregistration and articulation visits with feeder schools
- ❑ Identify prescheduled dates (with topics) for evening presentations, parenting classes, and other opportunities for family involvement or education
- ❑ Include prescheduled blocks of time set aside for parent, student, and teacher drop-ins
- ❑ Include prescheduled time for school counselors to meet as a team with administration, school staff, advisory council, and other district counselors
- ❑ Include school counselor attendance at important site leadership and grade-level meetings
- ❑ Ensure time is allocated for data analysis and program evaluation
- ❑ Are located in several prominent places, such as department bulletin boards, school or student bulletin boards, classroom bulletin boards, administrative offices, parent or guardian center, career center, student store, and other sites used to communicate school events
- ❑ Are published in newsletters, provided on the school and department website, and distributed to appropriate persons: students, staff, parents or guardians, and community
- ❑ Are reviewed and revised as needed and posted on a weekly or monthly basis
- ❑ Are compared at the end of the year with the year's goals for actual versus planned time spent in the delivery of system components
- ❑ Are used when designing and determining system priorities
- ❑ Are reviewed and approved by the principal as an indicator of leadership, advocacy, and foresight in the school counselor's professional approach
- ❑ Send a consistent and predictable message about activities school counselors perform within the school

and blocking out necessary planning and intervention time on the calendar ensures availability of facilities for group meetings and serves as an important reminder to all that this activity will occur (even if counselors get busy).

Imagine the impact that hard deadlines, such as those for college applications, will have on the use of school counselor time. Consider blocking out a certain amount of time as dedicated to assisting students in this process. If counselors know from experience they will spend a particular amount of time supporting last-minute student needs in these areas, it is best to indicate that immediately on the calendar to avoid conflicts later. If counselors know from experience the days following a presentation on "good touch, bad touch" will be filled with student referrals, reserving time on the calendar will prevent the need to cancel groups or classroom lessons.

Check online for dates of the annual, national, or state conference counselors desire to attend. When will district school counselor meetings be held? Inquire for dates from the central office in advance, so these important dates and times are protected. Remember to schedule school counselor department meetings and district school counselor meetings. Don't forget CORE team meetings, school leadership meetings, school site council meetings, grade-level meetings, PTA, or any other meetings counselors can be assets to and would benefit from attending. Finally, refer back to the Annual Agreement. Is anything missing? When the calendar is complete and approved by administration, determine which essential dates and times are important for students, parents, teachers and staff to know right away and the manner in which these important dates and the entire calendar will be distributed. Figures 9.2 and 9.3 show a few sample calendars. What do these calendars have that you like? What are they missing?

SCHOOL COUNSELOR MEETINGS AND SACRED COLLEGIAL TALK TIME

When building or maintaining efficient and effective school counseling programs, time must be scheduled on the school counselor meeting agenda for the "work" of creating the program. Without an agenda, school counselor meetings can be filled with random and unfocused items or become nonproductive spaces for airing grievances. Dividing the school counselor meeting agenda into specific topic areas can be very helpful. An agenda might include the following items:

1. *Information and Announcements* (e.g., discussion about new school or district policies, practices, or procedures, such as a new registration process or new report cards)

2. *Specific Student Concerns* (e.g., individual student issues; questions about handling certain student concerns, such as soliciting suggestions for a mentor for a new foster student)

3. *Program Management* (e.g., climate survey data analysis, finalizing action plans, scheduling groups)

4. *Counselor Concerns* (e.g., how to work with a teacher who appears stressed, how to talk with an angry parent)

Scheduling a consistent time for meetings is essential to minimizing interruptions. Some high school teams meet Friday mornings, as this is often used as a

Figure 9.2 Sample Calendar 1

Sun	Mon	Tue	Wed	Thu	Fri	Sat
1 Wk# 11	2	3 College Club Guest Speaker Series @ Lunch CAHSEE Retake 12 & 11	4 UC Workshop @ 3–5pm CAHSEE Retake 12 & 11	5	6	7
8 Wk# 12	9 PLC mtg	10 10th Group Intervention Presentation (Little Theater)	11	12	13	14
15 Wk# 13	16 PLC w/Liaison At-risk Small Group Counseling #1	17 10th: Sophomore Success Presentation (World History)	18 Dept. Meeting	19 10th: Sophomore Success Presentation (World History)	20 At-risk Small Group Counseling #1	21 Women Empowerment @ CSULB 100 Black Colleges @ UCI
22 Wk#14	23 All Counselors available UC/CSU Application	24 All Counselors available UC/CSU Application	25 No School	26 HOLIDAY	27 HOLIDAY	28
29 Wk# 15	30 PLC mtg At-risk Small Group Counseling #2	All Counselors available @ CCC & Library for UC/CSU Applications deadline				

Source: Paramount High School. Used with permission of Debbie Stark.

Figure 9.3 Sample Calendar 2

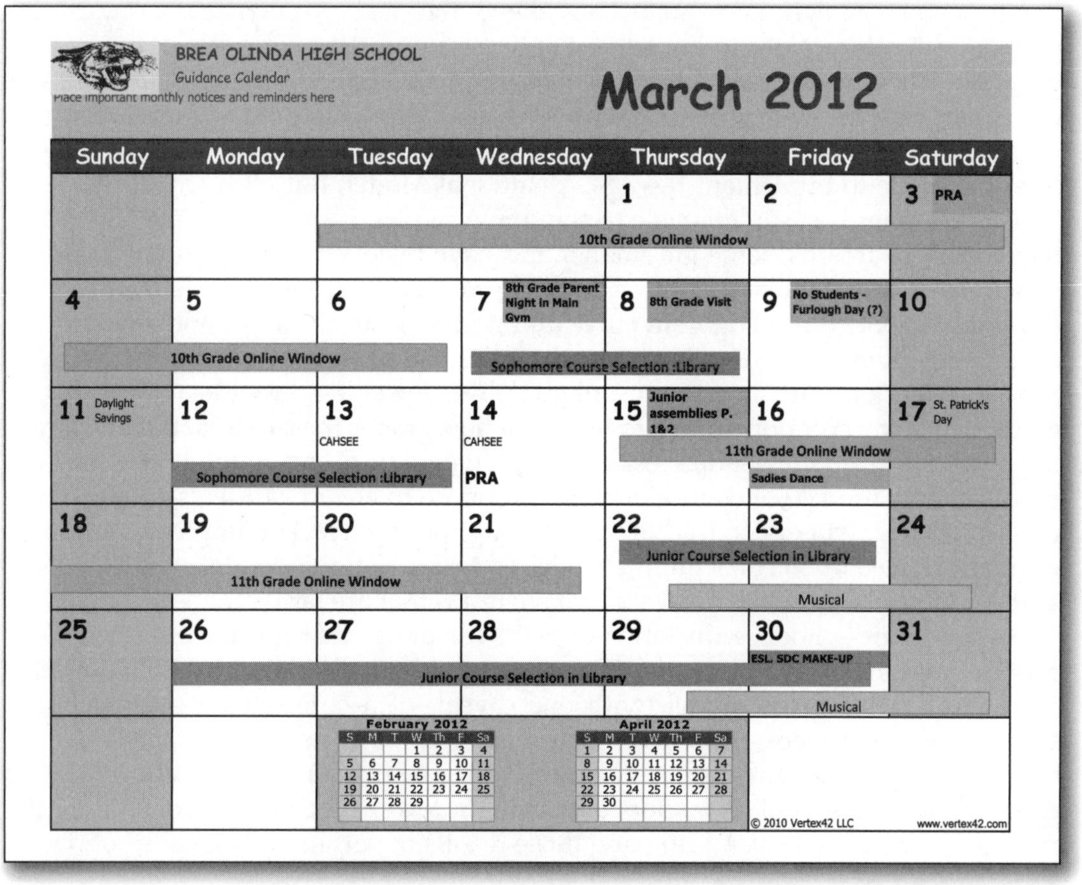

Source: Brea Olinda High School Guidance Calendar. Used with permission of Robert Stelmar.

testing time. School counselors who are the only counselor at their sites—such as those at rural, small, or elementary schools—need to schedule time off campus, as they are truly "lone rangers" in their schools. Each day, and especially during times of crisis, teachers, parents, and administrators look to school counselors to hold it together when others are falling apart. School counselors are not allowed to have a bad day or be seen in the teacher's lounge crying, "I have no idea what to do, Susie. I've tried everything. I give up!" That would not go very well. Lone ranger school counselors do not have a job-alike on site to meet with behind a closed office door to share professional concerns, vent about a student or parent, or seek personal support. "Sacred collegial talk time" is essential to helping professionals. School counselors are strongly encouraged to create time with their professional colleagues to share common concerns and challenges. The professional and personal support gained from these meetings is often invaluable. School counselors are helpers who are spread very thin at times and therefore prone to burnout. Take time for sacred collegial talk.

RATIOS AND TIME

Some school counselors mistakenly believe the way to manage a large student-to-counselor ratio is to implement only certain portions of a school counseling program. They might imagine providing group and individual counseling but not classroom lessons. Even when a counselor has a large ratio or is split between two sites (provided counselors are not assigned noncounselor responsibilities), it is absolutely possible to implement the ASCA National Model, but on a smaller scale. A house metaphor is easily relatable to the ASCA model. Some houses are larger and have many bedrooms; some are smaller and have fewer—but every home has bedrooms, bathrooms, and a kitchen. In the same way, every school counseling program provides school counseling core curriculum, group intervention, and every other direct and indirect activity central to the role of a professional school counselor. School counselors with larger ratios might deliver fewer lessons or be more selective about which intervention groups to hold in which grades (based on data). The larger the ratio, the fewer curriculum lessons are delivered or rooms in the house, and the more creative the school counselor will need to be to ensure students receive what they need (e.g., supervised advisories or support for teacher implementation of mutually agreed upon curriculum). While the ASCA National Model calls for a 250:1 student-to-counselor ratio, most states have ratios that are far larger (ASCA, 2012d). There are many schools with ratios of 500:1 (or more) that are Recognized ASCA Model Program (RAMP) schools. The ratio should not prevent a school counselor from implementing the model (with one caveat—if a counselor is assigned to a school one day a week—and yes, it does happen—it is no longer really a school counseling program anyway; it is purely crisis response). Instead, the model is designed to help school counselors advocate for lower ratios by demonstrating the results of their activities and utilizing those results to garner additional resources.

Making Choices on Spending Time

The school counselor's plate is always full. I remember as a school counselor seeing a day on my calendar that was empty and thinking "Okay, on Thursday I am going to catch up on everything!" Then, Thursday came, and I was "busy" all day, but didn't catch up. Why? Because it was impossible to ever imagine a moment without one or more students to see or parents to call. It always seemed like the pile grew higher and higher. As I write this I imagine the reader saying: "Yes! And now you are asking me to measure results too? And use data to find students I didn't know needed help and then survey them and make a PowerPoint of my results and . . . WHERE WILL I GET THE TIME?"

OK . . . deeeeep breath . . . deeeeeper . . . breathe in . . . and now out. OK, there, that is better. Now, sit back, relax, and let's pause for some story time. Story time? Yes, story time.

Once upon a time, many years ago, I took my three young sons (ages 6, 9, and 11 at the time) to the Circus Circus buffet in Las Vegas ($1.99 for all you can eat!). As you can imagine, they started filling their plates with many of the hundreds of items on the buffet, and before anyone knew it, although they were only 20% through the buffet, their plates were piled high and spilling. Typical kid behavior, right? This can happen to us as adults sometimes too! I have learned that sometimes the best (most desirous and expensive) food is often at the end of the buffet. So now, when I go to a buffet, I scan the entire buffet *first*, and *then* I decide what I will put first on my plate. I like to start with the prime rib, because I love it, and because it is the most expensive item, I get my money's worth. Then I choose from the remaining categories, attempt a balanced meal, and if I have room, I select a dessert.

Now, let's consider school counselors, and compare their days. Are school counselors like kids at the buffet? Do we add, add, and add some more until we can't hold it on the plate anymore? Do some items drop off when we try to balance the full plate? Many school counselors try to do it all and end up with an upset stomach or a spilled plate. Maybe it's time to rethink this approach.

Just as I scan the food line for "data" and select items to compose a balanced meal, the school counselor scans schoolwide data. Then, with a clean plate, school counselors determine their balanced meal of classroom curriculum, groups, individual planning, consultation, and so on. Decisions are made regarding what goes on the plate first, what is added second, and what is added at the end if there is room. There will always be days when crisis trumps all, but if counselors keep the metaphor in mind as they attempt to ration their time, they might find they feel healthier at the end of the day, week, and year.

Time Trackers

There are several new products available to assist school counselors with tracking time. Dr. Tim Poynton created EZAnalyze Time Tracker. It is a macro-enabled Excel workbook designed to perform note-keeping and time-tracking functions and to generate reports for accountability and improved service to students. It is available free of charge online at http://www.ezanalyze.com/tracktime/features.htm. Felipe Robinson-Zañartu created another time tracker that is currently being piloted by my graduate students at San Diego State University as well as students at DePaul University. One nice feature is the alignment with the third edition of the ASCA National Model (Figure 9.4) as well as the easy-to-read pie chart (Figure 9.5). For example, the time tracker pie chart in 9.5 shows the student counselor spending 40% of her time in individual students planning, 27% in program management, 23% in non-school counseling and 10% in indirect services, while spending no time in curriculum or responsive services. As a university supervisor, this provides me with an opportunity to guide the student and site supervisor to ensure the student is receiving an opportunity to implement a balanced program. Felipe's time tracker is available at http://digitalcounselor.com/.

The "Plates Are Full" activity in Figure 9.6 can assist you and your counseling team in a discussion of how full your individual and collective plates may be. What needs to stay? What goes? If something comes off the plate, who will take it on? Is there anything you need to add to the plate?

Figure 9.4 Time Tracker Page Showing Alignment With ASCA National Model

Weekly School Counselor Time Tracker											
Date											
69										**CODE KEY**	
Time		**Monday**		**Tuesday**		**Wednesday**		**Thursday**		**Friday**	**DIRECT STUDENT SERVICES**
7:00 AM	4	Parent Teacher Conference	8	Crosswalk Duty	4	IEP Review	8	Morning Supervision	4	Collaboration with 4th grade team	1 Core Counseling Curriculm
7:30 AM	5	Email/Planning	5	Email/Planning	5	Email/Planning	5	Email/Planning	5	Email/Planning	2 Individual Student Planning
8:00 AM	1	6th Grade Bullying	2	Goal Setting 7th	5	Email/Planning	4	Consultation about Student	5	Email/Planning	3 Responsive Services
8:30 AM	1	6th Grade Bullying	2	Goal Setting 7th	1	8th Grade Career Exploration	7	Attendance Data	1	4th Grade Guidance Lessons	**INDIRECT STDNT SERVICES**
9:00 AM	1	6th Grade Bullying	3	7th Grade Crisis	1	8th Grade Career Exploration	7	Disaggregating Academic Data	1	4th Grade Guidance Lessons	4 Refer Collaboration Consultation
9:30 AM	1	6th Grade Bullying	3	7th Grade Crisis	1	8th Grade Career Exploration	3	Meeting with D/F Students	1	4th Grade Guidance Lessons	**PRGRM MANAGE & SUPPORT**
10:00 AM	1	6th Grade Bullying	2	Goal Setting 7th	1	8th Grade Career Exploration	3	Meeting with D/F Students	1	4th Grade Guidance Lessons	5 Program Management
10:30 AM	1	6th Grade Bullying	2	Goal Setting 7th	1	8th Grade Career Exploration	3	Meeting with D/F Students	1	4th Grade Guidance Lessons	6 Professional Development
11:00 AM	1	6th Grade Bullying	1	8th Grade Academic Group	1	8th Grade Career Exploration	1	3rd Grade Social Skills Group	1	4th Grade Guidance Lessons	7 Data Analysis
11:30 AM	1	6th Grade Bullying	1	8th Grade Academic Group	1	8th Grade Career Exploration	1	3rd Grade Social Skills Group		Lunch	8 Fair Share

Figure 9.5 Time Tracker Pie Chart

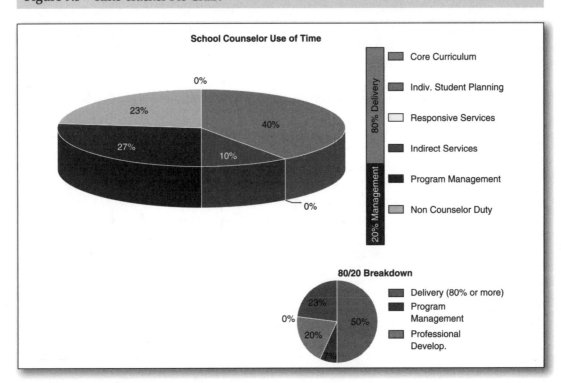

Figure 9.6 Our Plates Are Full

 What Stays? What Goes? What Gets Added?

ON PLATE	STAYS	UNSURE	TAKE OFF	WHO ADDS THIS?	ADDED TO PLATE	WHEN?

FAQS AND TIME SUCKERS

Regardless of the school, district, city, or state, school counselors and administrators have many of the same concerns and challenges when it comes to role definition for school counselors. The next section will provide thoughts and suggestions for handling some of these frequently asked questions regarding how school counselors spend their time, along with suggestions for ways for school counselors and others to manage these concerns.

School Counselors and Discipline

Do counselors have a role in discipline? *Yes*, a very important one. However, it is a different role than the administrator's. School administrators possess a license or credential providing them authority to mete out student discipline. Administrators take classes in due process and law and are employed to provide discipline as part of their expected responsibilities. The school counselors' role is fundamentally different, because their credential does not provide them the authority to suspend students. Rather, the school counselors' role in discipline is to support the teachers and administrators by ensuring students possess the knowledge, attitudes, and skills necessary to prevent and reduce the number of referrals requiring discipline. ASCA's position statement supports this perspective: "It is not the role of the professional school counselor to mete out punishment but to help create effective behavior change" (ASCA, 2010a, p. 21).

The school counselors' role in discipline is to provide a comprehensive program that includes systems of prevention and intervention as well as postsuspension follow-up.

School counselors are addressing discipline *prevention* when they

- Use data to locate trends in student behavior (e.g., referrals, suspensions, Youth Behavior Risk Surveys, climate surveys), present this important information to staff
- Advocate for evidence-based curriculum to be delivered in classrooms school-wide to address data-driven needs
- Coordinate, design, oversee, and evaluate the impact of conflict resolution/peer mediation/peer helper programs and services for students
- Participate in leadership conversations regarding schoolwide discipline issues
- Provide training for staff, students, and parents about conflict resolution, violence prevention, and early warning signs of violence
- Ensure systems are in place that allow anonymous referrals from concerned persons
- Participate in positive behavior intervention programs (PBIS)
- Advocate for classroom, school, and district consistency in discipline policies, practices, and procedures
- Promote accurate and consistent collection of discipline data

School counselors are addressing discipline *intervention* needs when they

- Query student discipline data records to determine which students need counseling interventions for frequent offenses (e.g., five or more referrals = anger management group)
- Ensure students who are identified by data (or referral) are provided with appropriate interventions (group/individual counseling)
- Refer students requiring more intensive intervention than is appropriate to provide in school to outside agencies (ASCA, 2010a, pp. 22, 50)
- Participate in meetings to create SSTs, 504 plans, and IEPs and to develop behavior contracts as appropriate and necessary
- Provide parent/teacher/administrator consultation and collaboration
- Follow up with feedback after receiving a referral from faculty member or administrator

School counselors are addressing discipline *postsuspension* needs when they

- Collaborate with administrators to ensure timely notification when students on their caseload have been suspended
- Provide a scheduled appointment following a suspension (upon return to school) to review and discuss:
  - What happened
  - What the student did to get the suspension
  - What the student could have done differently
  - What the student can do next time
  - Referrals as appropriate to group counseling, peer mediation, or outside counseling

Some school counselors state they are comfortable with the investigation portion of the discipline process so long as they don't actually mete out discipline. The concern with the school counselor providing even this part of the discipline process is the idea that the counselor is available to provide such assistance. As mentioned earlier, professional school counselors are not sitting in their offices waiting to investigate discipline problems or resolve minor "he said, she said" conflicts. Rather, they are implementing their programs, providing direct and indirect services such as classroom curriculum, group counseling, consultation, individual planning meetings, and so on. If the counselor has the time to mete out discipline, one might wonder why that is the case. The school counseling office is not an emergency room where trained counselors wait around to provide services to those who drop by in need. Rather, the professional school counselor's calendar should be filled with the activities previously mentioned to prevent, intervene in, and remediate issues leading to behaviors warranting a discipline referral.

That having been said, if one day the administrator *directs* the school counselor to perform a discipline-related investigation or to provide a first-level discipline consequence (not suspension), it is not in the best interest of the school counselor to refuse or to enlarge and laminate this page and paste it to the administrator's door, at least not as the first action anyway. It is recommended instead that the counselor follow the directive and then schedule a meeting to discuss the counselor's appropriate role in supporting the reduction of the need for discipline and the creation of safe climates for learning. Prior to the meeting, it might be a good idea for the school counselor to familiarize himself with his contract and with relevant portions of state education code, so he can show the administrator what the law allows. For example, California Education Code 48900 reads: "A pupil shall not be suspended from school or recommended for expulsion, unless the superintendent or the principal of the school in which the pupil is enrolled determines that the pupil has committed an act as defined pursuant to any of subdivisions."

Next, the counselor should get very busy collecting, disaggregating, and reviewing discipline and other youth behavior data. The counselor might offer to facilitate a data-based decision making (DBDM) team (Dimmit, Carey, & Hatch, 2007) and then create data-driven actions plans. The idea is to educate the administrator about the prevention, intervention, and postsuspension activities the school counselor *is* providing or will provide and show how those align with the counselor's professional training, relevant education code, and counseling professional organizations' recommendations.

Reviewing the data and sharing the plan will go a long way toward helping the administrator learn the value of the school counselor's appropriate role in reducing discipline. Start by collecting data on the impact of the interventions with students identified as (a) not attending, (b) not behaving, and (c) not achieving. Share the results and the difference the school counseling program is making.

TRUE STORY FROM THE FRONT LINES

(by a school counselor who was assigned discipline and decided to set up a meeting with his principal)

For our meeting with our principal, we were very organized and made sure that we presented the information as a united front. We had our own meeting prior to our meeting with our principal to discuss how we were going to go about explaining our perspective. We did a lot of research and gathered a lot of materials to back up our position. One of the counselors already had most of the research completed, as she knew that we would be facing this one day. Our district does not have an official policy stating that counselors are required to do low-level discipline, but in every school the counselors are handing out consequences. At our sister and much older high school, the counselors have always done discipline.

To make matters worse, our previous principal, who was with our school for many years before becoming our area administrator, took discipline from us because we finally realized that we should not be doing discipline based on the ASCA model. At that time, a new counselor had come into the office and was appalled that we were doing discipline. However, when that principal left, our new principal (came in last year) decided that the administrators were overwhelmed and wanted them more in the classroom, so he decided with the help of his administrators that we needed to do discipline.

It was important for me and the other counselors to understand the context in which we were working to better gauge how we were going to go about talking to our principal. The counseling staff put together a packet of information. We had a copy of EDCODE and what it says specifically about counselors; we had the ASCA position statement, which states in bold what counselors do and what they do not; we had a copy of the California Department of Education endorsement of ASCA; we had a copy of your first e-mail with advice to me; we had copies of our job description, which does not mention the word *discipline;* and we had copies of the assistant principal job description, which states that the assistant principal is in charge of "all discipline." Last, we had a copy of our action plan, something I created before the meeting to show the principal everything we are doing to help lower the number of suspensions and expulsions. In doing that, I also realized that we do not have a guidance lesson on violence——we need one. This is something that I am working on getting purchased in our district for grades 9–12. Anyhow, we came in very prepared.

We had an agenda that first started with the head counselor thanking the principal for coming to the meeting. Then we had another counselor go through our concerns. We had a last section where we were going to talk about our two recommendations, but before we got to that section of the meeting, the principal came up with his own solution. He took discipline from us, saying that the assistant principals needed to deal with the consequence end of things and that the counselors needed to go back to counseling. We were all very thankful. Since then I have not given a consequence but instead have counseled students as part of our postdiscipline role.

—E-mailed from counselor with approval to anonymously share

SSTs, 504 Plans, and IEPs

School counselors are important and necessary participants on SST, IEP, and 504 plan teams. Often, however, some counselors and/or their administrators are misinformed regarding the appropriate role of the school counselor. Consequently, these counselors are spending large amounts of time performing functions outside of their training and role—coordinating, facilitating, or serving as the authoritative LEA representative making decisions for placement and accommodations. Coordinating and scheduling meetings, collecting information from teachers, and calling parents is a time-consuming clerical task that is an inefficient use of valuable and expensive school counselors' time. These activities are most appropriately assigned to a classified employee. It is also unnecessary for a school counselor to attend every meeting. The school counselor's role is to serve as an expert team member at meetings, providing consultation, support, and assistance developing students' intervention plans. School counselors are encouraged to become well educated regarding their appropriate role when attending these meetings. According to ASCA, it is not appropriate for school counselors to serve as the decision makers or in a supervisory capacity. ASCA provides a position statement that includes directives on these issues:

> The professional school counselor has a responsibility to be a part of designing portions of these plans related to the comprehensive school counseling program, but it is *inappropriate* for the professional school counselor to serve in supervisory or administrative roles such as:
>
> — making decisions regarding placement or retention
> — serving in any supervisory capacity related to the implementation of IDEA
> — serving as the LEA representative for the team writing the IEP
> — coordinating the 504 planning team
> — supervising of the implementation of the 504 plan (ASCA, 2010a, p. 47)

School counselors, teachers, and other staff can put themselves at legal risk if they guarantee accommodations, programs, or services they do not possess the authority to require. Section 504 is a federal law that protects the rights of individuals with disabilities to ensure they receive appropriate accommodations in their education. School counselors are advised to educate themselves by reviewing their state's education code, district board policy, union contract, professional association's ethical guidelines, and position statements and the federal Office of Civil Rights before agreeing to serve in any administrative capacity (ASCA, 2012b; U.S. Department of Education, 2011b).

The Master Schedule

School counselors are vital to the master schedule process and serve as important participants on the scheduling team (ASCA, 2011). In some schools, however, building the school's master schedule is considered primarily the school counselor's responsibility. When school counselors carry the bulk of the responsibility in building the master schedule (by choice or requirement), many problems arise, but most important, the time used to serve students is impacted. School counselors report master schedules consume a considerable amount of time while providing little impact on improving student outcomes (Finkelstein, 2009).

As the coordinator of student services in my district, I became aware of the amount of time some school counselors were spending at the middle and high school levels on clerical and administrative responsibilities related to the master schedule, because it impacted their ability to implement essential components of the comprehensive program. Central office was asking them to implement data-driven interventions, provide classroom curriculum, and share results. The counselors wondered where they would find the time to complete these tasks with all the other responsibilities on their plates.

To address the issue, we held a series of meetings to identify specific problems impacting the school counselors' time. We learned that school counselors were spending two to three weeks of their time manually entering information from students' course registration forms into databases. This time-consuming and tedious task was counterproductive to improving student attendance, behavior, and achievement. We also discovered that some administrators did not understand how to create a master schedule and that many school counselors were the ones completing them at most sites. One school counselor reported, "Just when I finish training one assistant principal, they leave, and I have to train another. It's just easier to do it myself." Master schedule building also put the counselor in an inappropriate position of authority among the faculty, because decisions regarding prep periods, numbers of sections, and teaching loads had to be made. These and other issues also contributed to creating a teacher-driven, not student-driven, master schedule. Further, the imbalance of power and authority and the political maneuvering led to a failed outcome for all, but particularly for the students. At sites where the school counselors were not involved in the master schedule process, other problems arose. Administrators who worked alone and didn't consult with the counselors often created schedules that did not work for students, resulting in many weeks of schedule changes and lost instructional time well into the semester. Finally, the lack of clerical support at middle and high schools meant no one was available to assist school counselors with data entry, generating teacher and student schedules, and running tallies. All of this fell on the school counselor's plate.

Working collaboratively, the central office, site administrators, counselors, classified personnel, and union representatives developed a list of master schedule building responsibilities (see Figure 9.7). A new "guidance assistant" position was created to serve as the clerical support for any responsibility related to the master schedule. Training was provided for administrators, school counselors, and department chairs on how to build a student-driven master schedule using a team approach. While implementation took time, and many lessons were learned along the way, the impact of clarifying responsibilities proved successful in reducing time spent on schedule changes the following year.

Job Descriptions and Evaluation Tools

Finally, when completing the Annual Agreement, locate your job description and evaluation tools. Look for areas of alignment and areas of disconnect. Some job descriptions are very clear; others are not. Consider the language below, taken from a job description for a school counselor at Kipp Bay Area Schools:

> Be present and *willing to do whatever it takes* from 7:30 am to 5:00 pm, Monday through Friday, one Saturday a month, and 3–4 weeks during the summer to ensure that all students are on track to enter into competitive colleges. (Kipp Bay Area Schools, 2013)

The expectations of school counselors in this school will clearly be different than in the neighboring district with strong union representation. Consider working with the advisory council, school, district, union, and other school counselors to create alignment between what schools counselors are hired to do and evaluated for, and what the administrator signing the Annual Agreement expects or believes the school counselor will do. Readers are encouraged to review sample job descriptions and evaluation tools provided in the online appendix.

Online Resources Included

Figure 9.7   Master Schedule Building Responsibilities

Administrator

- Ensure training for key members of the scheduling team (counselor, minimum of two lead teachers, data specialist, administrator)
- Develop scheduling team (administrators, counselor representative[s], department chairs, guidance assistants)
- Make decisions on FTEs, assigning teachers to classes, reduction or enlargement of sections, when to put on caps, when to "run"
- Review staffing issues

Scheduling Team (administrators, counselor representative[s], department chairs, guidance assistants)

- Review course offerings and updates for next school year
- Review schedule parameters, construction tasks, and constraints
- Advertise curriculum to students
- Set registration process for students
- Edit/update student course selections
- Review scheduling software and capabilities if appropriate
- Finalize courses to be scheduled
- Make section decisions
- Construct master schedule (together)
- Analyze scheduling run

Guidance Assistant

- Enter data about student course selections (input)
- Produce course tallies
- Rerun tallies
- Produce conflict matrix
- Generate all student, teacher, and room schedules

School Counselors

- Review and revise registration forms
- Advertise course options to students and parents
- Teach curriculum on graduation and college requirements
- Explain registration process to students (curriculum)
- Oversee student course selection process
- Edit/update student four-year plans as students select courses
- Participate on the scheduling team (send representative(s) from the counseling office to serve as liaison to administrator in charge of scheduling team)
- Meet with students to ensure they have enrolled in the classes necessary to graduate
- Ensure students have appropriate placement with considerations for IEPs, 504 plans, language needs, and so on.
- Serve as advisors and consultants to scheduling team when conflicts arise
- Schedule students into appropriate classes

SCHOOL COUNSELING PROGRAM ORGANIZATIONAL QUESTIONNAIRE

When consulting with a school district, I often begin with a questionnaire designed to quickly gather a large amount of information regarding the organizational systems and functionality of the program. The questions below are not by any means an exhaustive list, as typically many more emerge once we begin, but they do provide a reference point for beginning conversations and a window into the policies, practices, and procedures that are working well as well as those that might benefit from revision during the training process. How might you answer them for your school?

1. How many credentialed school counselors are at your site?

2. How are caseloads organized? (alphabetically, grade level, domain, etc.)

3. What is the student-to-counselor ratio?

4. What other student support service professionals are at your site? (e.g., school social worker, school psychologist)

   a. What are their ratios or days of service?
   b. Have you delineated roles and responsibilities?

5. Do you have a school counseling program assistant/clerk/secretary?

   a. Who determines the responsibilities of the classified support for the school counseling program?
   b. Who does the classified person primarily work for?
   c. Do school counselors have input into the selection, training, mentoring, or evaluation of the classified person?

6. Do you have a person assigned to the career center? (clerical or certificated?)

7. Do you have a schoolwide curriculum action plan?

8. Do you have a set counseling curriculum? Do you have any assessment tools (pre/post) for it?

9. Who delivers the school counseling curriculum?

10. Do you have teacher advisory programs (model)?

    a. What role does advisory play in delivering school counseling curriculum?
    b. What role do the school counselors play in the delivery of advisory curriculum?

11. Do you run groups?

    a. What types (intervention groups? study skills? life issues? crisis?)
    b. How often do you run groups, and how many sessions are typically held?
    c. How are students in group counseling referred/identified?
    d. What curriculum do you use, and how was it selected?
    e. How do you evaluate groups?

12. Does each student have a four-year plan (or learning plan) on file?

    a. When do students first create their plan?
    b. How often is it reviewed and revised? What is the process?

    c. Are parents included, invited, and expected to attend to these meetings?

    d. What is the content of the meeting? How long is it scheduled for?

13. Do you provide parent evening presentations?

    a. How many are held?

    b. What topics are covered?

    c. Are the topics the same each year?

    d. When are presentations held?

    e. Do all school counselors participate?

    f. What is your rate of parent attendance?

14. May I see your yearly/monthly/weekly calendar?

    a. Who has access to your calendar?

    b. Who can make appointments on your calendar?

    c. How are decisions made about what will be scheduled on your calendar?

15. How do you use data to drive student interventions?

16. How do you use data to inform closing-the-gap activities?

17. How do you demonstrate accountability?

18. What results do you collect and/or share?

19. With whom do you share results?

20. What marketing strategies do you use to promote your program?

21. How do students let you know that they want or need to see you?

22. How do teachers or parents refer students to the school counselor?

23. What is your role in student discipline?

24. What is your role in the development of the master schedule?

25. What is your role in registering students for classes?

26. What is your role in testing (e.g., standardized, ASVAB, PSAT, AP, SAT, ACT)?

27. What is your role on the IEP team? Do you provide DIS counseling? What is the typical length of time you provide counseling (individual, group, etc.) to students on IEPs?

28. May I see your school counseling program brochure?

29. May I see your website? (review for depth, breadth, user friendliness, etc.)

30. What is your role on the site leadership or management team?

31. Who supervises you? Do you have a job description?

32. Do you have an evaluation that reflects your responsibilities?

33. When is the last time you attended professional development? Why did you attend?

34. Are you a member of your state and national professional association?

35. Do you attend regularly or have you attended a state or national conference? Why or why not?

10

Reporting Results

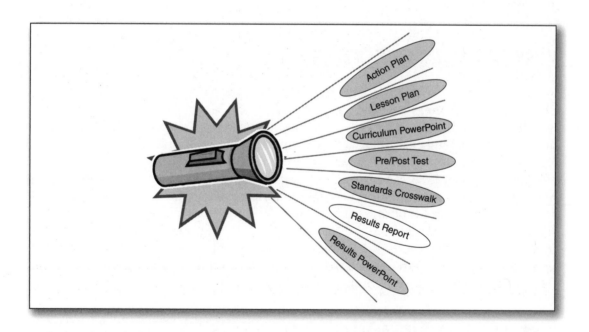

PROGRAM EVALUATION VERSUS RESEARCH

Since the 1960s, Carol Weiss, professor at Harvard University, has served as a pivotal researcher and theorist on evaluation and its role in federal policy. Weiss defines evaluation as "the systematic assessment of the operation and/or the outcomes of a program or a policy, as compared to a set of explicit or implicit standards, as a means of contributing to the improvement of the program or policy" (1998, p. 4). Stated more simply, evaluation is the review of results or of one particular program or policy designed to improve the lot of people.

What is the difference between research and evaluation? Program evaluation largely originated in 1965 with the passage of the Elementary and Secondary

Education Act (ESEA) and the need to account for the expenditure of funds for programs (Mathison, 2004). Educational psychologists and researchers found it difficult to utilize traditional hypothesis testing in school settings, which led to evaluation becoming a separate discipline. Some argue that research and evaluation are connected, because doing an evaluation requires doing research. Both evaluation and research describe, look for relationships, and trace sequences from one variable to another. Others draw the distinctions that research is highly detailed and strives for purity, while evaluation is applicable to the overall program and is more generalizable.

While there are many similarities, one central difference is that researchers formulate their own hypotheses and seek to test them; evaluators derive their questions from concerns of policy or problem communities. Research is intended for knowledge; program evaluation is intended for use. Simplistically stated, researchers prove; evaluators *im*prove (Mathison, 2004). Weiss describes five elements of evaluation: (a) systemic assessment (quantitative/qualitative), (b) process (the way a program was conducted), (c) outcomes (the effect), (d) standards for comparison (the set of expectations), and (e) improvement (increase program, improve resource allocation).

WHY RESULTS REPORTS?

Results reports serve as the tool for ensuring action plans were implemented and their impact was measured (ASCA, 2003, 2005, 2012a; Johnson & Johnson, 2001). Results reports document process, perception, and results data in three areas: standards and competencies data, achievement-related data, and achievement data. Results are measured immediately, intermediately, and over time (long range). Measuring results is vital to the school counseling program for several important reasons: (1) program evaluation, (2) program improvement, (3) student advocacy, (4) systemic change, and (5) program advocacy. Filling out a results report is relatively simple with the action plan and data in hand. While the action plan tells what was planned to do, the results report demonstrates what was actually accomplished (Johnson & Johnson, 2001). As they do with the action plan, school counselors enter the specifics of what they accomplished.

Program/Activity Evaluation

Similar in format to the curriculum action plan and the intentional guidance action plan, the end–of-the-year results report answers the following questions: How are students different as a result of the program/lesson/activity? Did the program assist every student in achieving competencies? Did it result in a change in students' attendance, behavior, and academic achievement?

- What short-term data were collected? (Pre/post test data on attitudes, knowledge, and skills)
- What intermediate data were collected? (Improved homework completion? Improved attendance? Improved quarter grades?)
- What long-term data (changes in data over time) were collected? (Increase in course completion rates? Increase in graduation rates?)

Program Improvement

Results data are used in analyzing the effects of the program. After implementing a schoolwide curriculum and intentional guidance, school counselors look at the results and ask, What worked? What went well? What didn't work? What went wrong with the activity? Is there any way to improve the activity next time? What needs to be changed or shifted to get the desired results?

All results—good or bad—are ultimately good, because they provide us feedback that can guide us, telling us what to do next and how to do it better . . . feedback is synonymous with results.

—Mike Schmoker (2001)

Student Advocacy

Results collected can be used to advocate for improved programs, policies, practices, or services to support students. If a particular school counseling activity or intervention has positively contributed to students' ability to attend, behave, or achieve, sharing these results could lead to increased support as well as increased allocation of counseling (or financial) resources to provide additional services. It may also lead to a better understanding of the value or lack of value in providing specific student interventions that interrupt valuable instructional learning time.

Systemic Change

When results are less significant than anticipated, it may have more to do with systems issues than student issues. For example, when results data indicate that despite attempts to deliver classroom presentations encouraging all students to take honors and AP courses, certain subgroups are still underrepresented, the data might lead to conversations regarding policies and procedures that may be gatekeeping some students from rigorous educational opportunities. By sharing results, the school counseling program can offer an opportunity for faculty to discuss access, opportunity, and attainment gaps and begin the process of systemically revising policies and procedures that may be contributing to the undesired outcomes. As was discussed in Chapter 8, addressing systems needs may lead to better outcomes for all students.

Program Advocacy

Finally, results are used for sharing successes and program advocacy. Sharing results with stakeholders allows school counselors to communicate the impact of their programs and services to the school community. Often, teachers and administrators are unaware of the counseling curriculum and interventions and the impact of these services provided by school counselors. Taking time to share results allows teachers and other stakeholders to understand the value of the program as well as how school counseling supports student achievement. Results are also used to market the school counseling program through the creation of advocacy tools such as a PowerPoint using the Flashlight approach (Hatch, 2004b; Lewis & Hatch, 2008). School counseling programs in many states are dependent on soft funds and local (site) decision making. Heart-wrenching anecdotes with little evidence of success will not garner the resources necessary. Policymakers will fund what works, not what feels good.

Multiple Tools for Sharing Results

The Flashlight approach is one of many ways school counselors can create presentations to be shared with sites, school boards, legislators, policymakers, and other stakeholders. The Flashlight approach, used in districts and states nationwide, is discussed in detail in Chapters 11 and 12.

While the Flashlight approach is the primary example presented in this text, there are other approaches available to school counselors for data collection and sharing results. As a school counselor educator, it is my responsibility to ensure, my graduate students utilize a variety of methods for marketing results, as schools and districts prefer different approaches, and counseling students are best prepared when they are proficient in multiple methods. Below are samples of additional resources:

The **SPARC** (Support Personnel Accountability Report Card) is a voluntary, continuous-improvement, one-page, two-sided document that identifies key college and career readiness outcomes for students (http://www.sparconline.net/). Recently two SDSU graduate students assisted Sweetwater Union High School in preparing a SPARC, which led to each receiving a certificate of recognition from Tom Torlakson, their state superintendent of public instruction. Their SPARC is located in Appendix A1.

MEASURE (Mission, Elements, Analyze, Stakeholders-Unite, Results, Educate) is a six-step process that helps school counselors organize their efforts and share their results (Stone & Dahir, 2007, 2011). A sample PowerPoint of the MEASURE is included in the online appendix.

Get a GRIP! is a one- or more-page organizing document that assists counselors with focusing on Goals, Results, Impact statements, and Program implications (Brott, 2008; Thompson, 2012). Appendices A2, A3, and A4 contain three GRIP templates that have been revised to align with the Flashlight Approach by Frieda Trujillo in Albuquerque Public Schools and further revised for this text.

PRoBE Projects (Partnership in Results-Based Evaluation) are designed to serve as models to evaluate the results of both the process and information delivery of counseling programs (http://www.missouricareereducation.org/project/probesample). At the University of Missouri-Kansas City, Deb Woodard encourages counseling candidates to tell a story to school stakeholders through the use of Prezi formats (http://prezi.com/v5srwmui6ld6/probe-project-6th-graders-at-plaza-middle-school/). Appendix A5 contains a PRoBE project rubric.

The online appendix contains additional samples of SPARCs, MEASUREs, PRoBEs, GRIPs, and Flashlight PowerPoints.

Recently, a counselor called from a nearby district in a panic: "The District is changing to the MEASURE; they are dropping the ASCA National Model!" I smiled and reassured her. I told her the ASCA National Model is a framework that calls for school counselors to use data to drive decision making, implement programs and activities, collect results, share successes, and use the results for program improvement. The MEASURE is a counselor-led systemic initiative that aligns with several components in the ASCA National Model (Stone & Dahir, 2007; 2011). Similarly, the Flashlight, SPARC, GRIP, and PRoBE are all methods for sharing results. Whatever format the district, school counselor, or graduate student selects, the most important message is not which tool is used, but that school counselors *measure something* they are doing (curriculum, intervention, closing-the-gap activity) and that they use the results to promote program improvement and sustainability.

FILLING OUT THE RESULTS REPORT

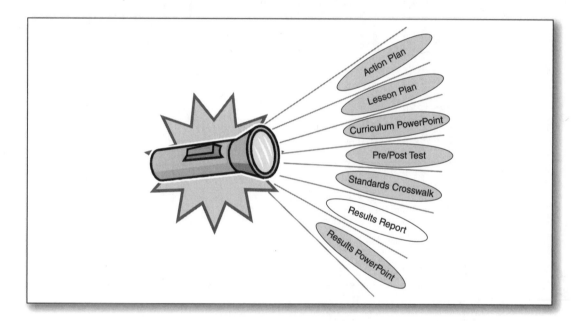

   Writing results reports is often a new skill for many school counselors. Figures 10.1 and 10.2 provide helpful guidelines for filling out results reports for both curriculum and intentional guidance. These samples will assist school counselors when preparing their Flashlight PowerPoints, as the information contained within them aligns with the rubric for the Flashlight. If the action plan has been filled out thoroughly, looking at it while completing these will be far easier. School counselors may also want to utilize a rubric for scoring results reports. When Julie Hartline assessed the impact of school counselors' results reports using a rubric she created, she found that more than half of the 100 results reports she assessed were missing important data elements. Some included postassessment data without preassessment data; others reported outcome data that didn't link conceptually to the activity (Hartline & Cobia, 2012). Almost half, however, were able to identify a data link between the intervention and improvements in achievement-related or achievement data. Readers are encouraged to discover more about Hartline's study (referenced in this text), and to utilize the core curriculum and closing-the-gap rubrics (Hartline & Cobia, 2012) located in Appendix A6.

Figure 10.1 Sample Results Rubric 1

_____ School District
School Counseling Curriculum Results Report 20XX–20XX

Grade Level	Lesson Content	Curriculum and Materials	Number of Lessons Delivered in What Class or Subject (or intervention provided)	Start Date/ End Date	Process Data: (number of students impacted)	Perception Data: Pre/Post Test, Activity, or Student Data (what they learned, believe, think or can demonstrate)	Results Data: How did students' behavior change because of the lesson? (improved behavior, attendance, or achievement)	Limitations/ Implications/ Recommendations (What do the data tell you?)
What grade level(s) did you service?	What was the content of your lesson? Describe the topics covered.	What materials did you use? Were they pre-packaged or counselor generated?	When was the curriculum or intervention delivered? Where was lesson held? In classrooms or lecture hall? How many lessons were delivered?	When did you begin and end the lesson?	How many students received the lessons?	Results of Pre/Post Test (Pick a few relevant samples to describe here, and attach the rest of the results to the report.) Attitude: Prior to lesson, ____% believed XYZ. After the lesson ____% indicated they believe XYZ. Skills: Prior to lesson, ____% demonstrated XYZ. After the lesson, ____% demonstrated XYZ Knowledge: Prior to lesson, ____% knew XYZ After the lesson, ____% know XYZ	Achievement-Related: Report any achievement-related data you collected or are monitoring for improvement. This will vary depending on activity but may include homework rates, attendance rates, discipline data, etc. Achievement: Report any academic achievement data you collected or are monitoring for improvement. This will vary depending on activity, but may include GPA, graduation rates, test scores, % of students passing classes, % of students scoring at or above grade level, etc.	What worked? What didn't? What will you do differently next time? Were there limitations to your results? What recommendations do you have for improvement?

_____   _____
Principal's Signature   Date

_____
Prepared By

Figure 10.2   Sample Results Rubric 2

School District
Intentional Guidance Results Report 20XX–20XX

Grade Level	Target Group/ Criteria Based on . . .	What intervention activities did you perform? Did you survey the at-risk group for barriers to learning? Group counseling?	Materials or Curriculum Used	Start Date/ End Date	Process Data: (number of students impacted)	Perception Data: Pre/Post Test, Activity, or Student Data (what they learned, believe, think, or can demonstrate)	Results Data: How did students' behavior change because of the lesson? (improved behavior, attendance, or achievement)	Limitations/ Implications/ Recommendations (What do the data tell you?)
What grade levels did you service?	What was the target group you selected for this intentional guidance? What were the specific data criteria you used to select this target group?	Include information gathered from needs survey (if you did one). What did the survey reveal students needed? Did you send parent letters home? Did you refer to other services or resources for intervention? Did you hold weekly group session? List everything you did to provide this intervention. (Remember this is the recipe part that will help others understand what you did, so they can learn from it and replicate it.)	Include the name of the specific curriculum if used (e.g., Why Try).	When did you begin and end the intervention?	How many students qualified to receive the intervention? How many actually received it?	Results of Pre/Post Test (Pick a few samples to describe here, and perhaps attach the rest of the results.) Attitude: Prior to the intervention, ___% believed XYZ After the intervention, ___% indicated they believe XYZ Skills: Prior to intervention, ___% demonstrated XYZ After the intervention, ___% demonstrated XYZ Knowledge: Prior to the intervention, ___% knew XYZ After the intervention, ___% know XYZ	Achievement-Related: Report any achievement-related data you collected or are monitoring for improvement. This will vary depending on activity, but may include homework rates, attendance rates, discipline data, etc. Achievement: Report any academic achievement data you collected or are monitoring for improvement. This will vary depending on activity, but may include GPA, graduation rates, test scores, % of students passing classes, % of students scoring at or above grade level on achievement tests, etc.	What worked? What didn't? What will you do differently next time? Were there limitations to your results? What recommendations do you have for improvement?

_____
Principal's Signature

_____
Date

_____
Prepared By

IMPACT OVER TIME

When designing schoolwide curriculum or intentional guidance activities for certain groups of students or systems, it may be helpful to look at the "Results Report: Impact Over Time" form (Figure 10.3), which serves as a summary sheet, listing site baseline and change data over time in all domain areas (academic, career, and personal/social). The data provide school counselors with a tool to review overall disaggregated student progress, providing a summary of the comprehensive program for the school site or district. Similar to the Data Profile (ASCA, 2012a), the Impact Over Time report also documents baseline data prior to programmatic restructuring.

While immediate results in attendance, behavior, and academic achievement may be seen with individual students or through intentional guidance for targeted student populations, schoolwide systemic change requires data that tell the larger story and present an evaluation of student progress overall. The choice of what to report depends on the school or school district's priorities and may include information such as demographic data, attendance data, suspension/expulsion rates, detention rates, graduation rates, underrepresented group data, and so on. As student populations and community demographics change, data may also shift. (Johnson & Johnson, 2001; Hatch & Holland, 2001; ASCA, 2002, 2005)

Tracking this information over time allows sites to evaluate and alter programs based on local needs. The implications of the data may stir a moral imperative for schools to implement new programs or policies designed to address the needs. It provides ready, necessary information for data-based decision making and calls into question whether the data reflect progress toward fulfilling the schoolwide mission and meeting the school's goals. The Impact Over Time report allows for use of data as a guide in continual program improvement, invites reflection and participation, and offers a systemic opportunity to share program achievements. The information provided is often in the school profile and is extremely valuable for all school counseling personnel. It indicates areas of strength and weakness, and growth or loss in overall program success.

CALCULATING PERCENTAGES USING THE "THE DAVID EFFECT"

When filling out the results report, it is important to accurately present the impact of the lessons or activities. Careful attention must be given to correct calculations of the pre/post test data and before/after data when computing the impact of the activity or lesson. One important point to remember is the distinction between the terms *increase* and *improvement*. For example, if someone had a quarter and was given an additional quarter, the *increase* would be 25 cents, but the *improvement* to the total amount of funds would be 100%, because the total amount of money doubled. In the same way, if the percentage of correct responses on a test shifted from 25% to 50%, this represents an *increase* of 25%, and an *improvement* of 100%.

Making a mathematical mistake in calculating the impact of school counselor activities could prove embarrassing. In the box that follows is an easy way to calculate percentages, affectionately called "The David Effect" because years ago, David, a school counselor, taught all the counselors in his district this way to calculate their

Figure 10.3 Results Report: Impact Over Time

	Results Reports: Impact Over Time				
School _____	School Year _____ Date _____				
		Academic Year			
	Measure	2012–2013	2013–2014	2014–2015	2015–2016
ACADEMIC					
	Graduation rate				
	Graduation rate (college eligible)				
	% of students taking SAT (or ACT)				
	Average score of students taking SAT (or ACT)				
	% of students taking AP classes				
	% of students with an AP score of 3 or better				
	% of underrepresented students taking AP classes				
	% of underrepresented students with an AP score of 3 or better				
	Amount of dollars in scholarships awarded				
	% of students accepted to four-year colleges				
	Dropout rate				
	# of students accepted to two-year colleges				
	# of students enlisted in the military after graduation				
CAREER DEVELOPMENT					
	% of students with interest inventories on file (completing Naviance, for example)				
	# of students attending career fair workshops				
	# of students completing resumes and job searches				

(Continued)

Figure 10.3 (Continued)

% of seniors participating in job shadowing	
% of students completing 100 hours or more of community service	

PERSONAL/SOCIAL

% of students suspended	
# of conflict mediations	
# of students referred for disciplinary reasons	
# of students participating in extracurricular activities	
% of students with positive attendance	

NONSTANDARDS-BASED DATA:

Other data:

Lead Counselor _____ **Principal Signature** _____

results (Hatch & Holland, 2001). This easy method not only yields correct results, it also assures the program will get accurate credit for the real improvement it has made!

---

1. Pretest number correct or beginning # = A

2. Posttest number correct or final # = B

3. B − A = C (change)

4. C/A = D (decimal change)

Move the decimal in the result from Step 4 two digits to right to get the percentage change. The result signifies the percentage improvement.

Example: Pretest A = 10 Posttest B = 25

25(B) − 10(A) = 15(C)

15(C)/10(A) = 1.5 (D)

Move the decimal two places to the right to get the percentage change: 1.5 = 150% change.

Now YOU try it!

Exercise #1:

1. 5 people answered question #5 correctly on pretest

2. 25 people answered question #5 correctly on posttest

What was the improvement in the percentage of students who answered question #5 correctly from the pretest to the posttest?

A = ___ B = ___

___ (B) − ___ (A) = ___ (C)

___(C)/___ (A) = ___ (D)

Move the decimal two places to the right to get % change:_____ = _____%

Exercise #2:

1. In Quarter 1, there were 33 discipline referrals.

2. In Quarter 2, there were 19 discipline referrals.

What was the percentage decrease in discipline referrals from Quarter 1 to Quarter 2?

A = ___ B = ___

___ (B) − ___ (A) = ___ (C)

___ (C)/___ (A) = ___ (D)

Move the decimal two places to the right to get % change ___ = ___%

[The answers are: #1= 400% improvement; #2 = − 42%, or a 42% decrease]

As a final reminder, care must be taken to avoid confusing the *improvement* with the *increase* (or *decrease*). If the average student score on an exam was 77% the first time it was given and 89% the second time, the average score increased by 12%. However, the improvement in student scoring was greater than 12%. The improvement would be 15.5%.

In summary, *improvement* is percentage as calculated in relationship to the original average score. *Increase* (or *decrease*) is the actual percentage increase/decrease from before the lesson or intervention to after. These calculations are also helpful when measuring the impact of behavior change in students. Counselors can compare improvements in students' attendance or number of F's before and after interventions.

CREATING GRAPHIC REPRESENTATIONS OF DATA

After calculating increases and improvements, it is time to find a way to present the data to constituents in a way that communicates the desired message. This can be done very effectively through text, or can be more creatively presented in charts and graphs. A PowerPoint presentation can often be a visually stimulating tool for organizing, representing, and comparing data. The PowerPoint slides below indicate, in text (Figure 10.4) and chart (Figure 10.5) form, a sample of a school counselor's results working with elementary students on Second Step skills. Both slides provide the same information; however, the bar chart (Figure 10.5) shows the improvement more dramatically.

Figure 10.4 Text Representation of Data

Second Step Care Curriculum

Problem-Solving Skills

Number of Students (Out of 70) who...

Know three ways to solve problems

Before: 5   After: 57

Identified steps in problem solving

Before: 12   After: 55

Demonstrated "calm down" strategy

Before: 4   After: 61

Data can be presented many ways using Excel programs to create charts. *Bar charts* are great for showing before-and-after data from pre/post tests, and for displaying data that show how knowledge or behavior has changed from before a lesson or intervention to after it. Arrows, data labels, and callouts help focus the readers' attention on the important information and on what the chart is intended to

Figure 10.5 Graphic Representation of Data

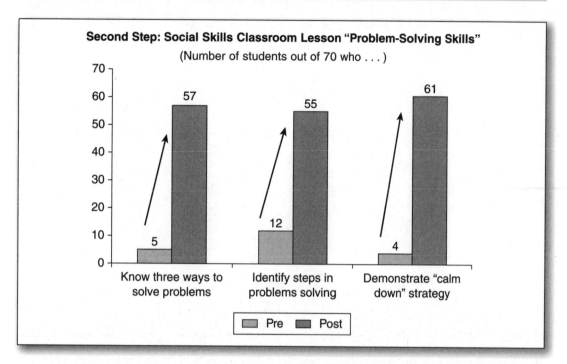

demonstrate. Note the callout in Figure 10.6: "More work is needed here." The arrows and callouts are found by clicking in the PowerPoint programs on the "inserts" tab and then on "shapes" and scrolling down.

Figure 10.6 Example of Use of a Callout in a Bar Chart

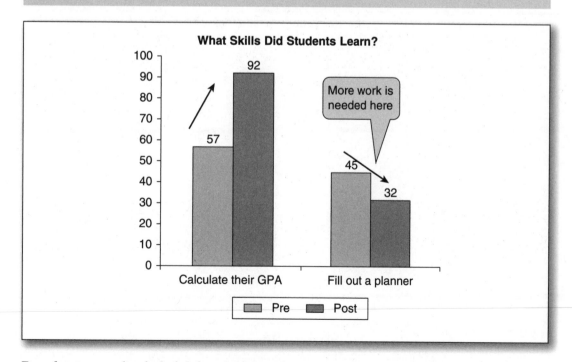

Bar charts are also helpful for showing data comparing one school to another and over a period of time (see Figure 10.7).

Figure 10.7   Example of Bar Chart Comparing Schools

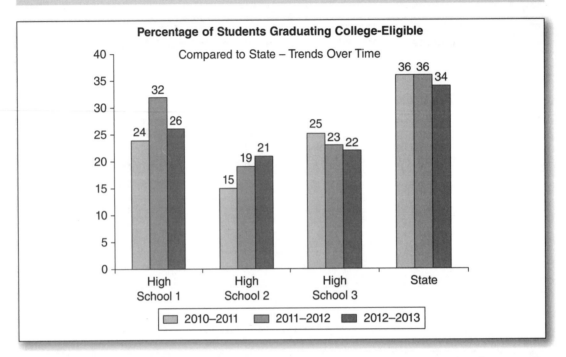

A *line graph* is helpful when comparing two variables over time (such as grade levels and months), as seen in Figure 10.8. A line graph shows trends in the data in a different way than a bar chart.

Figure 10.8   Sample Line Graph

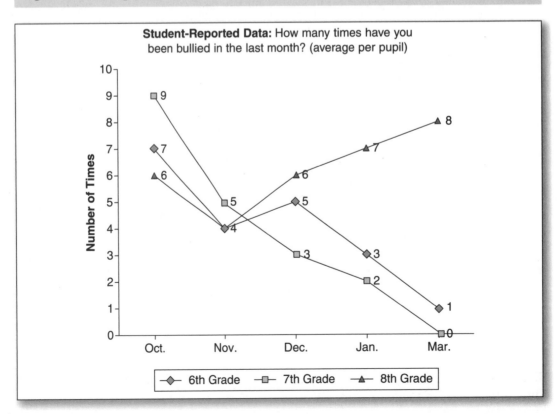

COMMON MISTAKES AND PITFALLS

When improvements are seen in attendance, behavior, and/or achievement data, it is tempting to rush to celebrate. Caution is recommended before assuming school counselors get all the credit. There may be other factors that contribute to improvements in, for example, attendance. Was a new attendance policy created? Was an attendance recovery program put into place? Any of these policy shifts could have contributed as well. Similarly, if discipline data reveal more referrals since school counselors started a violence prevention curriculum, it may not mean the curriculum is failing. It could be that students are less tolerant of bullying behavior and are now reporting it more often. Perhaps teachers are taking reporting discipline more seriously, or a new principal is encouraging more consistent documentation of discipline. Thinking through all the policies or contributing factors that may have influenced the shift in data will add credibility to the school counselors' report of the data.

> The school counselors at "Success High School" were elated to see the number of students graduating college eligible improved 21% over the previous three years. During that same time, the school counselors had started teaching classroom lessons and meeting with students individually to encourage students to take rigorous courses. Before presenting their success to the principal, they were reminded that another important event also occurred: Graduation requirements had shifted to align with college entrance requirements. Okay . . . so they don't get *all* the credit, but they contributed in a meaningful way.

PowerPoint slides are a powerful tool counselors can utilize when reporting results that are correlated with counseling activities to market their programs and earn legitimacy in schools. Caution is recommended, however, when results are reported as "proof" that a school counseling program "caused" the improvement in results data. Given the many internal and external variables as well as various teachers and educators that come into contact with students, it would be very difficult to "prove" that the only reason students attend, behave, or achieve differently is caused by the school counseling activity. Rather, it is appropriate to report these improvements as "correlated" with the intervention provided. Drawing the conceptual link between the activity and the outcomes is an important part of the reporting process. Taking all the credit is not. Therefore, school counselors are reminded to share credit with other educators working to support student achievement and to share how they are contributing in a meaningful way to the overall academic achievement of all students.

Finally, consider the many purposes of collecting and sharing results and imagine the impact of sharing these results with different stakeholders. Then ask yourself the following:

What RESULT do you want as a RESULT of sharing your RESULTS?

11

Reporting Results via the Flashlight Approach

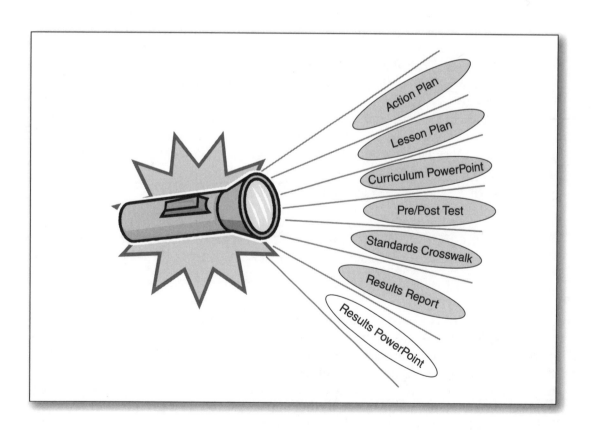

THE FLASHLIGHT APPROACH: MEASURING ONE THING—WELL

In many districts each year (Albuquerque Public Schools is just one example), it is expected that school counselors turn in action plans in the fall and results in the spring. The year culminates in a celebration day, when school counselors gather with administrators to share the successes of the year's activities. School counselors create presentations of their Flashlight PowerPoints for the year, and, divided into grade levels (high school, middle school, and elementary) they proudly share their results (Hatch, 2004b). Following each presentation, school counselors engage in collegial conversations about what worked, what didn't, and how they plan to improve their activities.

What is a Flashlight? Common knowledge suggests that a real flashlight does not light up an entire room; rather, it shines a beam of light on one area or in one direction on a specific target. In the same way, rather than school counselors showing the impact of everything they do, it is suggested school counselors select ONE thing they have done (one curriculum action plan and one intentional guidance action plan) and "shine the flashlight" on it.

The Flashlight was adapted from Weiss's logic model for evaluation (1998).

1. Describe the program; provide process data: who, what, when, how.
2. Did program follow original plan?
3. Did participants improve? (pre/post of knowledge, attitudes, and skills; behavior change)
4. Did participants do better than those who did not participate?
5. Is the change in perception or behavior due to the program or activity? What is the plausibility?
6. Disaggregate outcomes to show what characteristics are associated with success of the program recipients, services, or conditions.
7. What combination of factors, services, or conditions constituted success or failure?
8. Were there any unexpected events?
9. What are the limitations to generalizability?
10. Implications for future?
11. Recommendations?
12. Policy analysis: What new policy or programs are supported though this?
13. What was the value of the improvement? What is the cost/benefit analysis?

The Flashlight is a way to immediately begin to show results of a program using key concepts in the ASCA National Model, even if you are just beginning to understand it. Some school counselors may believe they need to finish each component of the model before moving forward. For example, they may want to take the first year to determine which standards to address, or write their entire curriculum and then connect it to standards, all before collecting impact data on their programs or activities. When counselors do this, they may be forced to wait years to have results to share with stakeholders. Professional school counselors simply cannot wait that long to gather data to show their programs are working. Instead of taking the first year to align all lessons to standards, and then waiting until the following year to collect results of the program, it is suggested counselors choose one thing they want to measure.

Selection of only one thing means the school counselors measure a lesson they already use in the program or a new lesson they would like to create and deliver. Then, using the Flashlight approach, they follow the counseling activity all the way through: standards, activity, process, perception, results data, and implications (just as presented in the action plan samples in the ASCA National Model). When counselors are learning to collect and use data to share program success, it is important they do not try to measure *everything*. While getting lost in the data can be fun when counselors are just beginning, it can also feel very overwhelming. Instead of measuring every lesson delivered or intervention conducted, it is suggested counselors use the Flashlight approach to focus on sharing the impact of a lesson or activity currently implemented, or an intervention the data indicate must be addressed in the area of attendance, behavior, or achievement. Then, create the PowerPoint and share successes with school staff. Finally, encourage other school counselors in the district to come together to celebrate and share successes. It's a great opportunity to learn, grow, and take pride in the value of the profession.

FLASHLIGHT RATING SCALE RUBRIC

If you would like to create your own Flashlight Results PowerPoint, follow the rubric in Figure 11.1, created as a guide to assist school counselors through the process (Hatch, 2010a). The sample in the figure is not intended to be a prescription; rather, it contains elements that can be interwoven to tell a story—*your* story. Note that the sample starts with the title slide and then calls for the ASCA Student Standards to be presented next. As the author of your Flashlight, you might prefer to present your lesson first, or some concerning schoolwide data that led to the decision to provide this specific intervention. Either way is fine, so long as each of the areas is explained. Presenting the standards, rationale (with data), and relevant research frames the story for the audience. After the content of the activity and results are presented, the rubric calls for slides that, much like the results report, share the lessons learned, next steps, and areas of improvement (Hatch, 2004b).

Figure 11.1 Flashlight Rating Scale Rubric

Category 1: Slide Contents Standard Met?	Yes	Somewhat	No
Title slide identifies name of presentation, school, and counselor(s).			
ASCA student counseling standards and competencies addressed. (Indicate the standard and competencies.)			
Lesson or intervention addresses a need identified by school data.			
Relevant research connecting need to activity presented.			
Complete process data for curriculum lesson activity are reported: Who, what, when, and how often was the activity conducted? (If Intentional guidance, specify target group and selection criteria.)			

(Continued)

Figure 11.1 (Continued)

Sampling of results of the pre/post tests (perception data) are reported, including graphic representations (e.g., bar graphs, line charts).			
Achievement-related data are presented and linked to perception data and the targeted achievement indicator.			
Achievement data that link to the activity are reported, including graphic representations.			
There is a slide summarizing the main points and the lessons learned (and their implications).			
One or more slides address limitations of the lesson and/or results.			
One or more slides address next steps and/or improvement.			
A thank-you slide acknowledges the contributions of teachers and staff to the work of school counselors.			

Category 2: Presentation Standard Met?	Yes	Somewhat	No
Presentation is easy to follow, and slides are in a logical order.			
Format is clear and consistent.			
There is a maximum of 25 slides.			
Text is concise and easy to read.			
Graphs are clearly labeled, accurate, and impactful.			
Conceptual link slides aid smooth transitions.			
Colors, graphics, and effects are used for maximal impact and minimal distraction.			

Category 3: Counseling Standard Met?	Yes	Somewhat	No
Lesson or intervention addresses a need identified by school data.			
Lesson/lesson plan is developmentally appropriate for desired results.			
Pre/post test questions are relevant and well written.			
Data collection and evaluation methods are appropriate (measure what they say they will measure).			

Supplemental Items	Yes	Somewhat	No
Action Plan			
Lesson Plan			
ASCA National Standards Crosswalk			

Lesson PowerPoint and/or Lesson Content			
Pre/Post Test			
Results Form			
Flashlight PowerPoint—see Slide Contents (Category 1) above			
Completed Rubric			

FLASHLIGHT INSTRUCTIONS

The sample Flashlight PowerPoint presentations shown in the next two sections are presented in a "skeleton" format, without pretty designs or bells and whistles. Presenting the slides stripped of clip art allows the creator to focus first on the content. When the content is completed, it is suggested simple designs be used rather than overly complicated designs, as this may distract from the presentation and results.

The two presentations—one for presenting results from a curriculum lesson and a second for presenting results from intentional guidance—are shared in "notes" form. Within the notes section, there are two specific areas: "slide content" and "what you say." The slide content provides a suggestion for what goes on each slide. First time "Flashlighters" are encouraged to follow the format as it is presented. Experienced school counselors may want to shift the slides to create their own more personalized Flashlight. The "what you say" section is provided to give counselors an idea of what they might say to their staff when they present this PowerPoint. It is helpful to prepare so as not to present longer than 10 minutes. Both PowerPoint presentations are designed to be presented within that time frame. Also, note alignment with Figures 5.2 (Curriculum Lesson) and 5.8 (Intentional Guidance).

CURRICULUM LESSON PRESENTATION: DETAILED WALKTHROUGH

XYZ Middle School

School Counseling Program

**Classroom Lesson on
Promotion Retention and Study Skills**

(Results sample)

Hatching Results® (2010)

Slide 1: Title Slide

List your school name, and indicate that this is a "results sample" (because it is only one sample of the many things that occur in the school counseling department).

What you say: Staff, thank you for coming and being here on time. Let's get started. First we would like to thank [Mr./Mrs./Dr. Principal] for having us here today and for supporting the work of the school counseling program. Today we will share with you an example of one of the many classroom lessons offered by the school counseling department. This year, we measured the impact of the curriculum we created to address our school's high failure and retention rates.

National Standard

Academic Standard A

Students will acquire the attitudes,
knowledge and skills that contribute
to effective learning in school and
across the life span.

A:A1 Improve Academic Self-Concept
A:A3 Achieve School Success

Hatching Results® (2010)

Slide 2: ASCA National Standard and Student Competencies Addressed

Indicate the ASCA National Standard you will be addressing in this activity. It might be more than one. Select the appropriate student competencies you are addressing in this classroom lesson. You may also want to show that you are addressing state standards by including your state's content standards on a slide.

What you say: Just as teachers have standards for what students should know and be able to do, so too do school counselors. School counseling standards are in three domain areas: academic, career, and personal/social development. Today's curriculum results presentation addresses National Standards A [read standard]. The competencies addressed in this lesson are Improving Academic Self-Concept and Achieving School Success.

What Did Students Receive?

Grades 6, 7, 8

- During October/November
- In Language Arts Class
- Two Lessons per Class
- Pre-Post Assessment

Hatching Results® (2010)

Slide 3: Process Data—What did the counselors do and for whom?

These data are located in the action plan and results report. Include what you did, when you did it, for whom you did it, and for how long (number of times and how long each time). You would also want to include the title of any curriculum used.

What you say: So what did we do? Well, as you know if you are a language arts teacher, we scheduled time to come into your classroom twice and delivered school counselor–generated lessons in October and November.

What Did Students Receive?

Schoolwide Core Curriculum

Lessons contained the following topics:
- –Retention criteria
- –How to avoid retention
- –How to calculate a GPA
- –Study skills that lead to success
- –Importance of homework completion
- –Positive attitude and success

Hatching Results® (2010)

Slide 4: Process Data—What did the counselors do and for whom? (continued)

What you say: Students received lessons on promotion/retention criteria, techniques for avoiding retention, and how to calculate their GPA. We also presented study skills and discussed the importance of a positive attitude and how it can lead to school success.

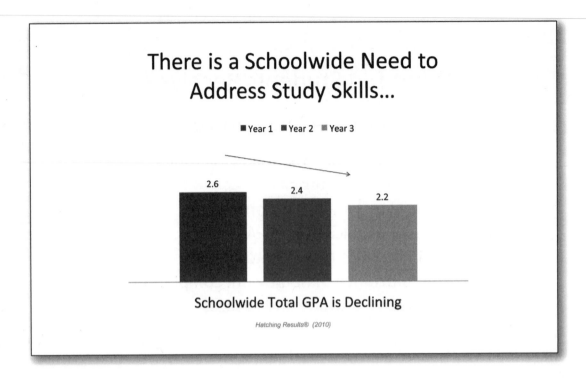

Slide 5: Why are you teaching this particular lesson?

Need addressed should be shown using school data. Provide a slide that tells why there is a need for this lesson. In this slide, counselors can share that schoolwide GPA is declining. However, if your lesson is on violence prevention, you may want to show school climate data.

What you say: As the graph indicates, our students' GPAs are declining, and we are concerned that this means more students will be up for retention this spring. We are hoping that students will use the skills we are teaching them, take their work seriously, and begin to perform better.

Why Are We Teaching Homework Strategies?

Research says:

Students who complete and turn in homework do better in school.

(Cooper, Lindsay, Nye & Greathouse, 1998).

Teachers report that the greatest barrier to passing grades is homework completion.

Hatching Results® (2010)

Slide 6: Why address this concern in this way? List relevant research.

The purpose of this slide is to share research that will help the audience understand why performing this activity or teaching this lesson links to the data you are trying to improve. (For more examples of research quotes or statements that can be used, see Appendix B).

What you say: Research indicates students who complete and turn in homework do better in school. We also surveyed the teachers and learned that the greatest barrier to passing grades is homework completion. Our goal is to encourage students to take homework seriously, so they can perform better in your classrooms.

What Do Students KNOW?

Pre	Post
Only **15%** of the students knew the retention criteria	**98%** of the students know the retention criteria

Hatching Results® (2010)

Slide 7: Perception Data (Attitude, Knowledge, or Skill)

List the results of your pre/post tests here.

What you say: Pre- and posttests were given to students. As you can see, before the lesson, on average, only 15% of students demonstrated knowledge of promotion/retention criteria; after the lesson, 98% of students demonstrated knowledge of retention criteria. This is because we worked with the students [thank you to the teachers who assisted us when we needed it] until every student knew the promotion requirements policy—after all, which student deserves not to know? In addition, we actually presented two lessons in each class, rather than just the one we originally planned, as we realized it would take longer than expected to get these results. Thank you for your flexibility with scheduling the second lesson.

What SKILL Did Students Learn?

Pre	Post
• **22%** could calculate a GPA	• **92%** can calculate a GPA
• **32%** could identify appropriate study strategies	• **85%** can identify appropriate study strategies

Hatching Results® (2010)

Slide 8: Perception Data (continued)

Add a couple more pre/post data pieces you believe will have the most impact and be the most beneficial to your presentation. While you may have collected results on several different ASK (attitudes, knowledge, and skills) items, it is best not to share every pre/post item, as it will make the presentation too long. Instead, select the most appropriate ones that will support your message, and share the others in a handout.

What you say: Before the lesson, only 22% of the students could calculate (skill) their GPA; afterward 92% could. Before the lessons, 32% could identify study strategies that would help them do better in school; afterward 85% did.

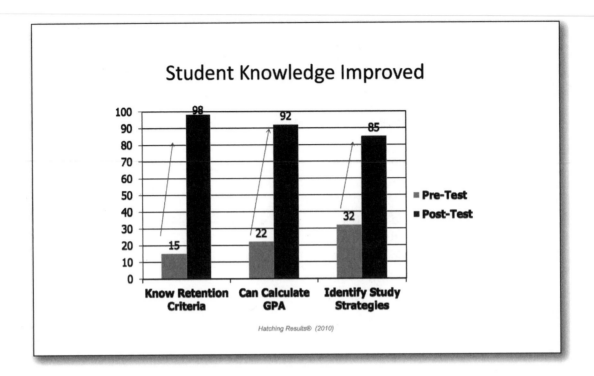

Slide 9: Graphic Representation of Perception Data

Presenting the data in graph form can really make the difference in enabling your audience to visualize student gains.

*What you say: As you can see in the graph, students learned a great deal in the lesson—it had an **immediate** impact.*

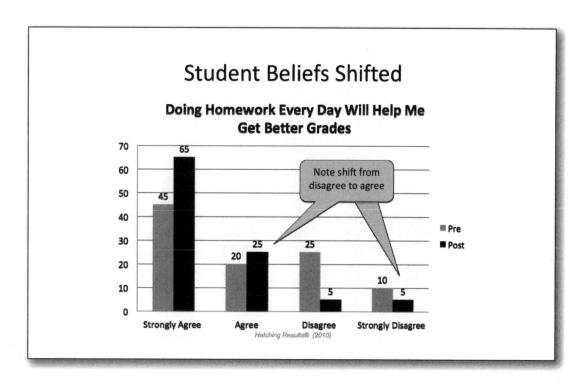

Slide 10: Include a "beliefs" graph that shows the shift from "disagree" to "agree" or "agree" to "disagree."

What you say: Note on this graph that students shifted their attitudes to agree that doing homework will help them earn better grades.

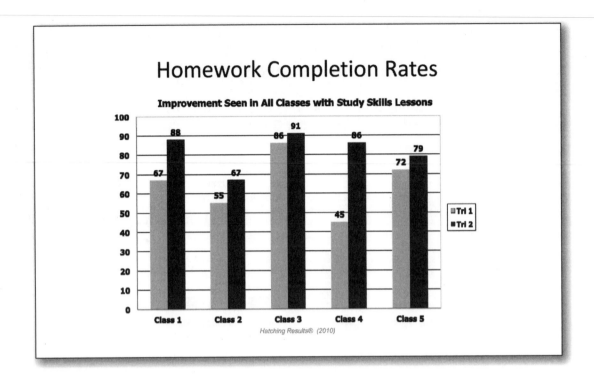

Slide 11: Achievement-Related Data

This slide will contain your achievement-related data—in this case, homework completion rates.

What you say: To see if we were making a difference in student behaviors, we looked at intermediate data, that is, whether students improved their homework habits in five language arts classes. As you can see, every class improved! While we can't take all of the credit for this—we know teachers are working on this too—we are excited to see that students are improving their homework completion rates! Thank you to the teachers who helped us gather these data.

Student Achievement Outcomes

From Trimester 1 – Trimester 2

Before Curriculum Lessons
20xx GPA's increased from 2.2 to 2.25

After Curriculum Lessons
20xx GPA's increased from 2.1 to 2.4

Hatching Results® (2010)

Slide 12: Results Data

This slide is where the achievement results data are located.

What you say: One of the goals of this lesson was to see if it could contribute to an increase in students' motivation to improve their grades. In 20XX, the average schoolwide GPA was 2.2 in Trimester 1 and 2.25 in Trimester 2. This year, interestingly, the average GPA was lower than last year. It was 2.1. However, I am pleased to share with you that we have calculated the second trimester GPAs, and our overall schoolwide GPA has increased to 2.4!

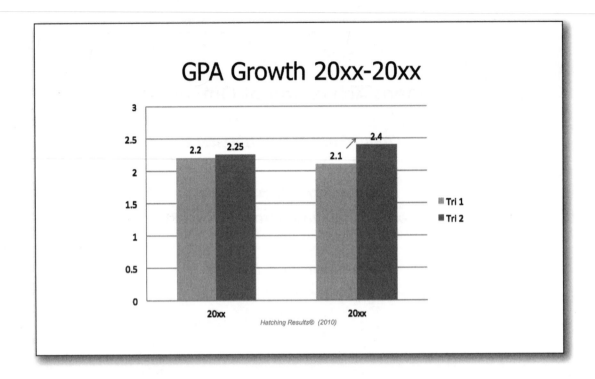

Slide 13: Graph Results

The visual effect of a bar or line graph is very powerful. Although you may be tempted to have an axis of 2.0 to 3.0 to enlarge the part of the graph with the shifts, this is not recommended, as the gain will then appear disproportionately greater than it actually is. Using a range from 0 to 3.0 ensures your data are not perceived as misrepresenting real gains.

What you say: The graph does show improvement—last year the average total school GPA was 2.2 at the end of the first trimester; at the end of second trimester, it was 2.25. This year, the total GPA at the end of the first trimester was lower—2.1. However, by the end of the second trimester, the total GPA rose to 2.4! This is something we should all be very proud of. I know we are all working on this goal as a school. Some of you are tutoring, mentoring, and spending extra time with your students to assist them. Overall, these efforts appear to be having an impact, and we are moving in the right direction.

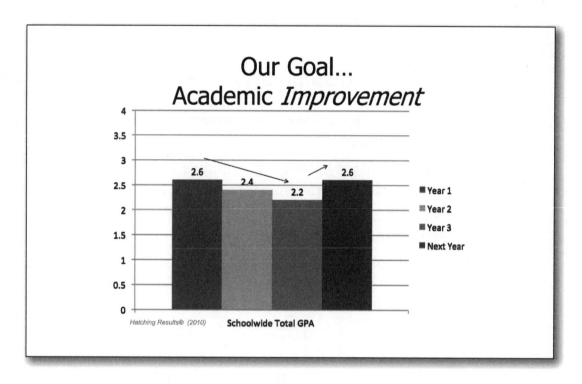

Slide 14: What are our goals for next year? What are we looking for as we move forward?

What you say: Our goal is to improve the school's overall GPA, so that fewer students will be up for retention or require summer school.

In Summary...

- Students received valuable information about study skills and retention criteria
- Students gained knowledge, attitudes and skills needed for academic success
- Lessons appear to contribute to student's improvement in homework completion rates
- The school's programs and interventions appear to support improvements in schoolwide GPA.

Hatching Results® (2010)

Slide 15: Summary

Tell what you learned from this. In this situation, the lesson was successful. Graciously share the following: The program was (or was not) effective. Remember not to take all credit. Finally, consider adding a student or faculty quote here to add an extra punch!

What you say: We are pleased to report that these lessons appear to be contributing to student success. As one seventh-grade boy shared after the lesson on calculating GPA: "Thanks! Now I can check my own GPA so I don't have to go to summer school!"

Limitations and Lessons Learned

- Do not schedule lessons on minimum days (ran out of time)
- Revise pre-post questions (wording was confusing for some students)
- Conduct pre-test a week prior to the lesson (provides more time to revise lesson content)
- Request teachers remain in class during lesson (to assist with students needing extra support)

Hatching Results® (2010)

Slide 16: Limitations and Lessons Learned

Tell what limitations you encountered. Was there enough time for the lesson? Were the pre/post questions flawed? Did you try to do too much? Did you try to teach too much too fast? What did you learn from this? Indicate what you might do differently next time.

What you say: Unfortunately we failed to provide enough time for the entire lesson in some classes due to the minimum day schedule. We need to make sure we do not schedule lessons on minimum days. We also need to revise some questions, as the wording was confusing for some students. We may want to do the pretest a week prior to the lesson, so we have more time to revise lesson content based on what we learn from the pretest. Finally, we may want to ask teachers to remain in class during our lesson to assist students who need extra support.

Next Steps

- We have queried the data on students in danger of failing

- We are currently working in small groups and meeting with parents

- We will report the impact of that intervention

Hatching Results® (2010)

Slide 17: Next Steps

What will you do next? Present to school board? Provide interventions?

What you say: Now we will move forward to start working with those students who have been identified as "in danger of failing," and we look forward to reporting those results to you at the end of the year!

**The school counseling program
is contributing in a meaningful way
to the academic achievement
of all students.**

*Thank you for your support of the school
counseling program.*

Hatching Results® (2010)

Slide 18: Thank You

Thank the staff for their support, and thank the administrator for her or his time. Offer to take questions at the end, and check to see that you stayed within the time you planned for the presentation (hopefully less than 10 minutes).

What you say: We wish to thank the school principal for [her/his] support and also thank all the language arts teachers for their support and collaboration.

Now that you have read through the first Flashlight, imagine yourself presenting something like this to faculty member at your school site. What might they learn about the school counseling program that they didn't know before?

When I ask this question at trainings, the most common responses are:

- *that we actually DO something!*
- *that we have standards too!*
- *that we use data in our program!*
- *that we aren't just winging it; that we have a plan!*
- *that we are working on the same goals and outcomes!*

What other comments might you imagine teachers having after your presentation?

INTENTIONAL GUIDANCE PRESENTATION: DETAILED WALKTHROUGH

XYZ Middle School

School Counseling Program
Intentional Guidance
(Results sample)

Hatching Results® (2010)

Slide 1: Title Slide

List your school's name, and indicate that this is a sample of results from your intentional guidance intervention (because it is only one sample of the many that occur in the school counseling department).

What you say: I'd like to thank [Mr./Ms./Dr. Principal] for validating the importance of the school counseling program by inviting us to present the results of our interventions to you. As you will recall, we presented the results of our promotion/retention curriculum earlier this year. At that time, we shared our plan to provide intentional guidance (intervention) to students identified as "needing more." We are here today to share these results with you.

Target Group

**All 6th, 7th and 8th Grade Students
in Danger of Failing.**

Hatching Results® (2010)

Slide 2: Target Group

Which students did you target to work with and why? (Students underachieving? Not attending? Not behaving?)

What you say: In consultation with the leadership team, we discussed the interventions we could do to address the needs shown by the data (attendance, behavior, achievement). The data indicated that the school had an increase in the number of students not meeting grade level promotion requirements—2.0 in math and language arts, and 2.0 overall. We decided to query the data to identify all sixth-, seventh-, and eighth-grade students who were in danger of failing.

> **Target Group selected on basis of following data:**
>
> **Students with a GPA of 1.3 or below on First Trimester Report Card.**
>
> *Hatching Results® (2010)*

Slide 3: Target group selected on basis of the following data. . . .

Specifically, how were the students identified? (e.g., students with a GPA below 1.3 on first trimester report card, with five or more absences, or with three or more referrals for fighting; or those with an N or U on their report cards in the Citizenship or Study Habits area)

What you say: In consultation with the administration and members of the leadership team, we decided to target those students with a 1.3 GPA or lower and provide them an intervention. Why 1.3?—best professional guess—it was our opinion that those above that point would benefit from other interventions and that these were the students with the most severe needs.

Why Intervene? Research Says...

Grade retention was found to be the *"single most powerful predictor"* of school dropout (Bridgeland, DiIulio, & Balfanz, 2009, p. 616).

Students from low socioeconomic status families are *twice as likely to drop out* of school as students from average social class families, even when controlling for other factors (Rumberger, 1995).

Hatching Results® (2010)

Slide 4: Why intervene? Why address this concern? What does the research say?

The purpose of this slide is to share research that will help the audience understand why performing this activity or teaching this lesson links to the data you are trying to improve. (For more examples of research quotes or statements that can be used, see Appendix B).

What you say: Research says students who complete and turn in homework do better in school. We surveyed the teachers and learned that the greatest barrier to passing grades is homework completion. Our goal is to encourage students to take homework seriously, so they can perform better in your classrooms.

A National *"On the Front Lines"* Report on Dropouts States...

- Schools need to <u>develop early warning systems</u> to help identify students at risk of dropping out and to <u>develop the mechanisms that trigger</u> appropriate supports for these students.

- By 9th grade, dropout can be predicted with 85 percent accuracy. The key indicators are <u>poor attendance, behavioral problems</u> and <u>course failure</u>.

(Bridgeland, Dilulio, & Balfanz, 2009)

Hatching Results® (2010)

Slide 5: It might be helpful to add a relevant and current message about the urgency of the need.

What you say: National dropout prevention experts are telling us we must create and implement early warning systems. This intervention is designed to do just that: create a mechanism to trigger an intervention.

National Standard
Academic Standard A

Students will acquire the attitudes,
knowledge and skills that contribute
to effective learning in school and
across the life span.

A:A1 Improve Academic Self-Concept
A:A3 Achieve School Success

Hatching Results® (2010)

Slide 6: ASCA National Standards and Student Competencies Addressed

Indicate the ASCA National Standard and student competencies you are addressing with this intervention.

What you say: Whenever school counselors provide services, we are working to address standards and competencies. In this case, the standard we addressed was Academic Standard A [read]. The competencies we addressed in this lesson were Improving Academic Self-Concept and Achieving School Success.

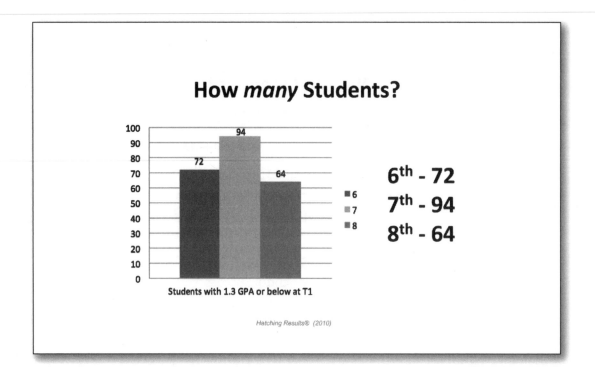

Slide 7: Process Data

Graph of the number of students you provided the intervention for.

What you say: [Tell your story if you have one.] Originally, we predicted we would provide intervention for 100 students total. However, when we queried the data, we soon realized that we had many more students who needed interventions than we predicted. We brainstormed ideas with our administrators:

a. *Maybe we should provide intervention only for sixth graders*
b. *Or only those with a GPA lower than 1.0 get the intervention*
c. *How about those with the best attendance (because they seem to want to be in school—maybe they have the best chance of improving)*
d. *Randomly selecting half to work with*

In collaboration with our administrator, we were able to renegotiate some of our responsibilities so that we could focus on providing direct services to all the students who qualified under our original criteria. We would like to thank our administrator for supporting that shift in responsibilities. We subsequently decided to meet with target group students in large groups first to discover what specific assistance they believed would help them.

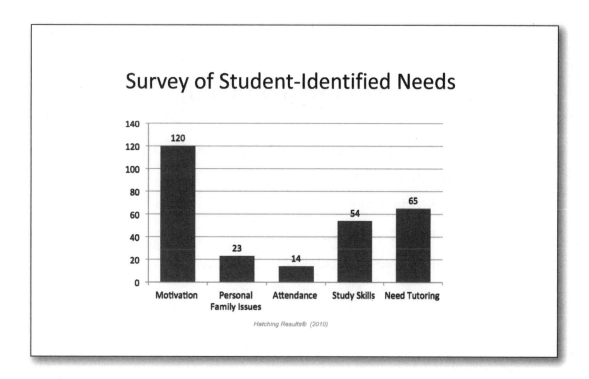

Slide 8: Surveying Needs

This slide can provide information about students identifying their needs and barriers.

What you say: We met with students in large and small groups in an effort to discover their barriers. Students who identified needing tutoring were placed in tutoring. Those requesting personal counseling received it or were referred to community-based services. Students who needed study strategies were provided large group lessons, and those who expressed concerns regarding motivation received a variety of interventions, including mentor match-up, small group counseling (Why Try? curriculum), and individual counseling as needed.

Study Strategies Groups

8 weeks: one class period a week on rotating basis
- –Study Strategies
- –Homework Tips
- –Positive Attitudes and Success
- –Using an Academic Planner

Hatching Results® (2010)

Slide 9: Process Data

Type of service delivered and in what manner? Group? Individual? What are you doing when? Where? How often? With what curriculum?

What you say: So, what did we do? We decided to work with the students who identified needing study skills and responsibility skills, using a prepackaged XYZ curriculum on these issues. We planned to meet with them for 12 weeks between the months of October and June, but with the number of students who needed assistance, we had to revise the curriculum to only 8 weeks.

**Results of Pre-Post Test
Knowledge of Study Strategies**

Pre	Post
• 6th - 55%	• 6th - 94%
• 7th - 48%	• 7th - 91%
• 8th - 35%	• 8th - 96%

Hatching Results® (2010)

Slide 10: Perception Data

List your pre/post data here for attitudes, skills, and knowledge. (Use charts and/or words.)

What you say: So what did we find? Well, interestingly, we found that our eighth-grade students who were struggling academically also scored lowest on our pretest. Specifically, students had little knowledge originally of the study strategies we taught (e.g., note-taking ideas) in the intervention. But in all grade levels, we did see great improvement in their ability to identify study strategies.

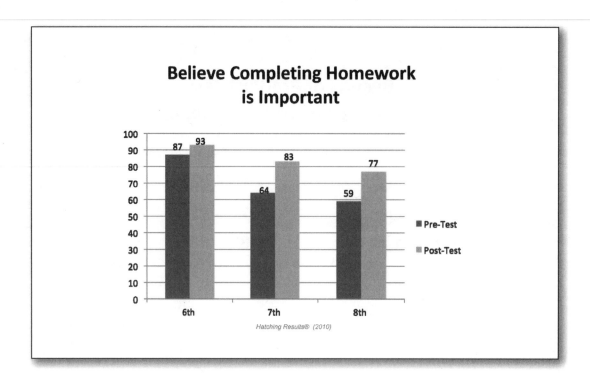

Slide 11: Perception Data (continued)

What you say: When asked if they believed doing and completing homework was important, again, fewer eighth graders responded positively than sixth or seventh graders, but all three groups reported shifts in their beliefs.

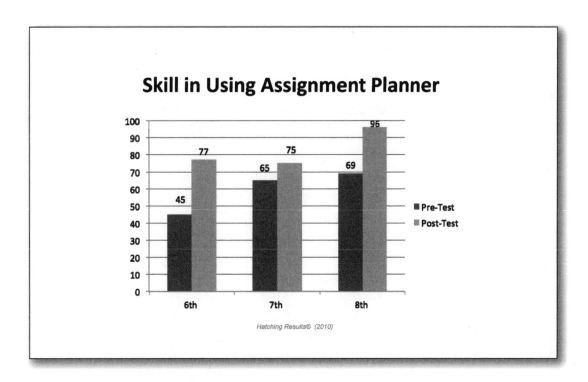

Slide 12: Perception Data (continued)

What you say: Finally, when we assessed their ability to use an academic planner, data indicated sixth graders needed the most help. All showed improvement, but as you can see, the gains were less in this area for seventh graders.

Our Goal...

- Students will gain knowledge of study strategies
- Students will gain skills they need to effectively use their planner
- Students will shift their attitudes regarding the importance of homework completion
- Improvement in these areas will result in better grades
- Improvement in grades will lead to reduction in number of students qualifying for retention

Hatching Results® (2010)

Slide 13: Remind them of the goal of the activity or the impact you are seeking.

What you say: Our goal is to assist the students in getting the support they need to get better grades and, hopefully, reduce the number of students qualifying for retention.

Results – **6th Grade** GPA Improvement

64 (37%) improved their GPA from Trimester 1 to Trimester 2.

<u>57%</u> of the targeted students earned a 2.0 or better GPA from Trimester 1 to Trimester 3.

Hatching Results® (2010)

Slide 14: Achievement Results

Indicate results obtained.

What you say: As you can read, 57% of the targeted sixth-grade students earned a 2.0 or better GPA from Trimester 1 to Trimester 3. Unfortunately, we did not obtain any achievement-related benchmarks, such as homework completion rates, resulting in a missing link in the causal chain of GPA improvement.

Results – **7th Grade** GPA Improvement

47 (24%) improved their GPA from Trimester 1 to Trimester 2.

<u>52%</u> of targeted students earned a 2.0 or better GPA from Trimester 1 to Trimester 3.

Hatching Results® (2010)

Slide 15: Achievement Results (continued)

What you say: In seventh grade, 52% of students earned a 2.0 or better by the end of Trimester 3.

Results – **8th Grade** GPA Improvement

46 (72%) improved their GPA from Trimester 1 to Trimester 2.

<u>85%</u> of targeted students earned a 2.0 or better GPA from Trimester 1 to Trimester 3.

Hatching Results® (2010)

Slide 16: Achievement Results (continued)

What you say: In eighth grade, 85% of students earned a 2.0 or better by the end of Trimester 3.

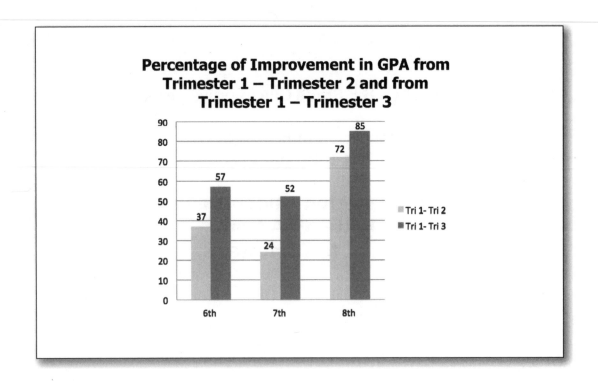

Slide 17: Graph Results (for impact)

What you say: Here you can see a graph showing that students' GPAs did improve. However, it appears that eighth graders improved more quickly, while it took longer for sixth graders and particularly for seventh graders to show improvement. One reality was that there were so many students in the seventh grade that they were not seen in small groups, but in larger groups. We believe this had an impact on the effectiveness of the intervention.

In Summary...

- By dividing students into groups with specific needs, we were able to provide specific targeted skill based interventions
- More students required interventions than we anticipated
- Every student received some type of intervention
- Students improved overall

Slide 18: Summary

Indicate your overall reflections of what worked.

What you say: [read slide]

Lessons Learned...Next Steps

- The smaller the number of students served, the greater the impact – we need smaller group sizes
- Disaggregating data in advance will help determine how many students qualify for interventions
- Large numbers of students at risk may mean we need to provide more prevention (get into classrooms earlier and teach study skills and motivational strategies)
- Look into impact of interventions on homework completion rates

Slide 19: Lessons Learned and Next Steps

What did you learn? What worked? What didn't? What would you do differently? (Perhaps measure homework?) How will you improve? Indicate areas needing improvement. Tell what you will do differently next time.

What you say: It was very difficult to manage this large number of students needing interventions. Therefore, we will have to seriously consider reviewing the criteria for selection next year and make decisions regarding how many students it is reasonable for us to work with at one time. It appears that with a smaller number of students, the intervention is more effective, but we don't have proof that this is the case. We believe it to be true, because we felt less effective in the larger groups, and the data tell us that the students in eighth grade performed better than others. Now, it could be that they had a greater incentive (promotion to high school), but it could also be group size. In order to find out, we need to try to find a way to decrease the number of students in each group. Maybe more sessions are needed in this area. Also, we'd like to see what impact the intervention has on homework completion rates.

Thank you!

- Teachers for collaborating on intervention schedules and providing grade checks
- Administrators for your consultation and support of the program
- Working together we are succeeding!

Slide 20: Thank You

Don't forget to mention that everyone at the school is working on these issues. Thank all those who are contributing to these efforts. Thank teachers and administration for supporting the school counseling program.

What you say: Again, we want to thank all of the teachers who diligently collaborated with us. We are continuing to use what we learned to improve our services for students and look forward to your feedback on this activity. Thank you again for your time, [Mr./Ms./Dr. Principal].

*The school counseling program
is committed to contributing
in a meaningful way
to the academic achievement
of all students*

The End

Slide: 21: Last Pitch

School counselors are contributing in a meaningful way to the overall academic achievement of students. The End! Applause!

What you say: [read slide] The end.

Note that this PowerPoint did not include achievement-related data. What could counselors have measured in this area? Homework completion, perhaps? What else? A slide could be inserted between slides 13 and 14 to include the results obtained in this area. Use graphs (comparable to the graph in Slide 17).

SHARING FLASHLIGHTS

Flashlight PowerPoint presentations provide a way for school counselors to share the impact of their activities with administrators, at school site faculty meetings, with central office administrators, and at school board meetings. Posting your Flashlight on your school or district website allows parents and community members to see the value of your work as well. But don't stop there! Encourage your colleagues to share their Flashlights as well, or suggest each school share a few results slides from their Flashlights and combine them into a districtwide presentation. Soon, all your Flashlights will shine like a large beam of light showcasing the benefits of your entire school counseling program.

Finally, consider sharing your Flashlight presentations at your local area school counseling association meeting, or include it as part of a presentation at your state or national conference. There has never been a better time to market the value of your school counseling program results. Samples of district Flashlight presentations are available in the online appendix.

12

Flashlight Packages: Putting It All Together

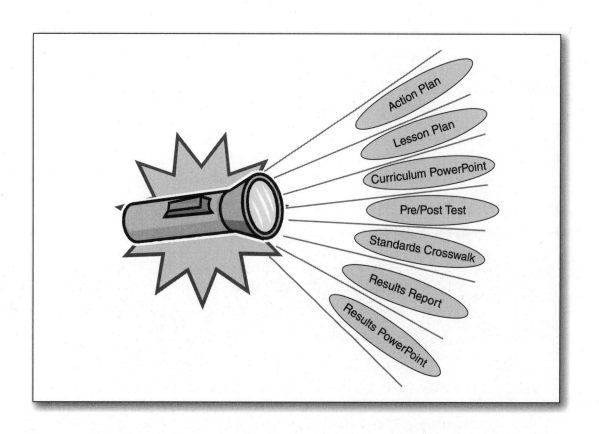

FLASHLIGHT PACKAGES INTRODUCTION

Throughout this text various components leading to the creation of a Flashlight PowerPoint were created. Now, it's time to put the Flashlight Package together. The *Flashlight Package* consists of the following components:

1. Action Plan (Curriculum and/or Intentional Guidance) (Chapter 5)

2. Lesson Plan (Chapter 6)

3. Curriculum (Lesson or PowerPoint of Lesson) (Chapter 6)

4. Pre/Post Test (Chapter 7)

5. Crosswalk of Lesson With ASCA National Standards (Chapter 5)

6. Results Report (Chapter 10)

7. Flashlight PowerPoint Presentation (Chapter 11)

As mentioned in Chapter 11, school counselors in Albuquerque Public Schools create action plans each year and share their results in the spring. Barbara Smith, MA, LPCC, NCC, who has created her own Flashlight Packages, was also awarded as a Recognized ASCA Model Program (RAMP) at John Baker Elementary School. The remainder of this chapter will share Barbara's guidance curriculum Flashlight followed by her intentional guidance Flashlight Packages. The topic areas of her two packages are related and provide both the grade-level curriculum (organizational skills) and an intervention for those who need more in a similar topic area (test-taking strategies). As a reminder, Barbara's documents use the terminology *Guidance Curriculum Action Plan,* as her Flashlight Package was completed prior to the release of the third edition of the ASCA National Model (2012a).

But first, with Barbara's permission, her *Program Evaluation Reflection,* which she submitted as part of her RAMP application, is presented here in its entirety. It tells her story about the changes that have occurred in the district since the ASCA National Model was implemented.

PROGRAM EVALUATION REFLECTION BY BARBARA SMITH

PROGRAM EVALUATION REFLECTION
John Baker Elementary School
Barbara A. Smith; MA, LPCC, NCC
Licensed Professional School Counselor

The Albuquerque Public School district first introduced the ASCA National Model to all Professional School Counselors at an in-service in 2004. Since that time, they have provided many opportunities to integrate the model into every school counseling program. The district is very supportive and has provided professional development with Trish Hatch, Carolyn Stone and Russ Sabella. The district Counseling Unit has provided support and advocacy for each school counseling program to have non-counseling duties shifted to more appropriate personnel, so the counselors are able to implement a comprehensive counseling program that benefits students, staff, parents and the community. The staff and administration at John Baker Elementary School have been very supportive and open to this "new" model for school counseling.

Advocacy

Advocacy is an essential part of the Counseling Program at John Baker Elementary. Ensuring student success is a fundamental part of the Philosophy and Mission Statement. The school counselor at John Baker Elementary advocates for all students continually through various committees, including Health and Wellness Team, retention meetings, 504 meetings, Multidisciplinary Team and Individual Education Plan (MDT/IEP) meetings, and Parent/Teacher conferences.

Schoolwide implementation of the *Steps to Respect* and *Second Step* programs has helped students learn how to advocate for themselves and each other. Small groups on Friendship, Relational Aggression, Anger Management and Study Strategies have offered some students more support in these areas. Advocacy for individual students occurs through collaboration with teachers and parents, mandated reporting, suicide and crisis intervention protocols and through the aforementioned committees and meetings.

Articles from the Counseling Program are included in every Broadcast Newsletter. The newsletter is sent to all families as well as district personnel. Article topics include: current classroom guidance units, strategies for parents to support these units, resource and referral information, any schoolwide Counseling Program information, and G.R.I.P. results reports.

Data from classroom guidance, small group and closing the gap activities have been utilized to advocate for increased funding for the counseling program. The counseling allocation has increased from part-time status to full-time status in just three years of implementation. By utilizing the ASCA National Model, the benefits of a comprehensive counseling program have been recognized by all stakeholders.

Leadership

At the school level, I am the Chairperson for the Health and Wellness Team, which provides an integrated, comprehensive system of care to address the barriers to learning for all students. I also serve on the School Wellness Committee, which sets schoolwide goals and action steps in the areas of family, school and community involvement, physical health and nutrition, and social/emotional well-being. I am a member of the Safety Committee, which creates and implements schoolwide prevention plans in many different areas. A few of these include: attendance, bullying, crisis response, suicide and violence prevention, conflict resolution and general behavioral health issues.

I provide annual training on Sexual Harassment, Identifying and Reporting Abuse and Neglect, Suicide and Crisis procedural directives, bullying prevention, and the Counseling Program. Other trainings have been presented on Student-led Conferences, Classroom Management strategies and the new district Attendance Policy.

At the district level I serve on several Elementary School Counselor Task Force groups, as I feel it is important to have a voice in district decisions. I also serve as a Traverse, Practicum, Intern and New School Counselor Supervisor. I have given presentations on various comprehensive counseling components at district-level meetings and in-services.

(Continued)

(Continued)

I feel it is important for all Professional School Counselors to be members of their local and national organizations. I have served on the New Mexico School Counseling Executive Board as Secretary (2006–2008), Membership Chair (2008–2009) and Elementary Level Vice President (2009–present). I maintain my National Board Certified Counselor (NBCC), Licensed Professional Clinical Mental Health Counselor (LPCC) and School Counseling licenses.

Systemic Change

There has been a significant systemic shift in the role the Counseling Program plays within the school. The counseling allocation at John Baker has been part-time status with just over 500 students for many years. In 2005–2006 the school counselor was on sabbatical. In 2006–2007 there was no counselor due to budget cuts. When I first came to John Baker in the fall of 2007, the staff and administration were not familiar with the ASCA National Model. I was able to utilize the Management Agreement as a tool to start a discussion with my Administrator on the benefits of a comprehensive school counseling program. These discussions continued throughout the year and also occurred at Staff Meetings and in Instructional Council meetings. I also utilized data and Results Reports to educate the staff on how we can partner to help students achieve academic success. The staff now has a better understanding of the framework from which the Counseling Program is based on. As a result, each year more teachers requested classroom guidance lessons.

This school year, I am in every classroom a minimum of twice a month. Many teachers have commented on the positive impact the consistent lessons have had on the students and the overall classroom climate. John Baker Elementary has a "Behavior Redirector" for students with disruptive and/or off-task classroom behavior. "The Redirector assists the teacher by providing an additional option of support in the classroom management plan. The Redirector assists the student by working with them to formulate a plan for maintaining appropriate behavior in a learning environment. Using a structured format, the Redirector guides the student toward making positive choices that will enable them to participate in and benefit from classroom instruction" (from the *Job Description for the Behavior Redirector;* APS). There were 172 referrals to the Redirector during the first semester of the 2007–2008 school year, and 171 during the same time period the following school year. Now that there is a more thorough implementation of the ASCA National Model, referrals are down to 87 for the first semester of the 2009–2010 school year.

My Administrator also realized the benefits and has worked to increase the Counseling allocation from part-time to full-time status. I have been delivering standardized lessons on topics such as bullying, problem-solving, anger management, empathy, study skills, and test-taking strategies that have resulted in positive changes in behavior and academics throughout the entire school. Continued analysis of data has helped to maintain this positive trend of becoming an integral part of the whole school program.

Collaboration

The school counselor collaborates with teachers through a Needs Assessment given at the beginning of the year. Individual student needs and classroom interventions for academic success are discussed at ongoing grade level meetings. Collaboration occurs at the leadership level at Instructional Council meetings, Administration meetings, Cluster Counseling meetings, District Counseling meetings, Transforming School Counseling meetings and New Mexico School Counseling Association meetings. At these meetings, various goals and objectives that impact the counseling program are identified and monitored. District meetings occur on a quarterly basis and allow for over 100 elementary school counselors to work together and discuss implementation strategies, data collection, lesson plans and other issues related to setting up and maintaining a comprehensive counseling program. Collaboration with parents occurs throughout the school counselor's daily work via conferences, phone contacts, Instructional Council, Health and Wellness and MDT/IEP meetings.

I am appreciative of the Staff and Administration at John Baker Elementary School for their commitment and support of the Counseling Program. They value the importance of a comprehensive program and realize the positive impact it has on the school. I also appreciate the invaluable support of the District Counseling Unit throughout this process. Completing this application has been a very rewarding experience.

GUIDANCE CURRICULUM FLASHLIGHT PACKAGE COMMENTS

The following are comments on Barbara's Flashlight Package for her guidance curriculum; her artifacts are below.

Action Plan (Figure 12.1): You'll note that Barbara's action plan is slightly different from other examples in this text. As many districts have done, Albuquerque Public Schools have adapted the action plan to meet their district's needs. Note the standards are on the left, and the intended effects (from the intentional guidance action plan) are added as a column. The majority of the action plan is the same, however, and all of the important evaluation measures are listed. Barbara has selected comparing "Student Responsibility" grades for (a) classwork responsibilities (b) homework responsibilities, and (c) organizing self and materials as a measurement for achievement-related outcomes. This is an excellent measurement, as completing assignments will most certainly support improved achievement.

Lesson Plan (Figure 12.2): Barbara's lesson plan is very well done. She has included not only the school counseling standards but the New Mexico teaching standards as well. She has chosen to implement the ASCA Organizational Boot Camp Curriculum. Thus, the entire lesson does not appear here; she refers to the curriculum for implementation. She outlines each lesson and describes ways she will measure the impact of these lessons. Finally, her decision to include her plan for data collection in the lesson plan sends a powerful accountability message to teachers and administrators.

Lesson PowerPoint (if applicable): Barbara does not have a lesson PowerPoint, as she implemented a prepackaged curriculum from ASCA.

Lesson Pre/Post Test (and follow-up survey if applicable, Figures 12.3 and 12.4): Barbara has decided to ask six questions in her pre/post test. She has indicated which questions are regarding attitude (A), knowledge (K), and skills (S). While this is not necessary, she has included it for her own use. Barbara also created a follow-up survey she administered to students some time after the lesson to provide feedback indicating how students utilized the knowledge, attitudes, and skills to change behavior.

Results Report (Figure 12.5): Barbara's results report is straightforward and easy to understand. She does a terrific job of explaining the impact, lessons learned, limitations, and next steps.

Flashlight PowerPoint (Figure 12.6): The highlight of the Flashlight Package is Barbara's Flashlight PowerPoint. Barbara does an exemplary job of telling her story. She begins by sharing a bit of research as to why organizational skills are important for students' success. She goes on to describe the content of her curriculum and share the data-driven need (19% of students needing improvement in organizational skills). After "cross-walking" her lesson to the standards, she then shares samples of pre/post assessments. A unique part of Barbara's plan is her decision to return to the classroom and survey the students to determine how many utilized the skills taught and which ones were most helpful. Although she knows she can't take all the credit for these gains, Barbara shares her impressive results (improvements on report cards as well as in proficiency levels). Next she shares the students' self-reports of improved behaviors as well as strategies used. Finally, Barbara summarizes and presents limitations, lessons learned, and next steps. This is followed by the school's mission statement, a reminder that the school counseling program is contributing in a meaningful way to the academic success of all students, and a thank you to staff. Although the components of her presentation are not in the same order as those in the rubric provided in Chapter 11, Barbara's Flashlight has every component of it included. Again, telling *your* story is important; don't be afraid to shift slides to make the PowerPoint your own.

GUIDANCE CURRICULUM FLASHLIGHT PACKAGE BY BARBARA SMITH

Figure 12.1   Action Plan

Albuquerque Public Schools [Action Plan]

John Baker Elementary School Guidance Curriculum Plan/Do/Study/Act (PDSA) for 2010–2011

ASCA Standards, Competencies and/or Indicators	Lesson Content (topic area)	Delivery Method	Curriculum and Materials	Start/End Date Frequency Number of Students Impacted	Number of Students Impacted	Intended Effect on Academics, Behavior, and/or Attendance	Evaluation Methods		Results Data: (What impact on achievement do you hope to have as a result?)
							Perception Data: (competency attainment)		
Academic Standard A: Students will acquire the attitudes, knowledge and skills that contribute to effective learning in school and across the life span (A:A1.1–1.5; A:A2.1–2.3; A:A3.1, 3.4) **Academic Standard B:** Students will complete school with the academic preparation essential to choose from a wide range of substantial post-secondary options, including college (A:B1.1, 1.3–1.5, 1.7; A:B2.1, 2.2, 2.4–2.6) **Academic Standard C:** Students will understand the relationship of academics to the world of work and to life at home and in the community (A:C1.1, 1.)	Organizational Skills Study Skills	Classroom Guidance Lessons (4–5)	Selected Lessons From ASCA *Organizational Skills Boot Camp* By Shawn Grime Counselor Generated Pre/Post Evaluation	October 2010 – December 2010 Twice a month (30 minute lessons)	Approx. 90 (All 5th graders)	Increase in organization skills which will help improve academic performance. Improved grades on the Standards Based Progress Report (SBPR) for work completion and organization	*Attitude:* ___% believe it is important to take home their agenda every night ___% believe being organized can help improve their grades *Skills:* ___% know how to correctly write an agenda entry ___% can identify the steps to breaking down a large assignment *Knowledge:* ___% know four organization strategies ___% know four ways to keep their desk organized		*Achievement Related:* T1 and T2 grades will be compared in "Student Responsibility" area *(Fulfills classwork responsibilities, Fulfills homework responsibilities, and Organizes self and materials)* on the New Mexico Standards Based Progress Report (SBPR) *Achievement:* Fall 2010 and Spring 2011 District Benchmark Assessment (DBA) scores will be compared

_____   _____   _____   _____
Principal's Signature   Date   Date of Staff Presentation   Prepared By

Figure 12.2 Lesson Plan

Organizational Skills—Fifth Grade—John Baker Elementary School

Barbara A. Smith, MA, LPCC, Professional School Counselor

ASCA National Standards/NM State Teaching Standards

Academic

Standard A: Students will acquire the attitudes, knowledge and skills that contribute to effective learning in school and across the life span: A:A1.1.1–1.5; A:A2.1–2.3; A:A3.1, 3.4

Standard B: Students will complete school with the academic preparation essential to choose from a wide range of substantial post-secondary options, including college: A:B1.1, 1.3–1.5, 1.7; A:B2.1, 2.2, 2.4–2.6

Standard C: Students will understand the relationship of academics to the world of work and to life at home and in the community: A:C1.1, 1.4

NM State Teaching Standards: Language Arts 1a-d, 2a-c, 3a-b; Health 1a-d; Science 10a, 11j-k

NOICC: Competencies: 4, 5, 6, 7 and 8

Materials Needed

Organizational Skills Boot Camp by Shawn Grime

Counselor generated pre/post evaluation

Goals

To improve students' attitudes, skills and knowledge about organizational skills

Improve organizational skills which will positively impact academics

Objectives

Students will learn ways to break down larger assignments.	Students will learn various organizational strategies.
Students will know how to accurately write lessons in agenda.	Students will understand the relationship of organization and grades.

Actions/Activities:

Lesson 1: Introduce topic of lesson and share objectives with students

Give Pre-evaluation

Session 2—"Keeping Track of Assignments," Activities 1 and 2

Questions and Answers, Wrap-up

Lesson 2: Review main ideas from previous lesson Introduce topic of lesson and share objectives Session 3—"Managing Your Time," Activity 2 Questions and Answers, Wrap-up
Lesson 3: Review main ideas from previous lesson Introduce topic of lesson and share objectives Session 3—"Managing Your Time," Activity 3 Questions and Answers, Wrap-up
Lesson 4: Review main ideas from previous lesson Introduce topic of lesson and share objectives Session 4—"Keeping Binders, Lockers, Desks and Book Bags Organized," Activity 1 Questions and Answers, Wrap-up
Lesson 5: Review main ideas from previous lesson Introduce topic of lesson and share objectives Session 5—"Creating a Productive Work Environment," Activity 1 Questions and Answers Give Post-evaluation, Wrap-up

Data Collection

Perception Data—Percentage change in Pre vs. Post Evaluation
Process Data—How many classes and students received lessons
Results Data—Compare "Student Responsibility" grades on Standards Based Progress Report and District Benchmark Assessment scores pre/post intervention

Figure 12.3   Lesson Pre/Post Test

Organization Skills

Pre/Post Evaluation

John Baker Elementary School

Directions: Circle the best response for each question.

1. I believe it is important to take home my agenda (planner) every night. (A)

   a. Strongly Agree
   b. Agree
   c. Disagree
   d. Strongly Disagree

2. I believe that being organized can improve my grades. (A)

   a Strongly Agree
   b Agree
   c Disagree
   d Strongly Disagree

3. Which of the following is a correct agenda (planner) entry? (S)

   a "Science due on Tuesday"
   b "Language Arts—all even numbered problems"
   c "Math, pgs. 58–59, even problems, due Tuesday"
   d "Social Studies, worksheet"
   e   All of the above are correct

4. When preparing to complete a large, long-term assignment it is important to: (K)

   a Write down the major steps in order
   b Break down the assignment into major steps
   c Set deadlines for each step
   d Break down each step into daily/weekly actions
   e All of the above are correct

5. Students with good organizational skills: (K)

   a Set long- and short-term goals
   b Use agenda (planner) correctly
   c Create a schedule
   d Break larger assignments into manageable tasks
   e All of the above are correct

6. Keeping my desk organized includes: (K)

   a Cleaning it out weekly
   b Replacing torn or broken materials
   c Putting items back where I got them when I am finished using them
   d Putting papers in their proper place
   e All of the above are correct

Figure 12.4 Follow-Up Survey

Organization Skills

Follow-Up Survey

John Baker Elementary School

Directions: Circle the best response for each question.

1. Since the organizational skills lessons, I am:

   a More organized

   b About the same

   c Less organized

   d I was already organized

2. Since the lessons, I take my agenda home:

   a More often

   b Less often

   c About the same

   d I already brought it home every night

3. Since the lessons, I am writing assignments down in my agenda with more detail:

   a Yes
   b No

4. Since the lessons, I have used the following organizational strategies (mark as many as apply):

   a Setting long-term goals

   b Setting short-term goals

   c Organizing my desk more often

   d Organizing my backpack more often

   e Breaking down long-term assignments

   f Creating a schedule

   g Replacing torn or broken materials

   h Putting papers in their proper place

   i Putting items back where they belong after using them

5. I believe the lessons have helped improve my grades:

   a Strongly agree

   b Agree

   c I already had good grades

   d Disagree

   e Strongly disagree

Figure 12.5 Results Report

John Baker Elementary School

Albuquerque Public Schools

Organizational Skills Guidance Curriculum RESULTS REPORT 2010–2011

Grade Level	Guidance Lesson Content	Curriculum and Materials	Number of Classes or Subjects in Which Guidance Lessons Are Delivered	Start Date End Date	Process Data (number of students impacted)	Perception Data: Pre/Post Test or Activity or Student Data (what they learned, believe, think, or can demonstrate)	Results Data: How did students' behavior change because of the lesson? (improved behavior, attendance. or achievement)	Limitations/ Implications/ Recommendations (So what do the data tell you?)
5th	Organizational Skills Study Skills	Selected Lessons from ASCA *Organizational Skills Boot Camp* By Shawn Grime Counselor Generated Pre/Post Evaluation	Five bi-weekly lessons	October 2010–January 2011	78 total students received the lessons, but only 70 students completed both the pre/post evaluation	*Attitude:* % believe it is important to take home their agenda every night **PRE: 59%** **POST: 69%** *Skills:* % know how to correctly write an agenda entry **PRE: 9%** **POST: 46%** % can identify the steps to breaking down a large assignment	*Achievement Related:* –**42%** increase in the number of students earning an "Excellent" grade "Fulfills classwork responsibilities" –**80%** increase in the number of students earning an "Excellent" grade on "Fulfills homework responsibilities" –**50%** increase in the number of students earning an "Excellent" grade on "Organizes self and materials" *Achievement:*	Students are receiving valuable information on organizational skills and time management. Students' attitudes have positively shifted, and they gained knowledge and skills necessary for their academic and future career success Lessons appear to be contributing to positive growth as evidence by the SBPR May need to revise some of the pre/post evaluation questions Collaborate more with teachers to better align expectations

Grade Level	Guidance Lesson Content	Curriculum and Materials	Number of Classes or Subjects in Which Guidance Lessons Are Delivered	Start Date End Date	Process Data (number of students impacted)	Perception Data: Pre/Post Test or Activity or Student Data (what they learned, believe, think, or can demonstrate)	Results Data: How did students' behavior change because of the lesson? (improved behavior, attendance, or achievement)	Limitations/ Implications/ Recommendations (So what do the data tell you?)
						PRE: 67% **POST: 67%** *Knowledge:* % know four organization strategies **PRE: 64%** **POST: 82%** % know four ways to keep their desk organized **PRE: 77%** **POST: 88%**	There was a **31%** increase in the number of students scoring proficient or above in math There was a **92%** increase in the number of students scoring proficient or above in reading	Time/scheduling is always a factor! There is a need to further disaggregate the data and create small groups for students who may "need more" Start lessons earlier in the year Implement periodic "check-ins" for support and reinforcement of skills taught

Principal's Signature   Date   **Prepared by**   * **Attach data, examples, and documentation**

Figure 12.6   Flashlight PowerPoint Presentation

John Baker Elementary School
2010-2011

Barbara A. Smith; MA, LPCC
Professional School Counselor
School Counseling Program
Classroom Guidance
(Results Sample)
Organizational Skills

Barbara A. Smith; MA, LPCC, Professional School Counselor (adapted from T. Hatch 2010)

Why Teach Organizational Skills?

Research states...

"In the classroom many students exhibit inadequate organizational skills that contribute to poor study habits which in turn lowers achievement" (Monahan, Ognibene, & Torrisi, 2000).

"Direct instruction of time-management skills is necessary because they are neither common knowledge or innate" (Bausch, & Becker, 2001).

Barbara A. Smith; MA, LPCC, Professional School Counselor (adapted from T. Hatch 2010)

Guidance Curriculum

❖ All fifth grade classes ~ 78 students total
   • 70 students completed pre/post evaluation

❖ American School Counseling Association curriculum - *Organizational Skills Boot Camp*

❖ Five lessons October 2010 – January 2011
   • How to correctly write assignments in agenda
   • How to organize desk and backpack
   • Time management skills
   • How to break down long term assignments

Barbara A. Smith; MA, LPCC, Professional School Counselor (adapted from T. Hatch 2010)

There is a need...

❖ Not only did fifth grade teachers request that the Counseling Department teach these skills, but...

   • After reviewing last year's Standards Based Progress Report **19%** of the students earned an *"Improvement Needed"* score under the "Organizes Self and Materials" section

Barbara A. Smith; MA, LPCC, Professional School Counselor (adapted from T. Hatch 2010)

National Standards

Academic Standard A

Students will acquire the attitudes, knowledge, and skills that contribute to effective learning in school and across the life span

Student Competencies
A:A1 Improve Academic Self-Concept
A:A2 Acquire Skills for Improving Learning
A:A3 Achieve School Success

Barbara A. Smith; MA, LPCC, Professional School Counselor (adapted from T. Hatch 2010)

National Standards

Academic Standard B

Students will complete school with the academic preparation essential to choose from a wide range of substantial post-secondary options, including college

Student Competencies
A:B1 Improve Learning
A:B2 Plan to Achieve Goals

Barbara A. Smith; MA, LPCC, Professional School Counselor (adapted from T. Hatch 2010)

National Standards

Academic Standard C

Students will understand the relationship of academics to the world of work and to life at home and in the community

Student Competencies
A:C1 Relate School to Life Experiences

Barbara A. Smith; MA, LPCC, Professional School Counselor (adapted from T. Hatch 2010)

What do they *KNOW*?

PRE

❖ **64%** knew the habits of a student with good organizational skills

POST

❖ **82%** knew the habits of a student with good organizational skills

Barbara A. Smith; MA, LPCC, Professional School Counselor (adapted from T. Hatch 2010)

What do they *BELIEVE*? What *SKILL* did they learn?

PRE

❖ **59%** believed it was important to take their agenda home every night

❖ **9%** could identify a correct agenda entry

POST

❖ **69%** believed it was important to take their agenda home every night

❖ **46%** could identify a correct agenda entry

While this is a nice improvement, the overall numbers may be low due to teachers having different classroom expectations

Barbara A. Smith; MA, LPCC, Professional School Counselor (adapted from T. Hatch 2010)

Pre-Post Evaluation Results

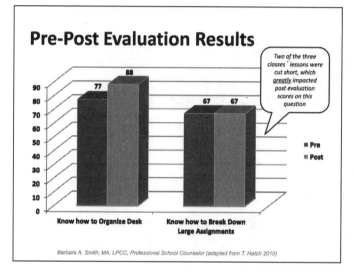

Two of the three classes' lessons were cut short, which greatly impacted post evaluation scores on this question

Barbara A. Smith; MA, LPCC, Professional School Counselor (adapted from T. Hatch 2010)

The intention of the lessons offered by the school counseling program, along with other contributing factors, is to have a positive effect on academics, behavior and/or attendance...

An increase in organizational skills will help improve academic performance.

Barbara A. Smith; MA, LPCC, Professional School Counselor (adapted from T. Hatch 2010)

Results - Achievement Related Data

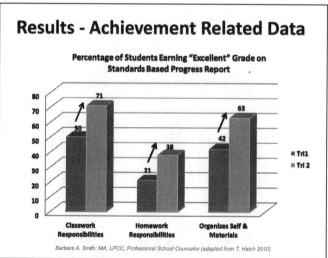

Barbara A. Smith; MA, LPCC, Professional School Counselor (adapted from T. Hatch 2010)

(Continued)

Figure 12.6 (Continued)

This is an _increase_ of:

❖ _42%_ in the number of students earning "Excellent" on the "Fulfills Classwork Responsibilities" section

❖_80%_ in the number of students earning "Excellent" on the "Fulfills Homework Responsibilities" section

❖_50%_ on the "Organizes Self and Materials" section

Barbara A. Smith; MA, LPCC, Professional School Counselor (adapted from T. Hatch 2010)

Results - Achievement Data

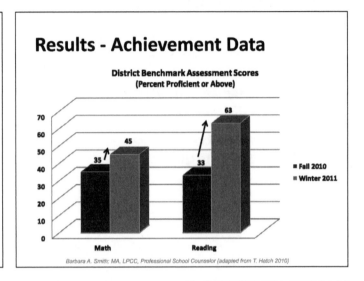

District Benchmark Assessment Scores (Percent Proficient or Above)

Barbara A. Smith; MA, LPCC, Professional School Counselor (adapted from T. Hatch 2010)

That is a **_31% increase_** in the number of students scoring Proficient or above in Math

AND...

A **_92% increase_** in the number of students scoring Proficient or above in Reading

Barbara A. Smith; MA, LPCC, Professional School Counselor (adapted from T. Hatch 2010)

Since the lessons...

Students self-reported:

❖_32%_ are **more organized** (36% reported they were already organized)

❖_41%_ bring their agenda home **more regularly**

❖_82%_ are writing assignments in their agenda with **greater detail**

❖_23%_ believe increased organizational skills have helped to **improve their grades** (23% reported they already had good grades)

Barbara A. Smith; MA, LPCC, Professional School Counselor (adapted from T. Hatch 2010)

Strategies used from lessons:

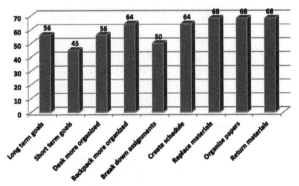

Barbara A. Smith; MA, LPCC, Professional School Counselor (adapted from T. Hatch 2010)

In summary...

❖Students are receiving valuable information about organizational skills and time management

❖Students' attitudes positively shifted, and they gained knowledge and skills necessary for their academic and future career success

❖Lessons appear to be contributing to positive growth as evidenced by Standards Based Progress Report

Barbara A. Smith; MA, LPCC, Professional School Counselor (adapted from T. Hatch 2010)

Limitations and Lessons Learned

❖ Some of the questions on the evaluation may have been confusing and might need to be revised to get the most accurate data

❖ Collaborate more with the teachers before the lessons as to their current expectations and those in the program to see how we can integrate the two into a more consistent message

❖ Time is always a factor!

Barbara A. Smith; MA, LPCC, Professional School Counselor (adapted from T. Hatch 2010)

Next Steps...

❖ Disaggregate data in order to create groups for those students who "just need more"

❖ Work with classes earlier in the year

❖ Implement periodic "check-ins" to see how students are doing and reinforce new skills

Barbara A. Smith; MA, LPCC, Professional School Counselor (adapted from T. Hatch 2010)

Mission Statement

John Baker Elementary School's comprehensive counseling program partners with staff, students and the community to reduce barriers to learning so that all students can achieve academic success and make responsible choices in life. All students are served at the prevention level in the areas of academic, personal/social and career awareness development.

Barbara A. Smith; MA, LPCC, Professional School Counselor (adapted from T. Hatch 2010)

Thank you to...

❖ Our 5th grade students for being open to learning new skills

❖ All 5th grade teachers for your support and time with your class

❖ Mrs. Brigman, Principal, and the Instructional Council for their continued support

❖ APS District Counseling Department for their technical assistance and support

Barbara A. Smith; MA, LPCC, Professional School Counselor (adapted from T. Hatch 2010)

The school counseling program is committed to contributing in a meaningful way to the academic achievement of all students

Your support is greatly appreciated!

Barbara A. Smith; MA, LPCC, Professional School Counselor (adapted from T. Hatch 2010)

INTENTIONAL GUIDANCE
FLASHLIGHT PACKAGE COMMENTS

The following are comments on Barbara's Flashlight Package for intentional guidance; her specific artifacts follow.

Action Plan (Figure 12.7): Similar to the guidance curriculum action plan, the intentional guidance action plan has been adapted by Albuquerque Public Schools to meet its needs. Specifically, because the teachers were being asked to design their curriculum using the Plan ➜ Do ➜ Study ➜ Act (PDSA) model, the action plan was revised to align with the district (smart move). Even with the minor revisions, the action plan is essentially the same as those presented in Chapter 2 and those in the ACSA National Model and contains all the necessary components.

Lesson Plan (Figure 12.8): Although Barbara created six lesson plans and full instructional lessons, only the first lesson plan is reprinted here. (The rest are provided in the online resources.) Again, the New Mexico teaching standards are referenced. Writing the lesson plan with clear objectives helps to maintain focus of the lesson on the main goals.

Lesson PowerPoint (if applicable): Again, Barbara does not have a lesson PowerPoint, as she is implementing curriculum she located online. If she had created a PowerPoint curriculum for her lesson, it would have been included here.

Pre/Post Test (Figure 12.9): This pre/post reflects the main objectives of the lesson(s). As you read it, think of ways you might improve the questions or what other ones you might have asked.

Results Report (Figure 12.10): The results report provides the template for organizing the information that will be put into the Flashlight PowerPoint. It is also a required component of the RAMP application.

Flashlight PowerPoint (Figure 12.11): Barbara's Flashlight PowerPoint for intentional guidance was an academic group intervention. She starts her PowerPoint presentation sharing the process data of her intervention. The next slides tell of the ASCA National Standards that align with the intervention. Her target group is identified as third through fifth graders who are "threshold students," who were selected based on "nearing proficient" test scores. After sharing research supporting her intervention, she ensures her audience knows the intended effects of her intervention and the goals for the students' academic achievement. Next, Barbara shares the number of students in the target group and the results of the pre/post tests. As she did in her guidance curriculum, Barbara performs a follow-up assessment and learns that 100% of the students report they used the test-taking and relaxation strategies she taught them, and 56% of the students also report being more organized. What is exciting to see is the 85% improvement in math scores and 52% increase in reading scores. Again, Barbara bullet points her implications and next steps, thanks her staff and administration, and reminds all of her listeners that the school counseling program is committed to partnering with teachers for student success!

INTENTIONAL GUIDANCE FLASHLIGHT PACKAGE BY BARBARA SMITH

Figure 12.7 Intentional Guidance Action Plan

Albuquerque Public Schools

John Baker Elementary School Intentional Guidance 2010–2011 (PDSA)

Target Group: Group participants will be 3rd—5th grade students identified by Research, Deployment and Accountability as "threshold students".

Target Group selection is based upon the following data: Analysis of District Benchmark Assessment (DBA) and Standards Based Assessment (SBA) scores, Academic Improvement Plan (AIP) qualification, and input from parents and teachers

PLAN → DO → STUDY → ACT →

ASCA Standards, Competencies, and/or Indicators	Type of Service and Delivery Method	Resources needed	Start/ End Dates	Number of Students Impacted	Intended Effect on Academics, Behavior and/ or Attendance	Evaluation Method		Results Data (What impact on achievement do you hope to have as a result?)
						Perception Data (competency attainment)		
Academic Standard A: Students will acquire the attitudes, knowledge and skills that contribute to effective learning in school and across the life span. **A:A1:** Improve Academic Self-Concept (1.3, 1.5) **A:A2:** Acquire Skills for Improving Learning (2.1, 2.2, 2.4) **Standard B:** Students will complete school with the academic preparation essential to choose from a wide range of substantial post-secondary options, including college.	Academic Groups focusing on Study Skills and Test-Taking Strategies Groups will meet for 6–8 sessions that are 30 minutes each.	Counselor gathered materials and Pre/ Post Evaluation *How to Do Homework Without Throwing Up* by Trevor Romain *Pigsty* by Mark Teague Collaboration with grade-level chairs on specific areas of need and pertinent vocabulary	Nov–Dec 2010 Jan–Feb 2011	Approx. 30 students	Students who participate in group will increase their study skills and knowledge of test-taking strategies. This intervention will help to improve test scores and decrease the number of students continuing to qualify for an Academic Improvement Plan (AIP).	*Attitude:* % of students believe that using test-taking strategies can help them do well on standardized tests % students believe that being organized can help them improve their grades *Skills:* % of students can follow the directions % of students can demonstrate the process of elimination		*Achievement Related:* As students' attitude, skills and knowledge of test-taking and study skills improve, so will their *"Fulfills Homework Responsibilities"* and *"Fulfills Classwork Responsibilities"* grades on their Standards Based Progress Report. Students will utilize the test-taking strategies and relaxation skills taught during testing. *Achievement:*

ASCA Standards, Competencies, and/or Indicators	Type of Service and Delivery Method	Resources needed	Start/ End Dates	Number of Students Impacted	Intended Effect on Academics, Behavior and/ or Attendance	Evaluation Method	
						Perception Data (competency attainment)	Results Data (What impact on achievement do you hope to have as a result?)
A:B1: Improve Learning (1.2–1.7) **A:B2:** Plan to Achieve Goals (2.2–2.4, 2.6) **Standard C:** Students will understand the relationship of academics to the world of work and to life at home and in the community. **A:C1:** Relate School to Life Experiences (1.1–1.6)		Office space for groups Letters to families DBA and SBA scores				*Knowledge:* % of students know what test anxiety is % know four ways to calm themselves down if they are feeling anxious	As homework and classwork completion grades increase, this will have a positive impact on Standards Based Assessment and District Benchmark Assessment scores.

_____ _____   _____ _____

Principal's Signature   Date   School Counselor's Signature   Date

Figure 12.8 Lesson Plan

Study Skills and Test-Taking Strategies Group

(Session 1)

John Baker Elementary School

Barbara A. Smith; MA, LPCC

Professional School Counselor

ASCA National Standards/NM State Teaching Standards

Academic Development

Standard A: Students will acquire the attitudes, knowledge and skills that contribute to effective learning in school and across the life span.

A:A1 Improve Academic Self-concept

A:A1.4

A:A2 Acquire Skills for Improving Learning

A:A2.4

Standard B: Students will complete school with the academic preparation essential to choose from a wide range of substantial post-secondary options, including college.

A:B1 Improve Learning

A:B1.2, A:B1.6, A:B1.7

A:B2 Plan to Achieve Goals

A:B2.2, A:B2.3, A:B2.4

NM State Teaching Standards: Language Arts 1a-d, 2a-c, 3a-b

NOICC: Competencies 4, 5, 6

Materials Needed

Counselor gathered materials:

- "Study Skills and Test-Taking Strategies Evaluation"—counselor made
- "Learning Style Inventory" (from www.gigglepotz.com)
- "Learning Styles—Types & Tips," "Study for Success" &"Study Methods: Which One Is Right for You" from www.montgomeryschoolsmd.org/schools/watkinsmillhs/ studyskills/files/studyskillshandbook06.pdf)
- "My Study Space" (from "Student Workshop: Study Skills for Kids 3–5" by Sunburst Visual Media)

Goals

Improve students' attitudes, skills and knowledge about their learning style and related study strategies

Improve test scores

Objectives

Students will know their learning style	Students will learn related study strategies
Students will be able to identify needed changes to improve their studying based on their learning style	Students will realize the impact their learning style has on how they learn and study

Lesson

Introduce topic of lesson and share objectives with students
Discuss group rules, confidentiality and limits, and group expectations
Have students complete "Pre/Post Evaluation"
Have students complete "Learning Style Inventory" (keep track of each student's learning style)
Discuss "Learning Styles—Types and Tips," individualizing for each student based on his or her learning style
Discuss "Study for Success" and "Study Methods: Which One Is Right for You"
Have students complete "My Study Space" and discuss
Question and Answers
Wrap up

Data Collection

Perception Data—Percentage change in Pre vs. Post Evaluation

Process Data—How many students participated in group

Results Data—Compare District Benchmark Assessment scores Pre vs. Post group intervention

Figure 12.9   Pre/Post Test

3rd–5th Study Skills & Test-Taking Strategies Group Grade (Pre-Post)

John Baker Elementary School

Barbara A. Smith; MA, LPCC

Licensed Professional School Counselor

Directions: Circle the best response to each statement. Write your initials on the bottom of the page.

1. I believe that using test-taking strategies can help me do well on standardized tests. (A)

   a Strongly agree
   b Agree
   c Disagree
   d Strongly Disagree

2. I believe that being organized can help improve my grades. (A)

   a Strongly agree
   b Agree
   c I don't know
   d Disagree
   e Strongly Disagree

3. Test anxiety (K)

   a is a worry or fear caused by having to take tests
   b can be physical or mental
   c is normal
   d can be controlled
   e all of the above are correct

4. If you are feeling stressed or anxious about a test, you could (K)

   a Take some deep breaths
   b Do some neck rolls
   c Do the "owl" technique
   d Do a hook-up
   e All of the above

5. Show how you would use the test-taking strategy of *elimination* for this question: (S) ($x = 22$, $z = 4$) $3x + 1y - 14z = 42$ $y =$

   a Yellow
   b 32
   c 49
   d Green
   e −129,457

6. On an essay test you should (K)

   a Read the questions first, then the story
   b Read the story first, then the questions
   c Write down the first thoughts that come to your mind after reading the questions
   d Use a graphic organizer to arrange the information
   e All but "b" are correct

Figure 12.10 Results Report

Albuquerque Public Schools

John Baker Elementary School—Academic Group Intentional Guidance RESULTS REPORT 2010–2011

Grade Level	Target Group and Criteria Based on . . .	What intervention activities did you perform? Did you survey the at-risk group for barriers to learning? Group counseling?	Materials or Curriculum Used	Start Date/ End Date	Process Data (number of students impacted)	Perception Data: Pre/Post Test or Activity or Student Data (what they learned, believe, think, or can demonstrate)	Results Data: How did students' behavior change because of the lesson? (improved behavior, attendance, or achievement)	Limitations/ Implications/ Recommendations (So what do the data tell you?)
3rd–5th grade	"Nearing Proficient" scores on the Spring 2010 Standards Based Assessment and/or District Benchmark Assessment in Reading and/ or Math Academic Improvement Plan qualification Teacher and parent input	Letters home to families Consultation with Regular and Special Education teachers 7 weekly 30-minute small group sessions Academic groups focusing on: Learning Styles Listening/Following Directions Study Skills Organization Test-Taking Strategies Test Anxiety and Relaxation	Counselor gathered materials Counselor generated Pre/ Post Evaluation *How to Do Homework Without Throwing Up* by Trevor Romain *Pigsty* by Mark Teague *Organizational Skills Bootcamp* by Shawn Grime	On-going Nov–Dec 2010 Jan–Feb 2011	**29** students attended the groups but 2 moved in-between the District Benchmark Assessment testing windows so their data are not included (74% of the students receive Special Education services)	*Attitude:* % of students believe that using test-taking strategies can help them do well on standardized tests **PRE: 82%** **POST: 96%** % of students believe that being organized can help them improve their grades **POST: 64%** *Skills:* % of students can demonstrate the process of elimination **PRE: 14%** **POST: 57%**	*Achievement Related:* As students' attitude, skills and knowledge of test taking and study skills improve, so will their *"Fulfills Homework Responsibilities"* and *"Fulfills Classwork Responsibilities"* grades on their Standards Based Progress Report Actual: Complete data are not available at this time *100% of the students* reported using one or more test-taking strategies	Lessons appear to be successful based on the data collected Look at scheduling issues May need to revise some pre/post questions to get more accurate data Review Standards Based Progress Reports for Achievement Related data Start groups earlier in the year and provide consistent feedback and support

Figure 12.10 (Continued)

Grade Level	Target Group and Criteria Based on . . .	What intervention activities did you perform? Did you survey the at-risk group for barriers to learning? Group counseling?	Materials or Curriculum Used	Start Date/ End Date	Process Data (number of students impacted)	Perception Data: Pre/Post Test or Activity or Student Data (what they learned, believe, think, or can demonstrate)	Results Data: How did students' behavior change because of the lesson? (improved behavior, attendance, or achievement)	Limitations/ Implications/ Recommendations (So what do the data tell you?)
						% of students followed the directions **PRE: 14%** **POST: 71%** *Knowledge:* % of students know what test anxiety is **PRE: ???** **POST: 43%** % know four ways to calm themselves down if they are feeling anxious **PRE: 39%** **POST: 64%**	*100% of the students reported using one or more relaxation strategies* *Achievement:* *As homework and classwork completion grades increase, this will have a positive impact on Standards Based Assessment and District Benchmark Assessment scores.* ***Actual:*** **52%** of the students' reading scores *increased* **85%** of the students' math scores *increased*	Review Standards Based Assessment data when it becomes available in the fall Look at separating groups into more specific topics (i.e. Test Taking, Study Skills, Organizational Skills, Motivation, etc.) Celebrate successes with students!

Prepared by _____   Date _____   *Attach data, examples, and documentation

Principal's Signature _____

Figure 12.11 Flashlight PowerPoint

John Baker Elementary School
Barbara Smith; MA, LPCC
Professional School Counselor
School Counseling Program
2010-2011

Academic Group Intervention
Intentional Guidance
(Results sample)
Barbara A. Smith; MA, LPCC, Professional School Counselor, 2011 (adapted from T. Hatch)

ACADEMIC COUNSELING GROUPS

7 weekly 30-minute lessons
❖ Learning Styles
❖ Listening/Following Directions
❖ Study Strategies/Homework Tips
❖ Organizational Skills
❖ Test Taking Strategies
❖ Test Anxiety/Relaxation
Barbara A. Smith; MA, LPCC, Professional School Counselor, 2011 (adapted from T. Hatch)

NATIONAL STANDARD

Academic Standard A:

Students will acquire the attitudes, knowledge, and skills that contribute to effective learning in school and across the life span.

A:A1: Improve Academic Self-concept
A:A2: Acquire Skills for Improving Learning
A:A3: Achieve School Success
Barbara A. Smith; MA, LPCC, Professional School Counselor, 2011 (adapted from T. Hatch)

NATIONAL STANDARDS - Continued

Academic Standard B:

Students will complete school with the academic preparation essential to choose from a wide range of substantial post-secondary options, including college.

A:B1: Improve Learning
A:B2: Plan to Achieve Goals
Barbara A. Smith; MA, LPCC, Professional School Counselor, 2011 (adapted from T. Hatch)

TARGET GROUP

Third - fifth grade students identified by Research, Deployment and Accountability as
"Threshold Students"
and
students at risk of qualifying for an Academic Improvement Plan
Barbara A. Smith; MA, LPCC, Professional School Counselor, 2011 (adapted from T. Hatch)

SELECTED ON FOLLOWING DATA:

Students were identified by a high *"Nearing Proficient"* score in Reading and/or Math on the Spring 2010 Standards Based Assessment or District Benchmark Assessment,
or
by Academic Improvement Plan qualification,
as well as teacher and family input
Barbara A. Smith; MA, LPCC, Professional School Counselor, 2011 (adapted from T. Hatch)

WHY INTERVENE?

Research states:

"...combined school counselor interventions of group counseling and classroom guidance were associated with a positive impact on student achievement and behavior."

Brigman, G. and Campbell, C. (2003). Professional School Counseling

Barbara A. Smith; MA, LPCC, Professional School Counselor, 2011 (adapted from T. Hatch)

INTENDED EFFECTS

❖Students who participate in group will *increase their study skills* and *knowledge of test taking strategies*

❖This intervention will *improve test scores*, therefore, the number of students who qualify for an Academic Improvement Plan will *decrease*

Barbara A. Smith; MA, LPCC, Professional School Counselor, 2011 (adapted from T. Hatch)

GOALS

❖Students' academic and responsibility grades will *improve* on Standards Based Progress Report

❖Students' standardized assessment scores will *improve*

Barbara A. Smith; MA, LPCC, Professional School Counselor, 2011 (adapted from T. Hatch)

HOW MANY STUDENTS?

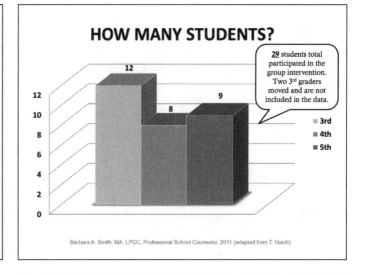

29 students total participated in the group intervention. Two 3rd graders moved and are not included in the data.

Barbara A. Smith; MA, LPCC, Professional School Counselor, 2011 (adapted from T. Hatch)

WHAT ARE THEIR ATTITUDES?

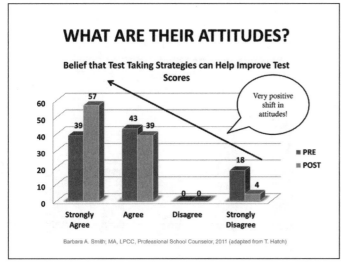

Barbara A. Smith; MA, LPCC, Professional School Counselor, 2011 (adapted from T. Hatch)

KNOWLEDGE OF RELAXATION STRATEGIES

PRE	POST
39% of the students knew four strategies to help them relax when experiencing test anxiety	**64%** of the students knew four strategies to help them relax when experiencing test anxiety

Barbara A. Smith; MA, LPCC, Professional School Counselor, 2011 (adapted from T. Hatch)

(Continued)

Figure 12.11 (Continued)

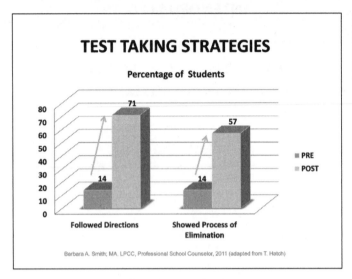

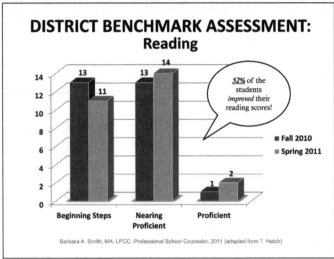

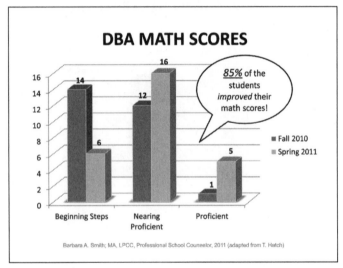

FOLLOW-UP RESULTS

Students were surveyed a few weeks after the Standards Based Assessment, and the following information was collected:

❖ *100% of the students* reported using one or more test taking strategies

❖ *100% of the students* reported using one or more relaxation strategies

Barbara A. Smith; MA, LPCC, Professional School Counselor, 2011 (adapted from T. Hatch)

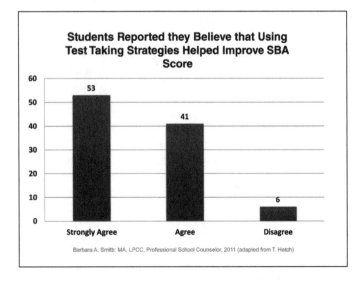

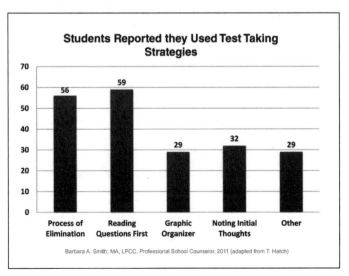

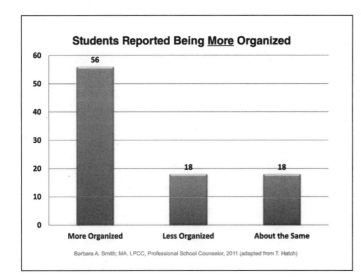

Students Reported Being <u>More</u> Organized

Barbara A. Smith; MA, LPCC, Professional School Counselor, 2011 (adapted from T. Hatch)

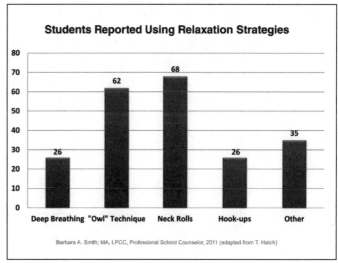

Students Reported Using Relaxation Strategies

Barbara A. Smith; MA, LPCC, Professional School Counselor, 2011 (adapted from T. Hatch)

IMPLICATIONS

❖ Program appears to be successful based on data collected

❖ Look at scheduling issues

❖ May need to revise some questions on pre/post evaluation

❖ Start lessons earlier in the year, and provide consistent feedback and support

Barbara A. Smith; MA, LPCC, Professional School Counselor, 2011 (adapted from T. Hatch)

NEXT STEPS

❖ Look at Standards Based Assessment scores when they become available

❖ Meetings with students discussing District Benchmark Assessment scores and celebrating their successes (letters home also!)

❖ Review academic and "Student Responsibility" grades on Standards Based Progress Report

Barbara A. Smith; MA, LPCC, Professional School Counselor, 2011 (adapted from T. Hatch)

THANK YOU!

❖ Teachers who participated and supported group process

❖ Instructional Council for their support and collaboration

❖ Administration for consultation and support of the program

Barbara A. Smith; MA, LPCC, Professional School Counselor, 2011 (adapted from T. Hatch)

John Baker's School Counseling Program is committed to partnering with teachers for student success!

Thank you!

John Baker Bobcats Try and Never Give Up!

Barbara A. Smith; MA, LPCC, Professional School Counselor, 2011 (adapted from T. Hatch)

REFLECTIONS

Below, Barbara Smith shares her thoughts about how implementing the ASCA National Model has impacted her professionally. She saw shifts in her faculty's response to the school counseling program after sharing her PowerPoint, and she was asked to come into many more classes. Barbara reminds school counselors in her last response to start slowly and to not take on too much at once. Good advice!

REFLECTIONS

By Barbara Smith, John Baker Elementary

1. *What were your first thoughts when training started in the ASCA National Model and when you were asked to move to data-driven practices?*

   I was excited to have a direction to take the program. I was working in an elementary school, alone, with over 600 students. I never had a school counseling class, so I was struggling with putting a program together. I had very little resources, so I was pulling anything I could find. Then, our district had a Professional Development workshop explaining the ASCA Model and how the district was moving in that direction. The following year, Trish Hatch provided two days of Professional Development and helped us put the theory into practice. It was very motivating to have a direction and way to show that our work is important and positively impacts students.

2. *What were the initial challenges, personally and professionally?*

   I had a great administration and staff, but there was still a struggle with shifting thoughts on what my role was. I started with a few teachers who were supportive. I gathered the data and presented my first PowerPoint at a staff meeting. After the presentation, a teacher asked how to sign up for me to deliver classroom guidance lessons. I pulled out my schedule for the month and passed it around. It was full by the end of the meeting!

3. *What did you learn along the way?*

   Data is your friend. It is a very persuasive tool! It is difficult to argue with positive shifts in the numbers. I also had to learn that there are always naysayers who will try to undermine you and turn others against you. I think some staff members see school counselors as a threat. If you are persistent and continue to focus on the data, it will take some of their power away. Stay with your allies; they are very powerful.

4. *Where are you now? How has implementing the ASCA Model and using the Flashlight approach changed your practice as a school counselor?*

   My school received RAMP designation in 2010. I continually refine and improve my program by adding new components, rewriting lesson plans, and revising data collection. It's a continually evolving process.

   (Continued)

(Continued)

5. *Since beginning implementation of the ASCA National Model, have any changes occurred overall in your school, with staff, or with administration regarding the perception of the school counseling program?*

When I first began at my current school, I was only working part-time. I continually shared my data with my administrator and collaborated with her on ways to integrate into the school program. Each year, she found money to increase my allocation until I was full-time. She saw the positive impact the counseling program had on the students and felt it was an important part of the educational process. I went from being in a few classes a month to being in all classes a minimum of bi-weekly. I am now part of the entire school program. There is more accountability with the program. I have the ability to prove that my work has an impact on students. I am now seen as a vital part of the educational process.

6 *What are you most proud of?*

I am most proud of the amount of time I now spend in classes. It speaks to how teachers feel about the program. I love knowing all the students in the school and having them see me as a positive part of their education.

7 *What are the ongoing benefits and challenges?*

Our district fully supports the counseling program now, because of the data. For the first time, we have minimum ratios, counselors in every school, and annual results presentations to district personnel. This would not have been possible without the ASCA Model, and the structure and direction it provides.

8 Do you have any suggestions or tips for school counselors just beginning this work?

Take it one step at a time. Implement the program in manageable pieces. Believe in yourself and the process. Change can be difficult, but there are positive results. Get support from other school counselors, or staff members. They can be great advocates.

CESCAL: FLASHLIGHT PACKAGES ONLINE

In 2007, the Center for Excellence in School Counseling and Leadership (CESCaL) was created to provide samples and examples of artifacts supporting the ASCA National Model. CESCaL began uploading Flashlight Packages on its website (cescal.org) for school counselors to refer to when creating their own. While artifacts were not required to be perfect to appear on the site, CESCaL has made efforts to ensure all samples are rated at least a grade of B or better. The Flashlight examples on the CESCaL website are clearly marked with a yellow Flashlight. When users click on the Flashlight, the group of documents is seen (Figure 12.13).

Figure 12.12   CESCaL Screenshot Showing Documents Linked to Flashlight Packages

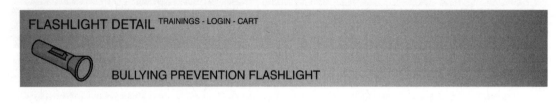

FLASHLIGHT DETAIL TRAININGS - LOGIN - CART

BULLYING PREVENTION FLASHLIGHT

Home // Flashlight Detail

Category	Description	Type	File Size	Created	Download
ACTION PLAN					
1 Action Plan Guidance Curriculum	Bullying Prevention Action Plan	W	34 kb	10/21/2013	⬇
LESSON PLANS					
2 Guidance Curriculum Lesson Plans	Bullying Prevention Curriculum	W	78 kb	10/21/2013	⬇
CURRICULUM					
3 Guidance Curriculum PowerPoints	Bullying Prevention PowerPoint		580 kb	10/21/2013	⬇
PRE-POST TESTS					
4 Pre-Post Tests	Bullying Prevention Pre-Post Tests	W	58 kb	10/21/2013	⬇
CROSSWALK OF LESSON					
5 Standards Curriculum Crosswalk	Bullying Prevention Standards Curriculum Crosswalk		125 kb	10/21/2013	⬇
RESULTS REPORTS					
6 Measure Results and Report on Results Report	Bullying Prevention Results Reports	W	25 kb	10/21/2013	⬇
FLASHLIGHT POWERPOINT PRESENTATION					
7 Flashlight Results PowerPoints (Do 1 Thing Well)	Bullying Prevention Results PowerPoints		110 kb	10/21/2013	⬇

Each year at San Diego State University, school counseling graduate students create school counseling curriculum and intentional guidance Flashlight Packages as a part of their culminating requirements in the program. School counselor educators will also find many materials to assist them in course development. These packages are uploaded to the CESCaL website to provide an opportunity for practicing school counselors to browse through and download samples to get ideas for their programs. Some of these Flashlights are also provided in the online appendix. It is CESCaL's hope that these samples and examples will serve as support to school counselors as they design, implement, evaluate, and improve their programs.

SUMMARY

Flashlight PowerPoint presentations are powerful marketing tools for any school counseling program. Additionally and perhaps most important, creating new Flashlight Packages each year can provide, over time, a resource bank of school core curriculum lessons and intentional guidance interventions. School counselors can deliver lessons and provide interventions with confidence that the lessons and interventions are linked to standards and have been effectively delivered, evaluated, and revised to improve results for students. Ideally, over time, staff in the school counseling program will have evaluated each of their curriculum lessons and interventions and feel confident the activities they perform support the outcomes they seek.

13

Today's Professional School Counselor Does Make a Difference

This text has thoroughly and systematically, through detailed instruction, stories, activities, and samples, provided a process for designing, implementing, evaluating, marketing, and improving school counseling in alignment with the ASCA National Model (ASCA, 2012a) and evidence-based practices (Dimmitt, Carey, & Hatch, 2007). This final chapter will address expectations for today's professional school counselors and address the challenges and opportunities for creating change in systems where school counselors, programs, or districts are hesitant, resistant, or struggling to change. Representing a slight shift from the previous chapters' intentionally casual register, this chapter will align new theories to the process of systems change, and offer original perspectives and considerations from leaders and change agents.

LOGIC MODEL FOR SUCCESS

Most new social programs are intended to address existing problems and create change. Realist evaluators Pawson and Tilley (1997, 2004) theorize programs are successful when participants (a) are allowed to make choices influenced by their prior experiences, beliefs, attitudes, and opportunities and (b) have access to resources. Making new choices requires a *change in the reasoning* of the participants (such as the participants' values, beliefs, attitudes, or logic they choose to apply to a specific situation), and a *change in the resources* available to them (such as information, skills, abilities, knowledge, training, and support).

The interaction of the participants' change in reasoning with the change in resources serves as the *mechanism* that allows programs to work in different ways for different people. Consequently, when schools start new programs, the change in reasoning and resources can prompt or inhibit different mechanisms of change for different participants. Additionally, the context in which the program operates can significantly impact the potential to get the desired results. Program *context* includes features such as social, economic, political, and organizational structures, program participants, program staffing, geographical and historical context, and so on (Pawson & Tilley, 1997, 2004).

Evaluating the outcomes of implementing a school counseling program based on the ASCA National Model, from a realistic evaluator perspective, requires looking at the context in which the school counseling program exists as well as the mechanism (change in reasoning and resources) being implemented. The interaction between the context and mechanism, which together shape the program's outcomes, are seen in Figure 13.1.

As schools and districts move toward implementing a data-driven ASCA National Model program, they may find program and student outcomes do not align with the expected or desired goals. When looking to shift school counseling program practices in light of disappointing outcomes, it is helpful to consider the contributing contextual variables. The logic model for program success in Figure 13.1 (adapted by Hatch from Pawson & Tilley, 1997) illustrates the necessary contributors to student and program outcomes. If contextual variables such as the organization's staffing ratios, program budget, and leadership buy-in are lacking,

Figure 13.1 Logic Model for Program Success

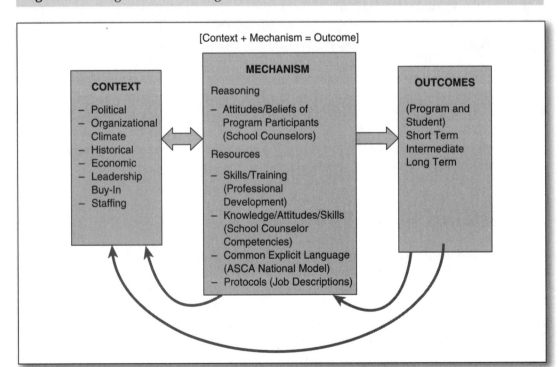

reasoning and resources within the mechanism will be impacted, leading to disappointing outcomes. However, if the organizational variables within the context are deemed suitable for change, and outcomes are still not forthcoming, then analyzing the strength of the mechanism is next. Do school counselors believe the staffing, administrator buy-in, and organizational variables are truly in place to support this change? Do their attitudes and beliefs align with those represented in the ASCA National Model? Do school counselors need professional development in data-driven practices or designing and implementing a school counseling program based on the ASCA National Model? Do protocols and job descriptions represent the new common language?

At a recent training, a school counselor shared he was excited to move in the direction of an ASCA National Model program but was reluctant to begin blocking time to become more proactive in calendaring his classroom lessons or groups. He feared his administrator would evaluate him poorly if he was not available at a moment's notice to assist students or parents. Successful transitions of behavior require conversations with key organizational personnel (e.g., superintendent, principal) to ensure expectations are aligned and employees can trust their supervisors will support their proactive work.

PREPARING THE SOIL

Metaphorically, imagine the context as preparing soil for grass seed. If a homeowner wants the outcome of a beautiful lawn, throwing grass seed on dry soil will not provide the result he or she is looking for. However, if the soil is tilled and fertilized, and a watering system is installed, the seed is more likely to flourish and produce the desired outcome of a beautiful lawn. In other words, a suitable context is necessary to develop the mechanism.

In schools, if a new program or mechanism is started in a context that is not prepared for change, then the program is less likely to produce desired results. To effectively implement a school counseling program based on the ASCA National Model and garner the positive program and student outcomes the school or district is looking to obtain, analyzing the context and the mechanism for potential limitations (political, economic, situational, etc.) is essential. If expected student and program outcomes are produced, then data-driven-practices training and the implementation of the ASCA National Model has likely aligned with the beliefs, values, and attitudes impacting the ability of the school counseling team to perform activities that influence the outcomes gained.

Because school counseling programs tend to work differently in different contexts with varying reasoning and resources (change mechanisms), programs cannot simply be replicated from one context to another and automatically achieve the same outcomes. Therefore, one of the tasks in realistic program evaluation is to learn what works for whom, and to discover in which contexts particular programs work or do not work, and what mechanisms are triggered by what programs in what contexts.

As Pawson and Tilley (2004) suggest,

For each decision point, the realist evaluators should be able to proffer the following kind of advice: 'remember A,' 'beware of B,' 'take care of C,' 'D can result in both E and F,' 'Gs and Hs are likely to interpret I quite differently,' 'if you try J make sure that K has also been considered.'

This logic model for change assumes programs are "theories in action," and when a program is implemented, it tests the theory to learn what might cause change, even though the theory itself may not be explicit (Pawson & Tilley, 1997). For that reason, one of the tasks of a program evaluation is to make the theories within a program very clear by developing explicit hypotheses about how and for whom these programs might work. The implementation of the program, and the subsequent evaluation of it, would then test those hypotheses. This means it is important to collect data not solely about program impacts or the processes of program implementation, but also about the specific aspects of the program context that might impact program outcomes and about the specific mechanisms that might be creating change.

In connecting this concept to the ASCA National Model, the theories for student outcomes are in the action plan(s). Theoretically, when school counselors implement the processes specified in the action plan, the intent is to garner positive perception data (ASK), which contributes to the students' behavior change, contributing to improvements in achievement-related data, which subsequently impact achievement data. Implementing and measuring the effect of the activity is like testing the hypothesis. Will the delivery of a violence prevention curriculum or the meetings of the anger management group really impact students' ability to change their behavior and lead to a decrease in the number of referrals?

Participants play a vital role in program implementation. Assessing program data may result in discovering different stakeholders have different beliefs, information, and understandings of how programs are supposed to work and whether the programs do, in fact, work. For instance, teachers and administrators might have different understandings or expectations of school counseling programs and services than school counselors have, and these differences impact the school counselor's ability to implement the mechanism (e.g., ASCA National Model).

Data collection processes (interviews, focus groups, surveys, etc.) could be constructed with stakeholders to collect the particular information those groups will have and thereby validate, refute, or refine theories about what stakeholders believe as well as how and for whom the program works (Pawson & Tilley, 1997). At a recent training, several high school counselors shared they hadn't provided classroom lessons because "teachers and administrators don't support classroom interruptions." A subsequent comprehensive survey of faculty, however, revealed overwhelming support from teachers to increase the frequency of classroom lessons by counselors (Hatch & Poynton, 2013). Interestingly, the strongest support for increased frequency of curriculum delivery came from administrators. In this case, the context (leadership buy-in) was blamed when deficiencies in the mechanism were certainly contributing factors to the lack of outcomes. Sharing the survey results led to productive discussions by counselors, which included addressing their own biases and needs for increased knowledge and skills for delivering classroom curriculum.

REALISTIC EVALUATION (ACTIVITY) QUESTIONS

Context

- What are the political issues impacting the call for change in the school counseling program?
- Is the organizational climate ready to accommodate a school counseling program change?
- What is the historical context of the school counseling program, and how will the program be impacted by change?
- What are the economic issues impacting the school and/or the school counseling program?
- Is there leadership buy-in for change within the school counseling program?
- Is staffing appropriate to accommodate activities expected of school counselors?

Mechanism (participant reasoning and resources)

- What are the beliefs, assumptions, and philosophies of the school counselors, teachers, and administrators?
- Is the school counseling program ready for change?
- Do school counselors value and believe in this change?
- Have school counselors been provided accurate information and training to implement the ASCA National Model?
- Do school counselors possess the knowledge, attitudes, and skills necessary to implement this program (data analysis, delivering classroom lessons, creating pre/post tests, measuring results, etc.)?
- Is there a common explicit language for the school counseling program among stakeholders?
- Are protocols, such as job descriptions and evaluation tools, in place to ensure consistent implementation?

Outcomes (short-term, intermediate, and long-term):

- Program (Are the program outcomes those desired?)
  - Are school counselors implementing the ASCA National Model by creating action plans and pre/post assessments, measuring the impact of their lessons, collecting results, and sharing results with faculty?
  - Are school counselors taking on fewer "utility player" responsibilities and spending more time in direct contact with students?

- Student (Are student outcomes meeting our goals?)
  - Has improvement been seen in students' competency attainment data (knowledge, attitudes, and skills)?
  - Has improvement been seen in students' behavior (achievement-related and achievement data)?
  - Do the outcome data appear to be shifting in the direction that aligns with the activities school counselors are performing and the data they are focused on improving?

OWNERS OR RENTERS?

School counselors implementing school counseling programs aligned with the ASCA National Model may discover their colleagues in the counseling department at their school or in the district have a "renter" rather than an "owner" reaction to the call for shift in professional identity, role, and function based on their personal or professional agendas, needs, life circumstances, or abilities. Are you an owner or a renter? Renters are more likely to see themselves as visitors or short-timers. They may be less inclined to invest in home improvement projects for property that is not "theirs." Owners tend to stay longer, and they are more likely to invest time, talent, and resources in their "property," taking great pride in their investment.

When it comes to the school counseling program or the students in school, are school counselors behaving as owners or renters? Earlier in the chapter, readers were presented with the metaphor describing the importance of preparing the soil (or the context) in preparation for spreading grass seed. Accordingly, the participant, in this case the homeowner, must also regularly water the lawn, proactively monitor the emergence of dry spots, and provide additional care in the most deprived areas.

> Owners accept full responsibility even when it is not formally assigned, believe deeply in their mission, collaborate with others, take initiative and hold coworkers accountable to the same high standards. Renters, meanwhile, approach their work with an "it's just a job" mentality, tend to make statements like "that's not my problem" and point the finger at others when things go wrong. (Ryan, 2011)

Owners inspire ownership in others. They hold themselves and others accountable to high standards of professionalism. Owners encourage and challenge renters to "own the turf"—improve their front yards, because it impacts the entire neighborhood (or district's school counseling program). In 2011, Secretary of Education Arne Duncan called on school counselors to "own the turf" in college- and career-readiness and implored them to take on the leadership role within their schools to become a central part of educational reform in preparing all students to be college- and career-ready (College Board, 2011). "Own the Turf" is a national advocacy campaign committed to galvanizing and mobilizing school counselors to establish a college-going culture in their schools and to take the lead in districts and communities (College Board, 2013). Duncan shared concerns that too few school counselor preparation programs adequately prepare graduate students, and he urged school counselors to redouble their efforts to "own the turf" as essential professionals in educational reform (College Board, 2011).

PROFESSIONAL SCHOOL COUNSELORS

Are school counselors professionals? What does it mean to be a professional? A quick search on Google provides the following as the top answer: "Professionals are obligated to operate according to high and strict standards of conduct in performing their work, both in terms of proficiency and ethics" (South Metro Denver Realtor Association, 2011). The American School Counselors Association provides clear ethical guidelines (2010b), using the title "professional school counselors" throughout the document. One of the ethical responsibilities of professional school counselors, as indicated below, is to belong to their professional association; others include to implement, evaluate, and share results of their school counseling programs.

F.2. Contribution to the Profession

Professional school counselors: a. Actively participate in professional associations and share results and best practices in assessing, implementing and annually evaluating the outcomes of data-driven school counseling programs with measurable academic, career/college and personal/social competencies for every student (ASCA, 2010b).

The membership rate for school counselors in state and national professional associations, however, as compared to that of other professions, is very poor. Seventy-five percent of school psychologists are members of their national professional association, but only 11% of school counselors belong to theirs (Bauman, 2008). How can school counselors expect to be treated as professionals when they actively choose to not follow the recommendations of their own ethical guidelines? Are school counselors really ready to own the turf?

According to Bing, the definition of *professional* is: "conforming to the standards of skill, competence, or character normally expected of a properly qualified and experienced person in a work environment" (Professional, 2013). ASCA's school counselor competencies (2012) are the professional standards for the profession and address both the program and student outcomes expected when professionals are at work. The competencies outline the knowledge, skills, and attitudes school counselors must possess to meet rigorous demands of both the profession and the needs of K–12 students (ASCA, 2012c). Interestingly, skill, competence, and character align well with attitudes, skills, and knowledge (ASK) with the intent of behavior change in the everyday practice of the professional school counselor (Figure 13.2).

Figure 13.2 Is School Counseling a Profession?

Is school counseling a Profession?
What does it mean to be a Professional?

Attitudes
Skills
Knowledge

Behavior Change

Professional: Conforming to the standards of skill, competence, or character normally expected of a properly qualified and experienced person in a work environment

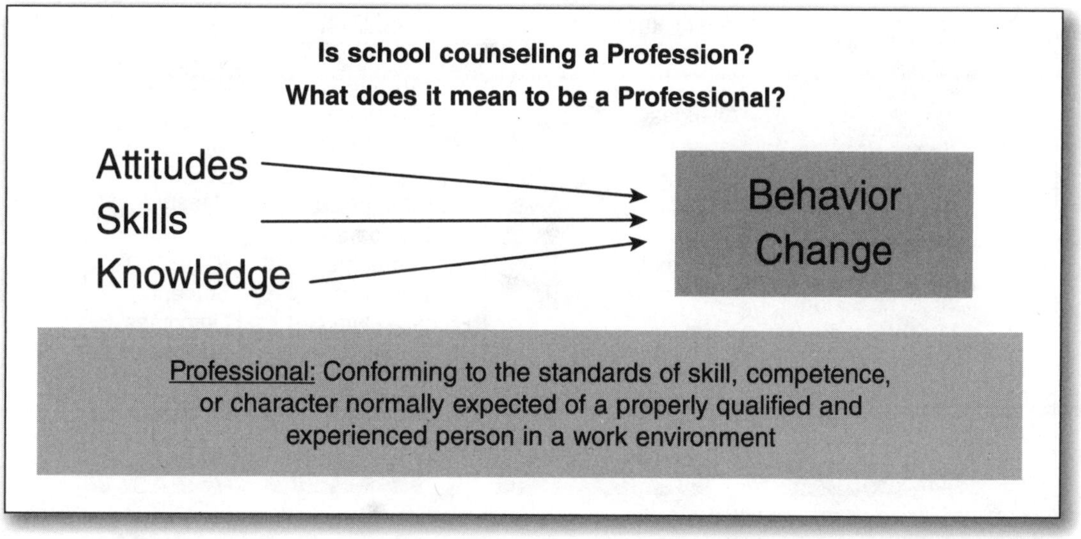

Aligning with the outcomes description in the logic model in Figure 13.1, the school counselor competencies reflect both the expectations for the *reasoning* and the *resources* in the mechanism. The competencies can be used by (a) school counselors as a self-assessment, (b) administrators as a tool for selecting and evaluating school counselors, and (c) school counselor educators as a benchmark for graduate program development (ASCA, 2012c).

As a self-assessment tool, the competencies can by used by school counselors to determine areas of confidence and areas of professional growth. In looking at a school site or district program, if outcomes are not gained as predicted, various contextual variables might be analyzed. Similar to the conceptual diagram in Figure 4.9 in Chapter 4, Figure 13.3 provides a logic model for the professional school counselor. If the context is prepared and the school counselor possesses the appropriate knowledge, attitudes, and skills, then implementing the activities suggested in this book and in the ASCA National Model ideally would lead to predicted student and program outcomes. In this case, the "professional school counselor" would be "ethical," as mentioned in the second part of the guideline (F.2) presented above, because the counselor is sharing the results of the implementation of data-driven school-counseling programs (ASCA, 2012a).

If program and student outcomes are lacking, it is appropriate to determine the extent to which artifacts (if any) might be contributing to the lack of results. Then the counselor may be assessed as student behavior is assessed, by asking the question, What knowledge, attitude, or skill does the school counselor need to acquire in order to perform the desired behavior? If knowledge or skills are needed, then professional development is in order. If the school counselors' beliefs conflict with performing the expected behaviors, then other factors, perhaps in the context (see Figure 13.3), may be contributing factors.

Figure 13.3   Hatching Results Logic Model: Professional School Counselor

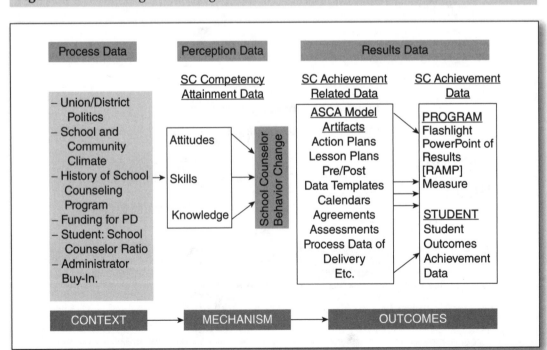

In the same way students need assistance to obtain the outcomes sought, so too do school counselors, who may be perfectly well intended and supportive of the movement toward data-driven school counseling programs, but who may lack the knowledge or skill to implement one. (Mason, Ockerman, & Chen-Hayes, 2013). For these issues, professional development is needed for school counselors.

Reasonable expectations for today's professional school counselors must be considered in light of current school counselor preparation programs and whether the preparation of today's school counselors is in line with competencies the profession seeks (ASCA, 2008; College Board, 2011; Hines & Lemon, 2011). Unfortunately, too many university training programs satisfy student competencies and practicum hours with tasks not appropriately performed in schools (e.g. long-term therapy) and in settings other than K–12 schools. Additionally, most university professors teaching school counselors have little, if any, training or background in school counseling.

Therefore, when new school counselors are hired or practicing school counselors are evaluated, close attention must be paid to the character, skills, and competencies normally expected of a properly qualified and experienced person in this work environment (Hatch, 2006). Does the prospective school counselor possess the attitudes, knowledge, and skills necessary to counsel students and produce both student and program outcomes? In areas in which school counselors (or their evaluators) believe they are unprepared, professional development training is recommended.

PILOTS, PASSENGERS, PRISONERS, AND HIJACKERS (P³H)

Airplane metaphors are often used when redesigning programs: "Building an airplane while it's flying"; getting participants "on board." Participants may respond differently than some leaders expect; some might be afraid of flying, others want to be in the cockpit, and some want the plane to have a different destination. When managing difficult leaders in an era of educational reform, an airplane metaphor can also be utilized to illustrate four archetypes, described briefly below (Hatch, 2005b).

Pilots love to be in charge. They possess a tremendous interest in helping to move the system forward. Give them a map, and tell them where to go, and they will get the plane there safely and on time. Pilots come early, sit up front, and offer to take charge of their team's forward movement. *Passengers* are along for the ride. They are thrilled there is a pilot in charge, as they have little interest in leading this activity or agenda. Passengers are content to perform the activities requested but prefer to let someone else take the lead. Passengers are compliant team members who focus on completing tasks assigned and supporting their leaders. *Prisoners* want off the plane. They are ready to retire, wish they could quit, and have grown to hate their work. Prisoners have been on the plane way too long; they are grumblers who complain the idea or program did not work before and will not work now. Prisoners can impact the morale of the team and make the work environment less pleasant. *Hijackers* are there to sabotage change to protect their interests and ensure they block forward movement at all costs. Hijackers believe they know what is best and think if everyone listened to them, situations would greatly improve. Because no one adheres to their approach, they ensure nothing moves the agenda in any direction other than the direction they want it to go. Hijackers have a map and plans of their own and are highly resistant employees who organizational leaders must watch out for. Hijackers would rather watch the organization crash and burn than follow a personally undesired direction. Inconvincible and never swayed, hijackers are to be managed and are best kept out of the cockpit (Hatch, 2005b).

THOUGHTS ON COMPLEX RESISTANCE

Redesigning the school counseling program within a district requires careful attention to the impact of change, especially for those who might be particularly resistant. Advice may be necessary about how to work more effectively with staff that resists change or thwarts or sabotages positive change-making efforts. In *Transforming School Culture*, Anthony Muhammad (2009) discusses what can be expected when educators, faculty, or staff are asked to make an unwanted change. Muhammad's four levels of resistance and suggestions for ways to address or eliminate resistance are presented below and adapted for the school counselor.

Level 1 resisters require rational understanding of why change is occurring. The basis of resistance is logical and easily addressed, as long as leaders resist the urge to coerce change. Change occurs for Level 1 resisters when they come to understand *why change is necessary*, and a meeting of the minds occurs. Articulating the rationale for redesigning a school counseling program and fulfilling the counselors' need to understand can quickly shift perspectives and result in new levels of commitment and productivity. For some school counselors, a thorough review of student data helps bring understanding about why change is necessary and propels them to try a new way of designing interventions. Others might be motivated by an opportunity to earn more respect within their school or district by sharing results or earning a RAMP award. Still, others might be swayed to try new ideas because of the move some schools are making toward merit pay based on student results (Goldstein, 2011).

Level 2 fundamentalists resist change because they do not trust the judgment or skills of the leader. When the credibility of the leader is called into question, participants are less likely to accept the leader's guidance. To earn trust, school counselor leaders are encouraged to know the school and the district's culture, history, policy, politics, and practices. They must stay abreast of local and national school and school counseling issues, including legislation, texts, journal articles, blogs, tweets, and any other relevant school counseling materials. School counselor leaders continue to improve their skills and garner additional credentials. They constantly demonstrate efforts to improve (such as by attempting to learn new technology skills), and they model professionalism by attending local, state, and national conferences. Finally, they pave the way and garner trust and respect by being active learners.

> People may keep familiar tools in a frightening situation because an unfamiliar alternative is even more frightening (Weick, 1996).

Level 3s resist change because they are unsure whether the proposed changes will cause more stress and perhaps, even worse, not achieve any better result than the current methodology.

When confronted with resisters who lack necessary skills, success will require ensuring adequate time is set aside to build their capacity, and adequate support is provided to make changes at their pace and with assistance they may need. Many school counselors were never trained in how to use, collect, or analyze data. Successful change requires the leader's patience and assistance to ensure appropriate counselor-focused professional development for those who are new to looking at data or using PowerPoint. Vertical learning curves can be very stressful; however, they are often necessary for vital self-improvement.

Level 4 resisters are the last ones to drop their tools and cooperate, because change would require redefining themselves to the other members of the organization.

To drop one's tools is to admit failure (Weick, 1996). Level four resisters pose a particularly challenging problem, because they are deeply and personally rooted in their opposition and have defined themselves within the organization by their resistance to change. In some of the most severe cases, the ideological resistance of a Level 4 resister will

> To drop one's tools may be to admit failure. To retain one's tools is to postpone this admission (Weick, 1996).

call the leaders into a battle of will. According to Muhammad (2009), it is a battle the leaders must win, because allowing Level 4s to operate within the culture in the midst of a transformation is akin to sanctioning the behavior.

For some school counselors, spending months each spring building the master schedule was considered appropriate. Learning that building the master schedule is now a noncounseling responsibility does not make school counselors who built the schedule for 20 years wrong. Rather, it makes them employees who were performing the task they were most likely hired, validated, reinforced, and evaluated to provide. The rationale for dropping the tool of schedule building and learning new data-driven school counseling practices must be connected to a respectful awareness that many school counselors were never expected to know anything about data, because it was never a part of their training program.

Similarly, dropping the tool of one-on-one weekly long term therapeutic counseling in favor of classroom lessons, skill-based groups, and short-term solution-focused brief counseling may be met with less resistance if counselors feel validated for performing the function they believe they were hired to perform. Care must be given to ensure counselors are valued and feel respected for the specialized training and skills they possess and appreciated for the difference they have made in the lives of students they served (albeit fewer students than they could have served).

SEEING OBSTACLES AS OPPORTUNITIES

When best efforts to shift paradigms result in less than favorable outcomes, it may be helpful to brainstorm obstacles, ideas, and opportunities for change and growth. In Figure 13.4, space is provided to list current challenges, obstacles, and barriers to implementing an evidenced-based school counseling program that aligns with the ASCA National Model. Sometimes, the challenge is identified as the school counselors' attitude, knowledge, or skill. Other times, there may be site-level or district concerns. Collaborate with your team to brainstorm ideas and possibilities. Imagine what might happen if a new idea is tested. Finally, take action today by committing to a timeline. Professional school counselors and their students can't wait any longer.

Figure 13.4 Obstacles, Ideas, and Opportunities Worksheet

Obstacles, Ideas, and Opportunities

School Counselor: _____

Site: _____

District: _____

Challenges/Obstacles/ Barriers (What gets in the way?)	School Counselor (ASK)	Site	District	Brainstorming Ideas (What if we tried___?)	Opportunities (Let's try ___)	When?
1.						
2.						
3.						
4.						

RESOLVING (AVOIDING) THE BERMUDA TRIANGLE

The introduction of this text presented the challenges in the school counseling profession, theorizing they are the consequence of organizational inefficiency, institutional illegitimacy, and subsequent political devaluing. If the profession is ever going to resolve these concerns, what steps are necessary to ensure the pilot flying the plane avoids the Bermuda Triangle?

First, school counseling programs must increase their *internal efficiency* and be respected for their accomplishments and efforts (Hatch, 2002). The program must become increasingly aligned with the school's educational goals, standards, objectives, and outcomes, and school counselors must engage in a continuous, self-reflective process that will result in the adoption of effective interventions and practices and the discarding of ineffective interventions and practices.

Second, student results must be communicated accurately and effectively for the program to gain *institutional legitimacy* (Hatch, 2004a). The program will become increasingly regarded as indispensable to the school by the leading opinion makers and decision makers, and the staff of the program will be increasingly regarded as professionals who are capable of self-direction and self-correction. As institutional legitimacy increases, the program will begin to attain *political legitimacy.* Increasingly, school counselors will have opportunities to participate in leadership activities that establish the policies, structure, and routines that define the appropriate role and work of school counselors.

Finally, the program and its personnel will be regarded as essential to the work of the school, and the value of the program will be worth far more than the cost of its personnel in terms resources. The centrality of the program will be dependent on school counselors' capacity to document important results, use these results to improve practice, and effectively communicate these results (and the processes used to obtain them) to the school community.

USING DATA DOES MAKE A DIFFERENCE!

Throughout the United States, hundreds of school counselors are not waiting for a miracle. They know that when budget cuts hit and financial resources are strained, difficult decisions must be made. They understand that if school counselors lack evidence of how their program activities support the mission and goals of their schools, the counselors may be seen as more dispensable than other school-level staff (Hurwitz & Howell, 2013). Instead, these school counselors are creating their own miracles by using data and sharing results with key stakeholders. Below are a few success stories. The first was received in May 2012 from "R," who asked that I not reference her school district, because, in cutting its counseling program, it was simply trying to meet its overwhelming financial obligations in extraordinary times like so many districts across the country; she did not want it to be seen in a bad light. The second, Debbie Stark's accounting, sheds light on the impact of data and accountability from a central office perspective. Many more success stories follow in this chapter and in the online appendix.

I am a high school counselor. I have been to several of your training sessions and I wanted to tell you that your advice on how to save school counselors worked!! Here's my story....

Our school counselors have received layoffs for the last four years, ever since the huge decline in state funding, in an effort to balance our district's strained budget.

This year our district offered a resolution to our school board to consider cutting *all five counselors* as a way to balance a tentative budget, in case the governor's tax initiative does not pass next November. This all happened back in March, when they had to notify certificated folks they may not have a position the following school year. Recently our school board held a special school board meeting to hear from the public about the proposed cuts.

Well, Trish, we fought back in the only way we knew how—with *data!*

We brought former school counselors, nearby high school counselors from surrounding districts, local CSU and community college reps, teachers, parents, and students together to implore the school board not to cut these counselors, because what we do makes a difference (and we could prove it).

When it was our turn to speak to the board members, we used our school's data to drive home our point—that we do make a difference. In our particular case, we have a fabulous graduation rate; it far exceeds the state averages. We showed them how, as school counselors, we have contributed to that success rate. We shared our program, our data, and our results, along with other information, to help persuade our school board to not make the proposed cut.

Well, bringing all these elements together worked! The board voted *unanimously* to keep all five school counselors! I hope you will share our story with other counselors!

Thank you again,

—A "professional" school counselor for at least another year.

Paramount Unified: One School District's Success Story

By Debbie Stark, Deputy Superintendent

What Was Our Reality?

Before an evidenced-based school counseling program was implemented at Paramount High School, counselors spent the majority of their time handling crisis and discipline issues. It may be said that random acts of counseling were performed, because plenty of time spent was during one-on-one interaction with students. The high school did not have an articulated plan for teaching guidance curriculum, providing intentional interventions, or collecting data on the impact of counselors' work. There were no collective agreements or commitments about the role and responsibilities of the counselor.

What Did We Do?

To improve the school's performance, staff at Paramount High School connected the high school's reform and PLC efforts, making it a priority to help meet the goal of increasing the graduation rate. Staff also committed their time to professional development on the ASCA National Model and standards, and on the counselor's role in providing curriculum and interventions and measuring results. Counselors outlined classroom lessons and interventions they would deliver, and they were responsible for showing their results at district meetings. School administrators responsible for supervising and supporting the counseling program at each school attended professional development sessions and followed up on site.

What Were the Results? What Has Changed?

High school counselors have begun working as a team to plan and implement common lessons. Counselors are spending more of their days teaching guidance lessons or leading intervention groups. High school students receive more consistent guidance support regardless of which counselor a student is assigned to. Counselors now routinely use pre- and posttests to measure the impact of what students learned as the result of their lesson or group intervention. District counselors' meetings focus exclusively on guidance interventions, lessons they teach, and data they are collecting. Counselors have a common language across schools for discussing their work and its impact. Throughout it all we have learned a few lessons:

- *Connect the work of the counselor with the greater vision and goals of the district and school.* We began our work with high school counselors, connecting the need for them to implement interventions to the school's goal to increase the number of students who pass classes. This provided some leverage for making change.
- *Make the school counselor's work a priority* by assigning an administrator to oversee the program at both school and district levels. Having an administrator attend the professional development sessions assured school counselors that their work would be continued and understood at the school. Having a district administrator involved meant that principals, assistant superintendents, and the superintendent would stay informed of the importance of this work.
- *Make the results public.* Counselors were asked to share the results of their work with school staff. In addition, their data were represented at a board of education meeting each spring.
- *Mine the data.* School districts are data rich—but too often, the data are underused or not used at all. Use the data the district already has to determine the interventions or curriculum to provide. How many students are failing multiple classes in middle or high school? How many students have excessive absences or tardies? How many disciplinary referrals are for fighting or bullying? This kind of information is readily available and can be used to determine where to begin.

Debbie's superintendent, Dr. Verdugo agreed:

Now that our counselors are monitoring the effect of their work with students, we have measurable results that clearly display they are making a difference. For the first time we have data that show more of our students are learning essential guidance lessons and fewer are being referred for behavioral or attendance interventions. By helping counselors focus on how to use data to identify each school's needs and measure the impact of their work, we now have a shared vision and common understanding of the vital role of the counselor in our school district.

Elementary School Counselor Positions Saved!

Sixty-four federal Elementary and Secondary School Counseling Program (ESSCP) grants were awarded in 2009. Typically these grants fund three to four elementary school counselors; however, most grant-funded districts are unable to sustain these positions when federal funding ends the third year. One awarded school district in California implemented a school counseling program based on the ASCA National Model (2005) and evidenced-based practices (Dimmit et al., 2007) at three high-needs elementary schools following the data outline shared in Chapter 3, Figure 3.8. Their program provided violence prevention curriculum for all students and intentional interventions for students with needs that had become evident through analysis of data. Predicted outcomes were achieved, including improved school climate, attendance, and behavior. The grant team strategically prepared and shared multiple results reports and presentations. In all three schools, the impact of these interventions contributed to significant decreases in truancy and discipline referrals and improvement on state achievement tests. Sharing these results was essential to keeping the monies that funded them.

Using the Flashlight approach to creating a school board presentation, the team presented the highlights of their work to key central office and school board members, who moved to sustain funding for the elementary team and expanded the program to district middle schools. Although many schools were losing school counselors in California, this school district committed to sustainable funding of this successful program after federal funds ended. Figures 13.5 through 13.7 are the "money slides" from the school board presentation, showing reduction in discipline referrals, improvement in attendance, and lower numbers of N's and U's on student report cards. Refer to the online appendix to view the entire school board presentation.

Figure 13.5   Slide Showing Reduction in Discipline Referrals

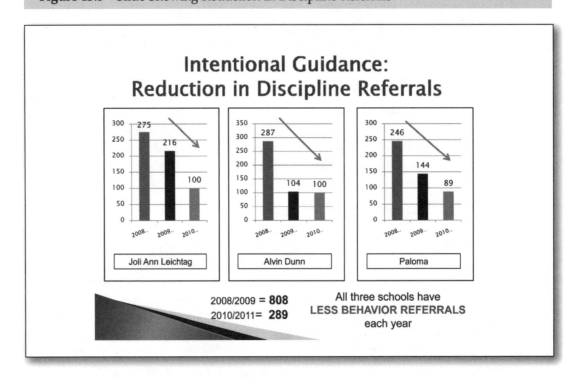

Figure 13.6   Slide Showing Improvement in Attendance

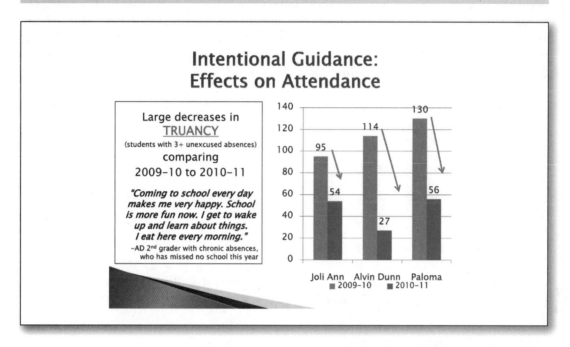

Figure 13.7   Slide Showing Improvement in Student Study Skills

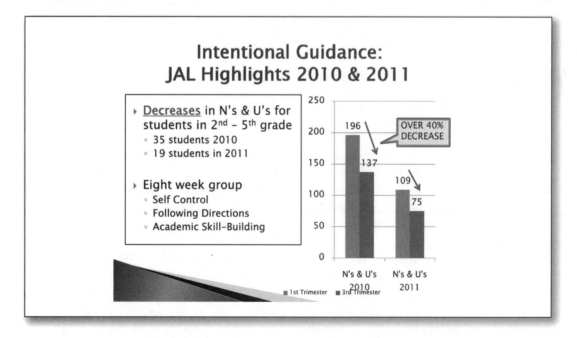

In Oceanside Unified School District, a similar federal grant was also implemented. The school counselors also presented their results to the school board (see online appendix). In an effort to provide even more support through a qualitative perspective, the district funded the creation of an 18-minute video to compliment the data shared at the school board meeting (http://www.youtube.com/watch?v= HplRzoP47Ag). The video shares stories of student resiliency, including a touching statement from a bullied student who proclaimed about his counselor, "Ms. Pablo is a way of life!" Attendees reported there was not a dry eye in the room. Following the presentation, school board members requested the superintendent find a way to maintain the program. These school counselors used data, collected results, and shared student outcomes, which lead to increased marketing by the district in the form of visual media. These efforts all contributed to maintaining elementary school counselor positions in this district. For more information on these and other districts successfully implementing elementary school counseling programs through federally funded grants, please see the online appendix or www.hatchingresults.com.

RAMP Leads to Sustainability!

Rob Stelmar, school counselor at a twice-awarded RAMP school in Brea Olinda, California, says

> A cut to the BOHS Guidance Department is always a last resort in the Brea Olinda Unified School District because we are able to prove that we are making a difference in the lives of our students by our ability to share our data with the faculty, principal, Superintendent and Board of Education.

Positions Saved in Georgia!

In Gail Smith's district in Cobb County, Georgia, 50 jobs at risk were saved. Smith reported the district was going to lose 60 or more positions, and ultimately, the only change was the ratio, from 464:1 to 500:1. According to Gail, measuring results and sharing successes saved more than 50 jobs!

School Counselors Lead the Way in Maryland!

Sarah Pelham, assistant superintendent for Anne Arundel County Public Schools (AACPS), reports that AACPS, with approximately 74,000 students, is the fifth-largest school district in the state. The philosophy of school counseling in AACPS is that all professional school counselors are expected to *lead* through their professional role by using data effectively to eliminate the achievement gap. This is accomplished through high levels of accountability and reaching targets established for targeted intervention plans for each level (elementary, middle, and high schools). School counselors have earned credibility and garnered sustainability. Pelham stated,

> It is our expectation that school counselors will serve all students by developing targeted intervention plans which requires analyzing data and becoming active partners with staff and community. . . . Data and the analysis of data is critical in understanding student progress. This process begins in elementary schools. School counselors focus their efforts based on data at all levels of the organization.

According to Dr. Gayle M. Cicero, director of student services, despite tough budget times, AACPS has not lost a single school counseling position. Data collected by professional school counselors demonstrate that students clearly benefit from school counseling services delivered at all grade levels, PreK–12. Demonstrating and sharing results through data collection and analysis builds credibility and sustainability.

Systemic Change in Chicago

by Lisa DeGregorio, Elementary School Counselor

In March 2011, the state of elementary (K–8) school counseling in Chicago Public Schools was a strong contrast to that of secondary (9–12) counseling. No elementary school counseling programs had achieved RAMP designation. There was a student-to-counselor ratio of approximately 1200:1. At the district level, there was a secondary counseling department, but no elementary counseling department; rather, elementary counseling was housed in the office of special education. The personnel had dwindled to one manager with multiple roles and me, citywide elementary school counselor, Lisa De Gregorio, to support approximately 425 elementary school counselors and provide professional development with no actual spending budget designated for elementary counseling.

In an effort to promote collaboration and form more of a K–12 model, Trish Hatch led a two-day American School Counselor Association (ASCA) National Model training to a limited number of elementary counselors. This professional development provided tools for the school counselors to implement a school counseling program aligned to the academic mission of the school. The program was comprehensive in design and was delivered systematically to all students, ensuring that every student had equitable program access. It identified and delivered to students the knowledge and skills needed to be socially, emotionally, and academically ready for high school.

Motivated by Dr. Hatch's message that taking action is crucial to our survival as a profession, those in attendance spoke out about the lack of support for elementary counseling. I created a sign-up list for those expressing enthusiasm and a commitment to use and begin collecting data to drive intervention decisions, monitor student progress, and demonstrate the impact of school counseling interventions on student achievement. Soon, we developed the Elementary School Counseling ASCA National Model Cohort Project, which has yearly goals, a vision, and a mission to

- Utilize leadership, advocacy, systemic change, and collaboration to implement the ASCA National Model framework in elementary schools.
- Advocate for comprehensive, developmental, and systematic programs available to all students.
- Use data to drive activities and collect evidence that objectives have been met in order to obtain results and demonstrate the value of school counseling in elementary programs.
- Develop a structured K–8 core guidance curriculum for school counselors to identify and deliver the knowledge and skills all students should acquire.

Group members dedicated themselves to their goals, meeting over the summer at libraries and each other's homes to develop the cohort and begin creating data projects. Graduate students were invited to assist in data collection and completing field activities and projects.

Ultimately, the majority of the cohort members completed Flashlight data projects; some completed two. Currently, the pioneering counselors mentor a growing base of new cohort members, attending project meetings, utilizing the ASCA National Model, completing data projects, and collaborating both with each other and administrators. They share their projects, Flashlights, and ideas through a Google group site. A handful of cohort members have joined an advisory council to the K–12 Counseling and Advising Department, and their data will be included in the group's executive summary.

Realization in Chicago!

Krish Mohip, principal of Walsh Elementary School in Chicago, shared

I never realized that a counselor could have such an impact in such a short amount of time. In just two years, Kirsten transformed our high school admissions process at Walsh. As a result we have a higher number of students attending selective schools this year than in years past. Our students and parents are more conscious of grades; the students are working hard in school and preparing for the future.

Because of Kirsten, I have reconsidered how I utilize the role of school counselor at Walsh. Many of our students have academic and socioemotional needs that are not being addressed, because our counselor is busy doing paperwork and case management. I am working on ways to eliminate these responsibilities so that Kirsten can spend more time with our students. As an administrator, I strive to address all factors that may negatively impact student access to learning so that my students have a well-rounded school experience and success in their pursuit of higher education. The work that school counselors do with students, staff, parents, and community members plays a vital role in this process.

FINAL THOUGHTS

Each year I "adopt" a new cohort of amazingly diverse and talented future professional school counselors. It is my honor to teach them as much as they teach me, every day. Some refer to themselves as "Hatchlings." That works. At the banquet when they share their results, I acknowledge that I do push them, hard, because the work they will need to do for students in school matters so much. We will need them to be the next generation of passionate leaders, advocates, and systems change agents. Perhaps, as you read this text, you felt a slight push too.

If so, thank you for hanging in there. To the graduate students, school counselors, school counselor educators, and school counselor administrators

Thank you for deciding to enter the profession of school counseling.
Thank you for being a school counselor.
Thank you for teaching and mentoring school counselors.
Thank you for hiring, supporting, and supervising school counselors.

And now that I am at the very end, I permit myself to write this part—the part where I tell you that believe it or not, *I do know* that some of the most amazing work school counselors will ever do, they will *never be able to measure.* I truly and deeply *know* that. Some of the "work" we do as school counselors is work we are called to do. I was called to be a school counselor. Some of my best days as a school counselor were truly the very worst days for others, and it was on those days, when I left my school, I knew, I *truly knew* that I was there for a reason. School counseling is a calling. It is *my* calling. It is my purpose on the planet.

When I began school at age six, I was thriving and excited to learn everything.

Trish Hatch @TrishHatch   72d
"If you are not uncomfortable in your work in as a leader ...you are not reaching your full potential."Godin. Love it. tinyurl.com/brygjbu
Details

Trish Hatch @TrishHatch   72d
"When you identify the discomfort, you have found the place where a leader is needed." Godin. Time for SC to Lead. tinyurl.com/brygjbu
Details

Trish Hatch @TrishHatch   72d
"Leadership is scarce bc few people are willing to go through discomfort required to lead." Time to get uncomfortable. tinyurl.com/brygjbu
Details

Trish Hatch @TrishHatch   72d
"Changing things—pushing the envelope ..at the same time you are criticized—requires bravery," Godin. Workn on that 2. tinyurl.com/brygjbu
Details

Trish Hatch @TrishHatch   72d
"Great leaders do not try to please everyone. Great leaders do not water down their message." I'm working on it. leadershipdevelopment.com/html/magazine2...
Details

Trish Hatch @TrishHatch   72d
Leadership is a choice, not a job. Anyone who cares, connects & has vision can make change happen. Great quick read: leadershipdevelopment.com/html/magazine2...
Details

When I was in seventh grade, however, I really needed a school counselor, and I didn't have one. There are lots of seventh-grade Trishes out there who need a school counselor. That is why we MUST measure the impact of our work—not all the work, but the work that is measureable—to ensure no student will ever again need a school counselor and not have one.

I thank you for the work you do for children.

I thank you for the immeasurable difference you have made and will continue to make in the lives of children each and every day.

Thank you for the efforts you have already made to move forward. This is hard work I am asking you to do. Most school counselors, administrators, and counselor educators were not trained to do this type of evidenced-based practice. So do your best, and give it your best professional effort, and don't be afraid to ask for help if you need it. That's all I ask, because it is all I ask of myself.

Writing a solo-authored text is hard work. Sharing professional wisdom is risky, because others might disagree. There were times when I was unsure if I would "go to the edge" (when I was writing Chapter 8 was one of those times). Thankfully Seth Godin had words of encouragement for me. Several quotes spoke to me, and I tweeted them to the world. I hope they will be as helpful to you as they were to me.

Ultimately, I know I gave this text my best professional effort. In areas I needed help, I asked for it. It is most certainly not perfect. I already see things I want to improve, revise, and shift. But if I keep at it, this text will never be published.

So, this is my best professional wisdom, today.

I look forward to receiving feedback on parts of the text that were particularly helpful to you as well as collegial suggestions for ways you might suggest it be improved. I particularly look forward to hearing ways in which readers have used data to hatch their own results for students, programs, or the profession. (Please send yours to trish@hatchingresults.com.)

One last miracle—recently, national leaders in school counseling met to serve as advisors and mentors at the first annual Evidenced-Based

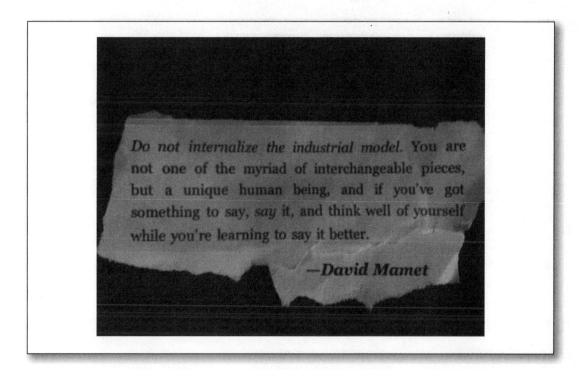

Do not internalize the industrial model. You are not one of the myriad of interchangeable pieces, but a unique human being, and if you've got something to say, say it, and think well of yourself while you're learning to say it better.

—David Mamet

School Counseling Conference in Kentucky (March 2013). What an amazing event it was! Almost 300 gathered to share ideas and best practices and to support each other and problem solve ways to support the next generation of professional school counselors through evidenced-based approaches.

At the end of each day, several of us just hadn't had enough. We sat and talked until the wee hours of the morning and tried to solve all of the problems in school counseling. It was one of the best conferences of my entire career, because it was so very evident that *every person really cared about the future of the profession and improving their practice.* The best part was sitting back imagining my graduate students, my former students, and those I have trained or those who will read this text as next year's presenters at the conference next year and someday becoming the next generation of school counselor leaders themselves at future conferences like this in every state!

What a miracle that would be!

"Come to the edge."
"We can't. We're afraid."
"Come to the edge."
"We can't. We will fall!"
"Come to the edge."
And they came.
And she pushed them.
And they flew.

—Guillaume Apollinaire (1880–1918)
French poet, philosopher

Appendix A

Sample Results Reports

SPARC Support Personnel Accountability Report Card, 2013
A continuous improvement document sponsored by the California Department of Education
Sweetwater Union High School
ADDRESS: 2900 Highland Avenue National City, CA 91950
WEB SITE: http://suh.sweetwaterschools.org/ **DISTRICT:** Sweetwater Union High School District
GRADE LEVELS: 9-12 **SCHOOL YEAR:** Modified-Traditional **ENROLLMENT:** 2,422
PRINCIPAL: Dr. Roman Del Rosario **ASSISTANT PRINCIPALS:** Monica Raczkowski, Richard Carreon, Hector Ornelas JR., and Patricia Perez
COUNSELORS: Brenda Chavez-Casas, Nancy Garcia, Vanessa Rico, Kevin Smith, Liliana, Silva, Lysabeth Luansing, and Dinnah Donato-Palmore
PHONE: 619-474-9700 **FAX:** 619-474-7635

Principals Message

The Sweetwater Union High School (SUH) Student Support Team (SST) prides itself on its efforts to ensure that all students are college and career ready. The SST also plays an instrumental role in providing a safe and secure learning environment that promotes a rigorous and enriching educational experience for all students. Through guidance lessons, individual student planning, parent information nights, and a plethora of other supports, students at SUH are increasing their college going rate and developing their personal/social skills. In addition to supporting students academically, the SST has created a School Safety Committee to oversee that SUH is a safe learning community. Through programs like: Every 15 Minutes, Red Ribbon Week and The No Place for Hate Campaign, students learn the importance of a healthy lifestyle, gain the skills to make good decisions, and develop tolerance for others. For our team, the SPARC is a reflective and evaluative tool that allows us to communicate information about school-wide goals and accomplishments to SUH students and the community. Our SST works tirelessly to support students in the areas of college and career readiness and members would like to continue to see improvement in the following areas: A-G completion rate, student involvement in peer mentor programs, and a revision of the school safety plan. As the School Support Team continues its valuable work on behalf of all students, I am proud to recognize their sacrifice and contributions to the students, parents, and community they serve.

Student Support Services Personnel Team

The Student Support Team at Sweetwater Union High School is dedicated to providing an equitable student support system to prepare students for career, college, and personal/social skill development. As a unit, the SST believes that in order to have a learning environment that is safe, productive, and educational for students, members must be educated and informed on current fluctuations and changes occurring in the educational system. For this reason members belong to professional associations including, but not limited to:

- o American School Counseling Association (ASCA)
- o California Association of School Counselors, Inc.
- o National Association of School Psychologists

Additionally, as members of the SST, the Sweetwater Union High School Counseling team provides student support using a comprehensive school counseling program based on the ASCA National Model. Classroom guidance lessons, small group sessions, and individual meetings allow students to obtain the knowledge, attitudes, and skills regarding their academic and personal/social success.

Principal	14 years, B.S., B.A., M.A., Ed. D.
Assistant Principals (4)	47 years, B.S. (2), B.A. (2), M.A. (3), M.S. (1), Teacher Credential (2), Administrative Credential (4)
School Counselors (7)	114 years, B.A. (6), B.S., M.A. (2), M.S. (5), Pupil Personnel Services Credential (7)
School Psychologist	12 years, B.A., M.A., Ed.S.
School Nurse	11 years, B.S., M.S.
Registrar	8 years, continuing education
Speech and Language Pathologist	48 years, B.A., B.S., M.A.(2), Certificate of Clinical Competency (2)
Counseling Clerical Support Staff	8 years, continuing education
Talent Search Site Coordinator	3 years, B.A., M.S., Pupil Personnel Services Credential

Career and College Readiness Student Outcomes

The SST at Sweetwater Union High School believes in promoting the advancement of 21st Century Skills, which includes the development of personal and social skills. The SST also emphasizes Career and College readiness to ensure graduates possess skills necessary for success in post-secondary education and career aspirations with the objective of becoming contributing members of their respective communities.

Career Readiness

The SST provides classroom guidance lessons, individual student planning, and information on career pathways to continue increasing graduation rates. As shown by graph A, Sweetwater's graduation rate is higher than the state's average. With the continued support of SST members, the goal is to continually increase the graduation rate year after year.

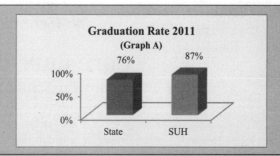

College Readiness

College readiness is an important goal for our SST. Over recent years, our team has provided support for all students through guidance lessons, individual counseling, and parent meetings that focus on A-G completion. As noted in graph B, the A-G completion rate has steadily increased over the past three years. The goal for the SST is to continue to increase the A-G completion rate over the coming years until all students are college ready.

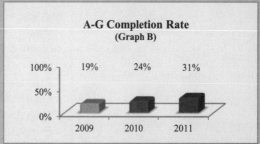

21st Century Skills

The SST believes that school involvement through extra-curriculum activities is important for students to feel connected to our school. Graph C demonstrates the increase of student involvement throughout the years. Our team encourages and supports students in their pursuit for extracurricular involvement through in class presentations that discuss the importance of being involved and its impact on college admission, personal development, and school connectedness.

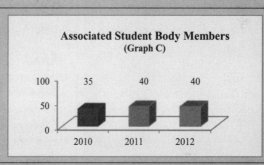

In addition to the student outcomes already listed above, we are proud that:
- 100% of SUH graduates have completed 30 or more community service hours
- More than $620,000 in scholarships were awarded in the 2012-2013 school year
- 65% of seniors completed the FAFSA for the 2012-2013 school year

Career and College Readiness School Site Programs and Community Partnerships

Career and College Readiness at Sweetwater Union High School is a team effort. School site programs and community partnerships collaborate to offer a wide array of services and programs for all students. If you would like to receive more information about our programs and partnerships, volunteer your time, or connect us with another resource for our students, please contact the SUH Counseling Department at (619) 474-9720.

School Site Program	*Community Partnerships*
Parent Workshops • Financial Aid, College Application Process, College Fair, Freshman Parent Orientation , Junior Night **Student Workshops/Classes** • Course selection, SAT/ACT preparation, FAFSA preparation **Peer Counseling Program** • Link Crew **College Readiness Program** • Advancement Via Individual Determination **Regional Occupation Program** • Health Academy • Welding **Personal/Social Counseling** • Project Samahan • South Bay Community Services	**Student Outreach** • San Diego State University • Southwestern College **Career Technical Training** • Regional Occupational Program (ROP) **Articulation Program** • San Diego State University, Compact for Success **Internship Program** • Scripps Hospital, Chula Vista • NASCO • American Lung Association • City of National City • La Vista Cemetery • Olive Wood Garden and Learning Center **Student Support Program** • A Reason to Survive (ARTS) • National City Adult School

[School Logo/Picture Here]

[School Title Here]

Core Curriculum G.R.I.P.
(Improving School Counseling Programs)

Goal: To increase/decrease _____ (achievement, attendance, behavior/safety, college /career readiness) by ___% or #.

School Data: (used to determine goal)

Why: (research supporting this type of intervention)

Focused Student Standards:

Implementation:
1. Grade Level:
2. Curriculum Title:
3. Where:
4. When:

Results: Based on the pre/post evaluations:
[Pick a couple of pre/posts to highlight in a bullet list and/or graph. Highlight key results (areas of strength and areas of improvement).]

- **Attitude:** (what students believe before/after the lesson)
- **Skills:** (what students can demonstrate before/after the lesson)
- **Knowledge:** (what students know before/after the lesson)

Impact: My curriculum activity contributed to these student outcomes:

Achievement-related data: (attendance, discipline referrals, parent involvement, homework completion, course enrollment patterns)

and/or

Achievement data: (grades, GPA, state test scores, SAT/ACT scores, college-prep course completion, passed AP exams)

[Type Your Name Here]
Professional School Counselor(s)
2013–2014 School Year

Program Implications
- What worked?
- What didn't work?
- What will you do differently next time?

Charted Results of Pre/Post Results or Outcome Data (Achievement or Achievement-Related)

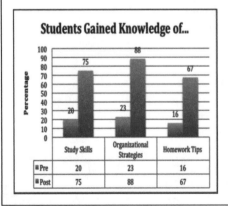

Students Gained Knowledge of...

	Study Skills	Organizational Strategies	Homework Tips
Pre	20	23	16
Post	75	88	67

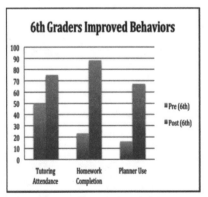

6th Graders Improved Behaviors

(Tutoring Attendance, Homework Completion, Planner Use) — Pre (6th), Post (6th)

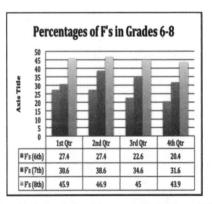

Percentages of F's in Grades 6-8

	1st Qtr	2nd Qtr	3rd Qtr	4th Qtr
F's (6th)	27.4	27.4	22.6	20.4
F's (7th)	30.6	38.6	34.6	31.6
F's (8th)	45.9	46.9	45	43.9

Adapted by Trujillo & Hatch from Thompson, 2012; Brott, 2008

[School Logo/Picture Here]

[School Title Here]

Intervention G.R.I.P.
(Improving School Counseling Programs)

Goal: To increase/decrease _____(achievement, attendance, behavior/safety, college/career readiness) by __% or #.

School Data: (used to determine goal)

Why: (research supporting this type of intervention)

Focused Student Standards:

Implementation:
1. Target Group:
2. Intervention (detailed so it can be duplicated):
3. How (small group, etc.):
4. When:
5. For how long:
6. Additional schoolwide activities that are being done to support this goal:

Results: Based on the pre/post evaluations:
Pick a couple of pre/posts to highlight in a bullet list and/or graph. Highlight key results (good or bad).

- **Attitude:** (what students believe before/after the intervention)
- **Skills:** (what students can demonstrate before/after the intervention)
- **Knowledge:** (what students know before/after the intervention)

Impact: My intervention contributed to these student outcomes:

Achievement-related data: (attendance, discipline referrals, parent involvement, homework completion, course enrollment patterns)

and/or

Achievement data: (grades, GPA, SBA test scores, SAT/ACT scores, college–prep course completion, passed AP exams)

[Type Your Name Here]
Professional School Counselor(s)
2013–2014 School Year

Program Implications
- What worked?
- What didn't work?
- What will you do differently next time?

Charted Results of Pre/Post Results or Outcome Data (Achievement or Achievement Related)

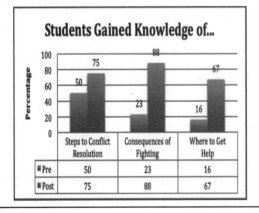

Students Gained Knowledge of...

	Steps to Conflict Resolution	Consequences of Fighting	Where to Get Help
Pre	50	23	16
Post	75	88	67

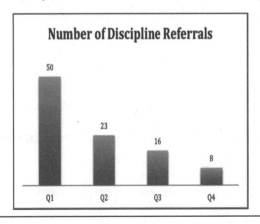

Number of Discipline Referrals

Q1: 50
Q2: 23
Q3: 16
Q4: 8

Adapted by Trujillo & Hatch from Thompson, 2012; Brott, 2008

Closing The College Going Gap G.R.I.P.
(Effectiveness of School Counseling Program)

Goal: To increase the number of students who complete the FAFSA by 8%age points.

School Data used to determine our goal: 2010-11 FAFSA Data

Why: Key studies have indicated that FAFSA completion correlates strongly with college enrolment, particularly among low-income populations.

Focused ASCA Standards:
Career Standard B: Students will employ strategies to achieve future career goals with success and satisfaction.

Implementation:
1. **Target Group:** 2012 Seniors
2. **Total number impacted:** 2677 seniors district-wide
3. **Intervention:** FAFSA Completion nights were held at every high school. Dates/times were listed on the school and APS website. College and Career Counselors (CCRCs) and School Counselors (SCs) helped families complete the FAFSA. Over the summer, the CCCRCs and SCs participated in Project SCOPE, where they continued to contact those students who had not completed the FAFSA and/or applied to a post-secondary institution yet.
4. **How:** Parents and students were walked through completing the FAFSA in computer labs. Over the summer they were contacted and assisted.
5. **For how long:** FAFSA Completion Nights ran from January through July, 2012.

6. **Additional School Wide Activities that are being done to support this goal:** School counselors and college and career readiness counselors also helped students individually during the school day and over the summer to complete the FAFSA and other college preparation items.

Results:
No pre-post tests were completed.

Impact: The CCRCs & School Counselor interventions contributed to these district-wide student outcomes:

Achievement Data - College Preparation Completion:

☑ Applied to College
☑ FAFSA Completed
☑ Males registered for selective service
☑ Students were connected with scholarship resources

District Wide Impact Results Are On The Back Side Of This GRIP

Program Implications
What worked:
❖ Having all the support from Ben Castleman, Laura Owen, and APS District Counseling Administrative Assistant, Janet Walters.

Work was done by all APS College and Career Readiness Counselors and most High School Counselors, 2011-2012

❖ The Google Site
❖ The College/University Partnerships & Collaborations
❖ Quick Tip Sheets for each NM College/ University
❖ Texting Students vs. E-mailing
❖ Calling students after noon

What didn't work:
❖ Initially getting our student list error free to upload to FSA site – Extremely difficult
❖ Student data from our School Max System was not always matched to completions
  ❖ Changed addresses so zip codes didn't match
  ❖ Legal names used in FAFSA vs. names they used to register at school
❖ Sending Counselors to sites other than their own school sites**
❖ Didn't have enough time to go back and make matches for those students who we knew completed, but School Max Data didn't match FSA data.**
❖ Having to call students after noon (for some)

What we will do differently next time:

- ❖ To the extent possible, have school counselors work out of their own schools with their own seniors.**
- ❖ Exit Survey – done on Survey Monkey so we can have them make corrections if their name and address are not correct.
- ❖ Set up time-lines for the FAFSA Completion Project/ Project SCOPE from January to last submission in October.
  - ❖ Include enough time to go back and make matches for those students who we knew completed, but School Max Data didn't match FSA data.**
- ❖ Seek more support from our Research, Deployment and Accountability (RDA) Department in our District Office so they are a bigger part of the data submission and returning the data back to the schools.

Districtwide Impact Results
Albuquerque Public Schools
FAFSA Completion Data for 2011 and 2012 Seniors

School	2010-2011 Seniors (as of October 2011)				2011-2012 Seniors (as of October 2012)			
	N	% Never Started	% Completed	% With Remaining Errors*	N	% Never Started	% Completed	% With Remaining Errors*
Albuquerque High School 590	375	45.3%	41.6%	13.1%	294	46.9%	52.4%	0.7%
Atrisco Heritage Academy High school	NA	NA	NA	NA	398	41.7%	55.3%	3.0%
Cibola High School 580	399	46.4%	46.4%	7.8%	394	39.1%	59.6%	1.3%
Del Norte High School 514	260	45.8%	45.8%	2.7%	205	36.1%	62.4%	1.5%
Early College Academy 593	26	38.5%	38.5%	23.1%	46	23.9%	76.1%	0.0%
Eldorado High School 515	411	35.5%	48.9%	15.6%	400	34.3%	63.3%	2.5%
Freedom, High School 596	91	61.5%	31.9%	6.6%	62	53.2%	46.8%	0.0%
Highland High school 520	324	55.6%	34.0%	10.5%	251	50.2%	47.0%	2.8%
La Cueva High School 525	517	41.8%	48.5%	9.7%	444	40.5%	58.6%	0.9%
Manzano High School 530	401	42.1%	45.9%	12.0%	308	32.8%	64.9%	2.3%
New Futures High School 549	80	57.5%	38.8%	3.8%	56	50.0%	46.4%	3.6%
Rio Grande High School 540	309	48.2%	39.2%	12.6%	226	44.7%	54.0%	1.3%
Sandia High School 550	424	38.0%	47.4%	14.6%	429	38.2%	59.7%	2.1%
School on Wheels 597	80	70.0%	25.0%	5.0%	40	40.0%	60.0%	0.0%
Valley High School 560	312	36.5%	50.3%	13.1%	253	39.5%	58.9%	1.6%
Volcano Vista High School 575	417	36.7%	51.1%	12.2%	409	40.3%	57.9%	1.7%
West Mesa High School 570	524	47.5%	42.4%	10.1%	279	44.1%	54.5%	1.4%
District-wide Totals	4950	2179	2210	548	4494	1817	2598	79
District –wide Percents		44.0%	44.6%	11.1%		40.4%	57.8%	1.8%

NA = No data in this year
*Expected Family Contribution (EFC) could not be calculated

School Counseling PRoBE Project Rubric: CPCE 5504 School Guidance Programs

Deb Woodard, Instructor
UMKC School Counseling Coordinator

	Exemplary (5 pts.)	Advanced (4 pts.)	Proficient (3 pts.)	Emerging (2 pts.)	Unacceptable (1 pt.)
	The student regularly demonstrates skills beyond what is expected based on his or her training to date.	The student intermittently demonstrates skills beyond what is expected based on his or her training to date.	The student demonstrates the skills sufficiently based on his or her training to date.	The student inconsistently demonstrates skills sufficiently based on his or her training to date.	The student regularly does not demonstrate skills sufficiently based on his or her training to date.
PRoBE Project Prep: Action Plan (15%) **MOStep 1.4.1.1.a – h Program Goal #1** **MOStep 1.4.2.1.a-c Program Goal #7** **SoE 1a,c, 2c, 5b NCATE 1e, 1f**	The **exemplary** PRoBE Project Action Plan includes all elements of the **advanced** one and: <ul><li>the addition of two or more tables (charts) to show the existing data</li><li>the addition of two or more tables (charts) to show the quantitative and qualitative data collected</li><li>APA citations, for references</li></ul>	The **advanced** PRoBE Project Action Plan includes all elements of the **proficient** one and: <ul><li>one or more tables (charts) to show the existing data</li><li>the inclusion of the needs assessment given to collect data</li><li>the addition of one or more tables (charts) to show the quantitative and qualitative data collected</li></ul>	The **proficient** PRoBE Project Action Plan includes the following: <ul><li>a description of the Foundation, including beliefs, philosophy, and a mission statement that matches that of the school</li><li>an explanation of the developmental level</li><li>a demonstration of knowledge of standards cross-walking</li><li>planning for the PRoBE Project (IDEAS, including SIMS)</li><li>a brief narrative discussion of existing data</li><li>a brief narrative discussion of quantitative and qualitative data collected by the group related to the intervention</li><li>completion of job targets</li></ul>	The **emerging** PRoBE Project Action Plan **does not include one or more** of the elements required for a **proficient** rating.	The **unacceptable** PRoBE Project Action Plan does not include **three or more** of the elements required for a **proficient or emerging** rating.
PRoBE Project Presentation: Foundation (15%) **MOStep 1.4.1.1.a – h Program Goal #1** **MOStep 1.4.2.1.a-c Program Goal #7** **SoE 1a,c, 2c, 5b NCATE 1e, 1f, 1g**	The **exemplary** PRoBE Project Foundation includes all elements of the **advanced** one and: <ul><li>shared hard copies of a related flier, brochure, or handout with fellow classmates</li></ul>	The **advanced** PRoBE Project Foundation includes all elements of the **proficient** one and: <ul><li>descriptions of the **physical, cognitive and social-emotional** developmental needs of the students involved in the project,</li><li>your resources in APA format</li></ul>	The **proficient** PRoBE Project Foundation includes about four to five slides including the following: <ul><li>the school's demographics</li><li>the school's mission statement</li><li>the school counseling department's beliefs and philosophy</li><li>your counseling mission statement for the school</li><li>the IDEAS model</li><li>the SIMS description</li><li>the developmental needs of the students involved in the project</li></ul>	The **emerging** PRoBE Project Foundation **does not include one or more** of the elements required for a **proficient** rating.	The **unacceptable** PRoBE Project Foundation does not include three or more of the elements required for a **proficient or emerging** rating.
PRoBE Project Presentation: Problem Identification	The **exemplary** problem identification includes all elements of the **advanced** one with: <ul><li>**three or more** charts illustrating the collection of</li></ul>	The **advanced** problem identification includes all elements of the **proficient** one with: <ul><li>**two or more** charts illustrating the collection of</li></ul>	The **proficient** problem identification includes the following: <ul><li>evidence of consultation with the administrator or</li></ul>	The **emerging** problem identification **does not include** one or more of the elements required for a **proficient** rating	The **unacceptable** problem identification **does not include three or more** of the elements required for a **proficient or emerging** rating.

Criteria	Exemplary	Advanced	Proficient	Emerging	Unacceptable
(10%) **MOStep 1.4.1.3.a-f Program Goal #3** **MOStep 1.4.2.2.3.a-e Program Goal #10** **MOStep 1.4.2.2.4.a-i Program Goal #11** **SoE 2c, 3a** **NCATE 1e**	both existing data and needs assessments	both existing data and needs assessments	counselor in the school where the project was completed (consultation agreement) • one or more charts illustrating the collection of existing data • a strong statement of the need or problem **that:** • is clear • shows how the problem is relevant to the student population and their assessed needs • utilizes correct spelling and grammar		
PRoBE Project Presentation: SIMS **(5%)** **MOStep 1.4.2.2.3.a-e Program Goal #10** **SoE 1a, 2c** **NCATE 1e**	The **exemplary** display of the SIMS process includes all elements of the **advanced** one with: • an explanation of **all** measurements created to analyze the impact of the intervention	The **advanced** display of the SIMS process includes all elements of the **proficient** one with: • one slide of information • an explanation of **more than one** of the measurements created to analyze the impact of the intervention	The **proficient** display of the SIMS process includes the following: • one or two slides of information • a description of the students involved in project • an outline of the intervention • an explanation of one of the measurements created to analyze the impact of the intervention • a list of the setting(s) used for the intervention • correct spelling and grammar	The **emerging** display of the SIMS process **does not include one or more** of the elements required for a **proficient** rating	The **unacceptable** display of the SIMS process **does not include three or more** of the elements required for a **proficient or emerging** rating.
PRoBE Project Presentation: Intervention Data Analysis & Summary **(15%)** **MOStep 1.4.1.3.a-f Program Goal #3** **SoE 1a, 2c, 3b** **NCATE 1e, 4a**	The **exemplary** intervention data analysis and summary includes all elements of the **advanced** one with: • **three or more** charts/graphs illustrating your intervention's pre and post survey results, including raw scores, means, and percentages • an explanation of how those results can be used to improve the school counseling program	The **advanced** intervention data analysis and summary includes all elements of the **proficient** one with: • **two or more** charts/graphs illustrating your intervention's pre and post survey results, including raw scores, means, and percentages • a clear analysis of the data on those charts, including what did and did not work (a data connection to the recommendations for improvements to the intervention)	The **proficient** intervention data analysis and summary includes the following: • a chart or graph illustrating your intervention's pre and post survey results, including raw scores, means, and percentages • an analysis of the data on those charts • statements using data to highlight the successes of the intervention • recommendations for improvements to the intervention	The **emerging** intervention data analysis and summary **does not include one or more** of the elements required for a **proficient** rating.	The **unacceptable** intervention data analysis and summary **does not include three or more** of the elements required for a **proficient or emerging** rating.
Collaboration with Other Team Members **(15%)**	The **exemplary** demonstration of collaboration includes all elements of the **advanced** one with: • service as a liaison with the school selected for the intervention	The **advanced** demonstration of collaboration summary includes all elements of the **proficient** one with: • willingness to agree to disagree on some points • willingness to take on more	The **proficient** demonstration of collaboration includes the following: • responsible completion of tasks in a timely manner • engagement during given	The **emerging** demonstration of collaboration **does not include one or more** of the elements required for a **proficient** rating.	The **unacceptable** demonstration of collaboration **does not include three or more** of the elements required for a **proficient or emerging** rating.

Criteria	Exemplary / Advanced	Proficient	Emerging	Unacceptable
SoE 3a	• work if necessary • involvement in the intervention at the school site	• work periods • professional communication with group members throughout the process • achievement of all assigned tasks on the job chart of the action plan • completion of self-evaluations of individual work • completion of group evaluations of the group process		The **unacceptable** representation of technology does **not include three or more** of the elements required for a **proficient or emerging** rating.
Use of Technology (10%) MOStep 1.4.2.5.a-b Program Goal #12 SoE 1c, 3b NCATE 1e	The **exemplary** representation of technology includes all elements of the **advanced** one with: • a non-traditional presentation format such as Prezi **which also includes:** • a pdf copy of the ppt. that is shared with fellow classmates The **advanced** representation of technology includes all elements of the **proficient** one with: • an unusual format and creative color usage **which also includes:** • an audio clip, video clip, or pictures of students involved (with permission) • one relevant example of a creation using zamzar, voki, myoats, photovisi, doInk, or other innovative technological resources • a hard copies of the ppt. presentation that is shared with fellow classmates	The **proficient** representation of technology is: • a traditional ppt. presentation **which also includes:** • clip art • graphics/ charts • pictures (other than students involved) • audio or visual clips retrieved from the web	The **emerging** representation of technology **does not include one or more** of the elements required for a **proficient** rating.	
Presentation (15%) SoE 1a, c NCATE 1e	The **exemplary** presentation is 5 – 7 minutes and the presenters include all elements of the **advanced** one and: **provide** the professor with a well-organized notebook that includes a copy of: • the action plan • the ppt. presentation • the needs assessment • the pre and post survey • any charts not included in the action plan • the lesson plan • any materials related to the lesson plan • the survey given to fellow classmate related to the lesson • the results of that survey in narrative and graph format • any additional relevant material(s) The **advanced** presentation is 7 minutes and the presenters include all elements of the **proficient** one and: • engage the audience from the introduction to the conclusion • appear relaxed throughout the presentation • elicit comments and questions and field them professionally and expeditiously • upload all project and lesson materials to Bb	The **proficient** presentation is 7 - 10 minutes and the presenters do the following: • address the audience of school board members, administrators, or teachers appropriately in the introduction • include all members of the group equally • rehearse and know the time line for the presentation • speak directly to the audience and do not read from the ppt. • explain all elements of the project in clear and concise detail • utilize technology to their advantage • field comments and question	The **emerging** presentation is **longer than 7 - 10 minutes** and the presenters **do not include one or more** of the elements required for a **proficient** rating.	The **unacceptable** presentation is **longer than 7 - 10 minutes** and the presenters do **not include three or more** of the elements required for a **proficient or emerging** rating.

CORE CURRICULUM RESULTS REPORT RUBRIC

	1 Emerging or Not Met	2 Adequate	3 Exceeds
Counselor led activity	The school counselor collected data on an activity that was conducted by another party.	The school counselor participated in the activity under the direction of another party.	The school counselor played a primary role in the design and implementation of the activity.
Activity	An activity for students was designed with some method to determine its success.	An activity based on an ASCA domain was designed and conducted. A method of assessment via perception or results data was established to determine if the activity was successful	An activity that addressed the need and was based on one or more of the ASCA domains was designed and conducted over a sufficient period of time. A method of assessment via both perception and results data was established to determine if the activity was successful.
Results	The report identified outcome data with conclusions. No future plans were identified.	The report identified perception and/or results data. At least one conclusion was drawn from the findings and some future plans were identified.	The report identified clear perception and results data. Logical conclusions were made based on the findings and realistic future plans were identified.

CLOSING THE GAP RESULTS REPORT RUBRIC

	1 Emerging or Not Met	2 Adequate	3 Exceeds
Counselor led intervention	The school counselor collected data on an intervention that was conducted by another party.	The school counselor participated in the intervention under the direction of another party.	The school counselor played a primary role in the design and implementation of the intervention.
Identification of an achievement gap	The report failed to identify students for whom a gap existed.	The report identified a group of students for whom a gap existed.	Based on school data, the report identified a group of specific students for whom a gap existed.
Intervention	An intervention for students was designed with some method to determine its success.	An intervention based on an ASCA domain was designed and conducted to close an achievement gap. A method of assessment via perception or results data was established to determine if the intervention was successful.	An intervention that addressed the need and was based on one or more of the ASCA domains was designed and conducted over a sufficient period of time to close an achievement gap for an identified population. A method of assessment via both perception and results data was established to determine if the intervention was successful.
Results	The report identified outcome data with conclusions. No future plans were identified.	The report identified perception and/or results data. At least one conclusion was drawn from the findings, and some future plans were identified.	The report identified clear perception and results data. Logical conclusions were made based on the findings and realistic future plans were identified.

(Hartline, J., & Cobia, D., 2012).

Appendix B

**Reference Listings
for Identifying
Appropriate Interventions
and for Flashlight Presentations**

Theme	Research Finding	Source
Attendance, Absenteeism	Truant students are at higher risk of being drawn into behavior involving drugs, alcohol, or violence (Garry, 1996).	Garry, E. M. (1996). *Truancy, first step to a lifetime of problems.* Washington, DC: US Department of Justice, Office of Justice Programs, Office of Juvenile Justice and Delinquency Prevention.
	Students who attend school perform better than those who do not (Easton & Englehard, 1982).	Easton, J. Q., & Engelhard, G. (1982). A longitudinal record of elementary school absence and its relationship to reading achievement. *Journal of Educational Research, 7*(5), 269–274.
	Poor attendance is linked to student alienation and disengagement, which may contribute to students dropping out of school (Lan & Lanthier, 2003).	Lan, W., & Lanthier, R. (2003). Changes in students' academic performance and perceptions of school and self before dropping out of schools. *Journal of Education for Students Placed at Risk, 8*(3), 309–332.
	Results show that a higher proportion of unexcused absences places the students at academic risk, especially in math achievement and as early as in elementary school (Gottfried, 2010).	Gottfried, M. A. (2010). Evaluating the relationship between student attendance and achievement in urban elementary and middle schools: An instrumental variables approach. *American Education Research Journal, 47*(2), 434–465.
	There is a direct correlation between attendance and academic achievement. Students who go to class invariably do better in school and maximize their chances for success down the road (Biegel, 2000).	Biegel, S. (2000). *The interfaces between attendance, academic achievement, and equal educational opportunity.* Report of Consent Decree Monitoring Team. US District Court, Northern District of California.
	Students who have poor attendance for reasons other than illness are also more likely to drop out. Students who miss school fall behind their peers in the classroom. This, in turn, leads to low self-esteem and increases the likelihood that at-risk students will drop out of school. (US Department of Education & ERIC, n.d.)	US Department of Education, The Educational Resources Information Clearinghouse (ERIC). (n.d.). *Identifying Potential Dropouts, ERIC Digest; School Dropouts, ERIC Digest #109; and Student Truancy,* ERIC Digest #125. Retrieved from http://ed.gov.databases/ERIC_Digests/ed
	A student's attitude towards the school is the single most important factor in combating truancy. It is the responsibility of school administrators to fashion a school where children want to attend as opposed to having to attend (Gullatt & Lemoine, 1997).	Gullatt, D., & Lemoine, D. (1997). Truancy: What's a principal to do? *American Secondary Education, 26*(1), 7–12.
	Excessive absences and truancies usually equate to poorer achievement, mediocre self-esteem, lower promotion and graduation rates and lesser employment potential, all of which frequently lead to a student dropping out of school (Walker, 2007).	Walker, K. (2007). Research brief: Attendance and truancy problems. *The Principals' Partnership.* Retrieved from http://oemanagement.com/data/_files/attendanceandtruancy.pdf
	Absences other than excused absences as defined by State regulations have a highly adverse effect on the student as well as the educational program (New York Educational Law, Section 3024).	New York Educational Law § 3024.
	Attendance has a stronger effect on grades and is more predictive of course failure than are students' test scores (Farrington et al., 2012).	Farrington, C. A., Roderick, M., Allensworth, E., Nagaoka, J., Keyes, T. S., Johnson, D. W., & Beechum, N. O. (2012). Teaching adolescents to become learners. The role of noncognitive factors in shaping school performance: A critical literature review. Chicago, IL: University of Chicago Consortium on Chicago School Research.

Theme	Research Finding	Source
Social Behavior (Personal/ Social Domain):	There is a strong relationship between social behavior and academic success. Social skills (getting along with peers, teamwork) positively predict academic achievement (Malecki & Elliott, 2002).	Malecki, C. K., & Elliott, S. N. (2002). Children's social behaviors as predictors of academic achievement: A longitudinal analysis. *School Psychology Quarterly, 17*, 1–23.
	Empathy training helps bring out more positive social behaviors and a more positive self-evaluation in both aggressive and nonaggressive students (Feshbach & Feshbach, 1982).	Feshbach, N., & Feshbach, S. (1982). Empathy training and the regulation of aggression: Potentialities and limitations. *Academic Psychology Bulletin, 4*, 399–413.
Bullying, Behavior, Discipline	Disruptive behavior (including hitting others) can affect academic achievement (Gibson, 2006).	Gibson, D. (2006). The association of students' academic efficacy, achievement goal orientation, and teacher rapport with disruptive behavior in the classroom. Doctor of Psychology Dissertation, St. John's University, New York. Retrieved from Dissertations & Theses: A&I database. (Publication No. AAT 3229029).
	Almost 30% of youth in the United States (or over 5.7 million) are estimated to be involved in bullying as either a bully, a target of bullying, or both (Nansel, Overpeck, Pilla, Ruan, Simons-Morton, & Scheidt, 2001).	Nansel, T. R., Overpeck, M., Pilla, R. S., Ruan, W. J., Simons-Morton, B., & Scheidt, P. (2001). Bullying behaviors among US youth: Prevalence and association with psychosocial adjustment. *JAMA, 285*(16), 2094–2100.
	At-risk children who can self-regulate have higher reading, math, and vocabulary achievement (Sektnan, McClelland, Acock, & Morrison, 2010).	Sektnan, M., McClelland, M. M., Acock, A., & Morrison, F. J. (2010). Relations between early family risk, children's behavioral regulation, and academic achievement. *Early Childhood Research Quarterly, 25*, 464–479. doi:10.1016/j.ecresq.2010.02.005
	Students who behave better achieve better (e.g., Van Horn, 2003).	Van Horn, M. L. (2003). Assessing the unit of measurement for school climate through psychometric and outcome analyses of the school climate. *Educational and Psychological Measurement, 63*(6), 1002–1019.
	Bullying may seriously affect the psychological functioning, academic work, and health of children who are targeted. Bully victimization has been found to be related to lower self-esteem, higher rates of depression, loneliness, and anxiety (Craig, 1998).	Craig, W. M. (1998). The relationship among bullying, victimization, depression, anxiety, and aggression in elementary school children. *Personality and Individual Differences, 24*, 123-130.
	Males are more likely than females to be the both perpetrators of bullying and the targets of bullying. Most frequently occurs in 6th-8. Both experiencing bullying and perpetuating are associated with poor psychosocial adjustment. (Nansel et al., 2001).	Nansel, T. R., Overpeck, M., Pilla, R. S., Ruan, W. J., Simons-Morton, B., & Scheidt, P. (2001). Bullying behaviors among US youth. *JAMA: The Journal of the American Medical Association, 285*(16), 2094–2100.
	Routinely victimized children exhibit depression, anxiety, and suicidal thoughts at higher levels than do non-victims. (Stanford University Medical Center, 2007).	Stanford University Medical Center. (2007, April 12). School bullying affects majority of elementary students. *ScienceDaily*. Retrieved from http://www.sciencedaily.com¬/releases/2007/04/070412072345.htm
	Individuals who habitually bully are at greater risk for having a criminal record by their mid-twenties. If bullying behavior continues into adulthood, there is an increased chance that the bully will also commit child abuse and/or domestic violence (Quiroz, Arnette, & Stephens, 2006).	Quiroz, H. C., Arnette, J. L., & Stephens, R. D. (2006). Bullying in schools: Fighting the bullying battle. Retrieved from http://www.schoolsafety.us/pubfiles/bullying_fact_sheets.pdf

Theme	Research Finding	Source
	The prevalence of bullying among elementary school children is substantial. Associations between bullying involvement and school problems indicate this is a serious issue for elementary schools (Glew, Fan, Katon, & Kernic, 2005).	Glew, G. M., Fan, M. Y., Katon, W. R., & Kernic, M. A. (2005). Bullying, psychosocial adjustment, and academic performance in elementary school. *Archives of Pediatrics and Adolescent Medicine, 159*(11), 1026–1031.
	Students stay home for fear of being bullied at school (Lazarus & Pfohl, 2010).	Lazarus, P. J., & Pfohl, W. (2010). *Bullying prevention and intervention: Information for educators.* Bethesda, MD: National Association of School Psychologists.
	Throughout their lives, both victims and bullies suffer higher levels of mental health problems, including depression (Lucile Packer Children's Hospital, 2007).	Lucile Packer Children's Hospital. (2007, April 12). *School bullying affects majority of elementary students, Stanford/Packard researchers find.* Retrieved from http://www.lpch.org/aboutus/news/releases/2007/bullying.html
	Students who are subjected to bullying on a regular basis can become isolated from friends and school and become vulnerable to risky behaviors (Sunburst Visual Media, 2002).	Sunburst Visual Media. (2002). *Own your anger.* (Video instruction kit).
	Students who are suspended are less likely to be high academic achievers (e.g., Williams & McGee, 1994).	Williams, S., & McGee, R. (1994). Reading attainment and juvenile delinquency. *Journal of Child Psychology and Psychiatry, 35,* 442–459.
Alcohol, Tobacco, and Other Drug Use	Students who use drugs or alcohol perform academically at a lower rate than those who do not (e.g., Jeynes, 2002).	Jeynes, W. (2002). The relationship between the consumption of various drugs by adolescents and their academic achievement. *The American Journal of Drug and Alcohol Abuse, 28*(1), 1–21.
Parent Involvement	Students whose parents are involved in meaningful ways in the school outperform those whose parents are not involved (e.g., Marchant, Paulson, & Rothlisberg, 2001).	Marchant, G. J., Paulson, S. E., & Rothlisberg, B. A. (2001). Relations of middle school students' perceptions of family and school contexts with academic achievement. *Psychology in the Schools, 38*(6), 505–519.
	Several family-school-community partnership practices predict an increase in daily attendance, a decrease in chronic absenteeism, or both. Schools may be able to increase student attendance in school by implementing specific family and community involvement activities (Epstein & Sheldon, 2002).	Epstein, J. L., & Sheldon, S. B. (2002). Present and accounted for: Improving student attendance through family and community involvement. *Journal of Educational Research, 95,* 308–318.
	Sixty-five percent of parents report checking to make sure their children finish their homework (Aud, 2011)	Aud, S. (2011). *America's youth: Transition to adulthood.* Washington, DC: US Department of Education, National Center for Education Statistics. Washington, DC: US Government Printing Office. Retrieved from http://nces.ed.gov/pubs2012/2012026.pdf
Course Enrollment Patterns	Students who take more rigorous coursework do better on standardized tests (e.g., Smith & Niemi, 2001).	Smith, J. B., & Niemi, R. (2001). Learning history in school: The impact of course work and instructional practice on achievement. *Theory and Research in Social Education, 29*(1)18–42.
	Forty-four percent of 2010 graduates surveyed by the College Board reported they wish they had taken different courses in high school (Hart Research Associates, 2011).	Hart Research Associates. (2011). *One year out: Findings from a national survey among members of the high school graduating class of 2010.* New York, NY: The College Board. Retrieved from http://media.collegeboard.com/homeOrg/content/pdf/One_Year_Out_key_findings%20report_final.pdf

Theme	Research Finding	Source
	"Nationally, over 1.8 million students in 2009–2010 took at least one Advanced Placement (AP) exam" (Aud, 2011, p. vi).	Aud, S. (2011). *America's youth: Transition to adulthood.* US Department of Education, National Center for Education Statistics. Washington, DC: US Government Printing Office. Retrieved from http://nces.ed.gov/pubs2012/2012026.pdf
Dropout and Retention	Grade retention was found to be the "single most powerful predictor" of school dropout (Bridgeland, DiIulio, & Balfanz, 2009, p. 616).	Bridgeland, J., DiIulio, Jr., J. J., & Balfanz, R. (2009). *Perspectives of teachers and principals on the high school dropout problem.* Washington, DC: Civic Enterprises, LLC. Retrieved from www.civicenterprises.net/pdfs/frontlines.pdf
	Students from low socioeconomic status families are twice as likely to drop out of school as students from average social class families, even when controlling for other factors (Rumberger, 1995).	Rumberger, R. (1995). Dropping out of middle school: A multilevel analysis of students and schools. *American Educational Research Journal, 32*(3), 583–625.
	Schools need to develop early warning systems to help them identify students at risk of dropping out and to develop the mechanisms that trigger appropriate supports for these students. (Bridgeland, DiIulio, & Balfanz, 2009).	Bridgeland, J., DiIulio, Jr., J. J., & Balfanz, R. (2009). *Perspectives of teachers and principals on the high school dropout problem.* Washington, DC: Civic Enterprises, LLC. Retrieved from www.civicenterprises.net/pdfs/frontlines.pdf
	The key indicators of dropout are poor attendance, behavioral problems, and course failure. (Bridgeland, DiIulio, & Balfanz, 2009)	Bridgeland, J., DiIulio, Jr., J. J., & Balfanz, R. (2009). *Perspectives of teachers and principals on the high school dropout problem.* Washington, DC: Civic Enterprises, LLC. Retrieved from www.civicenterprises.net/pdfs/frontlines.pdf
	Ninth grade is a critical year, because students need skills early to graduate (Cooper & Liou, 2007).	Cooper, R., & Liou, D. D. (2007). The structure and culture of information pathways: Rethinking opportunity to learn in urban high schools during the ninth grade transition. *The High School Journal, 91*(1), 43–56.
Ninth-Grade Interventions	By ninth grade, dropout can be predicted with 85% accuracy (Bridgeland, DiIulio, & Balfanz, 2009).	Bridgeland, J., DiIulio, Jr., J. J., & Balfanz, R. (2009). *Perspectives of teachers and principals on the high school dropout problem.* Washington, DC: Civic Enterprises, LLC. Retrieved from www.civicenterprises.net/pdfs/frontlines.pdf
	"Among students who sent their first serious distress signal in 9th grade, those who earned fewer than two credits or attended school less than 70 percent of the time had at least a 75 percent chance of dropping out of school" (Neild, Balfanz, & Herzog, 2007, p. 30).	Neild, R., Balfanz, R., & Herzog, L. (2007). An early warning system. *Educational Leadership, 65*(2), 28–33.
	Eighty percent of dropouts studied in Philadelphia sent a signal in the middle grades or during the first year of high school (Neild, Balfanz, & Herzog, 2007).	Neild, R., Balfanz, R., & Herzog L. (2007). An early warning system. *Educational Leadership, 65*(2), 28–33.
	Only 49% of 2010 graduates surveyed by the College Board reported "that their high school did a good job of preparing them for both work and school" (Hart Research Associates 2011, p. 3).	Hart Research Associates. (2011). *One year out: Findings from a national survey among members of the high school graduating class of 2010.* New York: The College Board. Retrieved from http://media.collegeboard.com/homeOrg/content/pdf/One_Year_Out_key_findings%20report_final.pdf

Theme	Research Finding	Source
College and Career Readiness	Twenty-four percent of 2010 graduates enrolled in college reported that they were required to take developmental or remedial courses (Hart Research Associates, 2011).	Hart Research Associates. (2011). *One Year Out: Findings from a National Survey Among Members of the High School Graduating Class of 2010.* New York: The College Board. Retrieved from http://media.collegeboard.com/homeOrg/content/pdf/One_Year_Out_key_findings%20report_final.pdf
	Only 66 percent of students met college readiness benchmarks in English in 2009–10 (Aud, 2011). "66 percent of male and 74 percent of female high school completers enrolled in college directly after high school in 2009" (Neild, Balfanz, & Herzog, 2007, p. vi).	Aud, S. (2011). *America's youth: Transition to adulthood.* US Department of Education, National Center for Education Statistics. Washington, DC: US Government Printing Office. Retrieved from http://nces.ed.gov/pubs2012/2012026.pdf
	Social skills have gained increasing attention as a critical factor for adolescents in connection with career readiness (Farrington et al., 2012).	Farrington, C. A., Roderick, M., Allensworth, E., Nagaoka, J., Keyes, T. S., Johnson, D. W., & Beechum, N. O. (2012). *Teaching adolescents to become learners. The role of noncognitive factors in shaping school performance: A critical literature review.* Chicago, IL: University of Chicago Consortium on Chicago School Research.
Homework	In 2007, 7% of parents reported that their children did no homework outside of school (Aud, 2011).	Aud, S. (2011). *America's youth: Transition to adulthood.* US Department of Education, National Center for Education Statistics. Washington, DC: US Government Printing Office. Retrieved from http://nces.ed.gov/pubs2012/2012026.pdf
	Academic behaviors (such as going to class, studying, doing homework) are a major determinant of course grades; improving academic behaviors can improve course performance (Farrington et al., 2012).	Farrington, C. A., Roderick, M., Allensworth, E., Nagaoka, J., Keyes, T. S., Johnson, D. W., & Beechum, N. O. (2012). *Teaching adolescents to become learners. The role of noncognitive factors in shaping school performance: A critical literature review.* Chicago, IL: University of Chicago Consortium on Chicago School Research.
	As a result of differences in self-control, girls spent about twice as much time on homework as boys (Duckworth & Seligman, 2006.)	Duckworth, A. L., & Seligman, M. E. P. (2006). Self-discipline gives girls the edge: Gender in self-discipline, grades, and achievement test scores. *Journal of Educational Psychology, 98*(1), 198–208.
Self-Control	Academic performance depends largely upon students' own self-control and conscientiousness; a failure to use self-discipline may contribute to many students' academic problems (Duckworth & Seligman, 2005).	Duckworth, A. L., & Seligman, M. E. P. (2005). Discipline outdoes IQ in predicting academic performance of adolescents. *Psychological Science, 16*, 939–44.
	Whether students exhibit self control-depends on context, the strategies they are given, and their own cognitive strategies (Farrington et al., 2012; Mischel & Mischel, 1983).	Farrington, C. A., Roderick, M., Allensworth, E., Nagaoka, J., Keyes, T. S., Johnson, D. W., & Beechum, N. O. (2012). *Teaching adolescents to become learners. The role of noncognitive factors in shaping school performance: A critical literature review.* Chicago, IL: University of Chicago Consortium on Chicago School Research. Mischel, H. N., & Mischel, W. (1983). The development of children's knowledge of self-controls strategies. *Child Development, 54*, 603–619.

Theme	Research Finding	Source
	Individuals tend to participate in activities that they feel that they can carry out and avoid those for which they lack confidence in their ability to complete (Bandura, 1986).	Bandura, A. (1986). *Social foundations of thought and action: A social cognitive theory.* Englewood Cliffs, NJ: Prentice-Hall.
Academic Perseverance and Beliefs	"One's beliefs about intelligence and attributions for academic success or failure are more strongly associated with school performance than is one's actual measured ability" (Farrington et al., 2012, p. 10).	Farrington, C. A., Roderick, M., Allensworth, E., Nagaoka, J., Keyes, T. S., Johnson, D. W., & Beechum, N. O. (2012). *Teaching adolescents to become learners. The role of noncognitive factors in shaping school performance: A critical literature review.* Chicago, IL: University of Chicago Consortium on Chicago School Research.
	Stereotype threat and learned helplessness can undermine positive academic mindsets and interfere with academic performance (Farrington et al., 2012).	
	Students exhibit different amounts of perseverance under different conditions, suggesting that school counselors and teachers can change conditions to promote academic perseverance (Farrington et al., 2012).	
	Correlational evidence suggests that student perseverance is an important mechanism in assignment completion (Farrington et al., 2012).	
	Academic perseverance can be increased by "supporting positive academic mindsets and helping students develop effective learning strategies" (Farrington et al., 2012, p. 17).	
	"When students value the work they are doing, they feel a sense of belonging in the classroom context in which they are working, feel capable of succeeding, and believe they will master challenging material with effort, they are much more likely to engage and difficult work and see it through to completion (Farrington et al., 2012, p. 26).	

Appendix C

Flashlight PowerPoints

Lin and Pereyra (2012).

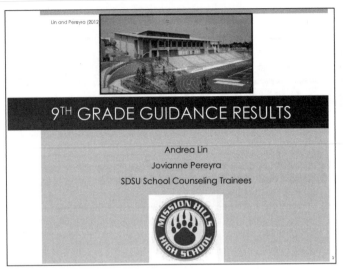

9TH GRADE GUIDANCE RESULTS

Andrea Lin

Jovianne Pereyra

SDSU School Counseling Trainees

Lin and Pereyra (2012).

Classroom Guidance Curriculum

- **Who**: 625 Ninth Graders
- **What**: 9th Grade Guidance Lesson
  - Graduation Requirements
  - GPA Calculation
  - Transcript Review
  - A-G Requirements
  - Pace Promise Requirements
- **When**: October 24th & 25th
- **Where**: 9th Grade History Classes

Lin and Pereyra (2012).

ASCA Standards

ACADEMIC

- **Standard A:** Students will acquire the attitudes, knowledge, and skills that contribute to effective learning in school and across the life span.
- **Standard B:** Students will complete school with the academic preparation essential to choose from a wide range of substantial range of post-secondary options, including college.

Lin and Pereyra (2012).

Student Competencies

- A:A3 Achieve School Success
  - A:A3.1 Take **responsibility** for their **actions**
- A:B2 Plan To Achieve Goals
  - A:B2.1 Establish **challenging academic goals** in elementary, middle/jr. high and high school
  - A:B2.2 Use **assessment results in educational planning**
  - A:B2.3 **Develop** and **implement annual plan of study** to maximize academic ability and achievement
  - A:B2.4 Apply knowledge of aptitudes and interests to **goal setting**
  - A:B2.5 Use **problem-solving** and **decision-making** skills to assess progress toward educational goals
  - A:B2.6 **Understand** the relationship between **classroom performance** and **success in school**
  - A:B2.7 **Identify post-secondary options** consistent with interests, achievement, aptitude and abilities

---

Lin and Pereyra (2012).

Why Did we Teach This Lesson?

- To create **more** awareness of the PACE Promise
- To **improve** grades in academic classes
- To **increase** A-G (college prep course) enrollments
- To **increase** high school graduation rates

Lin and Pereyra (2012).

Graduation Rates Comparison

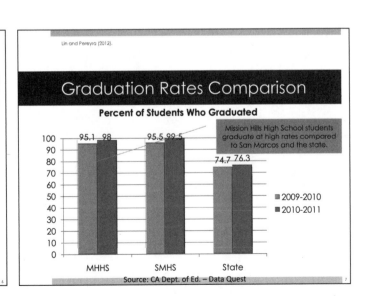

Percent of Students Who Graduated

Mission Hills High School students graduate at high rates compared to San Marcos and the state.

MHHS: 95.1, 98
SMHS: 95.5, 99.5
State: 74.7, 76.3

2009-2010
2010-2011

Source: CA Dept. of Ed. – Data Quest

Lin and Pereyra (2012).

But How Many Students graduated College Eligible (Completed A-Gs)?

Percent of students who graduated and completed A-Gs in 2010-2011

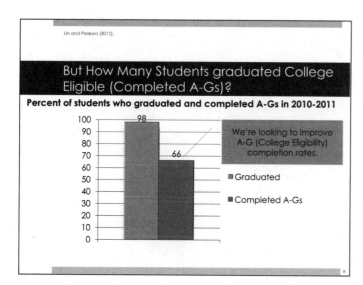

We're looking to improve A-G (College Eligibility) completion rates.

- Graduated
- Completed A-Gs

Lin and Pereyra (2012).

We Surveyed Students' Attitudes, Knowledge, and Skills

- ☐ And we found...
  - ☐ **49%** of students **strongly believed** that taking **A-G** courses will help prepare them for **college**
  - ☐ **32%** of students **strongly believed** that taking **A-G** courses will help prepare them for **career**
  - ☐ **26%** of students could **identify** MHHS's **graduation requirements**
  - ☐ **22%** of students could **read** a sample **transcript** and **identify** what classes the student would need to take to be **A-G** eligible

Lin and Pereyra (2012).

Also, Research Says...

"Students who have information about graduation requirements...are **more likely** to have higher aspirations and are **less likely** to fail" (Dimmitt, 2003).

"Ninth grade is a **critical** year because students need skills early to graduate" (Cooper & Liou, 2007).

School counselors provide **important** information about "courses required for college admission (McDonough, 2004). A **college-going culture** should be instilled for incoming ninth-grade students (The Education Trust, 2005)" (as cited by Banger, 2008).

Lin and Pereyra (2012).

What Were the Results?

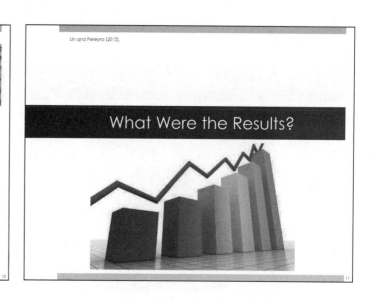

Lin and Pereyra (2012).

Attitudes

I believe taking A-G courses will help me prepare for...

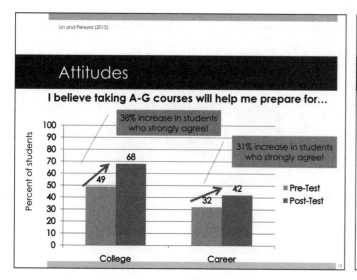

38% increase in students who strongly agree!

31% increase in students who strongly agree!

- Pre-Test
- Post-Test

Lin and Pereyra (2012).

Knowledge

% of students that knew how many credits they need to graduate from MHHS

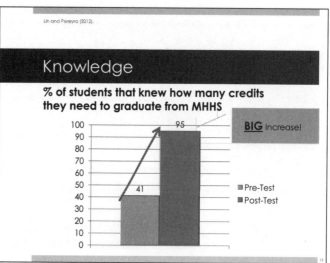

BIG Increase!

- Pre-Test
- Post-Test

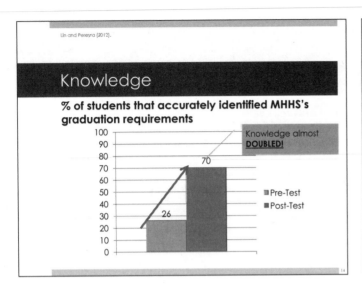

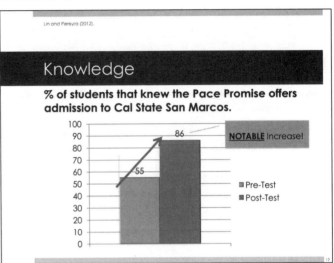

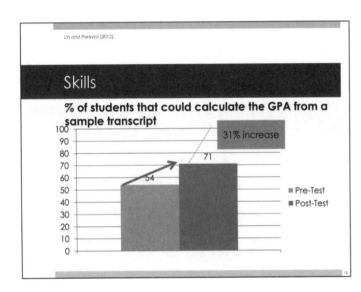

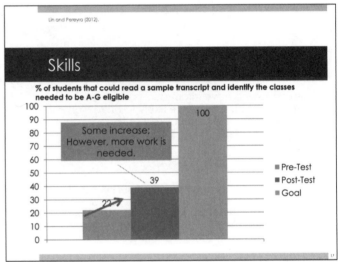

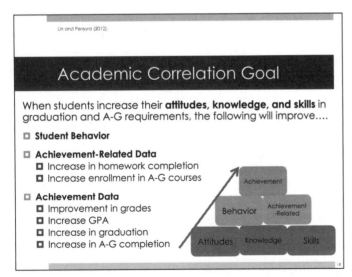

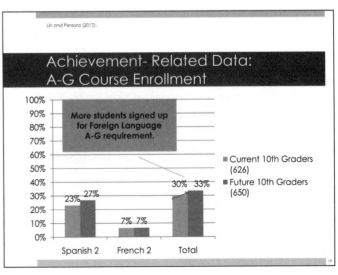

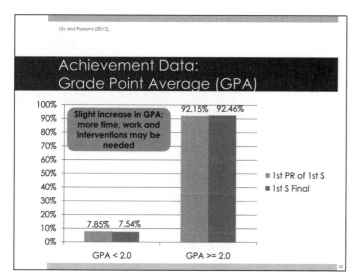

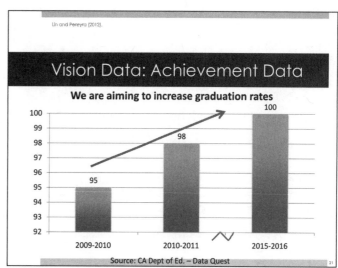

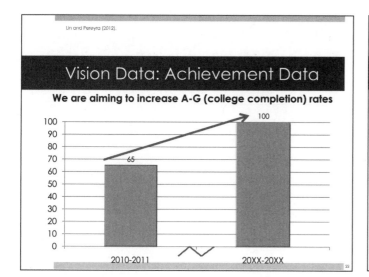

Summary

Lin and Pereyra (2012).

- More students were able to **make the connection** between rigorous course work to college and career readiness.

- More students accurately **identified** graduation requirements.

- Students received **valuable information** about how A-G courses align with high-school graduation requirements.

- Students learned that **their achievement affects their access** to postsecondary opportunities (e.g. guaranteed admission to Cal State San Marcos through the PACE Promise).

- **39%** of students were able to **analyze** a sample transcript, calculate GPA, and identify needed A-G coursework.

Lin and Pereyra (2012).

Implications and Limitations

- **What Worked...**
  - Across the board students increased their attitudes, knowledge, and skills in understanding graduation requirements, A-G requirements, Pace Promise requirements, and GPA calculation

- **What Didn't Work...**
  - Including "Essentials of Algebra" in skill question (#12) confused students
  - We did not address how going to college relates to advanced career options
  - Lack of Edusoft software to tally results of Pre-Test data impacted efficiency

---

Lin and Pereyra (2012).

What We Learned

- Follow up curriculum lesson is needed to show how going to college leads to advanced career opportunities

- Improvement needed on pre/post question #12:
  - Consider having students identify which course is an A-G (college prep) course
  - Consider having students determine if the grade in that course satisfies A-G (college prep) requirements

Lin and Pereyra (2012).

Next Steps

- Review with students how to analyze transcripts

- Collect, analyze, and report achievement and achievement/related data

- Use pre/post test data to make adjustments to our lesson plan (consider using student ID's to determine which students need more instruction)

- Create new curriculum lesson on college and career options

26

Lin and Pereyra (2012).

Thank You

<u>Thank you</u> to the principal, school counselors, and 9th grade History teachers for their collaboration and support.

And of course, thank you to all the students who participated in these presentations!

27

2011-2012

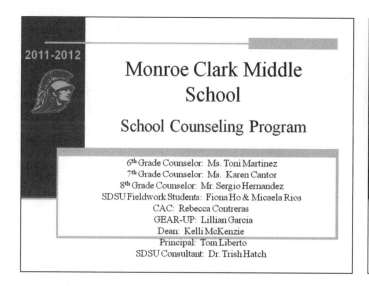

Monroe Clark Middle School

School Counseling Program

6th Grade Counselor: Ms. Toni Martinez
7th Grade Counselor: Ms. Karen Cantor
8th Grade Counselor: Mr. Sergio Hernandez
SDSU Fieldwork Students: Fiona Ho & Micaela Rios
CAC: Rebecca Contreras
GEAR-UP: Lillian Garcia
Dean: Kelli McKenzie
Principal: Tom Liberto
SDSU Consultant: Dr. Trish Hatch

School Counseling Mission

The Mission of Monroe Clark Middle School's Counseling Program to provide *all* students the *attitude, knowledge, and skills* for *academic, career, and personal/social development* in a safe and supportive environment. The comprehensive school counseling program will educate and empower a collaborative community of learners to *achieve academic success* and develop life skills to become life-long learners, creative thinkers, and responsible community members in a diverse, changing world.

The American School Counselor Association National Model

ASCA National Standards for Students
(Student Competencies & Indicators)

➢ Academic Development

➢ Career Development

➢ Personal/Social

Reforming the School Counseling Program

- **Align counseling program with** ASCA National Standards **and state standards**
- **More** collaboration with teachers and administrators **to address student needs**
- **Set** measurable goals
- **Implement a consistent** data driven **program**
- Classroom guidance **at all grade levels**
- Intentional Guidance **for at risk students**

Adapted from Trish Hatch, PhD (2006)

Delivery of Counseling Services

(Few Students)
Individual/Referral

(Some Students)
Intentional Guidance

(All Students)
Guidance Curriculum

2011-2012 Guidance Curriculum Plan

6th Grade	7th Grade	8th Grade
1) Study Skills (Academic, Personal/Social)	1) Goal Setting & CAC Benchmarks (Academic, Personal/Social, Career)	1) Goal Setting (CAC) (Academic, Career, Personal/Social)
2) Bullying & Cyber-Bullying Sexual Harassment (Academic, Personal/Social)	2) Ask for Help (Youth Suicide Prevention, Cyber-Bullying & Sexual Harassment) (Personal/Social)	2) Getting Ready for High School (Academic, Career, Personal/Social)
3) Respect & Conflict Resolution (Personal/Social)	3) Value of Education (CAC) & Roadway to Success Post-Secondary Options (Academic, Career, Personal/Social)	3) College Knowledge (CAC) (Academic, Career, Personal/Social)
4) Introduction to College Avenue Compact (CAC) (Academic, Career, Personal/Social)	4) Career Key/Naviance (CAC) (Academic, Personal/Social, Career)	4) Making Healthy Choices (Wellness Council) (Academic, Personal/Social)
5) Test Success & Motivation (Academic, Personal/Social)		5) My Dream/Naviance (CAC) (Academic, Personal/Social,

INTENTIONAL GUIDANCE ACTION PLAN:

On the Front Lines...

- **Dropping out begins in Elementary/Middle School**

- Schools need to <u>develop early warning systems</u> to help them identify students at risk of dropping out and to <u>develop the mechanisms that trigger</u> appropriate supports for these students.

- By 9th grade, dropout can be predicted with 85 percent accuracy. The key indicators are <u>poor attendance, behavioral problems</u>, and <u>course failure</u>.

       –John M. Bridgeland, John J. Dilulio, Jr. and Robert Balfanz (page 8)

Hatch, T. (2008)   8

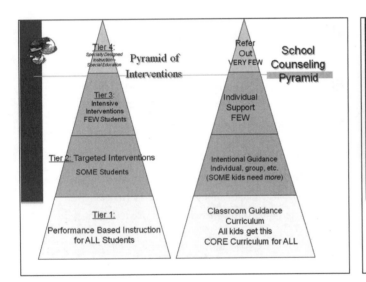

First Let's Review Monroe Clark School Counseling [GOALS 2010-2011]

From October 2010 to May 2011

- **20% reduction** in the number of students academically at risk (below a 2.0 GPA)

- **25% reduction** in the number of full day unexcused absences (3 or more)

- **25% reduction** in recidivism (repeat offenders) for behavior

DATA: First Progress Report (October 2010) all students

	# of Students Below 2.0	# of Students with 3 full day unexcused absences	# of students with 3 behavioral referrals
6th Grade	66	21	8
7th Grade	102	57	25
8th Grade	144	58	25

<u>15 Students have problems in all 3 Areas (School Wide)</u>

Eckenrod and Zeilano (2011)

Target Group selected on basis of following data:

Students with a GPA below 2.0 on first progress report.

ASCA National Standards

Academic Standard A

Students will acquire the attitudes, knowledge, and skills that contribute to effective learning in school and across the life span.

Personal/Social Standard A

Students will acquire the attitudes knowledge and interpersonal skills to help them understand and respect self and others

Student Competencies

- A:A1 Improve Academic Self-Concept
- A:A2 Acquire Skills for Improving Learning
- A:A3 Achieve School Success
- A:B2 Plan to Achieve Goals
- PS:A2 Acquire interpersonal skills

What DO we know?

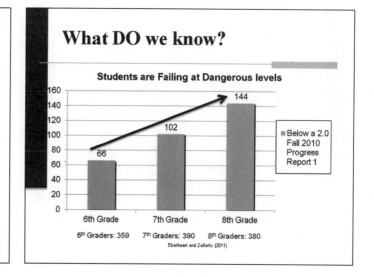

The Process

- Pre-screened students (surveyed needs)
- Sent letter home to parents
- Cooperated with teachers to create schedules
  - Created letter to be sent to participating teachers
- Created Hall Passes for students
- Developed group curriculum and weekly lessons
  - Using materials from Avid, College Board, Channing-Bete workbooks and the Why Try program
- Delivery of motivation and study skills groups

Eberheart and Zañartu (2011)

How *many* Students were placed in counseling groups?

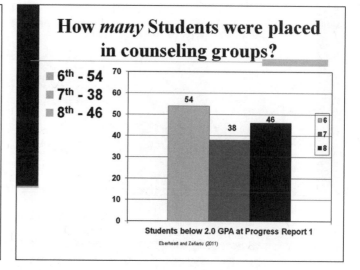

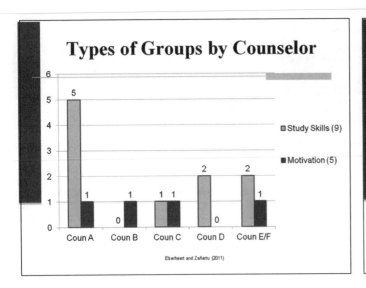

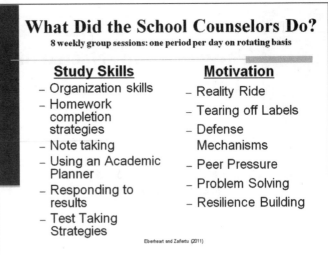

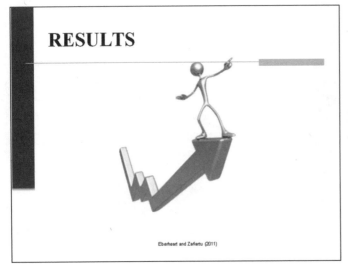

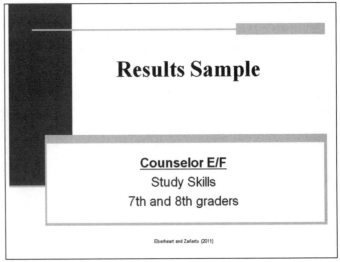

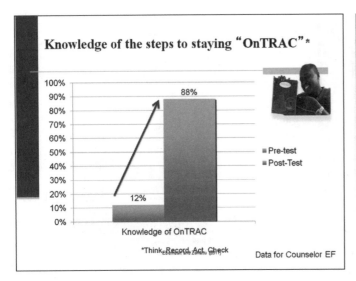

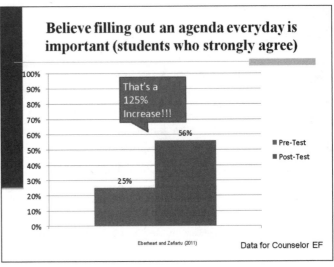

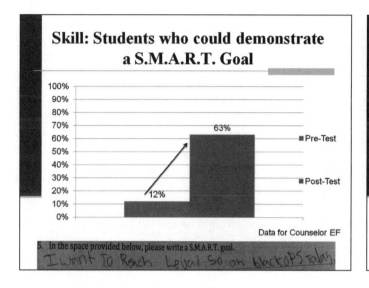

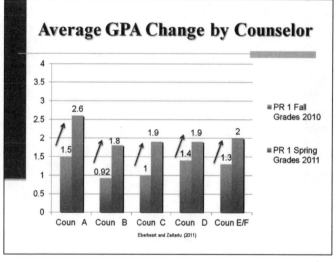

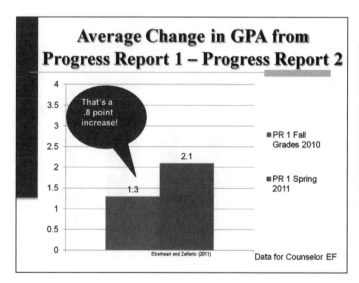

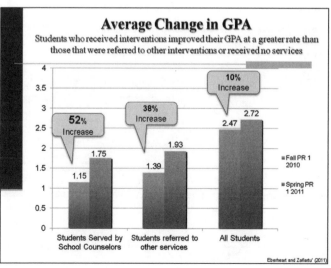

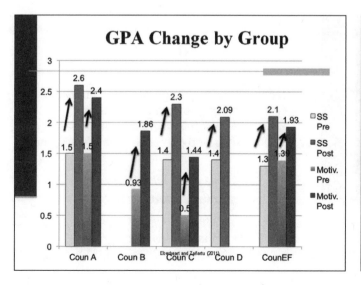

In Summary…

- Students are learning and retaining attitudes knowledge and skills with structured content lessons.
- Rotating class periods created minimal distraction from teachers.
- **Students did improve overall!!!**

Eberheart and Zañartu (2011)

NEW Monroe Clark School Counseling [GOALS 2011-2012]

From October 2012 to May 2012

- **20% reduction** of students failing Algebra from (PR 1 to Pr 2)
- **20% reduction** in the number of students academically at risk (below a 2.0 GPA)
- **25% reduction** in the number of full day unexcused absences (3 or more)
- **25% reduction** in recidivism (repeat offenders) for behavior

Comparing First Progress Report (October 2010 vs.2011)
Wow! Great Improvement!

	# of Students Below 2.0		# of Students with 3 full day unexcused absences		# of students with 3 behavioral referrals	
	2010	2011	2010	2011	2010	2011
6th Grade	66	39	21	2	8	3
7th Grade	102	74	57	8	25	11
8th Grade	144	134	58	8	25	7

But still much work to do…
Number of Students with a D or F in Algebra (S1 Progress)

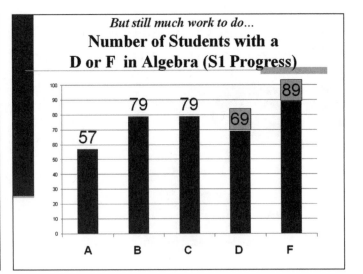

San Diego Unified School District
Clark Middle School Intentional Guidance Action Plan 2011-2012

Target Group: 8th grade students at risk of failing Algebra

Target Group selection is based upon the following data: students with a D or F on the first progress report in Algebra

THANK YOU!

Monroe Clark's Counseling Department is striving to guide all students to achieve their full potential in the areas of academic, career and personal/social development.

Thank you to all teachers and the leadership team for your support of the school counseling program.

References

Achieve. (2012a, December). *Implementing the common core standards: The role of the school counselor.* Retrieved from http://www.achieve.org/publications/implementing-common-core-state-standards-role-school-counselor-action-brief

Achieve. (2012b, December). *State college and career ready high school graduation requirements.* Retrieved from: http://achieve.org/files/CCR-Diploma-Grad-Reqs-Table-12–2012.pdf

Achieve. (2013, January). *New guides help school leaders support common core state standards implementation.* Retrieved from https://www.metlife.com/assets/cao/foundation/pressreleases/New-Guides-Help-School-Leaders-Support.pdf

Akos, P., Schuldt, H., & Walendin, M. (2009). School counselor assignment in secondary schools. *Professional School Counseling, 13*(1), 23–29. Retrieved from http://soe.unc.edu/fac_research/publications/journal_articles/professional_sch_counseling_akos.pdf

Allensworth, E., & Easton, J. (2005). *The on-track indicator as a predictor of high school graduation.* Chicago, IL: Consortium on Chicago School Research.

Allensworth, E., & Easton, J. (2007). *What matters for staying on-track and graduating in Chicago Public High Schools: A close look at course grades, failures and attendance in the freshman year.* Chicago, IL: Consortium on Chicago School Research.

American School Counselor Association. (2003). *The ASCA national model: A framework for school counseling programs.* Alexandria, VA: Author.

American School Counselor Association. (2004). *ASCA national standards for students.* Alexandria, VA: Author.

American School Counselor Association. (2005). *The ASCA national model: A framework for school counseling programs* (2nd ed.). Alexandria, VA: Author.

American School Counselor Association. (2008). *ASCA school counselor competencies.* Alexandria, VA: Author.

American School Counselor Association. (2010a). *ASCA position statements.* Alexandria, VA: Author.

American School Counselor Association. (2010b). *Ethical standards for school counselors.* Alexandria, VA: Author. Retrieved from http://www.schoolcounselor.org/files/EthicalStandards2010.pdf

American School Counselor Association. (2011). *The ASCA national model: Executive summary.* Alexandria, VA: Author. Retrieved from http://www.azed.gov/career-technical-education/files/2011/08/executive-summary.pdf

American School Counselor Association. (2012a). *The ASCA national model: A framework for school counseling programs* (3rd ed.). Alexandria, VA: Author.

American School Counselor Association. (2012b). *ASCA position statements.* Alexandria, VA: Author. Retrieved from: http://www.schoolcounselor.org/files/PositionStatements.pdf

American School Counselor Association. (2012c). *ASCA school counselor competencies.* Alexandria, VA: Author.

American School Counselor Association. (2012d). Student-to-school-counselor ratio 2010–2011. Retrieved from http://www.schoolcounselor.org/files/ratios10–11.pdf

An act to amend Title 20 of the Official Code of Georgia, H.R. 283. (2013).

American School Counselor Association. (2012e, July/August). ASCA national model 3.0: When it's time to change. *ASCA School Counselor, 49*(6), 10–13. Retrieved from http://www.ascaschoolcounselor.org/files/magazine/JulyAug2012.pdf

Balfanz, R., Bridgeland, J. M., Bruce, M., & Fox, J. H. (2012). *Building a grad nation: Progress and challenge in ending the high school dropout epidemic.* Washington, DC: Civic Enterprises. Retrieved fromhttp://www.americaspromise.org/~/media/Files/Our%20Work/Grad%20Nation/Building%20a%20Grad%20Nation/BuildingAGradNation2012.ashx

Balfanz, R., Bridgeland, J., Moore, L., & Fox, J. (2010). *Building a grad nation: Progress and challenge in ending the high school dropout epidemic.* Retrieved from America's Promise Alliance website: http://www.americaspromise.org/~/media/Files/Our%20Work/Grad%20Nation/Building%20a%20Grad%20Nation/Building%20a%20Grad%20Nation%20Executive%20Summary_FINAL_11–30–10.ashx

Balfanz, R., Herzog, L., & Mac Iver, D. J. (2007). Preventing student disengagement and keeping students on the graduation path in urban middle-grades schools: Early identification and effective interventions. *Educational Psychologist, 42*(4), 223–235.

Bauman, S. (2008). To join or not to join: School counselors as a case study in professional membership. *Journal of Counseling & Development, 86*(2), 164–177.

Bloom, B. S., Englehart, M. B., Furst, E. J., Hill, W. H., & Krathwohl, O. R. (1956). *Taxonomy of educational objectives: The classification of educational goals. Handbook 1: The cognitive domain.* New York: Longman.

Bowers, J. L., & Hatch, P. A. (2002). *Report of the Summit for School Counseling.* In American School Counselor Association (draft), *The ASCA national model: A framework for school counseling programs* (p. 73). Alexandria: VA.

Bowers, J., Hatch,T., & Schwallie-Giddis, P. (2001). The brainstorm. *ASCA School Counselor, 39*(1), 16–19.

Bridgeland, J., & Bruce, M. (2011). *National survey of school counselors: Counseling at a crossroads.* New York, NY: College Board Advocacy and Policy Center.

Bridgeland, J. M., Dilulio, J. J., & Balfanz, R. (2009). *On the frontlines of schools: Perspectives of teachers and principals on the high school dropout problem.* Washington, DC: Civic Enterprises.

Brigman, G., Campbell, C., & Webb, L. (2004). *Student success skills: Helping student develop the academic, social and self-management skills they need to succeed. Group counseling manual.* Boca Raton, FL: Atlantic Education Consultants.

Brigman, G., & Webb, L. (2007). Student success skills: Impacting achievement through large and small group work. *Journal of Group Dynamics: Theory, Practice and Research, 11,* 283–292.

Brott, P. E. (2008). Get a GRIP! In Virginia School Counselor Association (Ed.). *The Virginia Professional School Counseling Manual* (pp. 86–93). Yorktown, VA: Virginia School Counselor Association.

Brown, J. H., D'Emidio-Caston, M., & Benard, B. (2001). *Resilience education.* Thousand Oaks, CA: Corwin.

Bryan, J., & Holcomb-McCoy, C. (2004). School counselors' perceptions of their involvement in school-family-community partnerships. *Professional School Counseling, 7*(3), 162–171.

Campbell, C. A., & Dahir, C. A. (1997). *Sharing the vision: The ASCA national standards for school counseling programs.* Alexandria, VA: American School Counselor Association.

Carey, J. C., Dimmitt, C., Hatch, T. A., Lapan, R. T., & Whiston, S. C. (2008). Report of the national panel for evidence-based school counseling: Outcome research coding protocol and evaluation on student success skills and second step. *Professional School Counseling, 11*(3), 197–206.

College Board. (2011, November 14). *Own the turf: A message from secretary of education, Arne Duncan* [Video file]. Retrieved from http://www.youtube.com/watch?v=1pIkbo7pjTg

College Board. (2013). *Own the turf: College and career readiness training.* Retrieved from http://media.collegeboard.com/digitalServices/pdf/advocacy/own-the-turf-faq-010713.pdf

College Readiness Consortium. (2013). *Ramp up to readiness.* Minneapolis: University of Minnesota.

Committee for Children. (2010). *Second step violence prevention curriculum.* Retrieved from http://www.cfchildren.org/second-step.aspx

Cooper, H., Lindsay, J. J., Nye, B., & Greathouse, S. (1998). Relationships among attitudes about homework, amount of homework assigned and completed, and student achievement. *Journal of Educational Psychology, 90,* 70–83.

Darling-Hammond, L. (1998). Teacher learning that supports student learning. *Educational Leadership, 55*(5), 6–11.

DataDirector.(2012). *Empowering data driven instruction in districts, schools, and classrooms.* Retrieved from http://www.riversidepublishing.com/products/DataDirector/pdf/DD_Overview_Brochure_2012.pdf

DeKalb, J.(1999). *Student truancy.* ERIC Digest No.125. Eugene, OR: ERICClearinghouseon Educational Management.

Dimmitt, C., Carey, J. C., & Hatch, T. (2007). *Evidence-based school counseling: Making a difference with data-driven practices.* Thousand Oaks, CA: Corwin.

District of Columbia Public Schools. (2011). *Scope and sequence documents: Providing clear guidance on what your children's teachers should teach and when they should teach it.* Retrieved from http://dcps.dc.gov/DCPS/In+the+Classroom/The+DCPS+Academic+Plan/What+does+this++mean+for+my+child%E2%80%99s+teacher%3F/Scope+and+Sequence+Documents

Dooley, S. (2010, March 29). Counselor cuts loom as issue for schools. *Des Moines Register.* Retrieved from http://www.desmoinesregister.com/article/20100606/NEWS/6060353/Counselor-cuts-loom-as-issue-for-schools

Duarte, D., & Hatch, T. (2013). *Successful implementation of a federally funded elementary school counseling program: Results bring sustainability.* Manuscript submitted for publication.

Easton, J. Q., & Engelhard, G. (1982). A longitudinal record of elementary school absence and its relationship to reading achievement. *Journal of Educational Research, 7*(5), 269–274.

EdSource. (2013). *Standards-based education.* Oakland, CA: Author. Retrieved from http://www.edsource.org/iss_sta.html

Education Trust. (2009). *National center for transforming school counseling at the education trust.* Retrieved from http://www.edtrust.org/dc/tsc/

Education Trust and MetLife Foundation National School Counselor Training Initiative. (2002, October). *Challenging the myths: Rethinking the role of school counselors.* Retrieved from http://www2.edtrust.org/NR/rdonlyres/0EF57A7F-B336–46A8–898D981018AFBF11/0/counseling_train_broch.pdf

Efficiency. (2013). In *Merriam-Webster Dictionary.* Retrieved from http://www.merriam-webster.com/dictionary/efficiency

Elementary and secondary school counseling programs. (2011, November 3). Retrieved from http://www2.ed.gov/programs/elseccounseling/index.html

Fan, X., & Chen, M. (2001). Parental involvement and students' academic achievement: A meta-analysis. *Educational Psychology Review, 13*(1), 1–22.

Farrington, C. A., Roderick, M., Allensworth, E., Nagaoka, J., Keyes, T. S., Johnson, D. W., & Beechum, N. O. (2012). *Teaching adolescents to become learners. The role of noncognitive factors in shaping school performance: A critical literature review.* Chicago, IL: University of Chicago Consortium on Chicago School Research.

Field, J., & Baker, S. (2004). Defining and examining school counselor advocacy. *Professional School Counseling, 8,* 56–63.

Finkelstein, D. (2009). *A closer look at the principal–counselor relationship: A survey of principals and counselors.* New York, NY: National Office for School Counselor Advocacy, American School Counselor Association, and National Association of Secondary School Principals. Retrieved from http://advocacy.collegeboard.org/sites/default/files/a-closer-look_2.pdf

Fouad, N. A., Gerstein, L. H., & Toporek, R. L. (2006). Social justice and counseling psychology in context. In R. L. Toporek, L. Gerstein, N. Fouad, G. Roysircar, & T. Israel (Eds.), *Handbook for social justice in counseling psychology: Leadership, vision, and action* (pp. 1–16). Thousand Oaks, CA: Sage.

Fuller, S. (2012, August 5). School counselors: Our time and services are valuable! [Web log entry]. Retrieved from http://entirelyelementary.blogspot.com/2012/08/school-counselors-our-time-and-services.html

Garfat, T., & Van Bockern, S. (2010). Families and the circle of courage. *Reclaiming Children and Youth, 18*(4).

Gibson, D. (2006). *The association of students' academic efficacy, achievement goal orientation, and teacher rapport with disruptive behavior in the classroom* (Unpublished doctoral dissertation). St. John's University, New York.

Goldstein, D. (2011, April 4). The test generation. *The American Prospect*. Retrieved from http://prospect.org/article/test-generation

Guidance (n.d.a). In *Dictionary.com*. Retrieved from http://dictionary.reference.com/browse/guidance

Guidance (n.d.b). In *TheFreeDictionary*. Retrieved from http://www.thefreedictionary.com/Guidance

Gunn Guidance Advisory Committee. (2013). Supporting the success of all Gunn High School students: Report by the Gunn guidance advisory committee. Retrieved from http://www.gunngac.org/Gunn%20GAC%20Final%20Report%202013.pdf

Gysbers, N. (2010). *Remembering the past, shaping the future: School counseling principles.* Alexandria, VA: American School Counselor Association.

Gysbers, N., & Henderson, P. (2012). *Developing and managing your school guidance and counseling program* (5th ed.). Alexandria, VA: American Counseling Association.

Hart, P., & Jacobi, M. (1992). *From gatekeeper to advocate: Transforming the role of the school counselor.* New York, NY: College Examination Entrance Board.

Hartline, J., & Cobia, D. (2012). School counselors: Closing achievement gaps and writing results reports. *Professional School Counseling, 16*(1), 71–79.

Hatch, T. (2002). The ASCA national standards for school counseling programs: A source of legitimacy or reform? (Doctoral dissertation, University of California, Riverside). *Dissertation Abstracts International, 63*, 2798.

Hatch, T. (2004a, June). *Hatching Results. . . . School counseling: Moving the profession forward.* American School Counselor Association Conference: Reno, NV.

Hatch, T. (2004b). Writing school counselor action plans and sharing results: A two-pronged flashlight approach. In T. Hatch & L. Holland (Eds.), *National model workbook* (pp. 108–118). Retrieved from http://trishhatch.com/Documents/Hatch_National_Model_workbook.pdf

Hatch, T. (2005a, June). *Data made easy: Using data to effect change.* Paper presented at the American School Counselor Association, Orlando, FL.

Hatch, T. (2005b). *Pilots, passengers, prisoners and hijackers* [PowerPoint Slides]. Retrieved from www2.edutech.nodak.edu/ndca/conference/2006/files/trishhatch.ppt

Hatch, T. (2006). Today's school counselor. *School Counselor,44*(2), 28–34.

Hatch, T. (2008). Professional challenges in school counseling: Organizational, institutional and political. *Journal of School Counseling, 6*(22). Retrieved from http://www.jsc.montana.edu/articles/v6n22.pdf

Hatch, T. (2010a). *Hatching results: Flashlight sample XYZ* [PowerPoint slides]. Retrieved from http://www.cescal.org/resourceDetail.cfm?uploadedObjectKey=115

Hatch, T. (2010b). *Hatching results training manual: The ASCA national model: The changing role of the school counselor in educational reform and the use of data to effect change for student.* Ferndale, CA: Hatching Results.

Hatch, T. (2012a). Advocacy and social justice. In American School Counselor Association (Ed.), *The ASCA national model: A framework for school counseling programs* (3rd ed.) (pp. 14–16). Alexandria, VA: Author.

Hatch, T. (2012b). School counselors using data. In National Association for College Admission Counseling (Ed.). *Fundamentals of college admission counseling* (3rd ed.) (pp. 60–78). Alexandria, VA: Author.

Hatch, T., & Chen-Hayes, S. F. (2008). School counselor beliefs about ASCA model school counseling program components using the SCPSC scale. *Professional School Counseling, 12*(1), 34–42.

Hatch, T., & Holland, L. A. (2001). *Moreno Valley Unified District school counselor academy handbook.* Moreno Valley, CA: Moreno Valley Unified School District.

Hatch, T., & Lewis, R. E. (2011). *Promoting social justice with wisdom and data.* Retrieved from http://counselingoutfitters.com/vistas/vistas11/Article_91.pdf

Hatch, T., & Poynton, T. (2013). School Counseling Program Survey Findings and Impressions. Unpublished Manuscript.

Henderson, P. (2012). Fundamental questions and principles from the theory behind the ASCA national model. In American School Counselor Association (3rd ed.), *The ASCA national model: A framework for school counseling programs* (pp. 137–140). Alexandria: VA.

Heppen, J. B., & Therriault, S. B. (2008). *Developing early warning systems to identify potential high school dropouts.* Washington, DC: American Institutes for Research, National High School Center.

Hines, P., & Lemon, R. (2011, December). *Poised to lead: How school counselors can drive college and career readiness.* Washington, DC: The Education Trust. Retrieved from http://www.edtrust.org/sites/edtrust.org/files/publications/files/Poised_To_Lead_0.pdf

Holcomb-McCoy, C. (2007). *School counseling to close the achievement gap: A social justice framework for success.* Thousand Oaks, CA: Corwin.

Holcomb-McCoy, C., & Chen-Hayes, S. F. (2011). Culturally competent school counselors: Affirming diversity by challenging oppression. In B. T. Erford (Ed.),*Transforming the school counseling profession* (3rd ed.) (pp. 90–109). Boston, MA: Pearson.

Horner, R., Sugai, G., Smolkowski, K., Todd, A., Nakasato, J., & Esperanza, J. (2009). A randomized control trial of school-wide positive behavior support in elementary schools. *Journal of Positive Behavior Interventions, 11*(3), 133–144.

House, R. M., & Martin, P. J. (1998). Advocating for better futures for all students: A new vision for school counselors. *Education, 119,* 284–291.

Hurwitz, M., & Howell, J. (2013). *Measuring the impact of high school counselors on college enrollment.* College Board Advisory & Policy Center Research Brief.

Intention. (2013). In *Merriam-Webster Dictionary.* Retrieved from http://www.merriam-webster.com/dictionary/intention

Intentionally. (n.d.). In *Encarta dictionary.* Retrieved from http://encarta.msn.com/dictionary_1861621725/intentional.html

Iowa Department of Education. (2008). *Iowa school counseling: A program framework.* Des Moines: Author.

Jeynes, W. (2007). The relationship between parental involvement and urban secondary school student academic achievement: A meta-analysis. *Urban Education, 42,* 82–110.

Johns Hopkins University School of Education. (2012). *Robert Balfanz named "champion of change" by White House.* Retrieved from http://new.every1graduates.org/robert-balfanz-named-champion-of-change-by-white-house/

Johnson, C. D., & Johnson, S. K. (2001). *Results-based student support programs: Leadership academy workbook.* San Juan Capistrano, CA: Professional Update.

Johnson, R. (2002). *Using data to close the achievement gap: How to measure equity in our schools.* Thousand Oaks, CA: Corwin.

Kennelly, L., & Monrad, M. (2007). *Approaches to dropout prevention: Heeding early warning signs with appropriate interventions.* Washington, DC: American Institutes for Research, National High School Center. Retrieved from www.betterhighschools.org/docs/NHSC_ApproachestoDropoutPrevention.pdf

Kipp Bay Area Schools. (2013). *San Francisco college preparatory counselor job description.* Retrieved from http://www.kippbayarea.org/careers/sf/kipp-san-francisco-college-preparatory-counselor

Kingdon, J. (1984). *Agendas, alternatives, and public policies.* Boston: Little, Brown.

Krumboltz, J. D. (2009). The happenstance learning theory. *Journal of Career Assessment, 17*(2), 135–154. Retrieved from http://www.studentintegration.fi/filebank/77-The_Happenstance_Learning_Theory.pdf

Lee, J., & Ransom, T. (2011). *The educational experience of young men of color: A review of research, pathways, and progress.* New York, NY: The College Board.

Lee, V. V., & Goodnough, G. E. (2011). Systemic data-driven school counseling practice and-programming for equity. In B. T. Erford (Ed.),*Transforming the school counseling profession* (3rd ed.). Columbus, OH: Pearson Merrill Prentice-Hall.

LeFevre, A. L., & Shaw, T. V. (2011). Latino parent involvement and school success: Longitudinal effects of formal and informal support. *Education and Urban Society, 44,* 707–723.

Lewis, R. E., & Hatch, T. (2008). Cultivating strengths-based professional identities. *Professional School Counselor,12*(2), 115–118.

Ligon, M., & McDaniel, S. (1970). *The teacher's role in counseling.* Englewood Cliffs, NJ: Prentice-Hall.

Likert, R. A. (1932). A technique for the measurement of attitudes. *Archives of Psychology,140,*1–55.

Louis, K. S., Jones, L. M., & Barajas, H. (2001). *Districts and schools as a context for transformed counseling roles.* Minneapolis, MN: Center for Applied Research in Educational Improvement. Retrieved from https://www.cehd.umn.edu/carei/publications/documents/Report01–3.pdf

Malecki, C. K., & Elliott, S. N. (2002). Children's social behaviors as predictors of academic achievement: A longitudinal analysis. *School Psychology Quarterly, 17,* 1–23.

Mason, D. (2008). Solution focused therapy: What is the miracle question? Retrieved from http://www.key-hypnosis.com/Self-Help/Set-Your-Goals/Solution-Focused-Therapy-Miracle-Question.php

Mason, E. C. M., Ockerman, M. S., & Chen-Hayes, S. F. (2013). Change-Agent-for-Equity (CAFE) model: A framework for school counselor identity. *Journal of School Counseling, 11*(4). Retrieved from http://jsc.montana.edu/articles/v11n4.pdf

Mathison, S. (Ed.). (2004). *The encyclopedia of evaluation.* Thousand Oaks, CA: Sage.

Miller, S. R., Allensworth, E. M., & Kochanek, J. R. (2002). *Student performance: Course taking, test scores, and outcomes.* Chicago, IL: Consortium on Chicago School Research.

Muhammad, A. (2009). *Transforming school culture: How to overcome staff division.* Bloomington, IN: Solution Tree Press.

Myrick, R. D. (2003). Accountability: Counselors count. *Professional School Counseling,6*(3), 174–179.

National Career Development Association (NCDA). (2013). National career development guidelines framework. Retrieved from *http://ncda.org/aws/NCDA/asset_manager/get_file/3384?ver=16587*

National Commission on Excellence in Education. (1983). *A nation at risk.* Washington, DC: US Government Printing Office.

National Governors Association Center for Best Practices and Council of Chief State School Officers. (2012). *Common core state standards initiative.* Washington, DC: Author. Retrieved from http://www.corestandards.org/resources

National High School Center. (2012). *A demonstration of an early warning system implementation process and tool* [PowerPoint slides]. Retrieved from http://www.betterhighschools.org/documents/CECPresentation2012.pdf

National Office for School Counselor Advocacy (NOSCA). (2011). *High school counselor's guide: NOSCA's eight components of college and career readiness counseling.* New York, NY: The College Board.

National Office for School Counselor Advocacy (NOSCA). (2012). *Transforming the educational experience of young men of color.* New York, NY: The College Board.

Neild, R. C., & Balfanz, R. (2006). *Unfulfilled promise: The dimensions and characteristics of Philadelphia's dropout crisis, 2000–2005.* Philadelphia, PA: Philadelphia Youth Transitions Collaborative.

Neild, R. C., Balfanz, R., & Herzog L. (2007). An early warning system. *Educational Leadership, 65*(2), 28–33.

No Child Left Behind Act, Pub. L. No. 107–110 (2001).

Now is the time:The President's plan to protect our children and our communities by reducing gun violence. (2013). Retrieved from http://www.whitehouse.gov/issues/preventing-gun-violence

Ogawa, R. T. (1992). Institutional theory and examining leadership in schools. *International Journal of Educational Management, 6*(3), 14–21.

Ogawa, R. T. (1994). The institutional sources of educational reform: The case of site based management. *American Educational Research Journal, 31,* 519–548.

Pawson, R., & Tilley, N. (1997). *Realistic evaluation.* London, UK: Sage.

Pawson, R., & Tilley, N. (2004). *Realistic evaluation.* London, UK: British Cabinet Office. Retrieved from http://www.communitymatters.com.au/RE_chapter.pdf

Perkins, P. G., & Gelfer, J. I. (1995). Elementary to middle school: Planning for transition. *The Clearing House, 68*(3), 171–173.

Pinkus, L. M. (2009). *Moving beyond AYP: High school performance indicators.* Washington, DC: Alliance for Excellent Education. Retrieved from http://www.all4ed.org/files/SPIMovingBeyondAYP.pdf

Professional. (2013). In *Bing Dictionary.* Retrieved from http://www.bing.com/Dictionary/Search?q=define+professional

Railsback, J. (2004). *Increasing student attendance: Strategies from research and practice.* Portland, OR: Northwest Regional Educational Laboratory.

Ratts, M. J. (2009). Social justice counseling: Toward the development of a "fifth force" among counseling paradigms. *Journal of Humanistic Counseling, Education, and Development, 48,* 160–172.

Rennie Center for Education Research & Policy. (2011). *Student learning plans: Supporting every student's transition to college and career.* Cambridge, MA: Author. Retrieved from http://www.issuelab.org/click/kc_download1/student_learning_plans_supporting_every_students_transition_to_college_and_career/renniecenter

Reykdal, K. (n.d.). Joint taskforce on education funding. *Washington School Counselor Association.* Retrieved from http://www.wa-schoolcounselor.org/Files/Proposal2Jt.Cmte.Educ.pdf

Roby, D. E. (2003). Research on school attendance and student achievement: A study of Ohio schools. *Educational Research Quarterly, 28*(1), 4–15.

Rowan, B., & Miskel, C. G. (1999). Institutional theory and the study of educational organizations. In J. Murphy & K. S. Louis (Eds.), *Handbook of research in educational administration* (pp. 359–382). San Francisco, CA: Jossey-Bass.

Rumberger, R. W. (1995). Dropping out of middle school: A multilevel analysis of students and schools. *American Educational Research Journal, 32*(3), 583–625.

Ryan, J. (2011, March 30). Owners or renters: Which is your workforce? *Forbes.* Retrieved from http://www.forbes.com/2011/03/30/employee-loyalty-commitment-owner-renter-leadership-managing-team.html

Sabella, R. A. (2006). The ASCA national school counseling research center: A brief history and agenda. *Professional School Counseling, 9*(5), 412–415.

Sabella, R. A. (2012). Addressing RTI via ASCA national model implementation. In American School Counselor Association (Ed.), *The ASCA national model: A framework for school counseling programs* (3rd ed., pp. 73–74). Alexandria: VA.

Schmoker, M. (2001). *The results handbook: Practical strategies from dramatically improved schools.* Alexandria, VA: Association for Supervision and Curriculum Development.

Schumacher, D. (1998, June). *The transition to middle school.* ERIC Digest EDO-PS-98-6. Champaign: University of Illinois.

Siegle, D. (2010). *Likert scale.* Retrieved from http://www.gifted.uconn.edu/siegle/research/instrument%20reliability%20and%20validity/likert.html

Silva, L. (2005). *Sweetwater Union High School District school counseling program guidance curriculum results.* Retrieved from http://www.cescal.org/objects/accountability/19/Liliana Flashlight_New13.ppt

Sklare, G. (2004). *Brief counseling that works: A solution focused-approach for school counselors and administrators.* Thousand Oaks, CA: Corwin Press.

Smith, J., & Niemi, R. G. (2001). Learning history in school: The impact of course work and instructional practices on achievement. *Theory and Research in Social Education, 29*(1), 18–42.

South Metro Denver Realtor Association. (2011, October). What does it mean to be a professional? *SMDRA Education*. Retrieved from http://www.smdra.com/PDFs/Newspaper/October/1011.pdf

Stang, J. (2013, March 15). *Legislature is running out of places to hide from school funding decisions.* Retrieved from http://crosscut.com/2013/03/15/olympia-2013/113466/legislatures-evasion-school-costs-will-have-end/

Starting lineup. (n.d.). In *Wikipedia*. Retrieved from http://en.wikipedia.org/wiki/Starting_lineup

Stephens, D. L., & Lindsey, R. B. (2011). *Culturally proficient collaboration: Use and misuse of school counselors*. Thousand Oaks, CA: Corwin.

Stone, C., & Dahir, C. (2007). *School counselor accountability: A measure of student success* (2nd ed.). Upper Saddle River, NJ: Pearson Education.

Stone, C., & Dahir, C. (2011). *School counselor accountability: A measure of student success* (3rd ed.). Boston, MA: Pearson.

Therriault, S. B., O'Cummings, M., Heppen, J., Yerhot, L., & Scala, J. *High school early warning intervention monitoring system implementation guide*. Washington, DC: National High School Center. Retrieved from http://www.betterhighschools.org/documents/EWSHSImplementationguide.pdf

Thompson, R. A. (2012). *Professional school counseling: Best practices for working in the schools* (3rd ed.). New York, NY: Routledge.

Tierney, W. G., & Hagedorn, L. S. (2001). *Making the grade in college prep: A guide for improving college preparation programs.* Los Angeles: The Center for Higher Education Policy Analysis, Rossier School of Education, University of Southern California. Retrieved from http://www.usc.edu/dept/chepa/pdf/makinggrade.pdf

TurningTechnologies. (2013). *Response technology for K–12 students.* Retrieved from http://www.turningtechnologies.com/studentresponsesystems/studentclickers/

U.S. Department of Education. (2011a). *Elementary and secondary school counseling programs.* Retrieved from http://www2.ed.gov/programs/elseccounseling/index.html

U.S. Department of Education. (2011b). *Protecting students with disabilities.* Retrieved from http://www2.ed.gov/about/offices/list/ocr/504faq.html

Utility player. (n.d.). In *Wikipedia*. Retrieved from http://en.wikipedia.org/wiki/Utility_player

Van Horn, M. L. (2003). Assessing the unit of measurement for school climate through psychometric and outcome analyses of the school climate. *Educational and Psychological Measurement, 63*(6), 1002–1019.

Verdugo, A. (Producer). (2012, December 16). *Meet the press* [Television broadcast]. Washington, DC: National Broadcasting Company.

Webb, L., Brigman, G., & Campbell, C. (2005). Linking school counselors and student success: A replication of the Student Success Skills approach targeting the academic and social competence of students. *Professional School Counseling, 8,* 407–413.

Weick, K. E. (1996). Drop your tools: An allegory for organizational studies. *Administrative Science Quarterly, 41*(2), 301–303.

Weiss, C. (1998). *Evaluation: Methods for studying programs and practices.* Englewood Cliffs, NJ: Prentice-Hall.

Weldy, G. R. (1991). *Stronger school transitions improve student achievement: A final report on a three-year demonstration project "Strengthening School Transitions for Students K–13."* Reston, VA: National Association of Secondary School Principals.

Williams, S., & McGee, R. (1994). Reading attainment and juvenile delinquency. *Journal of Child Psychology and Psychiatry, 35,* 442–459.

Wirt, F. M., & Kirst, M. W. (1997). *The political dynamics of American education.* Berkeley, CA: McCutchan.

Wirt, F. M., & Kirst, M. W. (2001). *The political dynamics of American education* (2nd ed.). Richmond, CA: McCutchan.

Index

CORWIN
A SAGE Company

The Corwin logo—a raven striding across an open book—represents the union of courage and learning. Corwin is committed to improving education for all learners by publishing books and other professional development resources for those serving the field of PreK–12 education. By providing practical, hands-on materials, Corwin continues to carry out the promise of its motto: **"Helping Educators Do Their Work Better."**